The Political Economy of the Middle East

Volume I:
Economic Development

The Political Economy of the Middle East

Editors: Tim Niblock
Professor of Arab Gulf Studies and
Director of the Institute of Arab and Islamic Studies
University of Exeter, UK

Rodney Wilson
Professor of Economics
University of Durham, UK

I Economic Development

II International Economic Relations

III Islamic Economics

IV Economic and Political Liberalisation

V The Role of the State

VI Oil

Wherever possible, the articles in these volumes have been reproduced as originally published using facsimile reproduction, inclusive of footnotes and pagination to facilitate ease of reference.

For a list of all Edward Elgar published titles visit our site on the World Wide Web at http://www.e-elgar.co.uk

The Political Economy of the Middle East

Volume I: Economic Development

Edited by

Tim Niblock

Professor of Arab Gulf Studies and
Director of the Institute of Arab and Islamic Studies
University of Exeter, UK

and

Rodney Wilson

Professor of Economics
University of Durham, UK

An Elgar Reference Collection
Cheltenham, UK • Northampton, MA, USA

Published by
Edward Elgar Publishing Ltd
Glensanda House
Montpellier Parade
Cheltenham
Glos GL50 1UA
UK

Edward Elgar Publishing, Inc.
136 West Street
Suite 202
Northampton
Massachusetts 01060
USA

A catalogue record for this book is available from the British Library.

Library of Congress Cataloguing in Publication Data

The political economy of the Middle East / edited by Tim Niblock and Rodney Wilson.
Elgar mini series: 6 volume set. Includes bibliographical references and index.
1. Middle East—Economic conditions—1979–. 2. Middle East—Economic policy. 3. Middle East—Economic integration. 4. Arab cooperation. 5. Middle East—Politics and government—1979–. I. Niblock, Tim. II. Wilson, Rodney. III. Series. IV. Series: An Elgar reference collection.
HC415.15.P655 1999
338.956—dc21 99–34289
CIP

ISBN 1 85898 935 3
1 85898 443 2 (6 volume set)

Printed and bound in Great Britain by Biddles Ltd, Guildford and King's Lynn

Contents

Acknowledgements vii

Series Preface Tim Niblock and Rodney Wilson ix

Introduction Rodney Wilson xi

1. Unni Wikan (1985), 'Living Conditions Among Cairo's Poor – A View from Below', *Middle East Journal*, **39** (1), Winter, 7–26 1
2. Victor Levy (1986), 'The Distributional Impact of Economic Growth and Decline in Egypt', *Middle Eastern Studies*, **22** (1), January, 89–103 21
3. Rodney Wilson (1993), 'Whither the Egyptian Economy?', *British Journal of Middle Eastern Studies*, **25** (2), 204–13 36
4. Cassandra (1995), 'The Impending Crisis in Egypt', *Middle East Journal*, **49** (1), Winter, 9–27 46
5. Jahangir Amuzegar (1992), 'The Iranian Economy Before and After the Revolution', *Middle East Journal*, **46** (3), Summer, 413–25 65
6. A. Aydın Çeçen, A. Suut Doğruel and Fatma Doğruel (1994), 'Economic Growth and Structural Change in Turkey 1960–88', *International Journal of Middle East Studies*, **26** (1), 37–56 78
7. Volker Perthes (1992), 'The Syrian Economy in the 1980s', *Middle East Journal*, **46** (1), Winter, 37–58 98
8. M. Riad El-Ghonemy (1993), 'Food Security and Rural Development in North Africa', *Middle Eastern Studies*, **29** (3), July, 445–66 120
9. Alan Richards (1981), 'Agricultural Mechanization in Egypt: Hopes and Fears', *International Journal of Middle East Studies*, **13** (4), November, 409–25 142
10. Stephen Kontos (1990), 'Farmers and the Failure of Agribusiness in Sudan', *Middle East Journal*, **44** (4), Autumn, 649–67 159
11. Ziad Keilany (1980), 'Land Reform in Syria', *Middle Eastern Studies*, **16** (3), October, 209–24 178
12. M.G. Majd (1992), 'On the Relationship Between Land Reform and Rural–Urban Migration in Iran, 1966–1976', *Middle East Journal*, **46** (3), Summer, 440–55 194
13. E. Mine Cinar (1994), 'Unskilled Urban Migrant Women and Disguised Employment: Home-Working Women in Istanbul, Turkey', *World Development*, **22** (3), March, 369–80 210
14. Gil Feiler (1993), 'Palestinian Employment Prospects', *Middle East Journal*, **47** (4), Autumn, 633–51 222
15. Robert Bianchi (1986), 'The Corporatization of the Egyptian Labor Movement', *Middle East Journal*, **40** (3), Summer, 429–44 241

16. Delwin A. Roy and William T. Irelan (1992), 'Educational Policy and Human Resource Development in Jordan', *Middle Eastern Studies*, **28** (1), January, 178–215 257
17. Robert E. Looney (1991), 'Patterns of Human Resource Development in Saudi Arabia', *Middle Eastern Studies*, **27** (4), October, 668–78 295
18. Günter Meyer (1988), 'Employment in Small-Scale Manufacturing in Cairo: A Socio-Economic Survey', *British Society of Middle Eastern Studies Bulletin*, **14** (2), 136–46 306
19. Donald C. Mead (1982), 'Small Industries in Egypt: An Exploration of the Economics of Small Furniture Producers', *International Journal of Middle East Studies*, **14** (2), May, 159–71 317
20. Delwin A. Roy (1992), 'The Hidden Economy in Egypt', *Middle Eastern Studies*, **28** (4), October, 689–711 330

Name Index 353

Acknowledgements

The editors and publishers wish to thank the authors and the following publishers who have kindly given permission for the use of copyright material.

Cambridge University Press for articles: Alan Richards (1981), 'Agricultural Mechanization in Egypt: Hopes and Fears', *International Journal of Middle East Studies*, **13** (4), November, 409–25; Donald C. Mead (1982), 'Small Industries in Egypt: An Exploration of the Economics of Small Furniture Producers', *International Journal of Middle East Studies*, **14** (2), May, 159–71; A. Aydın Çeçen, A. Suut Doğruel and Fatma Doğruel (1994), 'Economic Growth and Structural Change in Turkey 1960–88', *International Journal of Middle East Studies*, **26** (1), 37–56.

Carfax Publishing Limited for articles: Günter Meyer (1988), 'Employment in Small Scale Manufacturing in Cairo: A Socio-Economic Survey', *British Society of Middle Eastern Studies Bulletin*, **14** (2), 136–46; Rodney Wilson (1993), 'Whither the Egyptian Economy?', *British Journal of Middle Eastern Studies*, **25** (2), 204–13.

Frank Cass & Co. Ltd for articles: Ziad Keilany (1980), 'Land Reform in Syria', *Middle Eastern Studies*, **16** (3), October, 209–24; Victor Levy (1986), 'The Distributional Impact of Economic Growth and Decline in Egypt', *Middle Eastern Studies*, **22** (1), January, 89–103; Robert E. Looney (1991), 'Patterns of Human Resource Development in Saudi Arabia', *Middle Eastern Studies*, **27** (4), October, 668–78; Delwin A. Roy and William T. Irelan (1992), 'Educational Policy and Human Resource Development in Jordan', *Middle Eastern Studies*, **28** (1), January, 178–215; Delwin A. Roy (1992), 'The Hidden Economy in Egypt', *Middle Eastern Studies*, **28** (4), October, 689–711; M. Riad El-Ghonemy (1993), 'Food Security and Rural Development in North Africa', *Middle Eastern Studies*, **29** (3), July, 445–66.

Elsevier Science Ltd for article: E. Mine Cinar (1994), 'Unskilled Urban Migrant Women and Disguised Employment: Home-Working Women in Istanbul, Turkey', *World Development*, **22** (3), March, 369–80.

Middle East Institute for articles: Unni Wikan (1985), 'Living Conditions Among Cairo's Poor – A View from Below', *Middle East Journal*, **39** (1), Winter, 7–26; Robert Bianchi (1986), 'The Corporatization of the Egyptian Labor Movement', *Middle East Journal*, **40** (3), Summer, 429–44; Stephen Kontos (1990), 'Farmers and the Failure of Agribusiness in Sudan', *Middle East Journal*, **44** (4), Autumn, 649–67; Volker Perthes (1992), 'The Syrian Economy in the 1980s', *Middle East Journal*, **46** (1), Winter, 37–58; Jahangir Amuzegar (1992), 'The Iranian Economy Before and After the Revolution', *Middle East Journal*, **46**

(3), Summer, 413–25; M.G. Majd (1992), 'On the Relationship Between Land Reform and Rural–Urban Migration in Iran, 1966–1976', *Middle East Journal*, **46** (3), Summer, 440–55; Gil Feiler (1993), 'Palestinian Employment Prospects', *Middle East Journal*, **47** (4), Autumn, 633–51; Cassandra (1995), 'The Impending Crisis in Egypt', *Middle East Journal*, **49** (1), Winter, 9–27.

Every effort has been made to trace all the copyright holders but if any have been inadvertently overlooked the publishers will be pleased to make the necessary arrangement at the first opportunity.

In addition the publishers wish to thank the Library of the London School of Economics and Political Science and the Marshall Library of Economics, Cambridge University for their assistance in obtaining these articles.

Series Preface

Tim Niblock and Rodney Wilson

The last two decades have seen more work by economists and political scientists on the Middle East than ever before. These volumes demonstrate the high quality of much of the work, and the major contribution it has made to the economic development and international relations literature more generally. There is a two way process however, as not only do those working on the Middle East contribute to the development of their own discipline, but even more importantly, their approaches are adapted to changes in thinking amongst economists and political scientists in the wider academic community.

It would have been tempting to have divided up these volumes on a country or sub-regional basis, as there is considerable heterogeneity within the region, and there is the danger of generalising from one country's experiences to another. The authors decided on a thematic approach however, as there are several important areas in which change has occurred throughout the region. Some of these, notably oil developments and the evolution of thinking in Islamic economics, have particular applicability to the region. The former may have applicability to other oil-dependent economies elsewhere, and the latter will certainly have applicability to other Muslim states.

As the state plays a greater role in the Middle East than in any other region of the developing world, it is appropriate that this should be a central theme of this set of books, as well as being the title of one of the volumes. As the articles show however, there has been a fundamental re-evaluation of the role of the state since the 1970s. Then the emphasis was on the oil boom, and how governments could apportion oil revenues. By the late 1980s the emphasis had shifted into how the state's role could be reduced, with a new emphasis on economic and political liberalisation, which involved privatisation and structural adjustment on the one hand, and democratisation and tentative steps towards political pluralism on the other hand.

It is clear from the analysis in these volumes that the poor performance of Middle Eastern economies cannot be attributed to the standard of the prognosis by economists and political scientists. There has been much excellent scholarship over the past two decades, and the shortcomings of the Middle East economies are well understood. The constraints on development are largely political in nature, which means more fundamental advance can only come through political reform.

Introduction

Rodney Wilson

The economic development record has been mediocre in the Middle East in relation to East and South East Asia and Latin America. Growth of per capita Gross Domestic Product (GDP) remains low, the average rate for the 1990–96 period being 2.2 per cent for Egypt, 1 per cent for Iran, –3.1 per cent for Saudi Arabia and 1.7 per cent for Turkey.[1] Oil distorts the GDP figures, especially for major oil exporting countries such as Saudi Arabia and Iran, but the continuing heavy dependence on oil could be regarded as a failure of economic development.[2]

The low level of investment in the region undoubtedly explains some of the poor economic growth, the rate in Egypt for example being a mere 17 per cent of GDP in 1996, less than half the rates recorded in South East Asia. Investment in people is also low, with 39 per cent of females of primary school age in Saudi Arabia still not actually attending school in 1995, and countries such as Iran not providing official figures on school enrollments. In these circumstances of limited physical investment and under-utilisation of human resources, economic advance is inevitably slow.

Development frustrations could be taken as a theme of this volume. The articles not only explain why there have been development failures, but the authors also convey some of the sense of what this means for living standards and employment. Of course, care has to be taken in interpreting development indicators when much economic activity is unrecorded, but articles have also been selected which deal with informal economic activity, sometimes referred to as the 'hidden economy'.

Poverty and Inequality

Poverty remains the lot of many people in the region, who seem to receive no benefit from any advance which does occur. It seems appropriate therefore to deal first with issues of poverty and income distribution in these readings on economic development, as they illustrate the scale of the challenge facing the economies of the Middle East.

Unni Wikan (Chapter 1) demonstrates what this deprivation involves for Cairo residents who typify the urban poor of the region. Their plight has not changed significantly since her article was published in 1985, or indeed from that depicted in her earlier book.[3] For Wikan the issue of poverty is as much social as economic, as it is not so much the problems of economic deprivation which the poor find difficult to bear, but rather the social exclusion experienced when they as a group have no distinct culture to take refuge in, which differentiates them from their more affluent neighbours. Therefore, even amongst the poor of a poor country such as Egypt, absolute living standards are not the overriding concern, but rather their relative economic position at the bottom of the income distribution.

Despite this, the plight of the poor was not tackled by government in the 1970s or 1980s as Victor Levy shows in Chapter 2, as this was not a policy priority. In any case, countries such as Egypt are arguably on the rising part of the Kuznets curve which traces out the relationship between the national average level of per capita income and the degree of income inequality.[4]

M. Riad El Ghonemy argues in a recent study that poverty in the Middle East is not caused by population growth,[5] demographic change being one factor supposedly explaining the Kuznets curve. Rather El-Ghonemy sees poverty resulting from highly unequal and deteriorating purchasing power. The proportion of the poor relative to the total population increased from 30.6 per cent in 1985 to 33.1 per cent in 1990 according to World Bank statistics cited by El-Ghonemy. Data from the early 1990s suggest that in Tunisia, Jordan, Morocco and Egypt the lowest 20 per cent of households only consume 5.9, 6.5, 6.6 and 7.3 per cent of income respectively, while the richest 20 per cent of households in the same four countries consume 46.3, 50.1, 46.3 and 44 per cent of income respectively.[6] Like Wikan, El-Ghonemy sees poverty not as simply caused by economic factors, but as reflecting the interaction of moral, historical and institutional factors with the economics within the social system. For this reason even if correctionist economic policies were pursued it is far from clear that they would meet with much success.

Other writers appear to share the views of Wikan and El-Ghonemy about the importance of the political and social factors in explaining the persistence of poverty in Egypt. Yet even during the time of Nasser little was done by government to rectify the inequalities as Mahmoud Abdel-Fadil showed.[7] The tax system became marginally more progressive, but tax evasion increased, and no real effort was made to curb this. Furthermore government price controls favoured consumer goods which the middle classes purchased rather than more basic wage goods, such as cooking oil, down-market clothing and footwear, which the poorer classes purchased.[8]

It can, of course, be argued that income inequalities favour economic development as the rich save more, and this finances investment on which economic growth ultimately depends. Galal Amin disputed the relevance of this to the Middle East, not least because of the consumerism of the wealthy and their low savings propensity.[9] In his more recent work Amin finds that savings have fallen further in Egypt since the mid-1980s and the share of consumption in national income has risen.[10] Again he attributes this to the social attitudes of the upwardly mobile who wish to demonstrate their success through their consumption pattern. In so far as the richer groups do save, much gets channelled into capital flight, which benefits economies outside the region rather than Egypt or other Middle East economies.

The views of Galal Amin are supported by the rather gloomy prognosis of the Egyptian economy I made in Chapter 3 of this volume, and the even more alarming picture given by an anonymous author in a *Middle East Journal* article which is also reproduced in this collection. More optimistic analyses are provided by World Bank economists, and some advocate that Egypt should try to follow the example of Turkey. As Chapter 6 by Aydın Çeçen, Suut Doğruel and Fatma Doğruel shows however, the situation in Turkey is very different to Egypt. In the end the lessons from Bent Hansen's monumental comparative study of Egypt and Turkey for the World Bank are far from clear as the circumstances of each country present enormous contrasts.[11]

Revolution and Economic Change

If evolutionary economic change produces such poor results, what about more revolutionary developments which have a greater chance of changing social structures? Again here the evidence from the Middle East is discouraging. It is not clear that a revolution such as that in Iran offers any easy solutions as the contributions by Jahangir Amuzegar (Chapter 5, this volume), Massoud Karshenas and Hashem Pesaran (Chapter 8, Volume IV, Economic and Political Liberalisation) to these volumes demonstrate. Although the Islamic revolution in Iran brought profound changes politically, and changes in institutional and administrative arrangements, there was remarkably little change in the direction of economic policy. Indeed in spite of the rhetoric about creating an Islamic economy, the stress, as Jahangir Amuzegar asserts in his most recent book, was on continuity.[12]

The Islamic banking law of 1983 was arguably the most significant piece of Islamic legislation in the economic sphere, but this changed the methods of banking rather than financing priorities. The effect on resource allocation was minimal, as money and credit policy was dictated according to the public sector's financial requirements.[13] Each bank was given a quantitative quota for its total credit and administrative guidelines were provided on how credit should be allocated between sectors. Credit charges were fixed by Bank Markazi, the central bank, and these varied between sectors, with lower charges for agriculture and higher charges for industry and services. The major change in the 1990s has been that banks were freed to lend to the private sector as much as their resources permitted, but the allocation of lending between sectors would still have to comply with government guidelines, which under recent plans have stressed lending to industry.

There appears to be remarkable similarities between economic developments in Iran since 1979 and earlier developments under the Shah as described by Massoud Karshenas in his work on oil, the role of the state and industrialisation.[14] Even the detail of policy was often the same in both the pre- and post-revolution periods. Amuzegar, for example, is able to draw parallels between earlier laws enacted by the Shah's government and the law of 1989 to control inflation which required shopkeepers to affix government controlled price labels on their goods, under the threat of being brought before the courts as 'hoarders and profiteers'.[15] This was remarkably similar to the fourteenth principle of the Shah's so called 'White Revolution', which stressed the need to achieve price stability through a campaign against profiteering. In both cases such admonishments were doomed to failure as they attacked the symptoms rather than the causes of the inflation: inadequate supply and excess demand brought about partly by the governments own spending. Inflation in Iran increased from 9 per cent to 23.2 per cent over the 1990–96 period making it one of the greatest economic challenges for economic policy makers which cannot simply be reduced in a sustainable manner through price controls.

Although starting from ideologically very different position there are a number of parallels between economic policy making in Iran and Syria. Volker Perthes shows how the Syrian economy marked time in the 1980s in Chapter 7. The stress was on exhortation rather than market incentives, and control by the state where exhortation did not work. Yet in the end that state had to resort to policies that opened up the economy to foreign capital and freed up the business community domestically. There were parallels with Rafsanjani's *perestroika*, the term Amuzegar uses to describe the Iranian President's change of direction from 1991 onward.[16] In the Iranian case these policies appear to have worked to some extent, despite the continuing pressures by the American government to keep US multinational companies out of Iran. The lure of lucrative contracts in oil-related projects was too much for other western companies to resist, especially those from Europe. In contrast Syria has been much less successful in opening up its economy, partly because of the stalled peace process and a lack of investor confidence.

Land Reform and Agricultural Development

Prior to the discovery and development of oil, agriculture was the major economic activity in most of the economies of the Middle East, and it remains significant for employment, although its share of gross domestic product has steadily decreased. In 1996 agriculture still accounted for 17 per cent of GDP in Egypt and Turkey and 25 per cent of GDP in Iran, but its share of GDP in the oil exporting countries of the Gulf was negligible.[17] The Middle East has become a substantial net importer of foodstuffs, especially grains, but given these purchases there are few food shortages, with the exception of the more remote regions of countries such as the Sudan where failures of food production and distribution are largely the result of the civil war.

Interest in Middle Eastern agriculture has declined in recent years and there is arguably less worthwhile writing now than there was 20 years ago. To some extent this reflects stagnation in the sector itself, as although much has been achieved with irrigation advance and higher yielding crops, there has been a lack of major innovation in the 1980s and 1990s. Yields compare favourably with other regions, and the land in the Nile Valley has some of the highest cereal yields in Mediterranean. Labour productivity remains low in agriculture however, and there are long periods of underemployment for rural workers given the seasonal nature of the activity.

Agricultural advance has been problematic, not only in Egypt as Alan Richards (Chapter 9) shows, but also in Sudan and Syria whose experiences are considered in this volume by Stephen Kontos (Chapter 10) and Ziad Keilany (Chapter 11). M. Riad El-Ghonemy's survey of food security and rural development in North Africa (Chapter 8) reaches similar conclusions to those of Marvin Weinbaum who surveyed the whole region a decade earlier,[18] indicating how little has changed. Little can be done about rainfall reliability and water is obviously the constraining factor on agriculture in the whole region, but the major policy debates centre on questions of the degree of government intervention in agriculture through subsidies on fertilizers and other inputs, and whether market prices should be charged for output, which has implications for urban consumers as well as rural producers.

Overall the effects of government intervention appear to have been counterproductive, as subsidies have encouraged a wasteful use of resources, including irrigation water. Large scale mechanisation schemes and subsidies to farmers purchasing tractors appear to have achieved little as Alan Richards asserts in Chapter 9 and in subsequent work.[19] The numerous large agribusiness schemes in the Sudan appear to have been especially badly planned as Chapter 10 by Stephen Kontos shows, a viewpoint shared by Alan Richards.

In the 1950s and 1960s there were numerous studies of land reform in the Middle East the most notable being by Doreen Warriner,[20] Ann Lambton[21] and Gabriel Saab.[22] By the 1970s the land reform movement has run out of steam however, partly because the governments had become less radical, but also because with the relative decline in agriculture, rural landlords were no longer a threat to political power. Although land reform is unlikely to become an issue again in the way it was in the 1950s and 1960s, the programmes of that period had a significant impact on the rural economy, as well as rural urban migration, which is why two articles are included on this topic dealing with Syria and Iran (Chapters 11 and 12).

Labour and Employment Issues

Rural failures have induced migration to urban areas, as M.G. Majd (Chapter 12) shows, where most get involved in informal sector activities of the type described by Günter Meyer, Donald Mead, Delwin Roy and Mine Cinar (Chapters 18, 19, 20 and 13, respectively). Neo-classical labour migration models from the economic development literature, notably the Todaro model,[23] would seem to have some applicability in the Middle East. There can be little doubt that it is financial incentives which attract people to the rapidly growing cities of the Middle East, although a critical factor is support from family members who have previously moved to the city while the new migrant searches for a job.

Labour markets in the Middle East are complex, and the steady stream of new migrants has not necessarily undermined the position of established workers, especially in the state industries, where the risk of being dismissed or laid off is low in comparison with many developed countries. In Chapter 15 Robert Bianchi looks at the corporatisation of the Egyptian labour movement, a topic dealt with by Marsha Pripstein Posusney in a recent study.[24] She stresses the power of the Egyptian labour movement to influence state policy despite government interference in union affairs, and the gap which often existed between ordinary workers and their union leaders.

Workers in small business and the informal sector are, of course, not unionised and it is in this sector where most job creation is needed. With potential labour force growth averaging between 3 and 4 per cent in most Middle East countries, and employment creation struggling to keep up, there is an enormous challenge ahead for the small business sector. Günter Meyer's survey of small scale manufacturing in Cairo (Chapter 18) and Donald Mead's work on small furniture producers in Egypt (Chapter 19) are included in this volume as it is in these type of activities that more jobs are most likely to be created. Arguably, there is too much focus on the macroeconomic policy in the Middle East, but too little on microeconomics and studies at the sectoral level.

Articles on human resource development by Delwin Roy and William Irelan (Chapter 16) and Robert Looney (Chapter 17) are also included as, ultimately, if the advocates of endogenous growth theory are to be believed, this may be the most important factor determining the level of development in the Middle East. There is certainly much that can be criticised in the education systems of the region, not least the methods of group rote learning rather than the encouragement of individual creative thinking. The latter may be a prerequisite for the emergence of entrepreneurs who can drive development forward in the manner identified by supporters of Schumpeterian growth theory. Another issue is the over concentration of resources on higher education rather than primary and vocational education. There are surprisingly few studies of education and training issues in the Middle East, in spite of its acknowledged importance in economic advance. Here resources do matter, and despite the deficiencies of the region's education systems, the improvement in knowledge and skills may well be the most lasting legacy of the oil boom era of the 1970s and early 1980s, especially in the Gulf states which have seen such dramatic changes in education, even though all too many girls continue to be excluded.

Notes

1. Figures from *World Bank Atlas*, Washington DC, 1998.
2. Rodney Wilson, *Economic Development in the Middle East*, London: Routledge, 1995, p. 28.
3. Unni Wikan, *Life Among the Poor in Cairo*, London: Tavistock Publications, 1980.
4. For an introductory discussion of the evidence on the Kuznets curve see Gerald M. Meier, *Leading Issues in Economic Development*, Oxford: Oxford University Press, Sixth edition, 1995, pp. 20–22.
5. M. Riad El-Ghonemy, *Affluence and Poverty in the Middle East*, London: Routledge, 1998, p. 25.
6. Ibid., p. 24.
7. Mahmoud Abdel-Fadil, *The Political Economy of Nasserism: a Study of Employment and Income Distribution Policies in Urban Egypt*, Cambridge: Cambridge University Press, 1980.
8. Ibid., pp. 80–81.
9. Galal Amin, *The Modernisation of Poverty: a Study in the Political Economy of Growth in Nine Arab Countries*, Leiden: E.J. Brill, 1974.
10. Galal Amin, *Egypt's Economic Predicament: A Study in the Interaction of Economic Pressure, Political Folly and Social Tension in Egypt, 1960–1990*, Leiden: E.J. Brill, 1995.
11. Bent Hansen, *The Political Economy of Poverty, Equity and Growth*, Oxford University Press, 1991.
12. Jahangir Amuzegar, *Iran's Economy under the Islamic Republic*, London: I.B. Tauris, 1993, pp. 320–25.
13. Ibid., p. 111.
14. Massoud Karshenas, *Oil, State and Industrialisation in Iran*, Cambridge: Cambridge University Press, 1990.
15. Jahangir Amuzegar, 1993, p. 322. See Note 12.
16. Jahangir Amuzegar, 1993, pp. 316–18. See Note 12.
17. Figures from *World Bank Atlas*, Washington DC, 1998.
18. Marvin G. Weinbaum, *Food, Development and Politics in the Middle East*, Boulder, Colorado: Westview Press, 1982.
19. Alan Richards and John Waterbury, *A Political Economy of the Middle East: State, Class and Economic Development*, Boulder, Colorado: Westview Press, 1990, pp. 172–6.
20. Doreen Warriner, *Land Reform and Development in the Middle East: A Study of Egypt, Syria and Iraq*, Oxford: Oxford University Press, 1957.
21. Ann Lambton, *The Persian Land Reform, 1962–66*, Oxford: Oxford University Press, 1969.
22. Gabriel Saab, *The Egyptian Land Reform, 1952–62*, Oxford: Oxford University Press, 1967.
23. Michael P. Todaro, 'A model of labour, migration and urban unemployment in less developed countries', *American Economic Review*, **59** (1), 1969, 138–48.
24. Marsha Pripstein Posusney, *Labour and the State in Egypt: Workers, Unions and Economic Restructuring*, New York: Columbia University Press, 1997.

[1]

LIVING CONDITIONS AMONG CAIRO'S POOR—A VIEW FROM BELOW

Unni Wikan

Whereas most scholarly and journalistic reports deplore the falling living conditions of Cairo's poor, according to the evidence I have obtained as a participant observer of their life since 1969, poor people themselves hold the contrary view that matters have improved greatly over the last 15 years.[1] How can this discrepancy be understood and what insights can it provide into the conditions of the urban poor and social science methods for recording or evaluating these conditions?

My analysis will show what I regard as a healthy bias in favor of the poor people's own point of view, and will leave it largely up to those who practice economics and social surveys to ponder the biases of *their* accounts—although I have to offer some criteria and guidelines of use to them. My primary materials come from a social anthropological field study in a small area of Cairo. My numerical coverage will be narrow; against statistics measuring pounds and people in vast numbers I shall pit a population of a score of families, totalling

1. Fieldwork has been conducted in a poor area of Cairo during a total of 21 months, beginning in 1969 and with yearly revisits until 1982. I have lived in Egypt (Cairo and Alexandria) a total of 4 years in all. See Wikan 1980 and 1983.

Unni Wikan is Associate Professor of Social Anthropology and Director of the Ethnographic Museum, University of Oslo. She is the author of Life among the Poor in Cairo *(1980),* Behind the Veil in Arabia—Women in Oman *(1982), and* Tomorrow, God Willing—Women's Lives in the Back Streets of Cairo *(in Norwegian) (1983).*

about one hundred people living in a dozen back streets in one of the poor areas of Cairo. But I have the advantage of having known them and followed them closely for 13 years; I have seen them through the ups and downs of life's stages as they have gone about their daily lives. They have voices and they should be listened to. And in judging most aspects of their lives, their own standards must be the measure. So I will claim that "small facts speak to big issues" (Geertz, 1973:23).

"The decline in standards of living is already serious in every aspect of life" says Yinon (1982:384) on Egypt, and Cairo in particular, in a judgment which is highly representative of expert opinion. But Cairo has grown so immense, population density has so increased, the rate of inflation is so high and national problems of resource management so staggering that it takes an in-depth study of poor people *over time* to recognize, against aggregate and surface evidence, that national problems and people's own problems do not necessarily coincide. I shall try to demonstrate how life as seen from below has a very different aspect, and that perhaps the state may even fare worse while people's lives in fact improve. In terms of their own values, the poor argue that they dress better, have better health, better entertainment, more and better education, more employment opportunities, better chances for savings and investments, less need than before for borrowing, and much, much more in the way of prestigious consumer goods. *And* they celebrate the Feast.

In 1969 I began a study of 17 families in a particular poor area of Cairo (Wikan 1980, 1983). Subsequently I have been back 11 times in 13 years. My aim was to learn how they conceived of themselves and their lives, as well as what the "objective" factors were that constrained and shaped their particular life situation and position in society. As a woman, committed to the method of participant observation, it followed that in a strictly sex-segregated society I would naturally take the perspective of women and children. This could be regarded as a bias in my data. But when it comes to assessing the standard or the level of living of the Cairo poor, such bias is probably less of a weakness than would be its opposite of one-sided concentration on men. First, neighborhood and domestic scenes are overwhelmingly woman-centered, though of course also vitally important to men. My access to women's circles thus offered privileged access to backstage information about both women and men and their actual level of living, as opposed to the life that men like to say that they lead, whether to impress companions or to flatter or fool officials (including enumerators who ask them about their standard of living).

Second, the women's role in the economy cannot be overestimated. They do not work outside the household and have no separate income. Yet they manage the domestic economy. They allocate the resources given them by their husbands and press the men to give more through threats of borrowing and public shaming. They are also in charge of all investments.

Third, they are the bankers, running intricate operations of savings clubs *(gam'iyyāt)* that cater to a host of living needs, both short-term and long-term.

Fourth, most indices of the level of living in the abstract have as their concrete input items of consumption and aspects of life that pertain to the domestic scene: health, education, sanitation, consumption patterns and clothing. To know these you must enter the houses, and you must speak to the women. The men will not know if a child has been sick, and with what. They cannot tell what the family had for dinner, for the members of the family may all have eaten different things at different times, and the men have brought home none of it, nor were they there to see. They do not know what the family owns in the way of clothes, and they know prices only imperfectly. Yet if you ask them, they like to give the impression that they are in charge. The women, for appearance's sake, may even support the illusion, secure in their knowledge that it is all an appearance; both men and women know that *issittāt byihkumū*—it is the women who rule.

What the men do know about, and better than women, are their actual incomes. Few women know exactly what their husbands earn, since most men have two jobs, at most one of which provides regular salary. To try to retain control over a sizable portion, men underreport their earnings to their wives. But often it is a losing game. The women's estimates of what their husbands earn are likely to be as accurate as are the men's reports to an official investigator who is an outsider.

My sample of 17 families in 1969 was not chosen by statistical methods. Rather, I followed natural networks of friendship and amity. This was both for practical reasons (cf. Wikan 1980:pp. 3–13) and because I wanted to build up rapport and to observe people in their natural surroundings. Nonetheless, I shall maintain that they are typical representatives of the Cairo poor in the patterns of live that they lead, the attitudes they hold, and the values that they display.

I have also spoken with and observed the men of those families and neighborhoods. Although in the early 1970s they did not use to spend much time in their own homes (times have changed: see below), they very often sit in their mothers' and sisters' homes, basking in the ego-strengthening comfort and consolation that the latter are only too ready to provide against what they and the men see as the wives' incessant complaints and demands (Wikan 1980:102).

My original sample of 17 families has shrunk over the years to 13; the members of two households have died and two have moved. However, six new families have been created through children's marriages. In addition I have no count of all the people I know as friends, neighbors or even enemies of the above families.

In 1969, these families all conceived of themselves as poor. They referred to themselves as "we, the poor" in contradistinction to those better-off (*al-zawāt:* lit. "those with a surplus"). They regarded themselves as falling towards the bottom of the range, since they inhabited the dirtiest, narrowest backlanes with the most decrepit houses. Regular monthly incomes ranged between £E10 and £E51.* Thus there were great differences among them, and they battled hard among themselves for status and prestige. Yet they all felt caught in the same trap. They felt shame at their situation, accepting their society's premise that material need is the most degrading of all conditions. They felt exploited and neglected by the government and voiced great bitterness towards those in power, President Nasser included (Wikan 1980, ch. 9).

Thirteen years later, two of the families no longer regard themselves as poor. On the contrary, they would be deeply offended if anyone alluded (as their neighbors do privately) to their dark past. Of the remainder, all but one of the families are definite that their lives have improved greatly. In general, they praise their improved conditions. That is, the women do, most of the men do, nearly all the old people do, but not all of the young. For in speaking of the level of living, it is necessary to differentiate. To use households as the unit of reference obscures the fact that separate members may fare very differently in regard to the same goods or aspirations.

While statistical measurement and evaluation may not agree with these perceptions, in many respects it is the latter which count. In forming a judgment we particularly need to consider the cultural factor and we need to be very clear and sensitive to the many ways in which culturally defined standards enter into the human facts that level and standard of living purport to measure. The remainder of this article is an attempt to go some way in showing what these cultural aspects are, and how they must affect any evaluation of changes in the conditions of life for the particular population represented by Cairo's poor.

A brief discussion of concepts may be necessary at this point. I have used the expressions "level of living," "standard of living" and even "living conditions" as if they were self-explanatory and interchangeable. Yet precision in social science is to be gained from a discriminating use of terms. It is now long ago that a UN committee advocated that the expression "level of living" replace "standard of living" when reference is made to actual conditions of life as contrasted with aspirations or ideas of what ought to be. This is a useful step, and I shall try to follow it. But "level of living" must also measure actual conditions with reference to the interests and priorities of the population concerned if it is to take account of legitimate differences in cultural factors.

The UN recommendation is that the following indicators be considered an acceptable international catalogue of the term, "although the precise connotation of each would to some extent be determined by national attitudes and standards

*£1.000 = $2.30 in 1970 at official rate of exchange.

resulting from peculiarities of environmental conditions, cultures, values and economic, political and social organization'' (United Nations 1954:p. 26):

1. Health, including demographic conditions
2. Food and nutrition
3. Education, including literacy and skills
4. Conditions of work
5. Employment situation
6. Aggregate consumption and savings
7. Transportation
8. Housing, including household facilities
9. Clothing
10. Recreation and entertainment
11. Social security
12. Human freedoms

Measuring the 13 remaining families on these accounts at only two points in time, 1969 and 1982, the results would be variable and inconclusive, even if valid measurements could be found. A requirement and limitation of the UN conceptualization is "that the data be expressible in measurable form" (op.cit.:27), and that which is measurable might be neither valid nor reliable. A further problem is the concept of national attitudes and standards that is introduced with the positive aim of avoiding global (in practice Western), judgmental biases. Yet the idea that countries constitute nations with national cultures is itself a Western, and for applied research purposes, an illusory concept. Egypt is a relatively homogeneous culture, yet even there, what are the "national attitudes and standards" concerning housing, education, relaxation, etc? On what "compromise" could the rich and the poor agree, not to speak of fellahin vs. urbanites, to take just some of the dimensions of variation in the population? And could any such compromise validly pass for "national standards"?

I shall in the following concentrate on what I know to be the standards, attitudes and actual conditions of the Cairo poor, meaning those particular people whom I have known intimately for years, and who, to the best of my judgment are representative also of other poor areas in Cairo that I have visited often when accompanying my friends to their relatives and friends. Insisting that actual living conditions are the key indicator of deterioration or improvement in the level of living, I shall concentrate my argument on this rather than on changes in ideals and aspirations, although the latter will also enter in, since people's assessments of changes in their lives are naturally linked with their ideals and aspirations.

Income level, housing, and calorie intake are measures always used to assess standard of living. On these measures, the families I know have not particularly improved their lot. They eat somewhat, but not significantly, better than before, measured in these objective terms. The regular income of the household heads has barely kept pace with inflation, except for two labor migrants. They all inhabit the same old flats; two even with a new family that they have had to take in, whereas in two other cases the old people died and the young ones have obtained both space and peace.

But housing hardly enters into people's own estimate of bettered or worsened lives; they accept the constraints on the housing market produced by the rent freeze which gives cheap flats at the cost of immobility. Consequently, the level of housing is not a meaningful measure of a family's standards or achievements (see below, p. 17–20). Clothing, on the other hand, is of signal importance. The families dress considerably better than before, which means in Cairene terms that they are also better able to think well of themselves.[2] And here we approach the crux of my argument: an assessment of changes in level of living must take *style* of living into account, and measure life in terms of the priorities that hold for people themselves. The measure can and should be objective, but with appropriate dimensions. What is more, it should measure real conditions of life, in these terms, whether resulting from goals consciously pursued and goods purposefully purchased, or from the unsought and unseen consequences of the patterns of allocation that are practiced. Durable consumer goods, for instance, are a feature of dramatic importance to the welfare and happiness, and therefore to the level of living, of poor Cairene families.

On page 14 is a tabular comparison of the major items of consumer goods in the possession of my sample of families in 1969 and 1982 respectively. The table shows a very marked increase in the stock of consumer goods available to the average poor family—and, incidentally, one that is easily enough measurable by enumerators and statisticians. Beside being counted, they may be measured in Egyptian pounds, and represent a not inconsiderable savings surplus.

More significantly, they provide relief and enjoyment which were previously lacking. Let us take TV as our example. The three TV sets listed for 1969 were recent acquisitions (1968, 1968 and 1969 respectively) and had only recently changed the daily pattern of life in those households. Now everyone shares in the enjoyment TV introduces into a life of urban poverty, where cinema visits are at best rare and memorable life experiences and holidays, vacations and even birthday celebrations are empty words only. The entertainment introduced in such lives by Egyptian TV comedy and soap opera genuinely changes the level of living.

Yet its significance goes even more deeply, and its consequences are even more profound. The overwhelming problem in the life of poor women in Cairo, and to a large extent also in the life of poor men, has centered on the conflict-ridden and often destructive relationship that has tended to obtain

2. On this point see Wikan 1980, ch. 8 and 1983, esp. pp. 110–112, 140–142, and 147–148.

between spouses trapped in a life of poverty (Wikan 1980, esp. ch. 7). The absence of loyalty and expressions of respect between spouses, and between father and children, regularly erodes the person's self-respect and impoverishes family life. Men respond by escaping from the home and spending time and money in cafés, or in the homes of mothers and sisters willing to support them against their wives. With the advent of TV in the home, family coherence suddenly increases. Husbands who previously spent their free time in cafés, now prefer to stay at home instead, and that in turn entails greater family commitment on his part; it leads to a greater appreciation of the home, and therefore to a much greater readiness to contribute financially to it.

Whereas in the beginning of the 1970s I estimated that husbands used between one fourth and one third of their personal incomes on private consumption, mainly cigarettes and coffee, my estimate today is that this fraction has sunk to between one fourth and one sixth. What is more, husbands whom I had never seen buy a thing for the house, but who showered their wives with complaints of spendthriftness and consumer mentality, have now come to embark upon "these ways" themselves. When a man comes home with a washing machine for his wife and daughter, the consequences for family loyalty and family coherence are immeasurable. Women and children feel more cared for, the husband feels more appreciated. The flat is no more a monument to his failings (Wikan, 1980:101), he now shares in making it into a home.

I am not saying that the acquisiton of TV *per se* has generated these changes. There is obviously more to it than that. This "more" will be discussed below. Noted here should be a general effect on the population of the fact of labor migration by a few men who have come home from Libya or Saudi Arabia laden with material things, with repercussions extending throughout neighborhoods of poor who measure themselves competitively against each other according to material standards. Thus, it is not only a question of what people earn, but how they spend their money. Patterns of acquisition have changed in ways that bring both direct and indirect benefits for the level of living.

The changes outlined above must not be read as drastic in extent. They are tendencies, but they are marked enough that the poor take note of them, and the observer should do likewise. Moreover, changes that may appear small from an outsider's point of view may have an entirely different import from the actor's point of view.

It is mainly since the mid-1970s that the families have acquired this impressive array of, by their standards, expensive consumer, utility and prestige goods. How have they bought it all, if incomes have not soared?

I have noted that regular incomes for the majority have barely kept pace with inflation. But every one of these men has, and has always had, two jobs and two incomes (Wikan, 1980:28–31). Secondary jobs are taxi driving, carpentry, electrical work, mechanical jobs and house painting, to name the most common. And

TABLE 1 *Major status-giving material possessions of 9 families as of 1969 and 1982 showing the range from best-off to worst-off.*

	Family	1	2	3	4	5	6	7	8	9
1969	Radio	x	x	x	x	x	x	x	x	
	TV	x	x	x						
	Sitting-room furniture		x		x					
	Land	x								
1982	Radio	x	x	x	x	x	x	x	x	x
	TV	*	*	*	*	*	*	x	x	x
	Butagaz	x	x	x	x	x	x	x		
	Refrigerator	x		x	x	x	x	x		
	Washing-machine	x	x	x	x	x	x	x		x
	Tape-recorder	x		x	x	x	x	x		
	Mixmaster				x	x	x			
	Juice presser	x			x	x	x			
	Sewing machine				x	x				
	Iron				x	x	x			
	Fan	x			x	x	x	x		
	Sitting-room furniture		x		x		x			
	Land	x		x						
	House share		x	x	x	x				
	Custom jewelry				x					
	Electric stove				x					

*Color TV

here incomes for some have soared. As a result of Sadat's *infitah,* the "opening" of Egypt to foreign business and investment, new opportunities have also opened for the poor in construction work, transport, and various irregular, semiskilled odd and part-time jobs. But how would such figures enter into statistics? I doubt that most men could give an account even of what they earned last week, for instance. But I know that some who before were driven up the wall from overwork to keep the family going, now take days off from time to time, even in the middle of the week, and many work shorter hours. Men who were drawn, their bodies thin as skeletons in the early 1970s, now look plump and relaxed by comparison. In the early 1970s people used to say "Egypt has become a country of school certificates, what is needed is a *shahāda* (diploma) above all." Today they say: "It's the technicians who excel. It's practical work, not education that pays." And they are right, if money is the issue.

A teacher who originates from among the poor will have spent some 25 years as a pupil in school (due to repeated failures at yearly exams stemming from a combination of circumstances: bad schools and hopeless situations for doing homework in the home). In the end, after getting his diploma, he will earn about £E25 a month. His brother who quits after 6th grade elementary school, or even 3rd year, can today earn £E60–70 a month painting walls or repairing TV sets. And there is work of this kind for everyone. I have not heard men in the slums complain of not finding work over the past 5 or 6 years. Previously, those who worked as taxi-drivers, for instance, used to complain that there were not enough taxis to go around for those who did not own but wanted to drive one. Today, again with the *infitah,* there is an influx of cars in the country, and well-paid work for drivers.

My estimate would be that when we take the regular and irregular jobs together, looking at total incomes, household heads among the poor earn about three times as much today as they did ten years ago. And they spend a proportionately greater share on those things—food, clothes and equipment—that benefit the family as a whole.

Family incomes in 1982, however, do not depend solely on the household head. Wives do not work, that is considered shameful unless one is educated, and married women in the poor quarters are not, but quite a few daughters work. This provides an appreciable supplement to family income. When sons work, there is no such automatic benefit to family income. Daughters feel loyalty to their mothers and recognize the latter's struggle to make ends meet. Sons, on the other hand, are more attuned to their comrades and want to impress them, which they do by spending money extravagantly. The irresponsibility accepted by parents in their sons is quite staggering. Mothers may as a last resort refuse to cook for them, but this in turn may simply mean that the son buys himself luxury foods which he brings home and sits eating in front of his family. Consequently, any estimate of family income would have to know these facts and reckon quite differently with the wages of daughters versus sons. Whereas in 1969 only two of the 17 families had unmarried daughters who worked outside the home, the figure today is six out of 13. Whether this development will continue will, of course, depend upon the employment situation in the country.

Income enters under the rubric "conditions of work" in the UN inventory. This, in turn, is spelled out as follows:

Conditions of work:
1. Hours of work per week.
2. Wages per week of industrial workers.
3. Real wages of industrial workers.
4. Normal hours of work per week as laid down by law or by collective agreements for workers in industry.
5. Number of paid holidays per year in industry.
6. Minimum age of eligibility for employment. (op.cit:S5)

The Commission recognizes difficulties, both of measurement and interpretation of items, one of which is that such information is available in the main only for industrial workers, and even for them such information is spotty and deficient. Another is in judging real incomes or buying power. But a further major difficulty which I cannot see that they recognize, is in judging real income *for whom*. The supposition seems to be that corresponding to each family is a household head with earning power, making his earnings available for a collective household budget. In Cairo it is true that the household head alone is economically responsible for the family. But what a family actually has to live on depends as much on whether it has daughters, rather than sons, who work, and above all what fraction of the household head's earnings is made available to shared consumption.

The above estimate of changes in income has not dealt with the lucky ones who have been off on labor migration. Of the 17 heads of families in 1969, four have subsequently been off to either Libya or Saudi Arabia, three sons have gone, and one unmarried daughter. Three of the four men returned after one and a half years to three years, having earned at least ten times as much a month as they did at home in their regular job, and having saved more than they knew what to do with. The fourth, the head of one of the two families referred to as "aspiring families" in my first book (1980:151), used to earn a total of about £E.25 a month when he was at home. He now works in Saudi Arabia and earns the equivalent of £E.500 a month. In Egypt he had no nighttime job, choosing instead to invest in education, with the aim of obtaining a lawyer's certificate. When, after countless attempts he had, in his 35th year, still gotten no further than the second year of law, he decided to quit, and went to Saudi Arabia to work as an electrician. The money seems to have gone to his head. To the chagrin of his wife, he still does not want to quit (and take up a job in Egypt paying about £E.30 a month). He sends home a minimum of £300 a month plus he has sent home two refrigerators, two stoves, two color TVs, etc. This might seem a wholly irresponsible use of money, but it must be understood in the context of people never before having been able to give vent to a self-indulgent buying spree and always having had to count each and every penny. For once they can buy what their hearts desire.

The effects of such incomes and forms of expenditure are profound. Envy and rivalry become inducements for men less fortunately positioned also to invest in prestige household equipment. Whereas before such envy was operative mainly among women, to the furious complaints of the men (Wikan, 1983:101–102), nowadays the men seem to have succumbed, with beneficial effects for the family. All things are bought on installment, and it is still the case that women run the savings clubs (see below) but men now see the point in saving, and they voluntarily contribute their share.

I have given above a list of acquisitions through the years, and I have sought to construct an argument to show that these items are indicators of improved level of living not because they cost money and may be counted. They enter because of the cultural and social value they carry for the Cairo poor. In their world they say, "Egyptians do not look to the person, they look to appearances only." They may scream at the injustice of such a view of people when directed towards themselves, and, as I have shown elsewhere (Wikan, 1980 and 1983:108–111), women try hard to escape ranking on material standards and substitute or add moral standards. Yet they are caught in a trap for reasons far too complicated to set out here, and they show it in their own priorities. The message to be read from the list of acquisitions is above all that these Cairo poor have gained greatly in self-esteem through these years. Self-esteem is not likely to enter into any international catalogue of components of "level of living," but surely it should.

I shall return below to some other implications of the list. Let us first address directly some of the UN-proposed indicators:

Housing: About this item the UN Committee writes: "Housing is an important component in the level of living and yet it is a field in which comparatively little statistical work has been done" (op.cit.:42). "The Committee is compelled to the negative conclusion that no international indicator of housing is possible in the light of existing information." More important than statistics is "a discussion of concepts and definitions, and analysis of the universal and the local elements in housing" (ibid:43).

"It is practically universally recognized that adequate shelter represents one of the most fundamental elements in the level of living, but the fact is . . . that there are no indicators available for any appreciable number of countries, permitting international comparisons of . . . conditions of housing. . . Sufficient experience has been accumulated both in the less-developed and developed parts of the world to justify the conclusion that useful and comparable data can, in effect, be obtained on housing through the census, or sample survey, method. On the substantive side, the Committee recommended that in the collection of housing information, consideration be given to the collection of the following types of data, although specific decisions must be a function of local conditions:

1. Types of dwelling, including indication of construction materials used.
2. Area per occupant.
3. Number of persons per dwelling unit.
4. Water supply—drinking water and for other purposes.
5. Toilet facilities and sewage disposal.
6. Utilities and community facilities.
7. Household facilities of significance in specific cultures."

Were one to follow these indicators, the neighborhoods I am discussing would score poorly, and, indeed, as viewed by Western eyes, it is the condition of housing that relegates them to the position of slum dwellers. The houses in which they live are, every one of them, more dilapidated than before. No landlord will pay money on house maintenance in a poor area. House rents, once they are fixed, are frozen by law, which means that the only way to increase the rent is to have the house fall down and build it up anew (with the opportunity of gaining sizable key money in the process). The law of course is intended to protect the tenants, and protected they are in that they pay the same for the flat now that some of them did 30 years back (see below).

But the appearance of the house counts little to the Cairo poor. What does matter to some women is the appearance of her particular apartment (for "the house" is considered to belong to the woman), but even that, for most, counts little. Whether the walls are painted or not, if the window panes are broken or whole, matter extremely little compared to other things in life. It is an indication of the over-all improved condition of life that flats today are somewhat better kept than in 1970, some rooms with walls brightly painted, etc.

I could count area per occupant and number of persons per dwelling unit. This would show bettered results for some, and badly worsened ones for others. Significantly, the family with least area per occupant, or highest density of persons, is considered one of the best off among the poor. What is more, ten years back when they would have scored considerably better, in that only two adults and three small children shared the flat that today six adults and four children are crammed into, they were extremely poor. Thus housing does not enter into these peoples' estimate of their standard of living. It is considered irrelevant and beyond their control; some were lucky some years ago and obtained good flats, others were not, and today there is nothing you can do about it except build, if you own a piece of land. Some do (see below), but more because it pays to escape paying rent to others, than because a home of one's own has cultural value. Most people are stuck with what they have, and a bad dwelling does not detract from their status. The above mentioned family which is suffering from its cramped quarters (and particularly from the lack of sexual privacy for the parents), would, to obtain a flat with one small room more, have to increase its rent 10 times, plus pay key money. This because of the housing crisis in Cairo and the discrepancy between old and new rents. No poor Cairene, even if he had money, would be so spendthrift.

In trying to assess major functional aspects of the housing in question, i.e. its use value for the occupants' purposes—which of course enters in as a component of their actual level of living—some cultural facts must be remembered which likewise tend to reduce the relative importance of housing in the total picture. Space in itself is of little value; people are gregarious and definitely do *not* wish to be alone. Full information on and participation in the activities, comings and goings of all family members are appreciated. A separation of functions is not much valued; even in those flats where separate rooms are available, many choose to cook, eat, sit and sleep in the same room. With respect to beds, most Cairo poor would no doubt make statements to the effect that every person above the age of five or so should have his or her own bed. Yet their actual preference is for several persons to sleep together in a bed even when space is available; crowding together provides comfort and security. Sleeping on floors and even under beds, as some must, does not seem to be experienced as serious hardships. Spouses, or rather wives, are unhappy to have intercourse in a bed shared with their children, and try to do so quietly, after the children are asleep. But only the extreme overcrowding that destroys this degree of privacy is regarded as truly troublesome. Location within the city, on the other hand, is important. Cairo is growing and spreading swiftly, with extensive new areas growing up on the peripheries, far away from public transport and poorly served by shops. I know poor families who have moved out to such areas and built simple houses of their own there. Such homes have increased tremendously in value because of the housing shortage in Cairo, but people in their former neighborhood of residence, though they are clearly envious of these investments, also deprecate the rural appearance of the area where these settlers now live. They are proud to be urbanites, and the centrality of their poor neighborhood, close to public transport and well served by shops and markets, always open and accessible, is highly valued.

The UN report further makes reference to a component identified as "household facilities of significance in specific cultures" (op.cit.: 42). Rather than describing lavatory facilities, the cold water tap and the electricity available in practically all of the flats in the neighborhood I am discussing, I shall return again to my list of consumer goods on page 14 to comment on the problem of "cultural significance." The problem is that different items have different kinds of significance in a culture, and neither relative price nor any other single measure seems adequate to capture these differences. I have already indicated, in the case of TV, the special cultural significance of that facility in the context of a largely joyless life. This might be called its acknowledged utility, but this does not reflect a range of very significant implications which might be described as the indirect benefits of introducing that facility into a particular context of family life and conflict. But there is, in Egyptian culture, a further significance which also needs to be considered—its prestige effect. Any new or flashy material item that is conspicuous in the flat has a value far beyond its utility. A pair of curtains or a color TV, a bedspread, washing machine or butagaz stove, each dramatizes—though to unequal extent—your material achievement and status. The requirement is only that the target be *conspicuous*, a target for the eye.

It is striking and problematical that the items found on the acquisition list for 1982 seem to be very dissimilar with respect to utility, conspicuousness and indirect benefits, and to come out very unequally if one tries to construct an aggregate or net value in terms of these components. To my sketch of the cultural significance of TV—high on utility and high on indirect benefits—I can obviously add a high score on conspicuousness. It is for looking at, and when TV sets were few, even served as a facility for such purposes for neighbors, who would congregate around the sets of the more fortunate. In other words, the prestige value for owners can be put as optimal.

Compare this to the washing-machine. The relief it provides in the task of washing a sizable family's laundry in a tray of cold water filled from the one tap can hardly be exaggerated. In terms of utility it represents a drastic improvement in the level of living for women and young girls. In a poor flat it also serves satisfactorily as an eye-catcher. Indirect benefits are less easily identified than for TV; it lacks the collective family aspect and there are no particularly significant uses for the time freed from chores.

The butagaz stove, on the contrary, has display value more than utility. It is expensive to run, compared to the primus, and women tend to be afraid it will explode. More importantly, they dislike standing up to make food. With the primus they can sit on the floor.

Why then the widespread acquisition of butagaz stoves, when most other conspicuous items could serve equally well for competitive purposes? That so many families have bought themselves butagaz stoves is an indication of "surplus money" and prestige competition as an overwhelming cultural concern. In order of acquisition, TV has been consistently first, but a butagaz stove has preceded the washing machine in all but one household. I am not sure what we can read from this. During the early 1970s, it was the stove that figured in plans and discussions, whereas washing machines only appeared later—perhaps because of simple availability. But there are also effects on interaction with neighbors and relatives to consider. While early TV owners were proud to show off their sets to begin with, the perpetual throng of viewers became increasingly tiresome. I have heard women declare that they would never buy a washing machine, since, if they did, their relatives would elbow in to do their wash there, and never pay for the electricity used. Food, on the other hand, is generally so poor and short that people are ashamed of it and often hide it, and so cannot make use of the neighbor's stove for cooking. A variety of cultural and social circumstances thus affect the significance of such facilities in the Cairene slum context, and steer people's priorities in complex ways. But the general picture of improvement in the level of living is undeniable, and can be given a simple gross measure merely by enumerating items of acquisitions.

Attempts to measure food and clothing must likewise proceed by other means than estimating average income, purchasing power and cost-of-living, if cultural factors are to be taken into account. Yet some relatively simple methods for enumeration and measurement can be designed, once this context is understood and taken seriously.

To take food first, Cairo's poor generally ate better in 1982 than in 1969, and they were aware that they did so. Ten years back they would eat what they call nourishing food *(ghidhā')*, that is meat, fish, eggs, cheese, milk, and other expensive foods, only three to four times a month. Today they have meat a couple of times a week and they have larger servings of it. Whereas in 1969 my estimates were that at these rare good meals the meat intake of each adult person was approximately 50 grams, ten years later I estimate it has doubled. They also have milk, cheese, eggs, etc. much more frequently. But these are still considered luxury items and not part of the daily diet. The latter consists of vegetable mixtures, sweetened tea and bread. Prices of these have doubled over these ten years, but they are heavily subsidized by the government, and prices are recognized to be low by the poor. Any measured estimate of the level of living as regards food among the Cairo poor must take account of what their diet in fact was, in 1969 and is now, not how prices for foods in Egypt have risen on the whole. "Food" *is* vegetable stew, rice, unleavened bread, tea and sugar—not primarily because of price but because of cultural convention and habituation. Increased consumption of *ghidhā'*, by having more meat more frequently in a stew is a cultural improvement in the level of living, as is the increased use of fresh fruits. A change to using meats, e.g. in the form of lamb chops, would no doubt entail increased protein intake, but would represent a change in food conventions and not a betterment in level of living in local cultural terms. A measure of improvement should therefore focus on the frequency and volume of ghidhā' within the conventions of poor Cairene cuisine.

On clothing the UN Commission reports: "The adequacy of clothing as an element in the level of living is significantly affected by climate, occupation, tradition and social status. . . Under the circumstances it is not possible to recommend at this stage indicators of this component that can be used for international comparison. . . It is, however, desirable that statements on the level of living should include available data in this field and be supplemented by descriptive materials to permit their interpretation in the context of national or local cultures." (op.cit.:44)

Had a concept like level of living any meaning for the Cairo poor, and should they be asked to gauge it, I have no doubt that they would consider clothing as one of the most significant items. This is because they are Egyptians, not because they are poor. Among comparable urban poor in Italy, food would seem to be stressed at the expense of clothing (Belmonte 1980). The Cairo poor live in a culture where clothing is the most significant item of appearance, and shame falls on him who reveals his poverty through his appearance.

There is no doubt that the population I am describing dresses significantly better today than in 1969. If it were possible to enumerate the number of items of clothing per person, not to speak of their quality, this could be documented. In 1969 and the early 1970s, situations repeatedly arose when some members or all members of a family had to refrain from attending weddings (and such nonappearance is inevitably interpreted as an unfriendly or even contemptuous act) because they lacked the clothes or shoes that would allow them to be present. But the simplest measure is presence vs. absence at the 'Id or feast at the end of

Ramadan. To participate in the feast, one must, according to convention, wear new clothes. In 1969 the families I knew were torn by conflicts over this issue during the weeks preceding the Feast, and only 6 of 17 were able to participate (see Wikan, 1980, esp. 12–15). Since 1980 all the families except one have participated[3].

My discussion of change in level of living so far has largely treated families as units, stressing changes that affect the members more or less collectively. Let us now break the population down. The lives of the old have significantly improved. New pensions have been established and old ones have risen. A widow who in 1974 had to live on her son's or daughter's mercy, now receives a pension of £E.10 a month. The difference between having ten pounds and having nothing is not ten pounds, it's a world.

Women's lives have significantly improved, both in terms of labor, leisure, material comforts and human rights. A decision by the president of the republic, dating from 1979, and modifying certain provisions of the laws of personal status, have improved women's status, and they know it. The security gained for them and their children is highly appreciated by them.

Men's lives have improved, but not to the extent of women's. They have lost some privileges. But they work less, earn more, eat better, go better dressed, have greater leisure, gamble less, assume greater responsibility and receive appreciable acknowledgement in return.

Young people are at a disadvantage. They need work, they need to marry, and they need a house. Many of them are educated and have unrealistic expectations of what education should bring. Young boys with a university education which it may have taken them a decade to obtain find they can earn less than does an electrical trainee. Girls who have finished secondary school might, if they are lucky, find a job. But they may also find that their value on the marriage market has declined. The picture is inconclusive. In the poor area I know intimately, more girls than boys have completed secondary education. These girls are attractive for some men, themselves educated, because of their income-earning potential. They are not acceptable to uneducated men: "She will be better than he and look down upon him." Moreover, most educated girls had hoped they could quit work once they married (see Wikan 1983:241–42). The men force them to go on. The reason is the rent. A young couple will have to pay about £E.25–30

3. The one family that has not participated, is, interestingly, the one that I reckoned to be the best off in 1969; the head had an exceptionally high income (£ E 51) and living quarters were good. What has happened since is that the father has been pensioned, and a son, an exceptionally hard-working and kind-hearted person, who looked after the family, is reported to be either dead or in prison in Saudi Arabia. The family has not been able to find out. Two other sons, both of them blind, who were in 1969 living at a boarding school for the blind, have since moved home. A daughter who after years of engagement could not find a flat, was finally given one room of the small family flat, so she could marry. Consequently the family's real income has been considerably reduced after the early 1970s, and living quarters are increasingly cramped.

for a flat comparable to the one for which their parents pay £E.3–5. £E.25 equals a regular monthly salary as an office worker. Hence the need for the women to continue working.

Young girls did not foresee such connections between education, marital value and marital life. They, and their mothers, thought education would better their life chances (their fathers disagreed). Strikingly, the girl in the area who made the best marriage in terms of its material advantages had not a year of elementary school and came from the poorest family. The boys who were considered the most eligible, two men with university education, both settled for uneducated girls.

But if we regard education as a value in itself, as one of the good things which enhance level of living, the young generation certainly also shows a dramatic improvement over the preceding generation.

In nearly all respects, we are thus witness to an improved level of living in terms of the standards and priorities embraced by Cairo's poor people. It is interesting to raise the question of how this improvement has come about, what have been the human and material sources and prime movers. Above all, the question arises as to the extent to which poor people themselves have been the driving force, or to what extent they have been the beneficiaries of fortuitous or government-directed and financed programs.

In my judgment, there can be no question but that the poor themselves have been significant agents in reshaping their own lives; my observations do not support the more extreme versions of a culture-of-poverty view which sees the poor as culturally preconditioned to reproduce their own poverty (Lewis, 1966:xlv). This is not to minimize the fact that reforms have been introduced from above to improve their lot, subsidies and price controls have been administered to aid them, and external factors have generated the better times to which they are responding. But this would all have availed little, had they not had the general and widespread capacity to respond and make swift use of marginal improvements in opportunities and circumstances.

It is notable that the main basis of this response has depended on the attitudes and activities of poor *women;* they have done the ground work, and it is their initial successes to which their husbands respond, and thereby also come increasingly to contribute. This interpretation agrees entirely with their own view. In the culture of the Cairo poor, it is regarded as self-evident that women, as wives and mothers, are the ones who must plan and think ahead; only they have the will and the ability to invest, whether in their children's futures or in their own homes. Men have no time or ability for such things; they must earn while "I, who have never earned a piastre, have always been the provider in the family!" (Wikan 1983:63) This is also reflected in the folk wisdom that women preach: God helps those who help themselves. It is no use expecting the world to change on its own for your sake. God rewards initiative and responsibility. But men, say women, are irresponsible and shortsighted, and unable to act as they should.

Over the years between 1969 and today, what have been the fields to which women have directed their efforts, and with what effects? The most important have been:

1. *Education for children.* "Egypt is the land of certificates and testimonials," they have all generally agreed, and so nearly every mother has set about trying to help her own children to secure such testimonials. Public school is free, except for uniforms and equipment (pencils, paper etc.), and women have saved and equipped and largely motivated their children for school. They have borrowed and saved to pay for private lessons often from first grade elementary school, when the children did poorly; and *they* have paid when the children failed annual exams twice, as most do sooner or later, and have been turned out from public schools. Fathers have been uninterested, or often negative; mothers have been firm in their belief that education was the grand road to betterment and largely convinced their children.

In material terms, these great investments have not been as advantageous as expected. As noted, salaries have developed recently in ways that have favored unskilled or craft-skilled men much more than office workers. One can hardly criticize Cairene women for not anticipating this, however, and in terms of Egyptian class and value standards, education remains a major source of prestige. For girls, it is still the main route to employment opportunities in offices and factories; unskilled employment as domestics, the only alternative, is regarded as extremely shameful.

It should be noted that mothers have also been in a position to anticipate benefits for themselves of such investments and potential mobility. Whereas the relationship between fathers and small children are often poor, and those between fathers and adult children are nearly non-existent, mothers and children remain close throughout life, and mothers have largely been supported in later life by their children.

2. *Protection and improvement of the home.* In many cases, women's mobilization of loans in financial crises have saved the 17 families of my sample from evictions. (e.g., Wikan 1983:67–70) Throughout, it is they who have saved and administered the investments in household appliances that have reshaped poor homes and lives. It started with TV's which they saw primarily as necessary to keep the children home and off the streets. As goods have accumulated, so have all family members' self-pride. Whereas previously men were too ashamed of their homes to bring acquaintances there, they now have items to show off, with pride. But for the efforts of wives, these homes would have remained monuments to men's failures as wage earners. But now, when the bases have been laid, men also join in the effort, and take pride in acquisitions. I can hardly overdramatize the turning-point it represented in the family with which I have lived most, when

the husband one day returned home with the first item he himself had purchased: an electric fan which cost him £E110.

3. *Purchase of building plots on the periphery of Cairo.* This has been the dream of many poor Cairo women, and three of my sample of 17 have succeeded. Husbands argued against it: "What's the use of this bit of land? We can never afford to build, and you can't take it with you!"

"Perhaps we will never be able to afford it, but then perhaps our children can." Two have managed to build so far, and a third would have, had she not inherited another slum tenement. The building sites have proved a very good investment, with soaring prices. The arrangement has also implied compulsory savings; installments have had to be paid, or the rights would be lost. Husbands have protested, and one even tried to steal the deed so as to sell it rather than pay on it. (Wikan 1983:95) The women originally were solely responsible for management of the transactions, saving for the installments, paying the registration fees, obtaining the building permits etc. Only in the last two years have I heard the men finally join in such plans and the man who in 1976 tried to steal the deed from his wife in 1982 said when I left: "Perhaps next year when you come back, we will have built!"

What are the cultural and institutional bases for such remarkable management and ability to respond to opportunities? Above all, I would identify them in the jungle of savings clubs *(gam'iyyāt)* which poor Cairene women administer for a number of small and large purposes (Wikan 1983:40–95). I shall not go into their complex structure and organization, but need only to emphasize the pressures and stimuli which they mobilize, particularly because of the necessity to enlist members. In need of money yourself, you start a club and you have the right to draw the first installment—but you have to mobilize a membership of others willing to pay their shares starting now but drawing their bonuses later. Alternatively, you go to someone recognized for being good at running such clubs, urging her to start one on your behalf. So the organizers circulate, encouraging one to save for a new bed here, and shaming another into saving for something else there, creating the network of commitments and motivation to manage to set aside some trifling daily or weekly sum, for a set, long-range purpose. Most members can only succeed in saving in their precarious economic condition because of these mutual commitments and pressures—and the houseplot installments, monthly school fees, TV payments and feast clothes could mostly never have been made without them.

In a social context of fierce rivalry and poor cooperation, the savings clubs dramatize long-term purposes and values and creates collective pressure for their achievement. Without these values and the cultural and social facilities, which the clubs provide, the results obtained would have been inconceivable. When they have succeeded to the extent they have, it is due to a fortunate consonance of external changes and embraced values, whereby the responses of the poor no longer simply reproduce their poverty but produce direct and indirect benefits to their level of living.

I have further tried to show where and how a macrostatistical approach to measurement of the level of living goes wrong, and how cultural factors must be taken into account to interpret changes and their import. Whereas my argument is overwhelmingly qualitative, it arrives at a number of indicators of a quantitative nature, very simple to enumerate and to determine. This would indicate that a cooperative effort between the social anthropologists and statisticians could lead to the development of a far more adequate instrument for measuring changes in level of living among Cairo's six to eight million poor citizens.

Bibliography

Belmonte, Thomas. 1979: *The Broken Fountain*. New York: Columbia University Press.

Geertz, Clifford. 1973: *The Interpretation of Cultures*. New York: Basic Books.

Heikal, Mohamed Hassanein. 1983: *Autumn of Fury*. London: Deutsch.

Lewis, Oscar. 1966: *La Vida: A Puerto Rican Family in the Culture of Poverty*. New York: Random House.

United Nations, 1954: Report on *International Definition and Measurement of Standards and Levels of Living*. New York.

Wikan, Unni. 1980: *Life among the Poor in Cairo*. London: Tavistock.

. . . . 1983: *Tomorrow, if God wills*. (in Norwegian) Oslo: Norwegian University Press.

Yinon, Oded. 1982: The Significance of Egypt's Population Problem. In *Middle Eastern Studies*. Vol. 18. p 378–386.

[2]

The Distributional Impact of Economic Growth and Decline in Egypt

Victor Levy

A growing body of evidence for the past two decades suggests that in many developing countries the benefit of economic growth has not been equitably distributed. In reaction to these findings, the main concern in development economics has been the nature of the income distribution and other measures of welfare. While there is some disagreement about the desired degree of overall equality, there is uniform concern about the need to improve the position of the poorest members of society.[1] As a result, the general feeling is that planners in developing countries ought to worry mainly about poverty and unemployment and that success in dealing with these social problems would result in an adequate overall rate of growth.[2] The underlying presumption is that social equity and economic growth are complementary objectives.[3]

The purpose of this paper is to analyse the experience of a developing country, Egypt, which since the late 1950s has committed itself to a development process aimed primarily at guaranteeing the equal distribution of income and increasing national income. This concern with equality and the social aspects of Egyptian economic development has so far produced too little evidence to evaluate the success or failure of past policies.[4] Here I attempt to analyse Egyptian time-series data on the income distribution, beginning in the late 1950s and stretching into the 1970s.

During the first part of this period (1958–64) Egypt achieved a substantial rate of growth by the standards of less developed countries, real private consumption increasing by 26 per cent. In the next decade, although real gross domestic product grew by over two per cent per annum, private consumption declined by six per cent. Since the population increased by 21 per cent over this decade, per capita private consumption declined by 27 per cent.

In this article I examine the distributional impact of economic growth during the period 1958–74. The analysis centers on the fundamental question: who (as classified by income) received what share of the proceeds of economic growth? In answering this question I follow Fields[5] in adopting an absolute income approach and comparing the results with measures of relative income inequality and Lorenz curves. The methodology used is basically that used by Fields in studying Brazil, including the calculation of the decomposition measures developed by him to show how income growth affects the poor. The present work differs from his analysis in the use of the household rather than individual recipients, the correction of the distribution of income among households for differences in family size, the method used to compute the mean income of the poor and non-poor, and the decomposition of the change in mean income into the parts attributable to changes in age structure, labor force participation rates and real wages. The problems pointed out by critics of Field's work are thus overcome.[6] The conceptual and statistical improvements are made possible by the better data available for Egypt from household budget surveys.

The results indicate that in 1958–64 Egypt experienced a significant reduction in poverty. However, the bulk of the income increment was received by those who were above the poverty standard at the beginning of the period. The evidence from the next decade is quite different. There was a marked increase in the fraction of the population below the poverty line. Those who remained non-poor received markedly lower incomes. However, the absolute improvement of the first period was accompanied by an increase in income inequality while the severe deterioration of the next decade was accompanied by a reduction in income inequality. These and other findings are presented in Section II; some of the reasons for the observed changes are discussed in Section III.

I. THE LEVEL AND DISTRIBUTION OF INCOME

The most consistent information on Egypt's income distribution comes from a series of three consumer budget surveys conducted in 1958/59, 1964/65 and 1974/75.[7] The surveys were stratified into separate urban and rural samples. Data were collected monthly on the value of regularly consumed items (food, beverages, fuel, electricity, clothes, etc.). Expenditures on consumer durables and services for a one-year period were collected during the third month of each round. Data on household size, age, sex and employment characteristics were also collected. For the purpose of this study the use of consumption or expenditure data rather than income data has been preferred; this is partly because consumption can be measured more reliably than income but chiefly because it serves as a better proxy for permanent income than current income (for convenience, the term income is used instead of expenditure throughout the article).

The data for all three surveys are summarized in Table 1, which presents the distribution of income by per capita household income, for the urban and rural sectors. Two measures of income inequality are used; the first is the simple measure suggested by Kuznets, the sum of the absolute differences between class shares in total income and total number, referred to as the TDM or total disparities measures;[8] the second is the Gini coefficient.

In general, the inequality measures in Table 1 indicate that the income distribution is fairly egalitarian by the standards of developing countries. There was some increase in equality in the rural income distribution between 1958/59 and 1964/65, and a slight reduction in the decade ending in 1974/75. The urban patterns was the converse, with an increase in income inequality in the first period, and a decrease in the second. An alternative measure of income inequality, the share of income accruing to the poorest 40 per cent, increased from 23 to 25 per cent during the first period but fell to 23 per cent in the next decade in the rural sector. The corresponding urban figures were 19 per cent in 1958/59 and 1964/65, rising to 20 per cent in 1974/75.

TABLE 1

INCOME DISTRIBUTION, PERSONS CLASSIFIED BY HOUSEHOLD PER CAPITA INCOME

Annual per capita income (£E) *	1958/9 Rural Per cent of Income	1958/9 Rural Per cent of Population	1958/9 Urban Per cent of Income	1958/9 Urban Per cent of Population	1964/65 Rural Per cent of Income	1964/65 Rural Per cent of Population	1964/65 Urban Per cent of Income	1964/65 Urban Per cent of Population	1974/75 Rural Per cent of Income	1974/75 Rural Per cent of Population	1974/75 Urban Per cent of Income	1974/75 Urban Per cent of Population
0–9	0.04	0.25	1.70	5.07	0.01	0.04	0.02	0.08				
10–19	3.73	12.04	15.70	28.28	0.86	3.39	3.17	7.78	0.04	0.34	0.32	1.52
20–29	11.02	21.63	27.04	31.17	5.82	14.62	16.75	26.34	0.51	1.95	2.76	6.64
30–39	9.81	14.28	23.38	19.00	10.01	18.15	25.76	29.55	2.13	6.09	9.34	16.61
40–49	13.31	15.70	16.17	9.69	8.55	12.37	16.67	14.84	4.80	10.99	13.73	19.34
50–59	17.72	16.45	2.36	1.10	10.53	12.87	14.47	10.67	6.38	11.82	13.41	15.42
60–69	11.23	7.92	7.93	3.37	16.18	15.58	9.27	5.66	14.01	20.67	22.36	20.36
80–99	9.81	5.27	3.68	1.17	9.80	7.18	6.63	2.95	13.08	15.03	12.83	9.10
100–149	6.64	2.48	1.36	0.31	16.29	8.79	4.84	1.72	20.43	17.34	14.75	7.86
150–199	9.95	3.08	0.32	0.06	10.87	3.91	0.75	0.17	12.23	7.27	5.44	2.08
200–249	0.29	0.07	0.05	0.02	5.04	1.48	0.60	0.12	7.01	3.24	1.92	0.57
250–299	0.83	0.17	0.35	0.05	1.68	0.42	0.19	0.03	5.88	2.22	0.91	0.20
300+	5.61	0.66			7.39	1.19	0.83	0.08	13.52	3.03	2.21	0.11
TDM		52.00		41.06		54.04		36.01		51.09		40.01
Gini		0.33		0.29		0.35		0.25		0.33		0.28

* At current prices.

However, the level of real income appears to tell another story. During the first period, per capita income (at 1964/65 prices) increased from £E62 to £E66 (or by six per cent) in the urban sector, and from £E35 to £E41 (or by 17 per cent) in the rural sector. In the next decade, per capita income declined to £E50 (by 24 per cent) and to £E30 (by 27 per cent) in the urban and rural sectors respectively. This deterioration appears to be more severe once demographic and employment changes are taken into account, changes that are summarized by the dependency ratio. The ratio of earners to household members is shown in the last column of Table 2, and it is higher in 1974/75 than in 1964/65 in almost every income bracket and in both sectors: the average urban ratio rose from 0.22 to 0.29 and the rural from 0.20 to 0.26. These changes imply that the number of persons supported by every earner has declined by more than 1: in urban areas from 4.5 to 3.4, and in rural areas from 5 to 3.8. The reduction in the dependency ratio is associated with stable average family size throughout the period.[9] The reduction in the dependency rate evidently has its origins in the changing age structure of the population and in changes in the employment ratio. In 1964/65, 18 and 59 per cent of the urban population were aged 0–5 and 14+, respectively. The corresponding 1974/75 figures are 11 and 68 per cent. In the rural sector the changes are less marked; the percentage of population aged 0–5 declined, and the percentage of adults (14+) also declined somewhat. The change in age structure is coupled with a marked increase in the employment ratio; the percentage of urban employed persons aged 14+ increased from 38 in 1964/65 to 43 in 1974/75; the corresponding rural figures are 33 and 44. The increase in the working-age population and in the employment ratio both reduce the dependency ratio.

To summarize this section, it is evident that although income is somewhat more equally distributed in 1974/75 than in 1964/65, there is a decline in the economic welfare of the population. How is this decline distributed among the different income classes? Who shared the benefits of growth in the first period? This is the subject of the next section.

II. THE DISTRIBUTION OF THE BENEFITS OF GROWTH

In comparing the changes in the incomes of the poor and non-poor, four related questions can be asked:

1. Did the fraction of the population classified as poor increase or decrease over the two periods, i.e., was the incidence of poverty reduced?
2. What were the rates of change of poor and non-poor income, i.e., were those who remained poor becoming less poor (absolutely and relatively)?
3. How much of the economic growth of the period went to the poor and how much to the non-poor?
4. How much of the poverty gap (the aggregate amount by which incomes below the povery line would have to be raised to bring them all up to the poverty line) was filled during the decade?

We begin by establishing a poverty line. The minimum level of per capita income required in Egypt to ensure a minimum diet (the destitution line)

TABLE 2
DEMOGRAPHIC AND EMPLOYMENT STRUCTURE, BY PER CAPITA INCOME
A. 1964/65

Per capita income (£E)	Age structure of household			Percent employed in 14+ age group	Household size	Ratio of earners per person
	0-5	6-13	14+			
Rural						
0-9	15	35	50	30	6.5	0.15
10-19	21	31	48	34	6.4	0.17
20-29	21	25	54	34	6.3	0.18
30-39	12	23	65	31	5.8	0.20
40-49	17	20	67	34	5.3	0.21
50-59	15	20	65	33	4.9	0.22
60-79	15	18	67	35	4.8	0.21
80-99	15	16	69	36	4.6	0.22
100-149	5	16	79	42	3.4	0.33
150-199	4	13	83	47	3.9	0.39
200-249		9	91	34	3.2	0.33
250-299		07	93	50	4.3	0.36
300+		11	89	50	2.3	0.55
Total	17	22	61	33	5.5	0.20
Urban						
0-9	35	15	50	30	6.7	0.15
10-19	24	34	42	40	6.8	0.16
20-29	23	28	49	37	6.4	0.18
30-39	21	27	52	37	6.1	0.19
40-49	20	24	56	37	5.8	0.17
50-59	18	24	58	37	5.6	0.21
60-79	16	21	63	38	5.1	0.24
80-99	13	18	69	40	4.6	0.27
100-149	13	16	71	59	4.5	0.28
150-199	10	15	75	39	4.2	0.29
200-249	11	13	76	42	3.6	0.32
250-299	7	11	82	39	3.9	0.32
300+	5	10	85	40	3.0	0.34
Total	18	23	59	38	5.4	0.22

(Table continued overleaf)

B. 1974/75

Per capita income (£E)	Age structure of household			Percent employed in 14+ age group	Household size	Ratio of earners per person
	0-5	6-13	14+			
Rural						
0-19	19	27	54	44	6.7	0.24
20-29	19	34	57	49	6.6	0.23
30-39	17	33	50	46	6.5	0.23
40-49	16	33	51	46	6.2	0.24
50-59	14	26	60	42	6.2	0.26
60-79	14	21	65	41	5.7	0.27
80-99	11	21	69	42	5.2	0.29
100-149	11	16	73	39	4.7	0.29
150-199	09	18	73	48	4.3	0.35
200-249	08	14	82	51	3.3	0.43
250-299	05	17	78	53	3.5	0.41
300+	07	16	79	48	3.5	0.45
Total	15	26	59	44	5.7	0.26
Urban						
0-19	12	26	62	41	5.7	0.26
20-29	18	26	56	39	6.6	0.21
30-39	15	28	57	37	6.5	0.22
40-49	14	24	62	38	6.5	0.24
50-59	13	25	62	41	5.2	0.25
60-79	11	24	66	40	5.9	0.26
80-99	11	21	68	42	5.6	0.28
100-149	10	26	74	44	5.0	0.32
150-199	08	16	76	50	4.4	0.38
200-249	11	10	79	53	4.1	0.42
250-299	07	14	79	54	4.1	0.42
300+	06	12	82	56	3.5	0.49
Total	11	21	68	43	5.4	0.29

was estimated by Radwan (1977) at £E13, £E16.6, and £E34.8 in 1958/59, 1964/65, and 1974/75, respectively.[10] To this was added the expenditure on non-food items of those survey households whose actual per capita expenditure on goods was closest to the value of the minimum diet. The minimum per capita cost of living was estimated for urban and rural Egypt at respectively £E20 and £E19 in 1958/59, £E25.5 and £E24 in 1964/65 and £E54 and £E50 in 1974/75.[11] Table 3 presents the percentage of population and households whose per capita income is equal to or below these minimum standards and the destitution line.[12]

TABLE 3
PERCENTAGE OF POPULATION AND HOUSEHOLDS BELOW THE DESTITUTION AND POVERTY LINES *

	1958/59		1964/65		1974/75	
	Rural	Urban	Rural	Urban	Rural	Urban
Population						
Destitute	17.1	5.0	6.3	2.8	17.9	6.0
Nondestitute poor	17.0	7.5	14.7	10.1	26.0	19.3
All poor	34.1	12.5	21.0	12.9	43.9	25.3
Households						
Destitute	16.7	4.6	5.2	1.9	15.7	4.0
Nondestitute poor	17.0	6.6	14.0	10.0	23.2	16.3
All poor	33.7	11.2	19.2	11.9	38.9	20.3

* For definition see text.

In answer to the first question, it is apparent that there was a large reduction in the incidence of rural poverty between 1958/59 and 1964/65. Total rural poverty declined by 38 per cent, reflecting mostly the significant reduction in the incidence of destitution. As can be seen in Table 3, the proportion of the destitute in the rural sector fell from 17 to six per cent, and the proportion of non-destitute poor from 17 to 15 per cent. The reduction in household poverty follows the same pattern. In the urban sector total poverty was practically constant. However, the proportion of urban destitute fell from 5 to 3 per cent, while the proportion of non-destitute poor rose from 8 to 10 per cent. In the following decade, the results are very different: the incidence of overall poverty doubled in both sectors. Most disturbing is the findings that in 1974/75, 18 per cent of the rural population was undernourished in comparison with only 6 per cent ten years earlier.

Next let us compare the rates of change of poor and non-poor incomes. Since the poverty line does not coincide with the income brackets of Tables 1 and 2, the following procedure was used to calculate the mean income of the destitute, the non-destitute poor, and the non-poor: in the rural sector in 1964 (for example), the poor in the £E20–29 income bracket were assigned a mean income of £E22 and the non-poor in the same bracket a mean income of £E27.

The results are summarized in Table 4. During the first period the rural poor became noticeably less poor. Their real per capita income rose by 24 per cent, reflecting a smaller share of destitution in total poverty and an increase of 23 per cent in the income of those between the destitution and poverty lines. The poverty of those who remained destitute was essentially constant. The income of the non-poor rose more slowly, by three per cent. The result was to narrow the gap between the poor and the non-poor: the

TABLE 4
MEAN ANNUAL INCOME OF POOR AND NON-POOR (1964/65 EL)

	1958/59		1964/65		1974/75	
	Rural	Urban	Rural	Urban	Rural	Urban
All poor	16.0	19.6	19.9	21.1	18.2	20.3
Destitute	13.5	14.4	13.5	13.4	14.0	14.3
Non-destitute	18.4	23.1	22.6	23.2	21.0	22.1
Non-poor	44.3	68.0	45.7	72.2	40.1	58.7
Total	34.6	62.0	40.3	65.6	30.1	49.0

ratio of non-poor to poor incomes fell from 2.8 to 2.3 and the absolute income gap between the two groups narrowed by nine per cent.

In the urban sector too, the mean income of all the poor rose by eight per cent, although that of the destitute fell by seven per cent and that of the non-destitute poor remained constant. The gain is thus the result of the marked decline in the proportion of destitutes. Unlike their rural counterparts, the urban non-poor gained as much as the poor, their mean per capita income increasing by six per cent. In consequence the absolute differences between poor and non-poor incomes increased and the income ratio remained constant. Thus, although the urban poor experienced an absolute improvement in income, the distribution of income between poor and non-poor was less equal in 1964/65 than in 1958/59.

In the next decade, the mean incomes of all four groups (urban and rural, poor and non-poor) declined, though not at the same rate. The non-poor paid the heaviest price, their income declining by 19 to 12 per cent in urban and rural areas respectively. The income of the rural destitute increased by four per cent, while the other poor experienced a seven per cent decline. The same is true of the urban sector: the income of the destitute increased, while that of the other poor declined by five per cent.

These changes made the urban distribution of income between poor and non-poor more equal, both in terms of absolute real income (the gap narrowed by 26 per cent) and in terms of relative income (the ratio declined by 15 per cent). This is in line with changes in income inequality reported in the preceding section. In rural areas, although the number of poor more than tripled in ten years, the distribution of income between poor and non-poor is more equal in 1974/75 than in 1964/65. The absolute real income differential narrowed by more than 16 per cent (from 26 to 22) but the ratio of non-poor to poor declined by four per cent.[13] Thus in 1974/75 income was more equally distributed (especially in the urban sector) at a much lower level, implying a considerably greater incidence of poverty. It is therefore evident that inequality and poverty measures move in opposite directions in both of the periods studied. Whether a relative inequality or an absolute poverty measure is chosen thus makes a considerable difference in assessing whether economic growth and decline have benefited or harmed the poor. Fields has suggested a welfare approach to growth and distribution based on a general welfare function with both relative and absolute measures of economic welfare as arguments.[14] It follows that any evaluation of the distributional effect of growth depends on whether we believe the narrowing of relative income inequality or the reduction of the incidence of poverty to be more important.

The next question is how much of the overall growth benefited the poor and the non-poor in the two periods. The total income growth of each group can be partitioned into two components: one attributable to the enlargement (or contraction) or the group to include a greater (or smaller) percentage of the population, the other attributable to the enrichment of the population of the group. The latter component results from a change in per capita income, which itself depends on the wage, employment or age structure of the population.[15] The analysis of total growth is summarized in Table 5. During the first period, the non-poor gained most of the benefit of growth: 63 per cent of the growth increased their real income, while 30 per cent raised the poor above the poverty line. Only eight per cent made those remaining poor somewhat less so. However, this overall pattern masks the differences between the urban and rural sectors. In the latter, the poor benefited most from growth: 67 per cent of the income increment raised poor persons above the poverty line and 14 per cent went to make those remaining poor better off. This means that 80 per cent of the growth benefited the poor. In the urban sector, since the non-poor enlargement effect was negative, the only significant benefit to the poor was an increase in the income of those who remained poor.

Most of the burden of the lack of growth of the following decade was

TABLE 5
ANALYSIS OF ECONOMIC GROWTH

	Non-poor		Poor	Percentage of growth benefiting the poor
	Enlargement	Enrichment	Enrichment	
	(1)	(2)	(3)	(1) + (3)
1958/59–1964/65				
Rural	66.5	19.9	13.6	80.1
Urban	-6.7	101.4	5.3	-1.4
Total	30.0	62.9	7.9	37.9
1964/65–1974/75				
Rural	-60.0	-32.0	-7.8	-67.8
Urban	-38.0	60.8	-1.2	-39.2
Total	-49.1	-47.9	-3.0	-52.1

borne by those who had been above the poverty line in 1964/65: of the total reduction in income, 48 per cent impoverished the non-poor and 49 per cent reduced non-poor to poverty. Only three per cent of the total reduction in income made the poor poorer. In this case, the rural and urban patterns are the same. In both sectors, it was the non-poor who paid the price of stagnation. However, in the rural sector it was mostly in the form of reducing non-poor to poverty (enlargement effect of −60), while in the urban sector it was mainly in the form of impoverishing those who remained non-poor (enrichment effect of −61), It can be seen that the enrichment effect would have been even more negative in both sectors without the increase in the employment ratio and the change in the age structure (described in the previous section) which compensated significantly for the fall in the real wage and kept income per capita from declining further.

Finally, we can examine the extent to which Egypt closed its poverty gap during the first period and widened it in the second. The poverty gap is defined as the total shortfall of poor incomes, that is, the sum of the differences between each poor person's income and the poverty line.[16] The poverty gap in the benchmark years was £E44, £E15, and £E53 in the rural sector and £E7, £E7, and £E19 in the urban sector. In the first period, 65 and six per cent of the gap was closed in the urban and rural sectors respectively. In the next decade the rural gap almost quadrupled and the urban gap tripled. As can be observed in Table 6, the reduction in the rural poverty gap is attributable in (roughly) equal measures in the increase in poor incomes and the decline in the number of poor; in the urban sector, the narrowing of the gap was due entirely to the first of these. In the second period, the two components are also roughly equal in importance, but they worked in the opposite direction and the poverty gap widened.

III. WHY IT HAPPENED: SOME ECONOMIC AND POLICY DEVELOPMENTS

In the early 1960s Egypt appeared to have embarked on the road to sustained growth. Since 1957 its national product per capita had increased steadily by over three per cent and annual aggregate output had increased by about seven per cent. In 1960/61 the first five-year plan was implemented and the government concentrated more, and more systematically, on development and growth. In general, the non-farm sector showed the highest growth rates. Electricity, with a growth rate of 18 per cent, was the most rapidly expanding sector. The next highest growth rate, 11.1 per cent, occurred in transport and communications, partly because of the vigorous expansion of Suez Canal traffic. Construction followed closely with 10.4 per cent, and industry came next with 8.5 per cent.

During this period the welfare and economic policies of the government had two aims: greater equality in the distribution of income and increased consumption of a number of goods and services. The principal measures for attaining the former were land reform, nationalization of all large private enterprises (except in agriculture) and public-sector employment. Land reform was the main factor changing the distribution of land ownership and

TABLE 6
AN ANALYSIS OF POVERTY GAP

	Percentage change during period in			Percent of change in poverty gap attributable to change in proportion of poor
	Poverty gap	Proportion of poor in population	Percentage difference between mean income of poor and poverty line	
1958/59–1964/65				
Rural	-65	-38	-58	-58
Urban	-6	4	-36	-67
Total	-63	-33	-59	54
1964/65–1974-75				
Rural	263	121	82	46
Urban	246	109	52	44
Total	198	96	28	48

agricultural wealth. The immediate effect of the series of laws was to remove the top bracket in the existing distribution of land ownership and to benefit the upper section of the poor group. The landless peasants (defined as neither owners or tenants) benefited very little from the direct measures of the reform. Nationalization of the large industrial enterprises did not in itself increase the wealth of the poor group, because the measures were 'essentially private rather than distributive',[17] but it did reduce the concentration at the wealthy end of society. Moreover, nationalization enabled the government to enact and enforce a number of laws granting substantial benefits to workers. These measures included a higher minimum wage, insurance plans for industrial workers, profit-sharing schemes whereby 25 per cent of the net profit was distributed among employees, higher sick pay, and a higher ceiling on sick leave.

The very poor in Egypt, those who owned no land either before or after the land reform and those not employed in the non-farm sector, did not benefit directly from these measures. However, their absolute and relative standard of living was improved by changes in the labor market. Because wages are higher in industry than in agriculture, and hence in urban than in rural areas, the movement of labor from agriculture to the higher income sectors reduced poverty. The proportion of the labor force employed in the lower-paid occupations (agriculture and construction) declined while the proportion with above-average earnings (manufacturing and public sector) increased significantly. The urban population grew faster than the rural because of substantial rural-to-urban migration. Very little unskilled rural labor moves directly to modern industry. An important route is via construction activities, since present techniques in canal and road works and in urban construction require a large volume of unskilled labor. Construction accounted for the largest relative increase of employment in Egypt in the early 1960s. This change was accompanied by a strong increase in wages of unskilled laborers in agriculture as well as in construction.

Egypt's war with the Yemen increased defense expenditure and reduced the rate of growth. The war of June 1967, resulting in considerable loss of factors of production, brought a further increase in defense expenditures, and economic growth came to a standstill. The basic dimensions of change are given in Table 7. From 1964/65 to 1973 the share of growth expenditure in GDP declined from 22.4 to 19.8 per cent and public non-growth expenditures rose from 14.6 to 27.4 per cent of GDP; the latter increase was due mainly to the increase in defense expenditure, which rose from 5.5 (in 1959/60) to 11.8 per cent. As a result of this increase which began in 1963/64 in connection with the Yemen War, combined with a sharp decline in net foreign borrowing, the share of growth expenditure stayed constant and there was a precipitous fall in the share of private consumption, from about 70 per cent in 1957/58 to 58 per cent in 1973. Egypt kept down private consumption and growth expenditures sufficiently to make room for the defense budget, within the limits set by the national product plus the balance-of-payments deficit. The significant reduction in per capita income and the sharp increase in the incidence of poverty during this decade indicate that self-financing development without foreign borrowing was not possible in Egypt. An attempt to increase the defense budget while simultaneously increasing national product and private consumption without increasing the external debt had failed.

The structural change in the labor market during the first period continued in the next decade. However, the shift to higher-paid occupations could not compensate for the almost universal reduction in real wages. The steepest decline was experienced in the public sector (electricity, transport, public utilities), the smallest was in industry and agriculture.[18] Thus the behavior of real wages confirms the results obtained from the expenditure surveys.

Government agricultural price policy has aggravated rural poverty. Since 1965 the government, through the co-operative marketing regulations, has kept down the prices received by farmers for many products. In view of the continuous increase in the world prices of these products and the cost of living in Egypt, this imposed a growing implicit tax on farm incomes.[19] However, it is the small farmer who has been hardest hit by this high implicit rate of taxation. There are significant differences in crop mix by size of farm. While small farmers usually grow traditional crops such as cotton, wheat, and rice, the large farmers are able to evade crop quotas (imposed on price-controlled products such as cotton) and to diversify their output with fruit, vegetables and livestock, which have never been subject to the co-operative

TABLE 7
THE PATTERN OF NATIONAL EXPENDITURE:
SELECTED YEARS, 1957/58–1973

	1957/58	1961/62	1964/65	1969/70	1973
1. Gross investment	1,224.1	1,513.0	2,213.5	2,971.3	3,644.6
2. Public consumption	13.5	16.6	17.2	14.0	13.7
3. Of which: Defense	16.3	17.3	19.8	24.1	33.5 *
4. Education and health	-	5.8	9.6	6.6	11.8 *
5. Growth expenditure (lines 1 + 4)	-	21.3	22.4	19.2	19.8
6. Private consumption	72.0	71.7	65.5	62.3	58.1
7. Import surplus	1.6	5.6	2.5	0.5	5.4
Total (lines 1+2+6-7)	100.0	100.0	100.0	100.0	100.0
Total GDP at current market prices (£E million)	1,224.1	1,513.0	2,213.5	2,971.3	3,644.6

(per cent of GDP)

* Includes deficit in the emergency defense fund set up in 1967/68.
Source: Ministry of Finance.

marketing regulations; since their prices have risen much faster than the prices of the traditional crops, the large farmers are able to increase their profit rate. For example, the net return per acre of cotton was £E54.5 in 1973/74, compared with £E100–150 for grapes, £E150–200 for tomatoes, and £E100 for water melons.[20]

IV. CONCLUSION

This paper has examined the changing patterns of income inequality and poverty in Egypt in the period 1958–74. The results indicate a U-shaped pattern of urban income distribution: greater inequality in the first period, the Gini and the TDM coefficients being somewhat higher in 1964 than in 1960, and more equality in the second period. The rural sector had the contrary pattern: a decline in inequality followed by an increase. However, using an explicitly poverty-oriented approach focusing on absolute rather than relative incomes, we find that in both rural and urban Egypt the poor shared in the benefits of economic development in the first period and in the hardship of the economic decline in the next. Among other things, during the first period, the percentage increase in income of those below the poverty line was double (urban) and triple (rural) the percentage increase above the line. In the next decade all groups suffered a decline in real income. The reduction in rural poverty in the first period is due to a combination of favorable developments: the rapid growth of the economy and the decline in rural income inequality. In the next decade, however, neither occurred in rural Egypt, that is, relative inequality increased in a declining economy, leading to a serious increase in the incidence of poverty and in the poverty gap. In this decade the urban sector experienced a decline in relative inequality combined with a drop in the standard of living. The decline in income more than offset rising equality, however, leading to lower absolute incomes for the poor and the non-poor and a higher incidence of poverty.

NOTES

I would like to thank Shlomo Yitzhaki for helpful discussion on the topic. S. Kuznets and R. Gronau made helpful comments on an earlier draft.

1. See Irma Adelman, 'Planning for Social Equity', in H.C. Bos, H. Linneman and P. de Wolff (eds.), *Economic Structure and Development: Essays in Honour of Jan Tinbergen* (Amsterdam and London: North-Holland; New York: American Elsevier, 1973), pp.181–200; Montek S. Ahluwalia, 'Inequality, Poverty and Development', *Journal of Development Economics*, III (December 1976), pp.307–42; M.S. Ahluwalia, N.G. Carter, and H.B. Chenery, 'Growth and Poverty in Developing Countries', *Journal of Development Economics,* VI (September 1979), pp.299–431; and Gary S. Fields, 'Who Benefits from Economic Development?–A Reexamination of Brazilian Growth in the 1960s,' *American Economic Review,* LXVII (September 1977), pp.570–82.
2. Annual address by Robert S. McNamara, 'Summary Proceedings', 1972 Annual Meeting of the Board of Governors (Washington, DC: International Bank for Reconstruction and Development, 1972).
3. This is in direct contradition to the widely accepted hypothesis, first stated by Simon Kuznets, 'Economic Growth and Income Inequality', American Economic Review, XLV (March 1955), pp.1–28, that the association between equality of income and the condition of the poorest, on the one hand, and economic development, on the other, is U-shaped: as the economy develops, income equality and the share of the poorest first falls, but eventually increases.
4. The most relevant studies on this issue are M. Abel-Fadil, *Income Distribution and Social Change in Rural Egypt 1952–1970* (Cambridge University Press, 1975); El-Kholie (1975), O.A. El-Kholie, 'Disparities of Egyptian Personal Income Distribution as Reflected by Family Budget Data', *L'Egypt Comtemporaine* (October 1975), pp.358–72, and Samir Radwan, Agrarian Reform and Rural Poverty, Egypt, 1952–1975 (Geneva: ILO, 1977).
5. Fields, op.cit.; Gary S. Fields, 'A Welfare Economic Approach to Growth and Distribution in the Dual Economy', *Quarterly Journal of Economics,* XCIII (August 1979), pp.325–53.
6. Notably, M. Ahluwalia, John H. Duloy, Graham Pyatt, and T.N. Srinivasan, 'Who Benefits from Economic Development?: Comment,' *American Economic Review,* LXX (March 1980), pp.242–5, and Albert Fishlow, 'Who Benefits from Economic Development?: Comment', LXX (March 1980), pp.250–56.
7. For description and data see National Bank of Egypt, 'Development of Standard of Living in Urban and Rural Egypt according to Family Budget Data between 1958/59 and 1974/75', *Economic Bulletin,* XXXI (No.4, 1978), pp.313–35.
8. For the advantages and limitations of this measure, see Simon Kuznets, 'Quantitative Aspects for the Economic Growth of Nations II. Industrial Distribution of National

Product and Labor Force', *Economic Development and Cultural Change, V* (Supplement to No.4, July 1957).

9. The results of the recently published 1976 population census confirm the budget-survey data regarding the stability of urban and rural family size, in spite of the reduction in fertility experienced in 1964–74.
10. Radwan (op.cit.) used the per capita food requirements prepared by the FAO regional office in Cairo in 1959. The FAO translated the 2250 calories recommended by FAP/WHO as the minimum energy requirements for the average Egyptian into a list containing quantities of the various types of foods that can satisfy it and that are usually consumed by the poorer classes. To obtain the value of the least-cost diet, the quantity of each type of food was multiplied by the unit price prevailing in the three benchmark years. Since there is no significant urban/rural difference in food prices, the same destitution line was used for both sectors. The cost of the minimum food expenditure thus increased by 27 per cent from 1958/59 to 1965/65 and by a further 110 per cent to 1974/75. Note that during the same two periods the official wholesale food price index increased by 14 and 114 per cent respectively. The difference in the first period between the official and the Radwan estimates of price increase is probably the result of differences in the weights used in the price index.
11. The higher minimum expenditure in the urban sector (which is technically due to the lower share of food expenditures in total consumption) neglects the fact that non-food items are more expensive in urban than in rural areas.
12. The destitution and poverty estimates in the table are derived from income distributions that take account of houshold size. Income per household member is total household income divided by the number of persons, not corrected for differences between children and adults or for economies of scale in comsumption. Limitations of the data for 1958/59 and 1964/65 prevented me from taking account of this factor.
13. This is in contrast to the deterioration in the overall rural income distribution indicated in the previous section.
14. Fields, op.cit.
15. For a detailed technical analyses see Victor Levy, 'The Distributional Impact of Economic Growth and Decline in A Developing Country–Egypt' (Discussion Paper No.82.02), Jerusalem Falk Institute, 1982.
16. See Amartya Sen, '"Poverty" An Ordinal Approach to Measurement", *Econometrica*, XLIV (March 1976), pp.219–31.
17. Robert Mabro, *The Egyptian Economy: 1952–1972* (Oxford: Clarendon Press, 1974), p.185.
18. Two price indices were used to compute real wages; the food price index which rose by 97 per cent (from 1964/65 to 1974/75) and the Cost-of-Living Index, which rose by 70 per cent. Real wages declined according to either price index; the decline ranged from 20 to 70 per cent across the various sectors.
19. Although many agricultural imports are subsidized by the government, a recent World Bank study, William Cuddihy, *Agricultural Price Management in Egypt* (Staff Working Paper No. 388), (Washington: World Bank, 1980), found that the negative effective protection coefficients do not differ much from the nominal coefficients. See Victor Levy 'The Welfare and Transfer Effects of Cotton Price Policies in Egypt: 1965–1978', *American Journal of Agricultural Economics*, August 1983, pp.576–80, for the magnitude of the welfare and transfer effects of this negative protection for Egyptian cotton growers.
20. International Bank for Reconstruction and Developments, 'Egyptian Agricultural Development Problems, Constraints and Alternatives', Unpublished Report, 1976, pp.32–3.

[3]

WHITHER THE EGYPTIAN ECONOMY?

Rodney Wilson

The Egyptian economy has changed considerably during the last two decades since the death of Nasser, but opinions vary over the direction in which it is heading. It is no longer correct to classify the country as a primary agricultural producer, since agriculture accounts for less than one-fifth of the gross national product, and over half the population now lives in urban areas. Raw cotton, the dominant export for over one hundred years until the 1960s, earns a mere 10 per cent of visible export receipts. Crude oil replaced cotton in the 1970s as the major visible export with the return of the Sinai oil fields following the Kissinger peace accords, but it is also diminishing in importance, partly reflecting the substantial relative fall in oil prices. Egypt in any case was never a large enough producer to gain admission to OPEC, and today it has only 13 years of reserves left at current production levels.[1]

Industrialization has a long history in Egypt, dating from the ill-fated attempt by Muhammad ʿAlī in the early nineteenth century to establish a mechanized textile industry.[2] The 1920s finally witnessed the opening of successful spinning and weaving plants with the help of finance from Bank Misr,[3] but it was only in the 1950s and 1960s under Nasser that a heavy industrial base was established, with the Helwan steel plant as its centrepiece. Nasser's industrialization was based on an import substitution strategy designed to secure economic independence,[4] a goal that was to some extent achieved despite the tensions with the West and the 1967 war with Israel.

Although a diversified range of industries was established, with reasonable input-output linkages, the state sector plants were much criticized for the poor quality of their output and their lack of price competitiveness by international standards. To some extent the criticism was misdirected, as this was not the objective of the industrial planners who envisaged continuing protectionist measures, including subsidies if necessary, to nurture the manufacturing sector. The gain was in the learning experience of using new technologies, not in providing the lowest cost output to disloyal customers.

Infitāḥ: *a means or an end?*

Under Sadat economic policy changed, with a new outward orientation designed to bring Gulf Arab capital into the country combined with Western

[1] BP, *Statistical Review of World Energy*, June 1992, p.2.

[2] Roger Owen, *The Middle East in the World Economy*, London, Methuen, 1981, pp.69–72.

[3] Marius Deeb, 'Bank Misr and the Emergence of the Local Bourgeoisie in Egypt', in Elie Kedourie (ed.), *The Middle Eastern Economy*, London, Cass, 1977, pp.70-86.

[4] Robert Mabro and Samir Radwan, *The Industrialisation of Egypt, 1939–1973*, Oxford, Clarendon Press, 1976, pp.191-210.

technology and know-how.[5] Though detailed incentives were drawn up to attract investment under law number 43 of 1974—the so called 'open door' or *infitāḥ* policy—it was by no means clear what the economic objectives of the policy actually were. No distinction was drawn between portfolio investment by individuals and institutions and direct investment by multinational companies. With the Cairo stock exchange virtually moribund, no domestic market in Egyptian government paper and a largely inconvertible currency, the former was unlikely. For multinationals these factors also mattered, but the overriding concern was the high perceived political risks in a volatile region such as the Middle East—risks which the peace treaty with Israel enhanced rather than dispelled.

The much heralded five-year plan for the 1978–82 period was a largely meaningless document which talked about establishing priorities, but did not indicate how this was to be done.[6] It was supposed to support *infitāḥ*, yet the policy is never mentioned in the document. Instead, in an effort to deflect popular discontent following the food riots of 1977, there was an emphasis on a 'social contract' between government and people. However, the contents of the contract were not defined, nor indeed its purpose. The authors of the document were clearly out of touch with reality when they stated that 'Egypt has come into the forefront of the welfare societies of the world'.[7] There is a recognition of past administrative weakness and production inefficiency, but this 'has been due to the sheer weight of the load which the government shoulders. It has been impossible to maintain quantity or quality in the services which must be extended so widely to so many'.[8]

This failure, which continued and worsened in the 1980s despite the admissions contained in the plan, resulted in Islamic groups providing basic welfare provision independently of government. As a consequence a parallel and growing Islamic economy developed in Egypt, with fundamentalist groups winning increased support from the urban poor and those in the countryside, especially in Upper Egypt. As a long-term strategy to win power from the grass roots up, this makes considerable sense. Government efforts to thwart this have not succeeded and have often been counter-productive. It was hoped, for example, that the collapse of the Al Rayan Islamic investment company, in which many middle- and low-income people placed their savings, might weaken support for Islamic financial institutions. This proved not to be the case: on the contrary, government officials were blamed for spreading rumours which helped destroy confidence in the institution. The government was forced to back-track and allow the state-owned commercial banks to offer Islamic deposit and funding facilities which were free of *ribā* or interest.[9]

[5] Yusuf Ahmad, *Absorptive Capacity of the Egyptian Economy*, Paris, OECD, 1976, pp.108–115.

[6] Ministry of Planning, *Five Year Plan for 1978-1982*, Cairo, 1977.

[7] Ibid., p.17.

[8] Ibid.

[9] Elias Kazarian, *Finance and Economic Development: Islamic Banking in Egypt*, Lund Economic Study, no.45, pp.148-149.

The policy of *infitāḥ* has resulted in some opening up of the formal sector which has benefited the few, but private financial inflows have been modest. Most private capital inflows have been of a short-term nature into the joint-venture banks, largely to finance imports. Although *infitāḥ* was designed to attract private capital rather than state assistance, many Egyptian officials saw it in terms of the latter. It was not so much a way of internationalizing Egyptian industry, or moving away from import substitution, as a means of building bridges to the West and the United States in particular. Without paying lip service to open markets, and 'playing the game', much less governmental assistance, especially from the United States, would have been forthcoming. Egypt has been by far the largest recipient of civilian aid from the United States in recent years, and in terms of military assistance is second only to Israel.[10] It is in these wider terms that the benefits of *infitāḥ* must be judged. *Infitāḥ* was never meant to be an end—indeed, there was little real desire to open up; rather, it was a means to overcome state financing difficulties, and in this it has been successful.[11]

Economic restructuring and privatization

The Mubarak government has congratulated itself on the way it has made *infitāḥ* help financial inflows without disrupting the state-sector companies established so painstakingly under Nasser. The debt write-offs as a reward for Egyptian assistance in the allied effort in the Gulf war were particularly welcome, especially as they were without strings—a recognition of past help rather than future intentions. It is clear that Egyptian state sector managers are even more resistant to change than their counterparts in Eastern Europe, and they are highly sceptical about the gains which restructuring or privatization will bring. The usual penalties which a market system brings for failure, bankruptcy, closures and lay-offs, would be unwelcome and politically unacceptable. Yet managers have little confidence that privatization would bring benefits, as it is difficult to see how Egyptian manufacturing could be internationally competitive with Far Eastern producers and maintain domestic market share without protection.

Most of the more buoyant enterprises in the private sector remain geared to the domestic market, and even the entrepreneurs themselves admit that without protection they would flounder. In order to encourage the domestic consumer industry in 1986 the Egyptian government re-imposed restrictions on imports which it was felt could be produced successfully in Egypt. These restrictions virtually stopped the importation of foreign quality casual clothing that had become fashionable amongst some upper- and middle-class youth.

10 Amounts are recorded in the *Statistical Abstracts of the United States*, Washington. In 1991, for example, US military aid to Egypt was worth $1.3 billion and civilian aid was worth over $2 billion. The comparable figures for Israel were $1.8 billion and $1.9 billion respectively.

11 The aid from the United States enabled subsidies to remain in place for longer than they otherwise might, even though the benefits were doubtful. See Iliya Harik, 'Subsidisation Policies in Egypt, Neither Growth Nor Distribution', *International Journal of Middle East Studies*, vol. 24, no. 3 (August 1992), 481–499.

In response a new Egyptian company, 'Mix-and-Match', was established to exploit the captive, though limited, niche market. This proved highly successful, but the designer, Shahira Fahmy, stated that 'when we started it was a monopoly, and that's why we grew so big'.[12] In seven years the company was able to open eleven shops in Cairo alone, but once local competitors appeared business actually contracted.

Making the break into exports has proved far from easy for Egyptian fashion houses. 'Mix-and-Match' exploited its knowledge of Arab tastes by opening two outlets in Kuwait and one in Bahrain. The Sahara clothing company, which has seven 'On Safari' clothing stores and three 'Shirt Shops' in Egypt, saw the potential of exploiting the favourable image of Egyptian cotton in Europe as a result of tourists purchasing from its Egyptian outlets. It opened two shops in Germany, but has experienced tough competition from Turkish garment exporters. Inconsistencies in fabric quality bought from local suppliers remain a major problem for Egypt's fashion houses. Towels and bath robes made from Egyptian cotton which are sold in House of Fraser stores in Britain bearing the 'Alexandria' label are actually manufactured in Canada. The Egyptian-born Al Fayed brothers who own the prestigious *Harrods* store in London have made some efforts to source cotton goods from Egypt but the spinning, weaving and sewing have usually been carried out in Italy.

The World Bank has been highly critical of the slow pace of state sector rationalization and the lack of private sell-offs in Egypt. The public enterprise office which was founded in 1992 has identified 20 small- and medium-sized enterprises for privatization, but some of these are joint ventures with foreign partners in areas such as food processing and textiles. None are heavy industries or large employers, as these are regarded as strategic and therefore outside the jurisdiction of the enterprise office.[13] The most prominent candidates for privatization such as Bank Misr, the National Bank of Egypt, the state insurance companies and Egypt Air have all been excluded as being of strategic importance, though it is difficult to see how this case can be made.

Although the five-year plan for the 1992/93–1996/97 period envisages a substantial increase in the role of the private sector, this is to come from the establishment of new enterprises rather than the transfer of existing public sector companies to the private sector. The reorganization of public sector companies in the 1980s under the control of 27 holding companies introduced a further level of bureaucracy. Indeed, this restructuring could be regarded as a move to at best thwart and possibly block potential privatization, despite the case argued by some Egyptian economists, notably Ibrahim Helmy Abdel-Rahman and Mohammed Sultan Abu Ali.[14] These economists stress the fiscal benefits of privatization rather than the efficiency gains. Experience elsewhere shows that this stress is probably correct, and in the case of Egypt, where the

12 Ann Hosier, 'The Rag Trade', *Cairo Today*, April 1993, p.80.

13 Tony Walker, 'Public Sector Liability for Egypt', *Financial Times*, 18 March 1993.

14 Ibrahim Helmy Abdel-Rahman and Mohammed Sultan Abu Ali, 'Role of the Public and Private Sectors with Special Reference to Privatisation: The Case of Egypt", in Said El-Naggar, *Privatisation and Structural Adjustment in the Arab Countries*, Washington, International Monetary Fund, 1989, pp.141-181.

large public sector companies are either monopolies or oligopolies, a change of ownership will not by itself ensure competition.

There have only been two minor privatizations in Egypt to date: the sale of the Meridien Hotel in Cairo for $75 million together with the Hurghada Sheraton, both to Saudi Arabian investors.[15] These, like other major hotels, were franchises, with the multi-national chains providing management service contracts. Such sell-offs involving hotels, which were only partially under Egyptian control in any case, can hardly be regarded as a precursor of widespread privatization.

The private sector has played an increasing role in the economy in recent years, though not as great as that envisaged in the previous 1987/88–1991/92 five-year plan. The construction industry accounts for a substantial part of private sector investment, as it has done since the time of Nasser. Although the five-year plan for 1992/93–1996/97 envisages 58 per cent of private investment being accounted for by the private sector, only a small proportion of this will be in manufacturing. The government and state sector industries are expected to invest £E 75 billion under the plan. This compares with a total private foreign investment of £E 8.5 billion over almost 20 years of *infitāḥ*,[16] a figure which helps put the contribution of the open door policy into perspective. Far from contracting, the public sector continues to grow, with the state sector industries constituting the backbone of Egyptian manufacturing. The hope of most in the state sector industries, and probably a majority in government, is that if they move slowly enough, the current world-wide fad for privatization will simply fade away.

Egypt as a newly industrializing country

With its cultivable area largely restricted to the Nile valley and with 97 per cent of its water resources utilized, the potential for greater employment in agriculture remains limited. Water could admittedly be used more effectively, but Egypt lacks the agricultural potential of Iraq or Syria where only 43 per cent and 9 per cent respectively of potential water resources were used over the 1970–87 period.[17] At the same time it is hardly feasible for a country with a population of 56 million inhabitants to become an economy based on service activities such as tourism. Further industrialization would appear to be the only realistic option available in an economy which must somehow create 600,000 new jobs every year.

The development success of the newly industrializing countries of South East Asia over the last two decades has been remarkable. How does Egypt measure up to these standards? Clearly, with a per capita gross national product of $620, Egypt is in a different league from South Korea and even Malaysia with figures of $6340 and $2490 respectively. Within the Middle East comparisons are often made between Turkey and Egypt, and the restructuring

[15] John G. Merriam and Anthony J. Fluellen, 'Arab World Privatisations: Key to Development?' *Arab Studies Quarterly*, vol. 14, nos. 2 and 3, p.58.

[16] Vanessa Kent, *Investing in Egypt*, London, Committee for Middle East Trade, 1993, p.17.

[17] *World Bank Atlas*, 25th edition, 1992, pp.26–27.

of the Turkish economy in the 1980s is often taken as a role model for Egypt to emulate.[18] Yet with a per capita gross national product figure of $1810, it also appears that Turkey is in a different league. Turkey's increasing international competitiveness is a great source of optimism for many,[19], but it is hard to take such a favourable view of Egypt's economic prospects, despite its positive real per capita gross national product growth of two per cent per annum over the 1980–91 period.

The magnitude of the task facing Egypt is clear from the World Bank definition of a newly industrializing country. Such economies are classified in terms of attaining, largely through industrialization, a favourable enough combination of income and growth to become high-income countries within two decades. A high income was defined as $7,620 in 1990, a goal clearly almost attainable by South Korea, but still some way ahead for the most rapidly advancing economies in the Islamic world, Malaysia and Turkey.

In structural terms the position of Egypt is more favourable, with 16 per cent of its gross national product accounted for by manufacturing in 1990, compared to a mere 8 per cent for Iran, but 24 per cent in Turkey—a higher figure than for many European Community countries, including the United Kingdom.[20] Investment rates are also relatively high in Egypt, at 20 per cent of gross national product in 1991, not far short of the Turkish figure of 22 per cent, though of course the absolute amount in Egypt is much smaller. As future growth ultimately depends on the level of investment, the figure for Egypt is encouraging. The effectiveness and quality of the investment may be questioned, but the indicators are relatively promising. Gross national product growth throughout the 1980s averaged over 4.5 per cent per annum. It was only the continuing high rate of population growth at 2.4 per cent per annum that brought the per capita figure down. With education a relatively low-cost sector in Egypt, and with the five million in school receiving a good basic education, it is important not to underestimate the amount of human capital formation taking place, which is arguably the most important aspect of investment.

An over-expanded service economy?

As already indicated, Egypt, because of its size, cannot realistically hope to develop on the basis of services, yet it could be argued that this is what has been happening over the last two decades. Much emphasis was placed on developing the tourist industry which was already a significant earner of hard currency, with favourable prospects for much higher revenues. Finance for hotel construction could be attracted from the oil-rich Gulf states, especially for four- and five-star ventures which were of interest to the international hotel management groups so respected in the region. Tourist receipts increased

18 Bent Hansen, *The Political Economy of Poverty, Equity and Growth: Egypt and Turkey*, Oxford University Press, 1991, p.435ff.

19 Dani Rodrik, 'Turkey: The Best is yet to Come', *International Economic Insights*, May/June 1993, pp.17–23.

20 World Development Report, *Development and the Environment*, Washington, World Bank, 1992, pp.216–217.

rapidly from £E404 million in 1980 to over £E1 billion ten years later.[21] By 1990 over 2.6 million tourists were visiting Egypt annually, with over half from the European Community, the United States and Japan and forty per cent from neighbouring Arab countries, mainly Saudi Arabia and the smaller Gulf states.[22]

The tourist industry is far from being a stable source of revenue, as Egypt has found to its cost during the 1990s. The Gulf War led to a substantial fall in visitors from the United States and the European Community, even though the war itself was very short-lived and all the action was a considerable distance from Egypt. The fact that the tensions coincided with the booking period for winter holidays was especially unfortunate, and the conflict was over at too late a point to save the 1990–91 winter season. Just as the industry was starting to revive in 1992 there were the actions of Muslim fundamentalists in killing and wounding British and German tourists. These actions were not because of hostility to the 'infidel' as such, but rather a way of waging economic warfare against the Egyptian government. In spite of the death sentences passed on some of those involved, and tight security measures to protect tourist buses, confidence has been seriously undermined. Holidays are an entirely discretionary purchase, and potential visitors have plenty of alternative choices. Many European Community visitors have substituted Turkey as a spring and summer destination which also has antiquities, and Morocco and even the Far East as winter destinations.

Evidence from elsewhere suggests that tourist memories are short, and if there are several incident-free months then tourists will return. Egyptian hoteliers have dropped their rates to try to encourage more bookings, and holidays to Luxor are now cheaper than many to Spain. Discounting room rates means less revenue per tourist, however, and it may be a doubtful strategy for Egypt to market itself as a cheap destination. Nearby Cyprus has managed to attract over two million tourists per year even though its currency is tied to the Exchange Rate Mechanism and prices are generally much higher than mainland Greece.[23] Egypt does not even benefit from the travel element, as most tourists from Europe arrive on charter airlines owned by the tour companies from their own countries.

It is important not to over-exaggerate the significance of tourist earnings for the Egyptian economy. Suez Canal transit fees are a more reliable and valuable source of revenue worth over £E 2.6 billion by 1991. These have depended less on tanker traffic in recent years as Sumed, the Suez-Mediterranean pipeline, has become more important. This also earns revenue for Egypt, the oil coming in shuttle tankers from Yanbu' on Saudi Arabia's Red Sea coast, which is the terminal of the trans-Arabian pipeline. The majority of shipping in the Suez Canal is now container vessels carrying Far East exports to European Community ports. The net tonnage of such vessels amounted to

[21] National Bank of Egypt, *Economic Bulletin*, vol.44, no.3, Cairo, 1991, p.233.

[22] Central Bank of Egypt, *Economic Review*, vol.31, no.3, Cairo, 1990–91, pp.157–158.

[23] Rodney Wilson, *Cyprus and the International Economy*, London, Macmillan, 1992, pp.99–115.

over 250 million tons in 1990 compared to 158 million tons accounted for by tankers.[24] The larger Japanese and Korean container vessels and car carriers sail around the Cape of Good Hope but Chinese, Taiwanese, Indonesian and Thai vessels transit through the Canal, as does most shipping from the Indian sub-continent.

Remittances are another valuable source of revenue for the Egyptian economy, but it is extremely difficult to estimate their worth as many do not pass through the formal banking system. The World Bank valued remittances into Egypt at $3.7 billion in 1990 compared with a figure of $2.8 billion a decade earlier.[25] This may well be an under-estimate, even though the 1990 figure exceeds the value of visible exports, which was just under $3 billion. Most remittances come from the two million Egyptian workers in the Arabian peninsula states and Libya, though some are sent by well-educated professionals such as doctors resident in the European Community and the United States, and some even come from the Coptic Christian community in Australia. Egyptian workers in neighbouring Arab states return home for visits at least every two years, and many once a year or more frequently. Often they travel back with large amounts of cash or consumer goods for their relatives in Egypt. Such transfers are not counted in official figures, nor are funds transferred through money-changers in the Gulf states such as Al Rajhi of Saudi Arabia. It is these transfers that fuelled the growth of the informal Islamic investment houses in Egypt whose activities are not monitored by the authorities.

As with tourist earnings, remittances have an uncertain future.[26] Egyptians working in Kuwait virtually all left following the Iraqi invasion, and few have returned since. In Saudi Arabia many of the positions occupied by Egyptians in the educational system and public administration are being increasingly filled by local nationals. Egyptians resident in Europe or the United States often bring out their relatives to join them, and the remittances gradually fall away. It is difficult to see how the current value of remittances can be sustained over the coming decade.

Remittances have certainly improved the living standards of the families of the migrants remaining in Egypt, but the wider social benefits have always been problematic. Much of the earnings went into real estate which drove up property values beyond the reach of the poor. The purchase of imported consumer goods did little to help the Egyptian economy. Often the best educated

24 National Bank of Egypt, *Economic Bulletin*, vol.44, no.3, Cairo, 1991, p.232.

25 World Bank, *World Tables*, Baltimore, Johns Hopkins University Press, 1992, pp.238–239.

26 There is an extensive literature on labour migration from Egypt dating from the work of Stace Birks and Clive Sinclair in the 1970s. See J.S. Birks and C.A. Sinclair, *International Migration and Development in the Arab Region*, Geneva, International Labour Office, 1980, pp.43–46. They took a somewhat negative view of Egyptian migration, but others were more positive. See for example Naiem A. Sherbiny and Ismail Serageldin, 'Expatriate Labour and Economic growth: Saudi demand for Egyptian Labour', in Malcolm Kerr and El Sayed Yassin (eds.), *Rich and Poor States in the Middle East: Egypt and the New Arab Order*, Colorado, Westview Press, 1982, pp.225–257.

migrated, which meant a brain drain and skills shortage.[27] There was also a fiscal loss, as those employed abroad did not pay tax in Egypt, although they had to pay for exit permits. The monetary loss occurred where conversion of Saudi Arabian riyals or dollars into Egyptian currency was delayed as long as possible, as with constant depreciation, the longer the lag, the greater the amount of Egyptian pounds obtained. More broadly it can be argued that the tradition of migration and remitting funds turned at least part of the Egyptian economy into a consumer society. Egypt became associated with rest and recreation rather than work. It was not that Egyptians did not produce, it was simply that they expended a large part of their efforts in other countries where the rewards were higher.

An outward or inward economic orientation?

Given the uncertainty over tourist earnings and the services which are dependent on remittances, should Egypt be trying harder to strengthen its productive base? Free market protagonists, including those in the International Monetary Fund, would argue that as long as Egypt's exchange rate is allowed to float at a realistic level, then the country's comparative advantage should become obvious. The abolition of the complex multiple exchange rate system in 1991 was seen as a move in the right direction, though substantial non-tariff barriers remained which allegedly penalised exports as well as imports because of regulations governing imported inputs.[28] Whether the removal of these would indeed bring gains is a debatable point. Any move towards a less interventionist policy would be counter to thousands of years of Egyptian history, as the historical power of government derived from its economic control of the irrigation system. The IMF is arguing for further fine tuning, as it has done for over a decade, when in the view of many the problems are fundamental. There is little point in trying to cure the symptoms, if the patient is in danger of dying.

This may be too dramatic a position, but it is clear that Egypt's fundamental economic problems are not being addressed, and perhaps the Mubarak government will never be capable of addressing them. The commitment to liberalization is half-hearted, but it is far from clear that this is the answer in any case. The economy is not generating sufficient new jobs for the increasing population, yet the escape valve of emigration is closing.[29] Agricultural exports are in steady decline,[30] and employment in rural areas, already declining in relative terms, may soon start to fall absolutely. The fall in agricultural exports was originally because raw cotton was used for the domestic textile industry, but now it is exacerbated by European Community restrictions on

[27] Ibrahim M. Oweiss, 'The Migration of Egyptians', in A.B. Zahlan (ed.), *The Arab Brain Drain*, London, Ithaca Press for the United Nations, 1981.

[28] Hanaa Kheir El-Din and Ahmed El-Dersh, 'Foreign Trade Policy of Egypt, 1986–91', in Said El-Naggar (ed.), *Foreign and Intertrade Policies of the Arab Countries*, International Monetary Fund, 1992, pp.206-241.

[29] Nagwa Aly Khashaba, 'Trade Strategy for Employment Growth in Egypt, 1960–86', *L'Egypte Contemporaine*, vol.81, nos.421–422, pp.5–34.

[30] Sami Baroudi, 'Egyptian Agricultural Exports', *Middle East Journal*, vol.47, no.1, Winter 1993, pp.63–76.

early vegetables and citrus produce. Preference is being given to Turkey rather than Egypt, in so far as concessions are being made to non-Community states.

It is often assumed that Egypt is becoming increasingly outward oriented, but recent economic indicators belie this fact. Although the ratio of imports to gross national product rose significantly over the 1970–80 decade from a mere 19 per cent to over 45 per cent, it has subsequently fallen back to 44 per cent. One option could be for Egypt to pursue an inward oriented development strategy like Iran, paying its way in the world but curtailing imports of western goods. The trading situation could be used to justify such action, even if it was internationally unpopular. The visible trade deficit is huge, with export receipts covering less than one quarter of import payments. Although the overall balance of payments has been less of a problem because of remittances, tourist earnings and assistance from the United States, there are now large questions over all of these. Visible exports are not going to take off, as although manufacturing is the best way forward, this is a long-term solution. A period of inward consolidation may be appropriate, so that the country can deal with the outside world from a position of greater economic strength rather than weakness. A begging bowl approach is not an economic policy, and it is inappropriate for a country with such a rich economic history and proud traditions.

[4]

THE IMPENDING CRISIS IN EGYPT

Cassandra

FOR Egypt to have severe political, social, and economic problems is nothing new. Those it is facing today are particularly acute, however, and the government is not dealing with them effectively. Instead of allowing increased opportunities for political participation to alleviate political pressure caused by economic austerity, the government of President Husni Mubarak is seeking to contain most manifestations of political autonomy, and the state's capacity for such containment is being sorely tested. If, ultimately, its containment capability proves to be inadequate, the Egyptian state will be more or less alone in confronting a revolutionary crisis. None of Egypt's allies, including the United States, is prepared or equipped to assist.

Economic and political correlates of potential systemic collapse are evident. First is a severe and protracted recession following a boom, a cyclical pattern often associated with political destabilization. The vast majority of Egyptians increasingly are suffering from relative deprivation, as the gap between their expectations and the reality of their living conditions widens. Relative deprivation often translates into political discontent, as the examples of Iran and Algeria have demonstrated.[1] A second indicator of serious trouble is the inappropriate governmental response to economic challenges. Although economic reform achieved considerable gains in stabilizing the macroeconomy following the 1991 Persian Gulf War, it has not been extended to the vital areas of institutionalization of the regulatory environment and privatization. In fact, the most difficult aspect of economic reform—structural adjustment—has yet to commence. The Egyptian economy is suspended between a rigid monetarism, on the one hand, and an inefficient state capitalism on the other. As a consequence, growth of the private sector continues to be

1. On the relationship between relative deprivation and the propensity to rebel, see Ted Robert Gurr, *Why Men Rebel* (Princeton, NJ: Princeton University Press, 1970).

retarded by a regulatory environment attuned to defending the interests of the public sector.

Third, political reform has not been successful. Instead of seeking to broaden its base of political support, the regime has resisted trying new ideas and bringing fresh recruits into the political elite. It has chosen to stand firm, betting that the state apparatus alone—without any support from civil society—is strong enough to eradicate any insurrection. Yet, sclerosis in channels of elite recruitment has produced a gerontocratic, unrepresentative elite.

A fourth and related development is the loss of legitimacy that has accompanied the growing political isolation of the regime. Intellectuals appear to have deserted it, a development which, in other settings, has been a harbinger of revolution. None of the major political tendencies—Nasserist, Communist, free marketeer, liberal democratic, or Islamist—considers the regime to be representative of its views or sympathetic to its interests. While Mubarak disposes of the state power he inherited from Gamal Abdul Nasser and Anwar al-Sadat, he can neither claim the legacy of either man, nor claim to be the progenitor of a new "ism." Many high-ranking officials complain uncharacteristically about the lack of leadership.[2] Rumors of corruption among high officials, including the office of the president, contribute to widespread disillusionment. Egypt seems to be in a state of "disequilibration," whereby the regime is not believed to share the ideas, aspirations, and values of society.[3]

A fifth correlate of political breakdown is the presence of an armed insurgency. Prior to the 1991 Persian Gulf War, Islamic militancy took the form of intermittent violent acts. Since 1992, however, sporadic terrorism has grown into an insurrection that has affected directly the lives of thousands of Egyptians. While the insurgents seem incapable of constituting an alternative government, they may succeed in destabilizing the incumbent one.

Sixth, the bedrock of the regime—the military and security services—shows signs of being fractured. The military is divided vertically and horizontally, i.e., within the officer corps and between officers and enlisted men. The security services are reportedly riven by internal disputes and worn down as a result of the extended campaign against Islamic activists, and there are questions about whether the 420,000 to 440,000-man army and the somewhat larger domestic security forces can be relied upon, in a condition of *extremis*, to defend the status quo or to secure the future.

Finally, the external patron of the regime, the United States, is so preoccupied with the Arab-Israeli peace process, that it is neglecting to monitor domestic developments in Egypt. Yet, even if the United States were sufficiently alert to Egypt's mounting problems, it has little capability to preserve Mubarak or to engineer a smooth and bloodless succession. In sum, in the absence of meaningful economic and political reforms, the

2. Even cabinet ministers are reported to have privately expressed such sentiments, as related in interviews with members of the Egyptian political elite, April and May 1994.

3. On disequilibrated social systems as a harbinger of revolution, see Chalmers Johnson, *Revolutionary Change*. 2d ed. (Palo Alto, CA: Stanford University Press, 1982), pp. 61–90.

Mubarak regime may collapse, opening the door to a military takeover or to an even more dramatic political change similar to what happened in Iran during 1978–79.

RELATIVE ECONOMIC DEPRIVATION

Per capita income in Egypt climbed steadily from the inception of the Nasser era in 1952 until the June 1967 War. It then rose rapidly from the onset of the oil boom in 1974 until oil revenues began to recede in the mid-1980s, at which time per capita income commenced a steady decline.[4] The rising expectations engendered by Nasser's rhetoric, the oil boom, American largesse, and Sadat's *infitah* (economic opening) policies, have been followed by bitter disappointment. This disappointment is aggravated further by a paradox that has come to characterize the post-1991 Gulf War Egyptian economy: macroeconomic performance has improved dramatically, but microeconomic performance has deteriorated sharply. Unfortunately for the government, it is performance at the microeconomic level that shapes individuals' perceptions. While economists are persuaded by data on balance of payments, levels of indebtedness, budget deficits, and other macroeconomic indicators, such data mean little to ordinary people concerned about the scarcity of jobs, low wages, high prices, and inadequate profits.

The relative success at the macro level is due to a huge infusion of aid following the Gulf war and to the accompanying stabilization package agreed to with the International Monetary Fund (IMF) in May 1991. This aid reduced the 1990 foreign debt of $50 billion to $26 billion by 1994. Fiscal reform has reduced the budget deficit from 20 percent of Gross Domestic Product (GDP) in 1990 to around 3 percent in 1993. Over that same period, inflation has fallen from 25 percent to less than 10 percent. Egypt's foreign currency reserves have risen dramatically, from $2.7 billion in 1990 to almost $12 billion in 1993.[5]

Success in economic stabilization has been bought at great cost to growth and equity. Real GDP growth slowed from 2.5 to 3 percent per annum during the period 1989–91, to 0.4 percent in 1992–93. Economists have estimated that growth will rise only slightly, to 1 percent, in 1993–94.[6] Since the population has been growing at a rate exceeding 2 percent per annum, the net effect on per capita GDP has been negative. Whereas per capita GDP was $680 in 1986, it had fallen to less than $600 by 1993.[7] Meanwhile, private investment has been inadequate to replace reduced government spending. Between 1974 and 1993, total private investment was only $2.3 billion, which in proportion to GDP is extremely low by Third World and Arab state standards.[8] Gross domestic investment as

4. For GNP per capita during these years, see relevant *World Development Reports*, published annually for the World Bank, Washington, DC.

5. *Egypt: Country Report*, First Quarter, 1994 (London: Economist Intelligence Unit, 11 February 1994), pp. 7–8.

6. *Egypt: Country Report*, Fourth Quarter, 1993 (London: Economist Intelligence Unit, 8 November 1993), p. 7.

7. The World Bank, *World Development Report, 1993* (Washington, DC, 1993), p. 238.

8. William E. Schmidt, "A Deluge of Foreign Assistance Fails to Revive Egypt's Stricken Economy," *New York Times*, 17 October 1993. D. Weigel, "Foreign Direct Investment: The Role of Joint Ventures and

a percentage of GDP has declined steadily since 1988.[9] Rather than adopt measures to stimulate the economy, the government's 1993–94 budget called for total spending to rise by only 5 percent, so that "public consumption will remain depressed as the government intends to meet its targets for a reduction in the budget deficit."[10]

The two most important, politically relevant consequences of budgetary austerity and inadequate private investment are growing unemployment and disparity of income between the rich and the poor. Since the unemployed constitute "a great proportion of those condemned for perpetrating terrorist acts," some amelioration of joblessness would appear to be a precondition for reducing political violence.[11] Yet, unemployment is steadily rising, reaching up to 17 percent by 1993, according to official figures, and over 20 percent by most other estimates.[12] The 1994 level of unemployment was between 1.5 and 2 million, and disguised unemployment in government departments and public-sector companies was extensive.

This unemployment problem cannot be resolved in the absence of a dramatic upturn in the economic growth rate, for which a major increase in private investment is a prerequisite. Private-sector employment opportunities are essential because both government and expatriate work—the source of 90 percent of new jobs between 1976 and 1986—have constricted.[13] Between 1987 and 1991, when the economy was more robust, a total of one million jobs was created, but that number represented only 50 percent of the jobs then required to accommodate all new entrants to the labor force.[14] While the government's current five-year plan has set a target of creating 400,000 new jobs annually, in actuality 700,000 jobs are needed to provide work for 500,000 new entrants each year and to reduce unemployment and underemployment. This number of new jobs would require an annual growth rate of 7–8 percent.[15]

Government job-creation programs have been inadequate. The 1993–94 budget allocated LE2.2 billion (LE1.00 equals approximately US$0.30) for job-creation schemes. During the 1980s, LE41,000 was the average capital requirement for the creation of each new job in companies operating under law 43, the private investment law, that inaugurated the infitah in 1974.[16] Assuming that job-creation costs have remained constant, the 1993–94 budget allocation is sufficient to create only 50,000 new jobs, barely adequate to provide employment for 10 percent of new entrants to the labor force.

Investment Authorities," in Said El-Naggar, *Investment Policies in the Arab Countries* (Washington, DC: International Monetary Fund, 1990), pp. 70–88.

9. *Trends in Developing Economies, 1993* (Washington, DC: The World Bank, 1993), p. 158.

10. *Egypt: Country Report*, First Quarter, 1994, p. 7.

11. Said El-Naggar, "Politics and Economic Reform in Egypt" (Paper presented to the nineteenth annual symposium of the Center for Contemporary Arab Studies, Georgetown University, Washington, DC, 7–8 April 1994).

12. Ibid., pp. 5–6.

13. Heba Handoussa, "The Burden of Public Sector Employment and Remuneration: A Case Study of Egypt" (Geneva: International Labor Organization, 1989).

14. "Grappling with Rising Unemployment," *al-Ahram Weekly*, 17–23 March 1994.

15. El-Naggar, "Politics and Economic Reform in Egypt," pp. 6–7.

16. For this figure, see Heba Handoussa, "Egypt's Investment Strategy, Policies and Performance since the Infitah," in Said El-Naggar, ed., *Investment Policies in the Arab Countries*, p. 143.

Increasing inequality and rising poverty closely track the growth of unemployment. Government spending priorities contribute to these interrelated phenomena. The 1993–94 budget, for example, calls for a 5 percent rise in total spending, but for a 19 percent increase in military expenditures. Expenditures on food subsidies, which have been identified as the single most important contributor to equity in Egypt, are to be reduced.[17] Salaries and wages, which amounted to 50 percent of GDP in 1970, had fallen to less than a third of GDP by the early 1990s, as yields from profits and investments rose proportionately.[18] Average real earnings of government employees by 1991 were 50 percent of their 1973 value, and real wages for workers in all sectors have declined steadily since 1985.[19] The incidence of poverty and malnutrition, which fell steadily from the early 1950s to the late 1980s, has risen in the 1990s.[20] By 1993, between 75 and 80 percent of the population had average monthly family incomes at or below $50.[21] Egypt was one of four countries listed in 1994 by the United Nations Development Program's annual Human Development Report as being "now in danger of joining the world's list of failed states because of wide income gaps between sections of their populations."[22]

Concerned by these developments and their political implications, the World Bank has channeled more than $600 million in donor funds to Egypt in order to create a Social Fund. The purpose of the Social Fund is to serve as a safety net for Egypt's poor and unemployed, particularly those forced into such conditions as a result of privatization of public-sector companies. The Social Fund is not large enough, however, to deal with problems of such magnitude, and has fallen victim to dissension within the cabinet, which has been unable to agree upon appropriate job-creation schemes.

While the economic wisdom of deflationary policies is debatable, their political consequences are manifest. Some jobless youths have joined a low-intensity civil insurrection against the government; many are alienated. Underlying both active opposition and despondency is perceived relative deprivation—relative in comparison to Egyptians' memories of earlier periods, relative in comparison to better-off fellow citizens, and relative to non-Egyptians. The perception that the government is insufficiently sensitive to the plight of the jobless, and unable or unwilling to do much about underlying causes of unemployment, contributes to the widening gap between ruler and ruled.

17. Bent Hansen, *Egypt and Turkey: The Political Economy of Poverty, Equity, and Growth* (Oxford: Oxford University Press, 1991), pp. 226–28.

18. Fawzy Mansour, "The Egyptian Economy: Restructuring or Destructuring?" (n.p., n.d.), p. 5.

19. *Al-Ahram Weekly*, "Grappling with Rising Unemployment."

20. Alan Richards, "Economic Policy and Egyptian Security: Dilatory Reform vs. Making a Break for the Market" (n.p., April 1994), p. 11.

21. The World Bank, *Trends in Developing Economies, 1993*, p. 156.

22. Paul Lewis, "UN Lists Four Nations at Risk Because of Wide Income Gaps," *New York Times*, 2 June 1994.

INAPPROPRIATE ECONOMIC POLICY

Egypt's economic problems are manifest in the disjunction between stabilization and structural adjustment—between macro and microeconomic policy. Reforms necessary to facilitate broadly based economic growth, including privatization, trade liberalization, and the creation of an appropriate regulatory environment within the context of accountable institutions following transparent practices, have proceeded slowly at best. Few of the more than 300 state-owned enterprises targeted for privatization have been sold to private investors. Public-sector holding companies have secured the right to retain proceeds from the sales of those companies they control. The consequence of this measure is to perpetuate the dominance of the public sector, which will sell off unprofitable enterprises and invest the proceeds in other undertakings. About half of the overall GDP, and two-thirds of non-agricultural GDP, are produced in the public sector. The primary beneficiaries of this sector are the approximately 5,000 comparatively wealthy Egyptians who comprise the senior management and members of the executive boards of the state-owned enterprises, in addition to the technocrat-politicians with whom they share economic rents.[23]

The government is not progressing toward creating a regulatory environment conducive to investment and growth. The absence of transparency—or clear and open procedures—throughout the administration is indicated by the manner in which economic data are treated. Ministers release statistics on a selective, rather than on a comprehensive, routine basis. Those data that are released invariably demonstrate how well a particular ministry or the national economy is performing and are unreliable.[24] Since the mid-1980s, for example, the Egyptian government has reported a rate of economic growth approximately double that estimated by the World Bank or other independent sources.[25] Egyptian economists who need authoritative statistics seek them, not from their own national bank, but from the World Bank or the US embassy in Cairo.[26]

A further indication of Egypt's reluctance to adopt an effective, market-oriented strategy of private sector-dominated, export-led growth, is its lack of a "change team." In comparing the rate and extent of structural adjustment in Egypt, India, Mexico, and Turkey, John Waterbury has noted the importance of such a team of economic technocrats, insulated from political pressures by powerful political patrons.[27] Although Egypt has a few prominent and well-qualified economists who publicly articulate the need for a thoroughgoing structural adjustment, they do not comprise a team and have not been backed by a political patron.

23. This figure is provided by Milad Hanna, "Nationalisation to Privatisation and Back," *al-Ahram Weekly*, 2–8 September 1993.

24. For a recent attack on the reliability of data released by the minister of tourism, see 'Abd al-Jawwad 'Ali, "Hadith fi Majlis al-Sha'b" (Discussion in the People's Assembly), *al-Ahram al-Iqtisadi*, 17 January 1994.

25. Hansen, *Egypt and Turkey*, pp. 489–90.

26. Interview with the chairman of an Egyptian bank, April 1994.

27. John Waterbury, *Exposed to Innumerable Delusions: Public Enterprise and State Power in Egypt, India, Mexico, and Turkey* (Cambridge: Cambridge University Press, 1993).

INAPPROPRIATE POLITICAL RESPONSE

The thrust of governmental policy since 1990 has been to restrict political participation. Most of the opposition boycotted the 1990 parliamentary elections in protest against an electoral law that favored the ruling National Democratic Party (NDP), and in protest against supervision of the elections by the ministry of interior. As a result, over 90 percent of the members of the current parliament represent the NDP.

The absence of competitive party politics in parliament has accentuated the importance of professional syndicates. Their politicized nature, and the fact that they hold comparatively free and fair elections for board members and officers, has made these syndicates ideal battlegrounds for contending forces seeking to demonstrate their strength and to broaden their appeal. Islamists have expanded their electoral presence progressively in these syndicates, dominating the most prestigious of them by 1992, including the syndicates of the commercial graduates, dentists, doctors, engineers, lawyers, and pharmacists. In February 1993, the government, alarmed by the growing influence of the Islamist movement within professional syndicates, enacted the Law to Guarantee Democracy within the Professional Syndicates. This law requires a minimum voter turnout of 50 percent of the members in professional syndicate elections, or, failing this, 33 percent in a second round. If these electoral thresholds are not met, voting results are voided and syndicates fall under the supervision of a panel of government-appointed judges. The NDP-dominated parliament passed the law despite a sustained campaign against it by the syndicates, including demonstrations attended by as many as 15,000 professionals.[28]

Constriction of political space has been accomplished in further ways. For example, the Emergency Law, initially decreed by Mubarak in the wake of Sadat's 1981 assassination, was extended by parliament for an additional three years in April 1994, with only 12 dissenting votes cast. The ministry of social affairs has been applying, with increased rigor, the restrictive provisions of the Nasserist-era Law 32 of 1964 that legalizes the ministry's control of voluntary associations.[29] Journalists have been the target of increasingly severe crackdowns. In April 1994, for example, the state security police arrested journalists who had written articles on corruption and the Islamist insurrection in the opposition newspapers *al-Sha'b* and *al-Wafd*. A journalist at *al-Wafd* claimed to have been beaten up when arrested.[30]

In October 1993, the government amended the Journalists Syndicate law to divide journalists into three categories. Promotion to a higher category or transfer to another post in the same organization was made contingent on authorization by a committee named by the Journalists Syndicate, which is government dominated. Journalists critical of this

28. On this law and reactions to it, see reports in *al-Hayat*, 15, 17, and 22 February 1993.

29. On this law and unsuccessful efforts to amend or nullify it, see Amir Salim, *Difa'an 'an Haqq wa Hurriyyat Takwin al-Gam'iyyat* (In Defense of the Right and Freedom to Form Associations) (Cairo: Center for Legal Studies and Information on Human Rights, 1991).

30. *Al-Wafd*, 13 April 1994. This act, along with the arrests themselves, were condemned by *al-Ahram* editor Salama Ahmad Salama, who drew parallels between these events and the "night visitors" of the Nasser era. See his column in *al-Ahram*, 14 April 1994.

measure—1,000 demonstrated against the proposed legislation when it was introduced in parliament—contend that it permits the government to muzzle journalists on the ostensible grounds that they are not qualified. The law also made employees of the ministry of information, who far outnumber professional journalists, members of the Journalists Syndicate, thereby making it easier for the government to manipulate elections and to prevent the syndicate from falling under the control of Islamists, or independent secularists.[31]

The government's aversion to autonomous political participation also is illustrated by its sponsorship of legislation, in March 1994, to terminate the century-old practice of villages electing their mayors and deputy mayors. Not even Nasser had meddled with this vestige of democracy. For the Mubarak regime to have done so suggests that it is anxious about rural political instability. It has reason to be. In the 1992 local government elections, Islamists won a few seats for the first time since local councils had become elected bodies during the Nasser era. In June 1992, parliament passed legislation that raised rents for agricultural land and abolished the provision of the 1952 agrarian reform law that guaranteed agricultural tenants security of tenure on rented land. Millions of peasants (if family members are included) may be affected negatively by these measures, either through dramatic rental increases, eviction, or forced purchase of land from the absentee owner at market prices.[32] Another potential contributing factor to rural political unrest was the cancellation of the United States Agency for International Development's (USAID) Local Development project, which was the largest such project USAID had ever undertaken. It funnelled hundreds of millions of dollars into rural Egypt, largely through provincial and district notables, the backbone of the NDP's rural presence.[33]

The effect of changes to the landlord-tenant law and cancellation of the USAID project has been to impose additional hardships on peasants, while stripping patronage resources away from rural notables, thus reducing their networks of peasant clienteles. Mindful of the Algerian experience in which Islamists first gained control of villages and towns through the ballot box, and fearful of the implications of these recent measures that have antagonized peasants while simultaneously eroding government-associated rural patronage networks, the regime has opted to appoint mayors, thereby converting them into employees of the ministry of interior. They will, therefore, lose much of their legitimacy,

31. For a report on the legislation and journalists' responses to it, see *al-Wafd*, 21 October 1993. For systematic descriptions of syndicate activities and laws governing them, see Center for Political and Strategic Studies, *al-Taqrir al-Istratiji al-Arabi* (Arab Strategic Report), published annually by al-Ahram Publishing, Cairo.

32. Robert Springborg mistakenly implied that the government, for political reasons, would be unable to amend the 1952 law. See his "State-Society Relations in Egypt: The Debate over Owner-Tenant Relations," *Middle East Journal* 45, no. 2 (Spring 1991), pp. 232–49. For a review of the consequences of amending the law, see Raymond A. Hinnebusch, "Class, State and the Reversal of Egypt's Agrarian Reform," *Middle East Report* 184 (September-October 1993), pp. 20–3.

33. For a description and analysis of this project, see Hanan Hamdy Radwan, "Democratization in Rural Egypt: A Study of the Village Local Popular Council," *Cairo Papers in Social Science*, 17, 1 (Spring, 1994).

further eroding already tenuous support for the government among the rural poor, who comprise the overwhelming majority of the village-dwelling population.[34]

The one governmental initiative that held out promise of expanding political participation was *al-Hiwar al-Qawmi*, or National Dialogue, which Mubarak called for in his acceptance speech before parliament in October 1993. The National Dialogue was intended to serve as a forum within which the government and the legal opposition could take up political reform. First scheduled to be held before the end of 1993, the Dialogue was postponed repeatedly until it was finally convened in early July 1994. In the event, it was stillborn, because the government forbade the Muslim Brotherhood or any other Islamist organization to participate, while the leading secular opposition political party, the Wafd, boycotted the proceedings. Resolutions that were passed took the form of recommendations to the president, which have yet to be acted upon.

As the political space available to the opposition has decreased, circulation within the governing elite has virtually ceased. The government of Prime Minister 'Atif Sidqi, first appointed in 1987, is the longest serving government since the first modern cabinet was formed in 1914. Excluding the interior portfolio, which Mubarak has changed about every two years—largely because of the unstable domestic political scene and the pressure this puts on that ministry—the cabinet turnover rate is at its lowest point in Egypt's modern history. Several ministers have held their portfolios for more than a decade, and five of them have been in the government longer than the prime minister. Excluding three younger (i.e., the average age is approximately 60) recruits to the cabinet in 1993, the average age of the cabinet is over 65.[35]

Finally, the insurgency has provided both cause and justification for wholesale violation of human rights, ranging from detention without charge or trial, to torture, the killing of suspects under interrogation, and the brutalization of entire villages and urban quarters by the security police.[36] An antiterrorism law has been adopted that, among other things, legalizes trials of suspected terrorists in military courts, from which there is no appeal. Those courts handed down 50 death sentences in the 15 months ending in April 1994. In one case alone, nine suspects were sentenced to death for attempting to kill Prime Minister Sidqi. Amnesty International reported in November 1993, that of the 39 death sentences handed down by military courts by that time, virtually all the defendants had been subjected to torture to force them to sign confessions.[37] In mid-March 1994, two suspects accused of seeking to plant a bomb at the Sidi Barrani military airfield in order

34. This and other criticisms of legislation amending the 1952 agrarian reform law were made by various opposition spokespersons. See *al-Ahram*, 30 March 1994; and Fikri El-Gazzar, "Beheading Democracy in Villages," *al-Ahram Weekly*, 31 March-6 April 1994.

35. For commentary on the negative consequences for the Sidqi government of its low turnover rate, see Adil Hamuda's column in *Ruz al-Yusuf*, 10 May 1993.

36. For a review of Middle East Watch's October 1993 testimony before a US congressional committee on human rights violations in Egypt, and for the Egyptian government's response, see *Mideast Mirror*, 22 October 1993, pp. 26–32.

37. Cited in *Mideast Mirror*, 11 November 1993, p. 15.

to blow up the president, were tried secretly and executed by firing squad, even before news of the attempt was made public.[38]

The regime's answer to its travails has been to curtail freedom of expression, restrict opportunities for political participation, and intimidate those who oppose the government. By failing to differentiate between the democratic opposition and antidemocratic insurgents, the government is converting reformers into revolutionaries, supporters into bystanders. Facing a political problem rooted in economic difficulties, the government continues to pursue economic policies that further stimulate political discontent, while bottling up that discontent rather than seeking to vent it.

DELEGITIMATION

Arab governments in the Maghreb and Mashriq have sought legitimacy in two main ways: by projecting a vision of the future, generating popular support for that vision, and convincing the public that the regime can attain it; or by introducing reforms from above. Mubarak's Egypt does not seem to possess the structural or personal prerequisites for either approach. The state neither has the resources to convince citizens to subscribe to its ostensible vision, nor can it provide tangible proofs that it could realize its goals. In fact, Mubarak has told those with whom he deals that he disdains grandiose visions and schemes, claiming that he is a practical man, a problem solver.[39] The cost of the failure to communicate a political vision seems to be the loss of popular support. Egyptians made sacrifices under Nasser and Sadat for reasons that were explained to them. Most people believed the sacrifices were necessary; current sacrifices, however, seem to be without purpose, and therefore are resented.

The principal alternative legitimation strategy pursued by Arab governments has been one of limited political reform, a major component of which typically has been for the government to seek to rise above the fray, much in the manner of King Hussein of Jordan or King Hassan of Morocco. These monarchs distance themselves from day-to-day politics. They delegate enough power and permit sufficient relaxation of the political system for a political class to emerge. That class debates low-level policy (i.e., excluding national security and foreign policy issues) and assumes some responsibility for it, thereby acting as shock absorber for the ruler and reinforcing his and the regime's legitimacy as the protector of the national interest.

Mubarak has not allowed a political class to emerge in Egypt. He is involved personally in all aspects of decision making. The restrictions on political participation hinder the emergence of representatives who can negotiate agreements on behalf of constituencies. All of Mubarak's cabinets have been comprised of technocrats, none of whom could claim to represent a nongovernmental constituency, or to have an extragovernmental base of political power. Since the population is aware that the government

38. Reuter dispatch cited in *Mideast Mirror*, 17 March 1994, pp. 18–19.
39. Interviews with members of the Egyptian political elite, April-May 1994.

cannot be changed by peaceful means, the secular political opposition, which lacks force to change the government, is perceived as marginal.

The legitimacy of the president himself has been undermined by rumors of corruption. Since the outbreak of the Islamist insurrection in the spring of 1992, important figures close to the president have been mired in revelations of corrupt behavior. For example, the previous Minister of Interior, 'Abd al-Halim Musa, was accused in January 1994 by his predecessor, Zaki Badr, of running a private security firm with public funds, bribing journalists, stealing foreign assistance monies, and committing various smaller transgressions.[40] Zakariya Azmi, chief of the Presidential Bureau and a member of the People's Assembly, was alleged by an opposition newspaper to be the partner of a notorious multi-millionaire developer accused of depriving the state treasury of LE100 million and of financing and running Azmi's election campaign.[41] While public tales of corruption and moral turpitude have been politically damaging, they are less destructive than rumors surrounding the president's family, especially rumors about commissions paid to his son and other relatives. Cabinet ministers are rumored to be disgruntled because lucrative commissions, which they had come to expect as a bonus of the job, are being diverted to the president's office.[42] The point of these rumors is that they cast doubt on Mubarak's principal virtue—that he is honest. Since his legitimacy rested not on his ability to articulate a vision, but on his managerial competence and personal integrity, he is facing an Islamist insurgency with inadequate personal legitimacy and insufficient political support.

ISLAMIST INSURGENCY

The Islamist insurrection has greatly exacerbated Egypt's economic problems. Income from tourism fell by one-third, or some $1 billion, from 1992 to 1993, and continued to stagnate in 1994.[43] Since tourism has, over the past two decades, created more jobs than any other sector of the economy—employing more than one million and indirectly as many as five million Egyptians by 1992—disruption to that industry has had profound consequences for employment and income distribution.

About 86 percent of the casualties resulting from civil disorder in the 41 years up to 1993 occurred during the Mubarak era, 92 percent of which occurred in the four years 1990–93, the bloodiest period of civil strife this century. The total of those killed and wounded in 1993 (1,106) was about three-and-a-half times that of 1992 (322). The death toll resulting from political violence rose from 139 in 1991 and 1992, to 207 in 1993, and to 225 in the first ten months of 1994.[44] The number of Islamist activists arrested leapt

40. This story was on the front pages of *al-Gumhuriyya*, *al-Akhbar*, and *al-Wafd*, on 3 February 1994.

41. *Al-Sha'b* ran articles on this connection on 11, 14, and 21 January 1994.

42. Interviews with members of the Egyptian political elite, April, May, and October 1994. See also, Jim Hoagland, "Cozy with Gadhafi," *Washington Post*, 3 November 1994.

43. *Egypt: Country Report*, Third Quarter, 1994 (London: Economist Intelligence Unit, 28 July 1994), p. 27.

44. *Annual Report of the Egyptian Organization for Human Rights*, cited in *al-Ahram Weekly*, 8–14 December 1994.

from some 3,600 in 1992 to over 17,000 in 1993.[45] Comparative casualty rates also suggest the growing potency of the insurrection and indiscriminate responses by security forces. In 1992, Islamist activists suffered twice the number of casualties as security forces (122 vs. 61). In 1993, however, more policemen were killed (120) than insurgents (111). The number of civilian bystanders killed by crossfire in 1992 and 1993 exceeded that of either police or insurgents.[46]

Of the 104 persons killed in shootouts in the first six months of 1994, a period in which security forces seemed gradually to be gaining the upper hand, 54 were alleged Islamic militants, 39 were policemen, 10 were bystanders, and one was a German tourist.[47] Islamic insurrectionists have pursued a campaign of assassinations that has resulted in the deaths of a former speaker of parliament, a leading secular intellectual, four police generals—including the undercover general in command of antiterrorist security forces—and scores of lower-ranking intelligence and security officials. They have narrowly missed killing the ministers of information and interior, the prime minister, and Naguib Mahfouz, Egypt's Nobel Prize-winning author. Although the intensity of violence tapered off in the spring and summer of 1994, with only nine deaths occurring in the April-June period, a string of attacks on foreigners and Egyptian security personnel commenced again in September. In the last quarter of 1994, Islamists engaged security forces in a series of skirmishes and small-scale battles in various villages, towns, and cities of the provinces of Asyut, Aswan, and Minya, and Islamist-related political violence resulted in 46 deaths in December, the third highest monthly total since 1992.

The qualitative change from a sporadic and limited terrorist campaign to a widespread, low-level insurgency being countered by large numbers of security personnel, is due, in part, to the changing social profile of the activists themselves. Compared to the 1970s, militants in the 1990s tend to be younger, less well educated, poorer, and more likely to reside in rural areas, shantytowns on urban outskirts, or urban slums. The average age of militants arrested and charged for acts of violence dropped from 27 years in the 1970s, to 21 years by 1990. Of the seven militants executed for attacks on tourists in 1993, three were below the age of 20. Whereas 80 percent of Islamist activists arrested in the 1970s were college students or graduates, by the 1990s they comprised only 20 percent. Those militants who had attended elite faculties, such as medicine or engineering, dropped from one-half of those arrested to 11 percent in the same time period.[48] In sum, the Islamist movement has become further radicalized and intensified because it increasingly reflects the interests of the lower classes, rather than those of the middle and upper-middle classes. Those youths most negatively affected by Egypt's faltering economy are the ones most likely to be Islamist insurgents.

45. Saad Eddin Ibrahim, "Governance and Structural Adjustment: The Egyptian Case" (Paper presented to the Governance and Successful Adjustment Conference at the World Bank, Washington, DC, 9–11 November 1994), p. 40.

46. *Al-mujtama' al-madani wa al-tahawwul al-dimuqrati fi al-watan al-arabi: al-taqrir al-sanawi* (Civil Society and the Democratic Transition in Arab Countries) (Cairo: Ibn Khaldun Center, 1994), pp. 419–22.

47. R. Clemente Holder, "Egyptian Human Rights Leader Calls for Moderation," *The Washington Report on Middle East Affairs* (September/October 1994), p. 62.

48. Ibrahim, "Governance and Structural Adjustment," p. 42.

Militant Islamists comprise not just small organizations capable of intermittent acts of violence, but, in fact, constitute an insurgency in which they, rather than the government, have controlled for extended periods the sociopolitical space within which they operate. Urban-fringe shantytowns in Lower Egypt and villages and provincial capitals in Upper Egypt constitute the battlegrounds on which Islamic militants and security forces vie for dominance. These so-called haphazard communities (shantytowns) in the governorates of Alexandria, Cairo, Giza, Port Said, and Suez, which house 16 percent of the overall population and 35 percent of Cairo's population, have "become hotbeds of terrorism," according to the NDP deputy for Nasr City.[49]

One such shantytown is Western Munira, which borders Imbaba, a suburb across the Nile from Cairo's wealthy island suburb of Zamalek. Western Munira is bereft of public services and home to an active Islamist organization that virtually ran it for several years, until December 1992, when 12,000 government troops, backed by scores of armored vehicles, battled with militants for three weeks to gain control.[50] Similar confrontations have occurred in other slum areas and in Upper Egypt. In December 1993, for example, Asyut became a battleground in the wake of a shootout that left three police officers, two policemen, and four militants dead.[51]

MILITARY AND SECURITY FORCES

The government's tactics are not counter-terrorism, but counterinsurgency warfare. This warfare directly engages the security forces. Ultimately, it may draw in the military, or force it to consider assuming a direct political role. Having almost a million men in total, divided more or less equally between military and security forces, these organizations are too large to be sustained adequately by available resources, even with annual US assistance in the form of Foreign Military Financing (FMF) of $1.3 billion—almost 39 percent of worldwide US security assistance monies. FMF funds are devoted exclusively to military procurement; other expenditures on the military, including salaries and associated personnel expenses, come from the general budget. Although the military's share of that budget has remained high during the Mubarak era, and is proportionately larger than it was during the last two years of the Sadat era, total funds available have been insufficient to prevent deterioration in pay and living conditions for officers and enlisted men. While officers still are privileged in comparison to civil servants, they, too, suffer from relative deprivation. Many officers' wives, for example, must work in order to cover the expenses of the private schooling necessary for their children to compete successfully for entrance to prestigious university faculties and to the military college.[52]

49. Gamal Essam El-Din, "Debate Puts Slums on the Map," *al-Ahram Weekly*, 5–11 May 1994.

50. On these events, see *al-Mussawar*, 1 January 1993, pp. 18, 20–1.

51. The Minister of Interior, Hassan al-Alfi, dispatched Major General Nassar Zaher and a detachment of 1,000 extra police troops to the city to reinforce several thousand troops of the province's security forces. All roads leading into and out of Asyut were sealed off, numerous shootouts occurred, and hundreds of arrests were made. Ahmed Moussa, "Police Conduct Massive Dragnet in Assiut," *al-Ahram Weekly*, 23–29 December 1993.

52. Interview with a former military attaché, May 1994.

Pay and conditions for officers and enlisted men in the security services are below those for equivalent military ranks. Conditions are especially inferior for the enlisted men in the 325,000-member Central Security Force, whose low living standards and harsh treatment by officers and the government caused key units stationed in Cairo to rebel in 1986. Three divisions of regular army troops—approximately one-quarter of the army—backed up by airforce helicopters, were required to put down that rebellion. The state, which already is spending a high portion of the budget on security, simply lacks the resources to sustain total military and security forces of one million men, which is 6–7 percent of the working-age population.

Conscripts into the Central Security Force typically are poor, uneducated peasants, unable to meet the army's higher education and health requirements. In the 1990s, the army has been taking 14 percent of the 580,000 young men who reach draft age every year.[53] It rejects illiterates, while men who can attend university typically avoid military service. Consequently, the median draftee is now drawn from the same lower- and lower-middle-class social strata that have been the primary recruitment base for the Islamist movement.

The social chasm that separates enlisted men from officers may underlie a growing political chasm based on the divide between secularism and Islam. Scores of enlisted men have been arrested for their participation in radical underground groups, including those involved in the 1981 assassination of Sadat and the attempted assassination of Mubarak in 1994.

The government has attempted to ensure the loyalty and obedience of officers, in part, through material rewards of dubious legality. Opportunities for commissions through procurement—the most lucrative area—are systematically rotated so that the wealth is spread among a reasonable number of the members of the general officer corps.[54] Military attaché positions in London, Paris, and Washington are the top plums, and, hence, are typically rotated on a biannual basis, about twice the turnover rate for equivalent foreign ministry positions. The military is, understandably, enormously sensitive about this issue. When, in November 1993, the opposition newspaper *al-Sha'b* published a summary report of a *Wall Street Journal* article about investigations by the US Federal Bureau of Investigation (FBI) and Congress into US companies' payment to Egyptian officers of commissions varying in amounts from $582,000 to $2.7 million, the Mubarak government

---

53. Central Intelligence Agency, *The World Factbook, 1993* (Washington, DC: The Central Intelligence Agency, 1993), pp. 114–15.

54. Since 1972, parliament has regularly passed legislation that authorizes the president to "issue law-decrees concerning armament allocations and other allocations for the armed forces." This provides the president with unrestricted powers (that he can then delegate) to purchase military goods from foreign countries without parliamentary or other forms of governmental oversight. Article 108 of the 1971 Constitution states that the president should be vested with such authority only in exceptional cases, and that the president must submit to the parliament reports on agreements reached in this manner. No such report has ever been received in parliament. In defense of the renewal of this authority for three years in May 1994, Gamal al-Sayid, a former minister of military production and currently an NDP member of parliament, declared, "We all know that Mubarak is an honest man and worthy of trust." The vote in favor of the legislation was 380 to 11. Cited in "Arms Mandate Renewed," *al-Ahram Weekly*, 12–18 May 1994.

arrested a leader of the Socialist Labor Party that publishes the paper. No independent Egyptian investigation of these charges was undertaken.[55]

The second major conduit of resources from the state to the officer corps is through economic enterprises under the military's control. In 1990, military industries produced about LE1 billion worth of military products, and LE622 million of civil commodities. The military's agricultural enterprises produced over 12,000 tons of meat and almost 11,000 tons of dairy products. Over 60 percent of military consumables (uniforms, food, footwear, etc.) are produced by military enterprises.[56] All of these economic activities are off budget and unsupervised by any civilian authority. Executive, managerial, and board positions on military enterprises provide hundreds of employment opportunities for retired officers. The huge amount of funds in circulation, with inadequate accounting supervision, virtually guarantees "leakage" into private pockets. The government seeks to ensure the loyalty of the officer corps through these more or less illicit rewards that are provided to those who go along with the system, and especially to those who attach themselves to powerful patrons within it. This modus operandi undoubtedly offends and alienates some officers, especially younger ones who have not been rewarded yet and whose values may be at variance with those of their seniors.

Military patrons compete with one another, a factor that introduces factionalism into the general officer corps. The continuing saga of former minister of defense, Field Marshal 'Abd al-Halim Abu Ghazala, reflects the general problem of maintaining military cohesion. Abu Ghazala built a sprawling patronage network that, in combination with his charisma and connections in Washington, made him a serious political threat to Mubarak. Despite his abrupt removal from the cabinet in 1989, Abu Ghazala continues to maintain the loyalty of many retired officers, whom he had placed in the military economy. Those officers, in turn, have friends and allies among serving officers.[57]

In order to counter the lingering threat of Abu Ghazala, Mubarak promoted General Hussein Tantawi, first to chief of staff, then to minister of defense, and finally to field marshal—only the fourth time in the history of the Egyptian army that the title of field marshal has been bestowed. Mubarak's intent was to build up Tantawi as a counterbalance to Abu Ghazala by downgrading the latter's field marshal title through conferring the same honorific on a relatively undistinguished general. Although Tantawi has support in the military, rumors that he owes his rapid promotions to the fact that he organized the security detachment around the presidential retreat in Ismailiyya have been unhelpful to his reputation in military circles.[58]

The existence of competitive patronage networks within the officer corps, combined with the lingering influence of Abu Ghazala, as well as Tantawi's limited popularity, have placed the higher circles of the general officer corps in a state of unease. In the event of the death or incapacitation of the president, factionalism within the high command could

55. The article appeared in the *Wall Street Journal*, 5 November 1993, and was cited in *al-Sha'b*, 19 November 1993.

56. Figures provided by a Pentagon official.

57. Interview with a former military attaché, May 1994.

58. Ibid. This is rumored to be the residence of President Mubarak's recently married second wife.

be a serious problem. Since the post of vice-president is vacant and no civilian has a sufficient political base within the state or civil society from which to make a claim for succession, the obvious successor is the minister of defense. Whether the high command would endorse Tantawi's nomination, or would divide on the issue, probably would be determined by the immediate circumstances surrounding succession. For the vital question of presidential succession to be so relatively open, and the military backstop even to be in question, suggests the political fragility of the system.[59]

Command of the security forces also is affected by competition over patronage and by disagreements over counterinsurgency strategy.[60] It is also possible that Islamist insurgents have succeeded in penetrating the highest ranks of the security forces. The assassination in 1994 of Major General Ra'uf Khayrat, a twenty-year undercover veteran of the feared and semi-autonomous State Security Agency, *Mabahith Amin al-Dawla*, may have depended on information to which only high-ranking officers in that agency would have had access.

Islamist penetration within the ranks of the security forces is most advanced in the South (Upper Egypt). The unreliability of southern troops has caused the ministry of interior increasingly to rely upon Cairo-based recruits to maintain security in Upper Egypt. While this reduces problems associated with relying upon local recruits, it alienates southerners, who resent what they perceive as a foreign army of occupation in their midst.[61]

THE US RESPONSE

Although the United States is concerned about Egypt's political situation, it is preoccupied with other matters. Moreover, because of the very nature of the bilateral relationship, a decisive US response in the event of a crisis is unlikely. Faced with a choice of supporting a destabilized and weakened incumbent regime, a military takeover, or reaching an accommodation with an Islamist-dominated opposition, Washington would, in those circumstances, find it hard to act, as it did when confronted with similar choices for Iran in late 1978.

The Clinton Administration is aware, at least at some levels, that the Mubarak government is in trouble. Not long after key Egypt-related appointments were made in the

59. A recent incident points to the sensitivity of relations between the military and the presidency. In June 1993, Brigadier General Murad Disuqi was placed under investigation for "revealing military secrets" for comments he made to a *Wall Street Journal* correspondent. He is quoted in the 14 June 1993 issue of that paper as saying that "the government's stupidity is the talk of the officers' clubs.... I deeply doubt the military will shoot the people for the sake of such an unpopular government." Cited in Carlyle Murphy, "Egypt Said to Question Two Critics," *Washington Post*, 22 June 1993.

60. As Minister of Interior Hassan al-Alfi was embarking on a draconian crackdown on Islamists, for example, former Minister Hassan Abu Basha, who Islamists tried to assassinate, said that "We must initiate a dialogue with the terrorists, even if they are killers." Abu Basha's comments appeared in *al-Wafd* and were reprinted in *al-Ahram Weekly*, 31 March-6 April 1994.

61. This interpretation of southern attitudes is based on discussions with academics teaching at Upper Egyptian universities. For a more detailed account of southern Egyptian attitudes, see Mamoun Fandy, "Egypt's Islamic Group: Regional Revenge?" *Middle East Journal* 48, no. 4 (Autumn 1994), pp. 607–25.

Department of State and other relevant agencies, a quiet review of Egypt's political situation commenced.[62] The *Sunday Times* of London exaggerated the importance of this review when it reported that a National Intelligence Estimate, which "represents the collective wisdom of all American intelligence agencies," was in the process of being drafted. According to the newspaper, this estimate would suggest "that Islamic fundamentalist terrorists will continue to make gains across Egypt, leading to the eventual collapse of the Mubarak government."[63] Cairo immediately sought clarification from Washington as to whether such an estimate did in fact exist, and was assured by Washington that it did not.[64] However, even if the *Sunday Times* sensationalized the findings of the interagency review, it did confirm that the US foreign policy bureaucracy was taking a reasonably close look at Egypt's security situation.

Egypt's problems, however, are overshadowed by the Arab-Israeli peace negotiations. The lens through which Washington views Egypt is designed to reveal what Egypt can contribute to the peace process, leaving in less clear focus purely national issues and challenges. US officials, including staff of the embassy in Cairo, whose capacities in other circumstances would be devoted to monitoring internal developments, have been assigned roles relevant to the peace process. Consequently, they have been providing comparatively little intelligence and analysis for Washington, which, in any case, has been distracted by the larger goal.[65]

Despite having provided $35 billion in foreign assistance to Egypt since 1975—of which about half has been to the military—despite having fought the Gulf war shoulder to shoulder with Egyptian troops, and despite having cooperated extensively to bring the Palestinians to the peace table, the United States possesses remarkably few Egyptian assets in the form of dedicated, reliable, and powerful supporters. Cairo has sought to restrict US influence in the Egyptian military as much as possible. The leading proponent of a closer alliance with the United States, Field Marshal Abu Ghazala, was sacked and discredited. Since his service as military attaché in Washington in the late 1970s, that post has ceased to be a stepping stone to an illustrious career in the Egyptian military. Indeed, the position appears to have been downgraded purposely by the Egyptian government, so as to send the message that US connections are a liability rather than an asset for a career in the military. Hundreds of young Egyptian officers have been trained at US military installations, yet almost all are still too young to occupy positions of command. Their careers have not been fast tracked. If anything, US-trained officers have been subjected to a form of loyalty testing, whereby they are expected to remain silent when commanded by less competent, less well trained senior officers.[66]

62. Interview with analyst consulted as part of that review, December 1993.

63. James Adams, "Mubarak at Grave Risk of Being Overthrown by March of Islam," *The Sunday Times*, 20 February 1994. See also, Marie Colvin, "Gun Law Spreads as 'Bearded Ones' Target Mubarak," *The Sunday Times*, 27 February 1994.

64. Interviews with various US and Egyptian government officials, Washington, DC, February-May 1994.

65. These observations were made to the author by relevant personnel of the Department of State, winter and spring, 1994.

66. Interview with a former military attaché, May 1994.

The Egyptian military has not been made over into a modern, highly mobile, technologically sophisticated fighting force led by US-trained officers. About half the army's equipment is still East bloc in origin. Aging T-55 tanks remain in operation. The high command, which Mubarak has reshuffled frequently, is in the hands of those influenced by Soviet methods and training. This anachronism in the command structure may be due, in part, to the desire of the political leadership to block potential expansion of US influence within the officer corps. While such influence has been restricted, the failure to promote US-trained officers into high command positions has entailed a cost to military capability and professionalism. Whether it has succeeded in ensuring loyalty in a time of crisis remains to be seen.

Virtually all the opposition parties are anti-American, to a greater or lesser extent. Those, such as the Wafd or the Liberals, whose ideology might predispose them to be pro-American, have become increasingly suspicious of the United States because its support for the authoritarian government has continued, while Washington has done little, if anything, to persuade Mubarak to expand the political space within which the opposition operates.

Within the public sector and the government itself, the younger generation of US-trained professionals has suffered the same fate as its US-trained military colleagues. Not only have the careers of these professionals not been fast tracked, but, in many cases, they have been sidetracked if they have tried to buck the seniority and old-boy systems within which they must operate. While some of the resistance to the US-trained younger generation is due to cultural and personal factors, some of it may also be due to the desire on the part of the political leadership to prevent US influence from pervading the public sector and governmental administration. At the cabinet level, Mubarak has drawn upon French- rather than US-educated technocrats, perhaps in order to lessen US influence at that level. The key players in cabinet-level politics have not been US-oriented and trained individuals, but Egyptian-educated apparatchiks or Francophile technocrats. In sum, there is neither a US-oriented "third force" of educated, moderate, secular political activists, nor a cadre of US-trained government officials, who could become significant assets in a time of political crisis.

WHAT IS TO BE DONE?

The United States can do relatively little to affect the course of events in Egypt. A major crisis can be avoided, however, if the government of Egypt adopts certain economic and political measures. At the economic level, Egypt should synchronize its macro and microeconomic policies. The government should slow, even temporarily reverse, some of its stabilization measures; or it should speed up structural adjustment in order to create real jobs over the medium and long term. At the political level, any of a number of measures would relieve some of the pressure: appointing new faces to the cabinet and the NDP leadership; nominating a vice-president to reduce current anxiety levels caused by the vacancy of that key post; holding a true National Dialogue; assigning to the judiciary the responsibility for election supervision; granting parliament greater authority to participate in the budgetary process; stopping flagrant abuses, including corruption, within the highest circles of the elite; terminating the systematic use of torture by the security forces and their brutalization of innocent civilian bystanders; and ending censorship, which serves no useful purpose because the news circulates anyway.

None of these steps requires a fundamental change in the regime, and none would result in a fundamental alteration of the status quo, at least immediately. Some combination of them would, over time, definitely improve the prospects for stability and even for gradual pluralization of the political process. In the absence of any such action, a political crisis of significant magnitude is likely to occur. When it does, it may come to US attention too late for Washington even to attempt a salvage operation, the success of which, in any case, would be uncertain, since the United States has so few resources with which to affect the course of events in Egypt.

[5]

THE IRANIAN ECONOMY BEFORE AND AFTER THE REVOLUTION

Jahangir Amuzegar

THE victory of Algeria's Islamic Salvation Front (FIS) in the December 1991 general elections—not long after the solidification of an Islamic government under General Umar Hassan al-Bashir in Sudan—has renewed fears of the rise to power of Islamists in North Africa and elsewhere. The FIS triumph has likewise emboldened religious militants, and raised their hopes of government takeovers through democratic means. Some Islamists in Asia, the Middle East, and Africa now confidently talk of a day when Islamic rule—some modeled after Iran's—will be established in their homelands and with it an era of spiritual liberation, economic prosperity, and social justice.

Curiously enough, of those who long for a theocratic government of the Iranian variety, few among the hundreds of thousands of demonstrators and political activists in Algeria, Egypt, Indonesia, Jordan, Morocco, Tunisia, and elsewhere seem to know much about Iran's past or present. The publicized picture of Iran before the 1979 revolution is often of an economy mired by stagnation, suffering from an intolerable chasm between the rich and the poor, with agriculture neglected for the sake of rapid industrialization, and oil revenues largely squandered on useless weaponry. In contrast, the publicized image of the new Iran is that of a balanced, prosperous economy, with reduced inequalities of wealth and income, relying on its own resources, defending Islam against a hostile world, standing up for the rights of the poor, and challenging the "forces of imperialism and Zionism."

Because such misconceptions can lead to a hasty rejection of the status quo, or the mistaken pursuit of an uncertain future, a realistic assessment of the Iranian experience should be of interest to those who now favor such a regime as well as

Jahangir Amuzegar is an international economic consultant.

those who dread its emergence. This article discusses the economic elements of the Iranian experience.

THE PAHLAVI YEARS AND POSTREVOLUTION DEVELOPMENTS

The story of Iran's economic development under the Pahlavis, with all its successes and setbacks, is well documented. Between 1946 and 1979, Iran was gradually transformed from a largely farm-based economy to a modern society by way of major changes in the traditional socioeconomic order. Through public planning, urbanization, industrialization, diversification, and infrastructural investment, the state guided the economy and achieved sustained growth. Through control of imports, management assistance, and low-cost credit, the government helped the private sector, and maintained an essentially free-market system. In those years, and particularly the decade and a half ending in 1978, the government was successful in achieving most of its economic, social, and military objectives.

Data published by the World Bank show that, compared with other Third World countries during 1960–1977, Iran's annual real growth rate of nearly 9.6 percent was about double the average of countries in its category, and higher than the average for any other group of countries in the world.[1] Impressive rates of growth were also achieved in other areas: investment, savings, consumption, employment, and per capita income. All sectors of the economy showed significant expansion, albeit at different rates. Inflation was kept at a low rate until 1974, when the oil boom pushed price indices to double-digit heights. The overall external payments balance for much of the 1970s was positive. The exchange and trading system was liberal even by Western standards. The Iranian rial became effectively a convertible currency toward the end of this period. Government finances, while in deficit, were in good order, and internal debt was easily manageable as was external borrowing. Thanks to considerable outlays allocated to education and health, great strides were made in improving social welfare. Infant mortality, malnutrition, endemic diseases, and illiteracy were significantly reduced. Caloric intake, life expectancy, and school enrollment were all markedly increased. While rural-urban income gaps (and income inequalities within each sector) did not narrow, indicators showed that absolute poverty was measurably reduced.

The shah's quest for military superiority in the region, combined with his drive to see Iran join the ranks of the world's major industrial powers within a generation, and his desire to create a West European-style welfare state—all simultaneously with the aid of oil money—proved to be too ambitious a target to reach and too heavy a burden. The country's significant socioeconomic achievements, and considerable military preparedness, thus failed to establish a solid base of support for the leadership. Despite an elaborate military-industrial superstructure, the regime's sociopolitical foundations were not strong enough to

1. *World Development Report, 1979* (Washington, DC: World Bank, August 1979), pp. 128–9.

withstand the onslaught of growing public dissatisfaction, or to ward off the challenge of a would-be savior. The country's sizeable investments in infrastructures, human resources, and defense under the shah, however, would enable the Islamic regime that came to power in 1979 to cope with many formidable problems much better than expected or imagined. The subsequent ability of the Islamic republic to defend Iran's territorial integrity against the Iraqi invasion, to sustain its fast-growing population (albeit at a reduced level), and to reduce its external debt was due to a very large extent to the enormous investments and capital accumulation during the shah's reign.

In short, while the shah's basic development strategy, and his principal socioeconomic policies, were a matter of controversy throughout the period—and the debates continue to this day—today's Islamic militants' image of pre-1979 Iran is skewed. Most specifically, Iran's prerevolution economy was far from stagnant: It was registering positive growth every year between 1963 and 1977, and unemployment was relatively small and localized. Domestic income distribution, while not ideal, was no worse than most developing, and some developed, countries'. Agricultural growth was higher than in all but a handful of nations. Industrialization was pushed through not at the expense of agriculture, but thanks to oil revenues. Although oil income was used to purchase a sizeable volume of sophisticated arms, it also served as the mainstay of foreign exchange needs for infrastructural expansion and for investments.[2]

The religious elements that coalesced behind Ayatollah Ruhollah Khomeini and ultimately triumphed over the other revolutionary groups opposed to the shah had no clear economic agenda beyond repudiating Pahlavi strategies and policies. The shah's regime was castigated for having adopted a Western development model that made the country's economic survival and prosperity dependent on foreign raw materials, managerial know-how, technology, and trade. The regime was further faulted for the too-rapid exploitation of oil reserves, insufficient investment in agriculture, an industrialization drive geared to assembly-plant operation, undue reliance on oil export revenues to finance domestic public expenditure, scant attention to non-oil exports, a widening gap between individuals, classes, and regions, and the promotion of a "consumerist" economy.[3]

An Islamic and appropriate model had thus to be found to right these wrongs, develop a healthy economy, and reduce the country's economic dependence on the outside world. This model—frequently idealized by the religious leadership, but never clearly delineated—was ultimately devined from different ideological tendencies within the clerical hierarchy. The 1979 constitution served as the initial

2. For a discussion of economic strategies and policies under the Pahlavis and their criticisms, see Jahangir Amuzegar, *The Dynamics of the Iranian Revolution* (Albany: SUNY Press, 1991), chapter 4 and part 2.

3. For a typical exposition of these criticisms, see *Bar-rasi-e tahavvolat-e eqtesadi-e keshvar baad az enqelab* (A review of economic developments after the revolution) (Tehran: Bank Markazi [Central Bank], [1984?]); see also Hooshang Amirahmadi, *Revolution and Economic Transition: The Iranian Experience* (Albany: SUNY Press, 1990), pp. 1–16.

step toward the Islamicization of the Iranian economy. The crucial difference between the new constitution and those of other contemporary nations—including Iran's own 1906 constitution—is in its emphasis on life's purpose. The economy, the 1979 constitution declares, is not an "end in itself" but only a "means" of moving toward God. To this end, it has to be planned in a proper and just manner to abolish all forms of unmet needs with respect to life's basic necessities and to attain national self-sufficiency in output, science, and technology. The chapters dealing exclusively with economic matters and the people's rights provide a mixture of "Big Brother" controls, comprehensive welfarism, cooperative associations, and private enterprise. The document as a whole prescribes an idealistic model wherein a benevolent theocratic government controls the commanding heights of the economy—basic industry, banking, insurance, foreign trade, and public utilities; cooperatives engage in vital production and distribution functions; and the private sector plays an important but residual role.

In line with these constitutional provisions, a series of measures were taken to expand the role of the state in the economy beyond what had been the case under the shah. All major industries were taken over from private owner-managers and placed in state hands. Banking and insurance were totally nationalized. Thousands of business firms in farming, industry, and trade that belonged to supporters of the previous regime were confiscated and turned over to a number of new revolutionary "foundations." In two principal areas, however—land reform and foreign trade—the conservative clergy rebuffed all moves toward radicalization; the matter is still in legal limbo. The most specific action taken in the direction of economic Islamicization was the enactment of interest-free banking legislation in 1982. Islamic transaction modes replaced regular bank lending practices, and bank depositors, instead of being creditors, subsequently became partners in profit-sharing. The nationalized banks also became owners of a large number of money-losing public industrial enterprises, previously confiscated from, or abandoned by, their former private owners.

The end of the war with Iraq in August 1988, the death of Ayatollah Khomeini in June 1989, the need for reconstruction, and problems from delayed development ushered in a new era. The ideological compass shifted in the direction of pragmatic considerations and fiscal realism. The election of Ali Akbar Hashemi-Rafsanjani to the presidency, following an amendment to the constitution, and the inauguration of the Five-Year Development Plan (1989/90–1993/94) provided impetus for a shift in development strategy, and changes in economic policy. Although deplored and denounced by the radical press and an articulate faction within the ruling clergy, the regime's new socioeconomic orientation and agenda began to overshadow revolutionary slogans and religious dogma. As a result, since 1989 the government's declarations and actions differ from the ideas and ideals expressed at the outset of the revolution. Except in inspirational terms, or in nomenclature, major economic policies now make scant reference to things specifically Islamic.

Talk in government circles as well as in the bazaar is no longer about rejection of materialism, the imposition of a frugal consumption model, the establishment of a classless society (*ommat-e vahed*), or a return to Islamic social justice, piety, and brotherhood according to the Prophet's prescriptions. The principal concerns are inflation, employment opportunities for college graduates, sales of state factories to the private sector, joint ventures with foreign firms for increased automobile production, expansion of electric power production, promotion of foreign investment in oil and petrochemicals, abolition of rationing and subsidies, deregulation of industry, establishment of free-trade zones, and promotion of non-oil exports.[4] The expansion of oil output, renewed emphasis on industrialization (including the assembly-plant variety), defense build-up, and the pre-1979 goal of "grow first, redistribute later" are again in vogue. Export promotion strategy seems to have replaced the import-substitution dogma.

THE STATISTICS

In the 13 years since the revolution, the Iranian economy has experienced four cycles: a deep recession immediately after the establishment of the Islamic republic in 1979; a strong revival between 1981 and 1986; a mild recession between 1987 and 1989; and a respectable recovery since the cease-fire with Iraq. Despite the regime's early intention of reducing dependence on the petroleum sector, during this entire 13-year period the economy has been closely tied to oil revenues. Several internal and external factors also affected the country's economic course.

Internal factors included political turmoil, the mass exodus of talent and capital, economic uncertainties regarding private property, ideological strictures relating to wealth and income, legal ambiguities concerning land tenure, and the preference for Islamic commitment over professional expertise in the choice of managers. Significant external considerations included the long and costly war with Iraq, major fluctuations in world oil prices, the freezing of Iranian foreign exchange assets abroad following the seizure of the US embassy and hostages, Western credit and trade sanctions, diplomatic isolation, and the influx of an estimated 3–4 million refugees from Afghanistan and Iraq.

Postrevolution economic developments reflect the impact of these adverse factors. Their influence, however, has been mitigated by an extensive infrastructure, a large industrial capacity, foreign exchange reserves, and trained bureaucratic cadres inherited from the previous regime. Nevertheless, as extensively reported in both the local and the foreign press, and widely acknowledged by the political leadership and high government officials, the economy's performance has been anything but laudatory.

4. See, for example, *Middle East Economic Digest* (MEED), November 15, 1991, p. 4.

According to the government's own figures,[5] Iran's gross domestic product (GDP) at constant prices declined by some 1.5 percent a year on average between 1977/78 and 1988/89, with the result that the total GDP in the latter year was approximately equal to that 15 years earlier, i.e., 1973/74. In the postwar period of reform and reconstruction, GDP registered 7.2 percent annual growth on average in 1989/90–1990/91. Real output at the end of the decade, however, was still below that of 1977/78. Due to an estimated average 3.5 percent annual rise in population during the postrevolutionary period—largely in response to an initial government policy of encouraging early marriages and high birth rates—per capital GDP at constant prices in 1988/89 was not much more than the level 21 years earlier. Private per capita consumption in real terms—as the best indicator of material well-being—dropped from 153,000 rials in 1977/78 to 125,000 rials in 1990/91. Added to this already reduced per capita consumption are such problems as periodic shortages of necessities, power blackouts, rationing, long waiting lines, polluted air, and other daily aggravations prevalent during the 1980s compared to the 1970s and 1960s.

Other major economic indices show similar unfavorable trends. The share of aggregate consumption in GDP rose from about 62 percent in 1977/78 to more than 77 percent in 1990/91 while that of total investment fell from 33 percent to about 12 percent during the same period, with public investment outlays down to 7 percent from more than 18 percent of GDP. Figures on employment are sketchy, but also discouraging. The 1986/87 official population survey showed a total population of 49.4 million, an active labor force of 13 million, and an employed portion of 11 million—indicating an official jobless rate of 14 percent. Private estimates put total unemployment at twice that figure. Nearly one-third of the jobs were in the public sector. According to unofficial estimates, between 1979 and 1991, employment in the agriculture sector increased by about 10 percent, while service sector employment nearly doubled. The largest number of workers in the private services was engaged in small retail and itinerant petty trade, with relatively low labor productivity.

Individual economic sectors showed vastly different rates of growth, and their share in GDP changed accordingly. Because of the attention and official priority attached to agriculture, and the adoption of policies designed to increase farm productivity, the agriculture sector performed better than the rest of the economy. Total farm output is shown by the authorities to have on average grown

5. Facts and figures cited in the following paragraphs are all compiled, calculated, and analyzed by the author from the following sources. I. Bank Markazi: *Hesabhaye melli-i Iran, 1353–1366* (Iran's national accounts) (Tehran, 1992); *Gozaresh-e eqtesadi va taraznameh* (Annual economic report and balance sheet), for each year from 1977/78 to 1989/90; *Annual Review, 1369* (1990/91). II. Plan and Budget Organization, *Gozaresh-e eqtesadi (Annual economic report)*, for each year from 1984/85 to 1990/91. III. Iranian Statistical Center, *Salnameh-e amari* (Statistical yearbook), various years 1977/78–1990/91. IV. Iran's Customs Administration, *Foreign Trade Statistics*, annual. V. Organization of Petroleum Exporting Countries, *Annual Statistical Bulletins*; International Monetary Fund, *International Financial Statistics*, monthly; *IMF Survey*, July 30, 1990; and other data; World Bank, *World Development Report*, annual; and other data.

by 4 percent a year between 1978/79 and 1990/91 due to an increase in yield per acre and area under foodgrain production. The share of farming in GDP thus rose from 12.4 percent in 1977/78 to more than 18 percent by the decade's end. Nevertheless, some 17 percent of the country's total annual imports on the average consisted of foodstuff. While this sector performed better than other sectors, its annual growth, according to World Bank data, was no more than the rates achieved in the 1970s and 1960s. Not only was self-sufficiency in agricultural staples not achieved by the end of the decade as promised, but national dependence on imported food items actually increased. Imports of cereals and grains—wheat, barley, rice, and corn—which amounted to less than 2.7 million tons in 1977/78 reached more than 8.2 million tons in 1989/90. Foreign purchases of sugar, red meat, and edible oil were also much larger than before.

Performance and growth in the oil and gas sector were severely affected by the war with Iraq and its damage to oil installations and facilities. Crude production fell to a low of 1.46 million barrels a day (b/d) in 1980/81 and 1981/82, compared to 5.6 million b/d in 1976, but subsequently ranged between 2.2–2.9 million b/d for the rest of the decade—less than Iran's Organization of Petroleum Exporting Countries quota in some years, and exceeding it in others. After the cease-fire with Iraq, production increased to some 3.2–3.4 million b/d but was still less than the peak volume in the 1970s. As a result, the share of the oil sector in GDP declined sharply from 30–40 percent in the mid-1970s to only 9–17 percent in the 1980s. Several diverse factors were responsible for the decline in petroleum production, exports, and oil revenues: the initial decision to save oil reserves by cutting output, damage suffered from the war, gyrations in world prices of crude petroleum, and poor maintenance of oil wells because of capital and other shortages. Oil income continued to account for about 90 percent of total foreign exchange receipts each year, and according to some estimates, no more than $50 billion of the $200 billion oil income received thus far since the revolution has been spent on fixed capital formation.[6]

The industrial sector experienced equally unfavorable developments after 1979. The political climate of the early years and revolutionary excesses led to a massive exodus of industrial entrepreneurs, managers, and skilled workers, as well as large-scale capital flight. The freezing of Iranian assets abroad, Western economic sanctions, and negative government policies toward multinational corporations resulted in the departure of foreign specialists and the cessation of foreign investment. Inexperienced new managers, labor disputes, and disruptive meddling by members of revolutionary *komitehs,* established in each factory, further reduced output. The situation was aggravated by the Iran-Iraq War, which damaged or destroyed production facilities. Reductions in oil revenues sharply cut into the import of industrial parts, raw materials, and processed goods. Added to the industrial sector's problems were the wholesale nationalization of hundreds of

6. See Majlis debates on the 1992/93 national budget, *Kayhan Havai,* January 22, 1992, p. 24.

privately owned enterprises, regulations impeding growth, and lack of coordination among government ministries and agencies in charge of industrial development. Uncertainty regarding the state's treatment of private property rights, lack of incentives, and the limited profitability of short-term commercial transactions discouraged new long-term investment by the private sector. In 6 of the 13 years in the postrevolutionary period, this sector experienced negative growth. Capacity utilization near the end of the decade was below 40 percent in many industries before it picked up after the cease-fire, thanks to a number of incentives and the availability of foreign exchange.

The service sector had a mixed record. While it was somewhat positively affected in terms of both output and employment shares in GDP, this sector also registered negative growth in 5 of the 13 years. The output share rose from 36 percent to 46 percent of GDP between 1979 and 1990. In terms of employment, the services' share went up from 33 percent to 46 percent of total employment. The sector was particularly noteworthy in absorbing the lion's share of new entrants into the job market. Positive growth was achieved in the trading subsector, but the picture was flat in banking, public services, and tourism.

The economy was also beset by a number of other adverse developments. All major indicators were negatively affected by unfavorable domestic and foreign events. Under the pressure of war, slow economic growth, and rising public expenditures, the central government has experienced a budget deficit every year since the revolution. The gap ranged from a huge 15 percent of GDP in 1980/81 to about 3 percent of GDP in 1991/92, with an average of about 7 percent. In some years, the deficit was larger than the government's total regular revenues. Since the budget shortfalls were almost totally financed by credit from the central bank, the money supply rose nearly 10 times during the period. This liquidity explosion pushed retail and wholesale prices upward year after year. With many items in the consumers basket subject to price ceilings, rationing, or subsidies, the true rate of inflation is not easy to determine. According to government statistics, the consumer price index rose by 637.5 percent between 1979 and 1991, or at an average annual rate of about 18 percent (compounded).[7] Unofficial estimates point to much larger figures. Official statistics show a steady decline in real wages and compensations in large-scale industrial establishments after 1980. There are other indications of similar reductions in the real incomes of middle- and lower-class workers.[8] The rising prices of goods and services, perennial shortages, and demands of war combined to cause an increase in the balance of payments deficit. The official external balance figures on current account show a deficit for 10 out of the 13 years.

Finally, despite the regime's declared policy of improving the lot of the poor (*mostazafan*), for whom the revolution itself was ostensibly launched, the

7. *Kayhan Havai*, January 15, 1992, p. 24.

8. For price and wage indices see Bank Markazi's annual reports each year from 1978/79 to 1989/90.

evidence suggests little or no measurable success. Data on wages and salaries are not adequate or reliable. Figures on family disposable incomes and rural-urban disparities are also frequently murky and unilluminating.[9] Based on all indications, however, nominal wages and salaries have persistently lagged behind inflation. According to a Majlis deputy, government employees' salaries and bonuses went up by only 142 percent between the revolution and 1991, while the cost-of-living soared more than six times, leaving "more than 90 percent of public servants below the poverty line."[10] In the absence of relevant and detailed information on wages and salaries, such claims cannot be easily verified or denied.

Regarding changes in the internal distribution of income, the official line is that the poor are now better off than before the revolution. This is undoubtedly true for certain groups of people who have been especially well positioned within the regime, such as most members of the Revolutionary Guards, many families of the war dead, some among the subsidized urban proletariat, a number of *basij* volunteers, and others coming from extremely low-income households. Whether or not this is true of the entire population is still an open question. In a study shortly after the revolution, it was found that in 1972 some 44 percent of the population were living "under the subsistence poverty line."[11] According to a former head of the government's Plan and Budget Organization, absolute poverty increased by 43 percent during the 1979-1985 period, and the trend was continuing.[12] Other reports indicate "absolute poverty" spreading among as many as 65–75 percent of the population in 1988.[13]

PERFORMANCE IN PROPER PERSPECTIVE

The foregoing data on Iran's postrevolution developments point to many undeniable economic shortfalls and setbacks.[14] An objective evaluation of this rather dark picture, however, must be made against the backdrop of the regime's numerous handicaps and disadvantages. The economy, in particular, must be given credit for its resilience in the face of enormous odds. As indicated earlier, immediately after its establishment, the Islamic republic faced the massive exodus of experienced businessmen and managers, thousands of leaderless enterprises bogged down for lack of working capital, a shaky banking system, flight of funds out of the country, management-labor disputes, and total chaos in intersectoral

9. Bank Markazi publishes average annual budgets of rural and urban households based on regular surveys, but the information is inadequate for a meaningful determination of disparities.

10. *Kayhan Havai,* January 15, 1992, p. 24.

11. Hossein Azimi, "Aspects of Poverty and Income Distribution in Iran, 1960–1972" (Ph.D diss., Oxford University, 1980), p. 145.

12. *Kayhan* (Tehran), March 19, 1986, p. 18.

13. See Amirahmadi, *Revolution and Economic Transition,* pp. 194–202 and 292; and *Iran Times* (Washington), 7 Aban 1367 [1987], p. 5.

14. For a candid reference to some of these failings see President Rafsanjani's Friday prayer sermon, *Kayhan Havai,* August 14, 1991, p. 9 ff.

relations. Shortly after that, the regime was confronted with a freeze on its badly needed foreign assets, a trade embargo, and harsh financial sanctions.

Before the disputes with the United States could be settled, the country was invaded by Iraqi forces in September 1980 with subsequent heavy damage to factories, power stations, oil installations, and other parts of its infrastructure—recently reported by a UN team, on the basis of official claims, to equal $97 billion (while the government puts the total at $1 trillion).[15] Meanwhile, the regime partially lost the core of its political leadership through internal uprising and terror tactics of the opposition. Finally, the oil industry, the mainstay of the economy, underwent disruptive fluctuations in output and price because of factors largely outside the regime's control.

Notwithstanding these handicaps and hardships, the economy—thanks to a continuous stream of oil export revenues—managed to avoid life-threatening shortages, runaway inflation, and mounting foreign debt. Even at the height of the Iran-Iraq War, food and other basic necessities were available for a modest level of living. There never was famine. Even "non-necessities" were adequate for those who could afford them at free-market prices. Inflation, even by outsiders' estimates, was never close to the level experienced in some developing economies in recent times. Despite the heavy cost of war, the regime avoided recourse to foreign borrowing on a large-scale, and even paid out some of its long-term debt—albeit partly from reserves inherited from the shah's regime. Public expenditures on defense were kept from rising steeply by mobilizing private financial contributions for the war effort. The budget deficit was held on average below 8 percent of GDP by cutting down on non-priority outlays, albeit at the expense of public services and investment. Adverse effects of inflation on low- and fixed-income groups were reduced through price subsidies, rationing, and direct distribution of certain essential goods, although at a reported cost of increased inefficiency and corruption.[16]

At the same time, it should be noted that while some of the adverse elements were beyond the government's control, other factors responsible for keeping both output and income down were of the regime's own making. Specifically, two policy decisions stand out. First, the regime's self-appointed mission as exporter of Islamic revolution throughout the Muslim world (and beyond) was clearly an overly ambitious and unrealistic objective for which the country was politically, financially, and technically ill-prepared. Not only was most of the world against such adventurism but, as the nearly universal support for the Baghdad government after its imminent collapse in 1982 made apparent, Tehran's own Muslim allies in Damascus, Tripoli, and Algiers were not ready to embrace Ayatollah Khomeini's brand of Islam and thus risk destabilization of their own regimes.

15. See UN Security Council, S/23322, December 24, 1991.

16. See Dilip Hiro, "War Unsettles Iran's Economy," *Washington Post*, January 9, 1986; see also, "A Teheran Spring," *New Yorker*, June 22, 1992.

Preoccupation with this unrealistic mission sapped a great deal of the country's energy and increased the government's diplomatic isolation.

The second policy decision that hampered economic growth was the choice of an old (and already discredited) Marxist economic model, long practiced in India and also in parts of Latin America with disastrous results. Largely under pressure from its radical faction, and partly due to war requirements and exigencies, the Islamic republic during 1982–88 resorted to public ownership, price control, industrial regulation, import substitution, and overall economic regimentation designed to produce an elusive self-sufficiency. Using wartime conditions as an excuse to harness the economy, the government tried everything to expand government ownership and operations. By 1987, an estimated 60–70 percent of the entire domestic economy and 90 percent of foreign trade were directly or indirectly in state hands. Although public expenditures by the central government as a percentage of GDP (at current market prices) fell from 42 percent in 1977/78 to 22 percent in 1990/91, the share of the general government (including public enterprises and parastatal "foundations") increased progressively.[17] The regime's foreign exchange system was, up to 1989, highly restrictive, complex, and arbitrary. There were a multitude of exchange rates for different transactions. The direction of trade was shifted deliberately from the United States and the West in favor of neighboring countries, the Eastern bloc, the Third World, and smaller partners. The result has been a mushrooming bureaucracy, which now employs twice as many people as there were in the shah's time, sheer inefficiency, lower per capita output, and related problems.

THE ROAD AHEAD

The period of "postwar reconstruction" began in earnest after the cease-fire with Iraq, the revision of the constitution, and the election of Rafsanjani to the presidency. A five-year plan has been underway since 1989. It targets 8 percent annual real growth for GDP, with promises of increased employment, and higher per capita income. Planned outlays are to be financed mainly from domestic resources and owned foreign income (i.e., earnings from oil and gas). Total gross fixed capital investment from central government sources is estimated at about 27 percent of total government expenditures.[18] While slightly larger than the last ten years' average, this share is measurably smaller than similar ratios in the prerevolution plans.

17. In the fiscal year 1992/93, the budget of public enterprises was one and one-half times the national budget. The budget of parastatal "foundations" was also an additional 50 percent. See *Kayhan Havai*, February 19, 1992, pp. 24–6.

18. See *A Summarized Version of the First Five-Year Economic, Social, and Cultural Development Plan of the Islamic Republic of Iran, 1989–1993* (Tehran: Plan and Budget Organization, 1990).

In a major policy shift from the past, the government and its top spokesmen now clearly admit that regulation and regimentation have been harmful to the economy.[19] Through a series of Majlis laws and cabinet decisions, the private sector is now asked to participate in non-strategic manufacturing, social services, transportation, tourism, and trade. One-fourth of state-owned enterprises have become candidates for privatization. Free trade zones have been established at Qeshm and Kish islands. The new strategy of "economic adjustment and reforms" aims at the establishment of a market mechanism for determining the prices of goods, foreign exchange, and money; privatization of non-strategic industries now under government control; deregulation of cumbersome bureaucratic rules; and reorganization of state machinery in the service of marketization. The policies designed to achieve some of these objectives relate to tax laws, import-export regulations, accounting procedures, exchange system, and monetary and banking guidelines. The ultimate goal is to enhance people's participation in economic activities and decision making, and reduce state controls.

Prospects for these new policies remain somewhat uncertain due to strong resistance from powerful vested interests already entrenched at the various levels of the bureaucracy and the economy as a whole. Apart from hurdles involved in the resolution of conflicting philosophies and approaches among various clerical factions to many essential policy issues, some of the targets of the 1989–1993 plan relating to inflation, balance-of-payments, budget deficit, housing, non-oil exports, job creation, and private investment seem rather ambitious. The government's reported determination to rebuild its shattered military, expand its regional assistance, and support Islamic groups in Afghanistan, Algeria, Lebanon, and Sudan may make the domestic task even more difficult.[20] The plan's performance in its first two and one-half years of operation is far from reassuring. Scattered information filtering through government offices and agencies indicate shortfalls from target goals in many areas.[21]

The plan's overall success will require in addition to the peaceful resolution of internal and external conflict, a series of sustained structural adjustment measures including the gradual unification of exchange rates; stringent fiscal reforms aimed at eliminating perennial budget deficits; speedy removal of price controls, rationing and subsidies; a serious demand management strategy to harness inflation; the dismantling of the regulatory mechanisms on credit, trade, and private enterprise; restoration of the accountability of the parastatal organizations; streamlining of public administration; and the adoption of clear long-term policies on energy, agriculture, industry, and foreign trade. Without such a substantial restructuring of the economy,

19. See *New York Times*, May 28, 1991, and July 2, 1991; *Iran Focus*, May 1990; and MEED, November 15, 1991, p. 4.

20. David Hoffman, "Iran's Rebuilding Seen as Challenge to West," *Washington Post*, February 2, 1992.

21. *Arzyabi amalkard barnameh aval dar salhaye, 1368 va 1369* (Performance evaluation of the first development plan for 1989/90–1990/91) (Tehran: The Plan and Budget Organization [1991?]).

the country is likely to face further inflation, larger fiscal deficits, reduced efficiency, a decline in output growth, a deterioration in the external account, and a possible recession. Even reasonable headway toward these objectives requires further rethinking of a number of political, ideological, and even constitutional preferences, priorities, and prescriptions.

Preparations are now being made for the second five-year economic plan (1994/95–1998/99) to be submitted to the Majlis later this year or in early 1993. Thus far, significant deviations from current plan targets have raised questions at home and abroad regarding the usefulness and relevance of the Iranian planning mechanism in helping to shape the country's economic development. These questions have become even more pertinent now that the private sector is officially mandated to serve as a main force for growth in the next plan.

The results of the April-May 1992 nationwide elections for the fourth Majlis have been widely interpreted as a confirmation of President Rafsanjani's pragmatic economic policies and a good omen for the country's sustained growth and political calm. Some Western observers have seen the hardliners' defeat as a mandate to proceed with industrial privatization, government deregulation, and the economy's integration into the global market. While this prognosis seems plausible, its optimistic undertones remain to be tested. Iran's current economic problems need much more than a friendly Majlis; they call for an improved international political image of the Tehran regime, greater private sector confidence, increased foreign exchange, newer technologies, higher labor productivity, a cleaner bureaucracy, and less income disparity. An accommodating Majlis can at best be a catalyst for change, but it cannot be an ultimate solution.

The new "moderate" Majlis may support the government in further opening the country to the West—even to the United States—streamlining the bureaucracy, shedding some money-losing enterprises and clostly regulations, and seeking foreign assistance. These reforms, however, are not without cost. If the experience of Eastern Europe and the former Soviet Union serves as a guide, Rafsanjani's *perestroika*—raising taxes, rationalizing interest rates, cutting off subsidies, unifying the exchange rate, liberalizing trade, and linking wage hikes to productivity—will have similar widely unpopular repercussions. These restructuring measures, although ultimately rewarding, are bound in the short term to produce further inflation, unemployment, bankruptcies, and deprivations unwelcome not only to opposition politicians but to an overwhelming majority of the rank and file Iranians who, after 13 years of patient waiting, would like to see the regime's promises of prosperity and plenty fulfiled. In the fluid political climate of today's Iran, it is too soon to count the new Majlis's blessings.[22]

---

22. For full details see Jahangir Amuzegar, *Iran's Economy under the Islamic Republic* (London: I.B. Tauris, forthcoming 1993).

[6]

Int. J. Middle East Stud. **26** (1994), 37–56. *Printed in the United States of America*

A. Aydın Çeçen, A. Suut Doğruel, and Fatma Doğruel

ECONOMIC GROWTH AND STRUCTURAL CHANGE IN TURKEY 1960–88

After almost five decades of industrialization—characterized, on the one hand, by considerable state intervention and, on the other, by protectionist import-substituting policies in domestic capital formation—in the early 1980s Turkey ostensibly entered a new era of export-led economic growth. Since 1960, the Turkish democracy has experienced a series of crises with astonishingly regular ten-year cycles of recurrence. The 1980 military intervention, however, brought about a radical attempt to restructure the economy, hardly comparable with the rather gradual changes in its recent economic history. Its ten years of experimentation with economic liberalization and structural adjustment provide us today with an adequate record to identify and discuss at least the salient features of this period by comparing the performance of the economy in different years.

The purpose of the study is to offer a fairly general discussion of the patterns of development in Turkey between 1960 and 1988 by contrasting the 1960–80 period with the postliberalization era of the 1980s and analyze the dynamics of economic growth and the concomitant mutation the economy underwent during these years. It also strives to demonstrate that, despite some salutary effects, these liberalization attempts and structural adjustment policies failed to remedy some of the most important structural problems of the Turkish economy. We do not claim, however, to have captured the sociopolitical correlates of this complex transformation, nor to have given a *histoire raisonnée* of this dichotomous period from an economic perspective. Much of the analysis elaborated in this study concentrates on the macro developmental aspects of the Turkish experience, without losing sight, insofar as possible, of the historical specificity of the underlying processes.

The article is organized as follows. The first section focuses on the 1960–78 import-substitution period and investigates the dynamics of growth and structural change by striving to identify the demand and supply side determinants of economic growth. The second section reviews the new developments in the Turkish economy in relation to the stabilization and structural adjustment programs introduced in 1980. The third section gives a brief evaluation of the results obtained in light of the continuing internal disequilibria and the drastic changes in the distribution

A. Aydın Çeçen teaches at the Department of Economics, Central Michigan University, Mt. Pleasant, Mich. 48859, U.S.A., and A. Suut Doğruel and Fatma Doğruel teach at the Department of Economics, Marmara University, Kuyubaşi, Istanbul, Turkey 81040.

of income. Finally, the last section concludes with some remarks regarding the character of the post-1980 period and the salient features of the Turkish economy.

IMPORT-SUBSTITUTING STRATEGIES AND ECONOMIC GROWTH, 1960–78

After a period of postwar expansion, the Turkish economy showed sluggish growth and trade imbalances during the years between the mid-1950s and the beginning of the 1960s. Annual growth rates of industrial production averaged 4.3 percent in the second part of the 1950s, while that of agriculture remained only at 1.8 percent. Exports and imports fell below their 1953 levels and did not recover until 1960. It is during this period that comprehensive protectionist measures were introduced to overcome the persistent deficits in the balance of payments, together with price control programs to curtail inflation. Although the origin of strong state intervention in the economy dates back to the early 1930s, one can argue that a stronger orientation toward import-substituting development strategies and interventionist development programs generated a revival of interest in the stagnant economic conditions of this period, despite the official policy of the government that preached laissez-faire and free competition. In sharp contrast to the pre-1960 years, however, the 1960s enjoyed a vigorous economic recovery together with high growth rates in GNP. More specifically, the growth rates of GNP were 6.4 percent (1963–67), 6.7 percent (1968–72) and 7.2 percent (1973–77) during the three successive five-year-plan periods. These growth rates, compared to those of fifty-five countries that are within the same income category, appear to be higher than their overall average rate of 6 percent per annum.[1]

With the implementation of the three five-year development plans, the economy continued to expand throughout this period, thanks to the unprecedented growth in the manufacturing and service sectors. The growth rate of agriculture, although relatively modest, stayed consistently above that of the population, with an average of 3.3 percent per annum. In the early 1970s, record high workers' remittances (originating mostly from the Turkish guest workers in Germany) together with the aggressive investment plans of the government enabled the domestic output to keep on growing for a few more years, until the end of 1976, when the oil crisis threw the economy into a deep recession. Throughout the rest of the decade, Turkey struggled with severe balance of payments difficulties coupled with rising inflation. By the end of the 1970s, the Turkish economy found itself in a full-fledged economic crisis accompanied by political instability and social unrest.

Concomitant with these developments, the economy underwent a far-reaching transformation in its structure during the same period. While the share of agriculture in total output (at 1968 prices) declined from 38.4 percent in 1962 to 23.3 percent in 1977, that of the industrial sector (including manufacturing, mining, energy, and construction) rose rapidly from 22.3 percent to 31.5 percent.[2] Nevertheless, this economic expansion, it is argued, did not give rise to the "expected" outcomes, when the results obtained are compared to the international norms of the same period.[3] First and foremost, the growth in manufacturing did not succeed in generating adequate employment opportunities to absorb the labor force released by the shrinking agricultural sector. Second, compared to other developing coun-

TABLE 1 *Sectoral distribution of investments and savings*

	Growth Rates (%)			Shares in GDP at 1968 Prices (%)			
	1963–67	1968–72	1973–77	1962	1967	1972	1977
Total gross investment	8.5	7.2	15.3	15.8	17.4	17.9	26.1
private	4.8	9.1	13.1	8.6	7.8	9.0	10.5
public	12.5	5.4	18.0	7.1	9.6	8.9	14.6
Total gross savings	12.7	5.2	8.8	12.3	16.4	15.4	16.7
private	11.9	3.6	12.2	6.7	8.6	7.5	9.3
public	13.7	6.8	6.9	5.6	7.8	7.9	7.4

Sources: State Institute of Statistics, State Planning Organization.

tries in the same income category, the share of agriculture in GNP continued to remain relatively high, which hampered the growth of total factor productivity. Third, in spite of this impressive growth record of output, the share of total gross savings in gross domestic product (GDP) at 1968 prices did not show any substantial improvement and remained stagnant throughout this period (see Table 1). Fourth, international comparisons also reveal that exports remained well below those of other developing countries with similar characteristics. Last but not least, one should also point to the continuing dominance of the public sector over domestic industrial production throughout this period, despite all the incentive programs directed to the private sector.

During the 1960–78 period, two major and interrelated developments are discernible in the expansion of the Turkish economy. One is the impact of five-year development plans on industrialization and capital accumulation.[4] The other is the end of the "easy" stage of import substitution and the beginning of its "complex" stage, characterized by the replacement of imported intermediate and capital goods, consumer durables, and the domestic production of related technologies. While much of Turkey's economic growth in 1947–53 was made possible by a rapid expansion in agricultural production and exports under relatively liberal trade policies buttressed by the Korean boom, the main thrust of the planning years originated from inward-looking import-substituting programs that relied heavily on public investments in both manufacturing—through State Economic Enterprises (SEEs)—and infrastructure and resulted in a steady growth of domestic total demand.[5]

On the foreign-trade front, however, the performance of the economy was far from impressive. Except for the 1971–74 period, during which the dollar value of total exports more than doubled, due to the 1970 devaluation of the Turkish lira (TL) and the accompanying export-promotion measures, the share of manufactured exports in total exports did not show any spectacular improvement. Between 1962 and 1970, it remained around 18 percent of total exports, whereas for the 1970–78 period it fluctuated around 32 percent. Finally, it should be mentioned that the 1963–70 period corresponded to a "positive" import substitution mostly financed by domestic savings, and the 1971–77 period can be defined as a "negative" import-substitution era, which gave rise to increasing current account deficits over time.[6]

TABLE 2 *Population and employment characteristics*

					Growth Rates (%)		
	1962	1967	1972	1977	1963–67	1968–72	1973–77
Total population (million)	28.9	32.7	37.1	42.0	2.5	2.5	2.5
Active population (million) I	16.4	18.5	21.2	23.9	2.4	2.8	2.4
Labor force (million) II	13.1	13.9	15.0	16.2	1.1	1.6	1.6
Participation rate (% II/I)	80.1	75.0	70.6	67.7	—	—	—
Total employment (million)	12.6	13.2	13.9	14.7	0.9	1.0	1.1
Unemployment (million)	1.4	1.7	2.0	2.2	4.0	3.3	1.9
in agriculture	1.0	1.1	0.9	0.7	—	—	—
Unemployment rate (%)	11.1	12.1	13.3	13.1	—	—	—
Workers abroad (thousand)	13.0	204.0	634.0	815.0	73.4	25.5	5.2

Sources: State Institute of Statistics, State Planning Organization.

In order to investigate the contribution of different factors to economic growth, one can decompose the proportional increase in total value added by using a neoclassical aggregate-production-function approach.[7] Based on the aggregate data for the 1963–75 period, the results obtained by Chenery et al. indicate that the growth rate of total aggregate output amounted to 6.4 percent and the rate of increase in capital and labor were 6.82 percent and 1.02 percent, respectively. While the share of capital in total aggregate output was 55 percent, that of labor stood at 45 percent. Finally, the rate of technological change was found to be 2.23 percent. These figures demonstrate that more than half of the 6.4 percent average annual growth rate of value added was due to capital accumulation. On the other hand, technological change accounts for almost one-third of the growth rate of output. The contribution of labor growth was the most modest one, which may seem to be paradoxical in view of high population growth rates in Turkey during this period. As we shall try to explain below, this situation is directly related to the emergence of a highly capital intensive manufacturing sector in the economy. In light of these findings, we can now turn to a more detailed analysis of these factors.

Since 1955, the average growth rate of population in Turkey has been approximately 2.5 percent per annum. This high and gradually rising growth rate of population was due to an increase in birth rates and a decrease in death rates, mainly as a result of improved nutrition and the diffusion of health facilities during these years.[8] In spite of the family-planning programs introduced in the five-year plans, progress has been marginal in this area. Meanwhile, a very rapid rural–urban migration increased the urban population share from 18.8 percent in 1950 to over 40 percent by 1978. Table 2 summarizes the changes in population characteristics, labor force, and employment levels for the years 1962–77.

As can be observed from the figures in Table 2, the growth rate of the labor force has remained consistently below that of the economically active and total population. This can be explained by the rising proportion of the young, the rapid increase in the school population, and the growing number of workers emigrating abroad. Parallel to this rapid population growth, the sectoral distribution of the labor force has undergone a radical change during the same years. As the proportion of the labor force in agriculture fell from 77 percent in 1962 to 61.8 percent in 1977, the corresponding share of the manufacturing sector rose from 7.2 percent to 11 percent and that of the service sector increased from 15.1 percent to 25.6 percent.[9] Given the marginal character of most of the jobs created in the service sector (in terms of factor productivity growth), these results point to the fact that the growth in manufacturing has not been able to absorb the growing labor force in the economy.

The fact that structural and disguised unemployment remained quite high despite the rapid pace of industrialization can be partly explained by the relatively low growth rate in manufacturing, compared to that of some southern European countries such as Spain, Portugal, and Greece. Yet, the highly capital-intensive structure of Turkish manufacturing is a factor that cannot be discounted. Undoubtedly, high tariff and quota regimes, together with unrealistic exchange-rate and interest-rate policies, are the major causes behind this nonoptimal capital intensiveness of the manufacturing sector.[10] This process is well epitomized by the following statistics: in 1976 constant prices, while a TL 373,000 investment per job was needed in the 1963–67 first five-year-plan period, this amount rose to TL 772,000 in the second five-year plan.[11]

As to the accumulation of capital and investment patterns, one can distinguish two subperiods in 1963–79: the 1963–73 period, during which capital accumulation relied to a large extent on domestic savings; and the post-1974 period, when reliance on foreign financial resources increased substantially to continue to sustain economic growth. With the implementation of the first three five-year plans, the proportion of gross fixed investments in GNP rose rapidly from 15.8 percent in 1962 to 26.1 percent in 1977. However, while there has been some increase in gross domestic savings, their growth rates have remained consistently below those of investments, with the divergence between them becoming more pronounced toward the end of the 1970s. The sectoral distribution of investments and savings, as well as their growth rates, are given in Table 1.

The reasons behind these dismal saving ratios are complex. Suffice it to say here that their causes should be sought in the structure of income distribution and the characteristics of capital and assets markets together with the introverted nature of oligopolistic holding companies in Turkey.[12] Furthermore, the analysis of the sectoral distribution of investments reveals that the manufacturing sector absorbed the largest portion of total investment, followed by the construction, transportation, and communications sectors. Meanwhile, investments in the areas of health and education showed a steady decline.

Moreover, in order to complete our discussion of the supply-side factors affecting economic growth, we must also consider the impact of technological change. Indeed, the introduction of new technologies into domestic production, skill deepening, and modern production-management techniques greatly contributed to productivity growth during these years. For instance, Krueger and Tuncer[13] show that for the 1963–76 period, total factor productivity increased at an average rate of 2.10 percent per annum in various branches of manufacturing, the most successful ones being the tobacco, rubber, metal, and textile industries. An interesting result

TABLE 3 *The sources of the growth of GNP (%)*

	1963–68	1968–73	1973–77
Domestic final demand	83.6	81.6	100.4
The effects of trade			
export growth	4.9	16.3	-1.0
import substitution	8.3	-1.4	0.6
Technological change	3.2	3.3	—
Total	100.0	100.0	100.0

Source: World Bank, *Policies and Prospects*, 8 (see n. 1).

that transpires from the same analysis pertains to the performance of the public sector. They found that total factor productivity growth in the public manufacturing sector was around 2.65 percent, whereas that of the private sector was only 1.84 percent. One can therefore argue that, despite their chronic deficits and losses, the public sector has made important contributions to productivity growth during these years.

Finally, another issue that should be addressed in this context is the nature of the import-substitution process. By the end of the mid-1960s, the "easy" stage of import substitution—during which the domestic production of most consumer nondurables and of their intermediate products was achieved utilizing mostly unskilled labor—came to an end. Because these products were mostly labor intensive and did not require large-scale production for efficient operations, they were well suited to the conditions in Turkey.[14] Yet, in the 1970s the Turkish economy was already in the "complex" stage of import substitution where the domestic production of most consumer durables—which started in the mid-1960s in the form of so-called assembly industries—and the production of intermediate and capital goods was at stake. Because the production of these goods depends critically on the implementation of high technology and the use of highly skilled labor, the deficiencies in labor training, technology adaptation, and management had very strong negative effects on efficiency and productivity growth. Indeed, the sharp drop in total factor productivity growth from 3.2 percent (1963–67) to -1.18 percent (1973–76) in manufacturing is, beyond the oil-price shocks of this period, attributable to the characteristics of this new phase of import substitution. This period reveals as well the increasing dependence of domestic production and investment on imported intermediate and capital goods.

The industrialization process that gained momentum after the 1940s has also deeply affected the composition of domestic demand. As the proportion of manufactured goods in total demand continued to rise throughout these years, the share of foodstuffs in consumer products declined sharply. One also observes, during the same period, a steady expansion in the demand for investment goods, as well as the strengthening of sectoral interlinkages. A more careful examination of the statistics reveals that the increase in final demand has been the overwhelming force behind economic expansion. The decomposition results given in Table 3 also demonstrate that the contribution of exports to the growth of GNP was very modest at the beginning of the planning period and tended to increase between 1968 and 1973. The impact of the oil crisis in 1974 is visible as well, in the abrupt decline of the effects of exports on output growth. Moreover, despite the heavy emphasis of the third five-year plan on import substitution in intermediate and capital goods, these figures shed light on the declining importance of import-substituting policies and appear to vindicate our contention that these policies became gradually ineffective in promoting the domestic production of consumer durables and investment goods (the second phase of import substitution).

In connection with the demand-side sources of economic growth, another point that needs to be stressed is the particular nature of the excess-capacity phenomenon and its relationship to economic growth. In fact, a casual look at the growth patterns in the Turkish economy is sufficient to reveal that the emergence and exhaustion of the excess capacity in infrastructure, as well as in manufacturing, is indeed at the very heart of the cyclical growth the economy has experienced since the late 1940s. Without going into the details, the story can be told, in a highly stylized fashion, in the following way.

In the course of the industrialization process, the state appears to be periodically compelled to initiate extensive investment projects in both infrastructure and key primary and intermediate products industries, which eventually give rise to the formation of excess capacity in the economy. Subsequently, due to expansionary policies, on the one hand, and to a certain extent to the existing favorable trade conditions, on the other, aggregate demand starts to rise and exhausts this excess capacity over time. Consequently, the boom periods often correspond to the years during which the excess capacity produced in previous years is being used up gradually, whereas the crises seem to emerge in the aftermath of the excess-capacity exhaustion. Meanwhile, the same phenomenon is observable in manufacturing. Independent of the fluctuations in domestic demand, there seems to exist an "autonomous" excess capacity in manufacturing that goes beyond optimal excess-capacity levels. It is possible to argue that there are two major reasons behind this maladjustment process. One is the relatively low domestic prices of imported capital goods, determined mostly by import-substituting policies. The second is the oligopolistic-monopolistic character of these industries. In this context, one can point to three key variables that determine simultaneously the relative prices of capital (investment) goods in Turkey: real effective exchange rates, import restrictions, and real interest rates. Under the fixed-exchange (multiple) rate regime, effective exchange rates applied to capital-goods imports declined steadily from the beginning of the 1950s onward. In the 1960s, by means of credit-rationing policies, selective credits were channeled to various branches in manufacturing with practically nonexistent or negative real lending rates.[15] It is no wonder that during the 1963–76 period there was a 6.3 percent annual average increase in manpower utilization in the manufacturing sector, whereas the capital stock grew at an average rate of 12.8 percent per annum. This observation is particularly striking in view of the high unemployment and population growth rates that prevailed in the economy, which hindered any spectacular increase in per capita income.

Furthermore, from a microeconomic viewpoint, the existence of the excess capacity in manufacturing can be attributed to the oligopolistic-monopolistic structure of these markets. As is well known, since the level of production does not correspond to the minimum level of average cost, in such markets output is below competitive levels and the price is above these levels, which gives rise to the buildup of unused capital stocks. It should be emphasized here that we are not talking about the classical version of the excess-capacity theorem that is applicable to monopolistically competitive markets. Rather, it is the small-group case concerning competition among a small number of oligopolistic firms that is relevant in the case of Turkey. Hence, the excess-capacity phenomenon is not about the existence of too many firms producing differentiated products but rather pertains to the behavior of oligopolistic firms that create more capital than they need for their own production—both as a barrier to entry and as a response to the aforementioned import-substituting policies.

CRISIS, STABILIZATION POLICIES, AND ECONOMIC RESTRUCTURING

The Turkish economy entered the 1970s with rapid growth, a current-account surplus, and a relatively high rate of inflation. Record-high workers' remittances together with increasing export revenues enabled the government to continue with its ambitious investment projects and rapid-growth targets. This performance was interrupted by the first oil crisis in 1974, but the reluctance of the government to adjust to the new international environment and to pass the deterioration in the terms of trade on to domestic prices of oil and other imported intermediate products created strong internal and external imbalances over the rest of the decade.

In the second part of the 1970s, Turkey had to resort to short-term foreign borrowing to finance current-account deficits in the face of falling workers' remittances and stagnant export proceeds. With rapidly declining exchange reserves, rising import bills, and debt-servicing payments, the Turkish economy was thrown into a full-fledged payments crisis, which brought about a total collapse of its credit worthiness in international markets.

From 1978 onward the government introduced a series of stabilization programs under the protection of the International Monetary Fund (IMF) that centered around various contractionary measures and export-promotion policies. Accordingly, the Turkish lira was devaluated twice (23% in March 1978 and 44% in June 1979), and stronger export-tax-rebate schemes were introduced to improve the trade balance. Moreover, some debt restructuring was achieved under the auspices of the Organization of Economic Cooperation and Development (OECD), and this was accompanied by a new syndicated loan. These stabilization and adjustment packages did not, however, succeed in reversing the declining performance of the economy. The growth of real GNP continued to decline and became negative during 1979–80. While inflation gathered momentum and reached an unprecedented triple-digit rate in 1980, unemployment soared to 14.8 percent. This economic crisis, compounded by political and social unrest, prepared the ground for the third military intervention in the history of the republic.

The stabilization and adjustment programs introduced on 24 January 1980, under the aegis of the IMF, the World Bank, and OECD were designed to curb inflation and circumvent the balance of payments difficulties in the short run and to restore equilibrium and economic growth in the long run. Financial assistance was provided by these international institutions as well as by bilateral donors, and happened to be one of the largest operations of its kind: between 1980 and 1985 the IMF made available $1.7 billion in special drawing rights (SDR) under a series of stand-by arrangements, and the World Bank extended $1.6 billion in structural adjustment loans. It is possible to argue that although initially these programs left an impression of déjà vu in Turkey, it shortly became apparent that these policies were aimed at achieving a radical break with the inward-looking, import-substituting development strategies of the past.[16]

A voluminous literature exists on the description of these policies.[17] Therefore, it suffices here to say that most of these programs may be studied under the following four headings: (1) short-run stabilization packages aimed at curbing inflation and alleviating payments difficulties; (2) liberalization of the domestic-pricing mechanism; (3) rationalization of the public and financial sectors; and (4) promotion of exports and foreign trade in general. The developments in these four areas will be sketched seriatim.

As far as the stabilization programs are concerned, these policies sought to curb inflation and remedy-payments difficulties by eliminating the excess demand in domestic markets, which is consistent with the spirit of orthodox IMF anti-inflationary measures. In practice, this implied a drastic reduction in the Central Bank credits extended to the public sector, hence a sudden drop in public investments and spending. During the initial years of the program, contractionary demand-management policies depended heavily on monetary programs. Since the use of open-market operations is limited by the lack of developed money and capital markets in Turkey, these contractionary programs had to rely on credit reduction and interest-management operations. Accordingly, as Central Bank discount rates as well as reserve requirements on time and sight deposits were adjusted upward, interest rates were deregulated to arrest financial disintermediation, which emerged as a result of negative real interest rates.[18]

To strengthen the anti-inflationary effects of these fiscal and monetary measures, further steps were taken to introduce various comprehensive structural reforms into commodity and factor markets. Consequently, in 1980 private-sector prices were freed and those of basic commodities and services provided by state monopolies and SEEs were substantially adjusted upward. Agricultural subsidies were reduced and support lists were redefined. Yet, similar liberalization attempts did not follow in the reorganization of the labor markets. Instead, the military rule banned a large section of the trade-union movement and established the High Arbitration Council (Yüksek Hakem Kurulu) to handle most wage determinations and labor disputes.[19] As a result of these policies and the continuing inflation, real wages declined from TL 100 in 1979 to TL 74.0 in 1985, and unemployment soared to 16.3 percent in 1985 in the face of this economic contraction.

The most comprehensive and probably the most radical steps have been taken in the foreign-trade sector of the economy, and they have been quite instrumental in promoting exports and hence alleviating current-account deficits. Ostensibly, these efforts also marked the end of inward-looking development strategies and the beginning of export-led growth. The major developments in this period can be summarized under two categories: first, reforms and programs aimed at trade liberalization and export promotion; second, the concomitant exchange-rate policies directed at restoring external equilibrium and expenditure switching. As a first step toward dismantling the existing trade restrictions, the quota list was abolished in January 1981; advanced-deposit requirements on industrial imports were reduced, and tariff exemptions on imported intermediate products were granted. Furthermore, in an effort to promote exports, export credits were introduced and export-licensing requirements were eliminated. Yet, with the growing practice of the "fictitious exports" (i.e., over invoicing), export credits were ended in 1984 and were replaced by direct subsidies in 1985.[20] Indeed, the Turkish export miracle owed much to the active exchange-rate policies of this period. After a 33 percent nominal devaluation of the Turkish lira in 1980, multiple-exchange rates were abolished and a flexible-exchange-rate regime was established. In 1984, commercial banks were allowed to determine their exchange rates within certain limits set by the Central Bank. Finally, in August 1988 exchange-rate determination was totally left to market forces by means of the newly established Foreign-Exchange Market.

THE POSTLIBERALIZATION ERA

From the debt crisis, which has plagued much of the Third World since the early 1980s, Turkey has emerged as the "paragon of export-led growth" and an inspiring example of stabilization and liberalization. In sharp contrast to Latin American countries, its rapid convalescence made it possible to restore its credit worthiness in international markets and regain relatively high growth rates. In the words of one economist, Turkey presented "the single most important case of a 'life after debt'."[21] After more than a decade of economic stabilization and structural adjustment, however, it is possible to argue that the results of these programs left much to be desired. Some of the most relevant statistics describing the performance of the Turkish economy during the 1979–88 period are given in Table 4.

The reduction of inflation from its peak rate of 104 percent in 1980 to 28 percent in two years, the restoration of positive growth rates, the elimination of foreign-exchange bottlenecks, and especially the unprecedented growth in exports are, without doubt, remarkable results that deserve much praise in appreciating the effects of these programs. Yet, an objective evaluation of these policies would be incomplete without taking into account the overall performance of the economy in other areas as well.

First, as can be observed from the growth rates of GNP in Table 4, this success story ought to be qualified in a number of ways. It is true that economic growth owed much to these policies in the aftermath of the payments crisis: from 1981 onward, the growth rate of real GNP increased steadily and reached a peak value of 8.1 in 1986, declining later to 4.1 in 1988. However, one should also note that for the 1980–88 period, the average annual growth rate has been 4.61 percent, which is well below rates observed between 1963 and 1972 (6.6%) and those during the 1972–77 period (7.2%). Indeed, the post-1980 growth rates should be viewed in the context of the worldwide stagflation of this period and should be contrasted with the failure of many Latin American economies that, despite similar attempts, have not succeeded in arresting sharp declines in their GNPs. Yet, one should be reminded of the fact that none of these countries benefited from external financial

TABLE 4 *Selected statistics for the 1979–88 period*

	1979	1980	1981	1982	1983	1984	1985	1986	1987	1988
Real GNP[a]	-0.4	-1.1	4.1	4.6	3.3	5.9	5.1	8.1	7.4	4.1
Real domestic demand[a]	-2.2	-1.2	1.6	2.8	4.7	5.5	4.4	11.4	6.1	1.5
Implicit GNP deflator[a]	71.1	103.8	41.9	27.5	28.0	50.1	43.9	30.9	38.3	63.2
Private investment[a]	-3.1	-10.0	1.7	3.4	3.0	2.0	4.3	17.8	14.1	13.6
Interest rate[b]	10.8	13.5	40.5	40.5	40.5	46.8	45.0	36.9	34.2	74.7
CB credits to public sector[a]	72.6	71.0	35.2	5.5	12.8	-4.1	62.1	38.0	71.4	45.9
Tax revenue[c]	18.4	16.9	18.1	17.9	16.7	12.9	13.8	15.2	15.5	13.9
Merchandise exports[c]	2.3	2.9	4.7	5.7	5.7	7.1	7.9	7.5	10.2	11.7
External debt at year end[d]	15.8	16.2	16.9	17.6	18.4	21.3	25.3	31.2	38.3	37.7
Real wage index[e]	100.0	68.8	79.5	75.0	79.7	78.5	74.0	75.9	67.8	56.9
Unemployment rate[f]	13.6	14.8	15.2	15.6	16.1	16.1	16.3	15.8	15.2	14.4

Sources: State Institute of Statistics, State Planning Organization, Central Bank, IMF estimates.
Notes: [a]Annual percentage change; [b]after tax six-month time deposit rate; [c]percentage of GNP; [d]in billions of U.S. dollars; [e]based on the Social Security Institute data and Consumer Price Indices; [f]percentage of domestic civilian labor force.

supports commensurate with the ones Turkey managed to receive during this period. It seems therefore fair to calibrate the growth performance of the Turkish economy by saying that it has been a success relative to the failure of other debt-ridden developing economies. It is also important to recognize that external financial support played a crucial role in pulling the economy from the acute payment crisis. In addition, another point that needs to be addressed is the nature and determinants of growth in this period. The growth success of Turkey in the post-stabilization era is due mainly to the reduction of consumption and the shift of government expenditure from public consumption to investment. In other words, in contrast to other high-debt countries, in the aftermath of the debt crisis Turkey adopted a growth-oriented debt strategy rather than relying on sustained high surpluses in the noninterest account to keep the debt–output ratio under control. In fact, the estimation results of Anand, Chhibber, and van Wijnbergen[22] demonstrate that the government, by reducing consumption, succeeded in maintaining output growth at the expense of external targets and that public investment has played an important role in the strong-growth performance of the economy. It is therefore possible to argue that, despite various privatization and liberalization attempts, the role of the public sector did not wither in the post-1980 period.[23]

Second, although impressive by any standard at the beginning of the crisis period, these anti-inflationary policies did not fare well during the rest of the decade. From 1981 to 1988 the average rate of inflation (the rate of change in the implicit GNP deflator) remained around 40.5 percent per annum and once again accelerated during 1988. What are the reasons behind this failure? How should one tackle the problem of sustained inflation in the face of relatively contractionary policies? Although the determinants of inflation change over time and its analysis is far from being facile, it can be briefly pointed out that, in general, the failure of these policies stems from a neglect of the supply-side effects of these programs and to a certain extent from the insistence on a strict monetarist explanation of inflation that tautologically blames it on the growth in nominal money balances. Recent economic research shows that contractionary policies may fuel rather than dampen inflationary tendencies. For instance, restrictive monetary policies and devaluations may increase the price level while decreasing output, hence triggering a stagflationary process in a developing economy.[24] In other words, inflation cannot be curbed by reducing the growth rate of the money supply and the value of the Turkish lira vis-à-vis other foreign currencies. In the absence of well-developed capital markets, long-term investment plans of domestic firms depend critically on the availability of official and private bank credits, which are bound to decline as a result of contractionary monetary policies. On the other hand, due to the strong import dependence of the manufacturing sector, depreciation of the Turkish lira tends to increase the domestic cost of imported inputs, which in turn validates the price hikes in manufacturing, thereby contributing to overall inflation.

Moreover, casual empiricism suggests that even the relationship between aggregate demand and inflation is far from being direct. In fact, after a peak rate of 60 percent (consumer price index) in 1985, inflation slowed down gradually until 1987. During the same period, however, domestic demand was continuously increasing. In this context, one can point to the price structure of Turkish manufacturing to better understand the dynamics of inflation in Turkey. Clearly, the estimation results of the following equations demonstrate that price increases in this sector are particularly sensitive to the changes in imported input prices, the variations in the supply of industrial credits, as well as the capacity-utilization levels.

$$\frac{\dot{P}_I}{P_I} = \underset{(2.861)}{.4259} + \underset{(2.01)}{.4347}\left(\frac{\dot{W}}{W}\right) + \underset{(7.86)}{.3316}\left(\frac{PM\dot{T}L}{PMTL}\right) - \underset{(-3.28)}{.4050}\ CUI - \underset{(-2.63)}{.4156}\left(\frac{C\dot{R}S}{CRS}\right)$$

$$R^2 = .8905 \quad DW = 1.557 \qquad (1)$$

$$CUI = \underset{(-0.52)}{-.0541} + \underset{(5.77)}{.9580}\left(\frac{MINT \times EXRM/PMTL}{KI}\right) + \underset{(2.20)}{.1190}\left(\frac{YD}{KI}\right)$$

$$R^2 = .7372 \quad DW = 1.07 \qquad (2)$$

In Equation 1, $(\dot{P}_I/P_I)$ denotes the proportional rate of change in the price index for manufacturing; $(\dot{W}/W)$, $(PMTL/PMTL)$, and $(C\dot{R}S/CRS)$ are, respectively, the proportional rates of change in wages, the domestic price index for imported inputs, and the supply of industrial credits. *CUI* is the capacity-utilization index for the manufacturing sector. In Equation 2 *MINT* and *EXRM* stand for, respectively, the imports of intermediate products in \$U.S. and the average nominal-exchange rate for manufactured goods (TL/\$). The numerator of the first ratio in Equation 2 simply gives the real value of imported intermediate goods in Turkish lira. *YD* and *KI* denote disposable private national income and the fixed-capital stock in manufacturing. The figures in parentheses are the *t* statistics.[25]

In light of these estimations, one can argue that imported input prices as well as capacity-utilization levels and the availability of credits strongly determine the price variations in the manufacturing sector. It is also important to note that the level of capacity utilization is negatively related to price increases. This is explained by Equation 2, which demonstrates that the capacity-utilization index is more strongly influenced by the availability of imported intermediate products than by domestic-demand pressures.

In addition to these results, the decomposition analysis of Conway shows that, for the 1980–83 period, devaluation alone contributed to inflation by an average of 58.4 percent in Turkey. For the whole 1973–83 period, increases in imported input prices, external inflation, and devaluation appear to explain as much as 63.2 percent of the rate of inflation.[26] Consequently, it is not possible to ignore the impact of those stabilization policies on the price level.

Furthermore, another subject pertinent to the discussion of inflation in Turkey is the rationalization and performance of SEEs. The prices of various final and intermediate products produced by the SEEs have been adjusted in an effort to rationalize production and eliminate losses. This would reduce the burden of SEEs on the government budget and hence alleviate the pressure on the Central Bank to finance the deficit through money creation. However, since many of the SEE products are intermediate goods used by public and private firms in manufacturing, these price hikes affect the price level in this sector and therefore contribute to inflation in general. We should parenthetically point out here that, abstracting from the intricacies of public-enterprise economics, it may be rational to determine the output prices on the basis of the cost of production and productivity. Yet, it is also true that efficiency cannot be achieved through mere price adjustments in a monopolistic market. In other words, without changing the micro structure of SEEs, it is not possible to attain high efficiency and the optimal allocation of resources.

A thorough analysis of inflation in Turkey that also incorporates its political economy is more complex and goes beyond the confines of the cursory discussion given earlier. For instance, the inflation tax on domestic-currency holdings is a major source of government revenue and hence cannot be omitted in the investigation of the determinants of sustained inflation. This point is particularly important in view of the growing debt burden that requires new sources of financing. On the other hand, there is (perhaps paradoxically) the counterpressure of the IMF that requires the borrowing countries to reduce inflation to enhance their repayment capacity. The opposition (or support) of different social strata to the persistence of sustained inflation—with its effects on the domestic terms of trade and the redistribution of income—is another dimension that should be taken into account.

Probably the most spectacular results of the liberalization programs have been in the area of foreign trade. During the 1980s, Turkey witnessed an unprecedented export boom by international and domestic standards whereby total exports rose rapidly from $2.9 billion in 1980 to $11.7 billion by the end of 1988. This was accompanied by a drastic change in the composition of exports: in five years, the share of manufactured products in total exports increased from 36 percent in 1980 to 80 percent by the end of 1985. Apparently, a number of factors contributed to this export drive: the fast depreciation of the Turkish lira, various export incentives in the form of tax rebates and direct export credits, the Iran–Iraq war, and, finally, the sudden drop in domestic demand. Whether there really was an export "miracle" and, if so, which of these factors has been the most important driving force behind this miracle has been a matter of debate among economists. Some economists have attributed this export boom to the liberal use of export incentives. Others have drawn attention to Turkey's exchange-rate policy. For instance, Celasun and Rodrik[27] argue that Turkey's export success had little to do with either the incentive regime or exchange-rate policy, but was mostly a consequence of its geographical location and the Iraq–Iran war. Arslan and van Wijnbergen,[28] on the other hand, hold the view that this export boom can be explained by the trade reforms and the macroeconomic policies Turkey followed during this period. Nonetheless, one point is now clear: Turkey has not yet succeeded in penetrating into the world export markets as, for instance, Taiwan and Korea did in the 1960s and 1970s. In fact, the share of Turkish exports in the total exports of non-oil developing countries to industrialized economies increased from 1.1 percent in 1977 to only 1.6 percent in 1988.[29]

There exists a vast literature on the nature and possibility of export-led growth in developing economies.[30] In the case of Turkey, given the overwhelming impact of domestic demand on economic growth, among other things, one has every reason to have mixed feelings about the euphoria of export-led growth. In this context, Yeldan's CGE (Computable General Equilibrium) analysis demonstrates that Turkey can achieve a superior growth performance over the export-led growth

TABLE 5 *Functional distribution of income (%) 1975–88*

	Profits and Rental Income	Wages	Agriculture
1975	37.73	31.51	30.76
1976	35.60	33.11	31.28
1977	34.07	36.81	29.12
1978	38.15	35.19	26.66
1979	42.88	32.79	24.33
1980	49.47	26.66	23.87
1981	52.15	24.68	23.17
1982	53.65	24.56	21.79
1983	54.69	24.78	20.52
1984	57.99	21.57	20.44
1985	62.02	18.84	19.08
1986	64.21	17.70	18.09
1987	65.40	17.00	17.60
1988	70.20	14.00	15.80

Sources: S. Özmucur, "Türkiye'de Gelir Dağılımı," *Iktisat Dergisi* 258 (1986): 13–25; idem, *Milli Gelirin Üç Aylık Dönemler itibariyle Tahmini* (Istanbul: Istanbul Ticaret Odası Y., 1987); Petrol-İş, *1988 Yıllığı* (Istanbul, 1988).

strategy by adopting a program based on domestic demand and sectoral interlinkage promotion policies.[31]

Another important point that should be addressed in this context is the impact of these stabilization and liberalization programs on the distribution of income. Not only did these policies not succeed in bringing about any improvement in terms of income distribution, they made it even worse by reducing both the share of wage earners and the agricultural sector in national income by almost 50 percent in just eight years. While the results of various studies reveal that the personal distribution of income did not substantially worsen in Turkey during this period (see, e.g., the CGE model estimations of Celasun[32]), the total collapse of wages and salaries caused the functional distribution of income to deteriorate rapidly in the course of these years. Table 5 summarizes this trend in the distribution of income in Turkey between 1975 and 1988. As one can observe from these estimates from 1978 to 1988, while the share of profits and rental income rose from 38.15 percent to an unprecedented level of 70.2 percent, that of wages and salaries declined from 35.19 percent to 14.00 percent. A similar collapse can be seen in the share of the agricultural sector.[33] Apart from the equity and welfare implications of this state of affairs, it is possible to argue that the worsening of income distribution will further render any future improvement in domestic savings impossible, a factor crucial for any prospective balanced growth of the Turkey economy.[34]

Finally, another new development that needs to be taken into account in evaluating the performance of the Turkish economy in the post-1980 period is the growing external debt. In spite of the export boom and the improvement of the current account, external debt continued to grow and reached $37.7 billion in 1988, or 53 percent of GNP. What is at stake here is not so much the potential risks associated with short-run illiquidity or insolvency of the economy—at present, the secondary market quotation of Turkey's debt does not seem to threaten its credit worthiness—but its repercussions in the domestic markets. First, there is the equity question. The recent experience of Latin American countries indicates that, in addition to exchange-rate adjustments, real-wage cuts in debtor countries are needed to assure trade surpluses and dollars earnings necessary to service foreign debt.[35] The rapid deterioration of the functional distribution of income since 1980 (Table 5) demonstrates that indeed Turkey has been no exception to this rule. Second, there is the problem of inflation. In the face of growing internal and external debt, the inflation tax may become an attractive source of revenue for the government, which may erode the incentives to arrest inflation.[36] Third, the existence of growing foreign debt makes domestic markets extremely sensitive to the external performance of the economy, namely the control of imports and the promotion of export growth. With regard to exports, the problem stems from the fact that the depression of domestic demand—to create the necessary surplus for foreign markets—becomes more difficult during a recovery period, and hence requires further steps toward export promotion. Given the ambiguous results as to the nature and the determinants of the recent export boom, it is not clear whether Turkey can afford enhancing its export capacity without jeopardizing its domestic equilibrium.

CONCLUSION

We have attempted in this study to give an overview of the patterns of economic growth and structural change in Turkey between 1960 and 1980 by contrasting the import-substitution era of the 1960s and 1970s with the export-led growth orientation of the post-1980s period. Some tentative conclusions can now be drawn as to the development prospects for the Turkish economy. First, the brief analysis of the sources of growth during the 1960s and 1970s revealed that domestic demand was indeed the most important driving force behind economic growth. Therefore, given the structural characteristics of the Turkish economy, it is not possible to discount the importance of domestic markets in terms of growth and get on the bandwagon of export-led development. This, of course, neither implies a plea for a return to export-discriminating policies nor a defense of neomercantilism. A more carefully designed long-term capital-formation program that emphasizes the sectoral interlinkages and domestic demand is needed in Turkey under current conditions.

Second, it should be recognized that in an economy integrated into the world markets, as the Turkish economy is, it is not possible to ignore the repercussions of external economic conditions and therefore avoid the necessary internal adjustments indefinitely. Both the recent maladjustments during the second phase of import substitution and the ensuing debt crisis have demonstrated that the need for necessary adjustment policies in the economy is crucial for the long-term growth prospects of the country. Third, in spite of all incentive programs adopted by the government, the private sector did not show much responsiveness to new investments and domestic-capital formation. Consequently, despite concerted efforts to dismantle the public sector, its decisive position remains almost as powerful as ever in the economy—so much so that the label frequently used to depict the post-1980s developments such as "free-market orientation" becomes rather meaningless in terms of putting them into a historical perspective. (Needless to say, this is due to the sociopolitical and historical characteristics of the state and the entrepreneurial classes in Turkey.) This should not be construed as contending that nothing has changed and that *plus ça change, plus c'est la même chose*, but rather emphasizes our view that, given the stubborn nature of the underlying institutions, it is too early to characterize this period as a historically distinct phase of capitalist development in Turkey.

Finally, in closing we should point to a number of recent developments in the Middle East and the world economy that may strongly affect the performance of the Turkish economy in the 1990s. One such development concerns the new export markets and investment opportunities that have emerged as a result of the demise of the Soviet Union and other neighboring socialist economies. Because of its proximity to these countries and its export structure, Turkey may greatly benefit from this new environment. This may also alleviate the export losses incurred by Turkey as a result of the Gulf War. Moreover, the emergence of independent Turkic states in the former Soviet Union is already giving rise to closer economic cooperation between these countries and Turkey. Also, in the longer run, full membership in the European Economic Community, however remote it might be, offers another challenge to the Turkish economy. Yet, the expansionary effects of these new circumstances may be countervailed, on the one hand, by the deepening of the mild recession that has started to affect the industrialized economies since the beginning of 1990, and, on the other hand, by the intensification of protectionist sentiments in the United States and in some European countries.

NOTES

[1]World Bank, *Turkey: Policies and Prospects for Growth* (Washington, D.C.: World Bank Publication, 1980), 1.

[2]Ibid., 2.

[3]H. D. Chenery and M. Syrquin, *Patterns of Development: 1950–1970* (Oxford: Oxford University Press, 1975).

[4]These five-year development plans, their various shortcomings notwithstanding, should be contrasted with the previous planning programs that were, for the most part, motivated by short-term policy responses to existing internal and external economic conditions, devoid of any long-term view of industrialization. For an in-depth analysis of these five-year plans, see M. Durdağ, *Some Problems of Development Financing* (Dordrecht: D. Reidel Publishing Co., 1973); E. Günce, "Türkiye'de Planlamanin Dünü, Bugünü, Yarını," *ODTÜ Gelişme Dergisi*, Özel sayi (1981): 117–32.

[5]For a discussion of the political factors behind the introduction and evolution of central planning during 1960–71, see F. Ahmad, *The Turkish Experiment in Democracy: 1950–1975* (London: Hurst and Company, 1977), chap. 10. On the other hand, Boratav and Keyder define the five-year plan periods as "populist" economic policies, based on a fragile compromise between capital owners, workers, and peasants; K. Boratav, *Türkiye Iktisat Tarihi 1908–1985* (Istanbul: Gerçek Y., 1988); Ç. Keyder, "Ithal Ikameci Sanayileşme ve Çelişkileri," in *Krizin Gelişimi ve Turkiye'nin Alternatif Sorunu*, ed. K. Boratav, Ç. Keyder, and S. Pamuk (Istanbul: Kaynak Y., 1984), 13–32.

[6]Ş. Pamuk, "Ithal Ikamesi, Döviz Darboğazlari ve Türkiye: 1947–1979," in *Krizin Gelişimi ve Türkiye'nin Alternatif Sorunu*, 36–68.

[7]The growth rate of total output (value added) $\dot{Q}/Q$ can be written as

$$\frac{\dot{Q}}{Q} = \frac{\dot{A}}{A} + e_K\frac{\dot{K}}{K} + e_L\frac{\dot{L}}{L}$$

where $\dot{A}/A$ denotes the rate of technological change, $\dot{K}/K$ and $\dot{L}/L$ are the rates of increase in capital and labor inputs, respectively; e_K and e_L are the share of capital and labor in total output. Using the aggregate data for the 1963–75 period, the following results (%) are obtained: $\dot{Q}/Q = 6.4$, $\dot{K}/K = 6.82$, $\dot{L}/L = 1.02$, $e_K = 55$, $e_L = 45$, $\dot{A}/A = 2.23$. See H. D. Chenery, S. Robinson, and M. Syrquin, *Industrialization and Growth* (London: Oxford University Press, 1986), 22.

[8]World Bank, *Turkey: Prospects and Problems of an Expanding Economy* (Washington, D.C.: World Bank Publication, 1975).

[9]These percentages do not add up to 100.0 because the mining and energy sectors are left out; see various publications of the State Institute of Statistics and the State Planning Organization.

[10]For detailed discussion of factor-price distortions and capital intensity in the Turkish economy, see A. Krueger, *Foreign Trade Regimes and Economic Development: Turkey* (New York: National Bureau of Economic Research, 1974); and B. Balassa, *The Newly Industrialized Countries in the World Economy* (New York: Pergamon Press, 1981), essay 13.

[11]World Bank, *Turkey: Policies and Prospects*, 129.

[12]Given the nature of our discussion, we cannot go into a detailed analysis of these intricate issues here. For a more in-depth discussion, see A. A. Çeçen, A. A. Doğruel, and F. Doğruel, *Türkiye'de Ekonomik Büyüme, Yapisal Değişim ve Kriz* (Istanbul: Egemen Y., 1990); L. Rittenberg, "Financial Liberalization and Savings in Turkey," in *Liberalization in the Turkish Economy*, ed. T. Nas and M. Odekon (New York: Greenwood Press, 1988), 115–27.

[13]A. Krueger and B. Tuncer, *Estimating Total Productivity Growth in a Developing Country* (Washington, D.C.: World Bank Staff Working Paper, 1980).

[14]World Bank, *Turkey: Policies and Prospects*.

[15]For a detailed discussion of the incentive structure and protectionist measures in Turkish manufacturing, see F. Yağcı, *Protection and Incentives in Turkish Manufacturing* (Washington, D.C.: World Bank Staff Working Paper, 1984). Krueger, on the other hand, argues that excess capacity in manufacturing could be the result of firms' deliberate overexpansion; *Foreign Trade Regimes*, 230.

[16]For a discussion on the previous stabilization programs in Turkey, see N. Ekzen, "1980 Stabilizasyon Paketinin 1958, 1970 ve 1978–79 Paketleriyle Karşılaştırmalı Analizi," in I. Tekeli et al., *Türkiye'de ve Dünyada Yaşanan Ekonomik Bunalım* (Ankara: Yurt Y., 1984), 168–88.

[17]See, among others, M. Durdağ, "1980 Yılı Uygulamasının Işığında İstikrar Programının Genel bir Değerlendirmesi," *Toplum ve Bilim* 14 (1981): 98–124; Nas and Odekon, *Liberalization in the Turkish Economy*; F. Şenses, "An Assessment of Turkey's Liberalization Attempts since 1980 against the Background of Her Stabilization Program," *METU Studies in Development* 10 (1983): 271–322; P. Wolff, *Stabilization Policy and Structural Adjustment in Turkey, 1980–85: The Role of the IMF and World Bank in an Externally Supported Adjustment Process* (Berlin: German Development Institute, 1987).

[18]For a more detailed discussion of these financial reforms, see G. Kopits, *Structural Reform, Stabilization and Growth in Turkey* (Washington, D.C.: IMF, 1987).

[19]Wage determinations by the council were mandatory for the public sector and were used as guidelines in the private sector. However, in the face of growing labor unrest, the role of the council declined and collective bargaining was liberalized somewhat after 1987.

[20]For a detailed discussion of the determinants of exports during this period, see D. Rodrik, "External Debt and Economic Performance in Turkey," in *Liberalization in the Turkish Economy*, 161–85, esp. 175–80. For an analysis and description of export-incentive programs, see B. Milanovic, *Export Incentives and Turkish Manufactured Exports, 1980–84* (Washington, D.C.: World Bank Staff Working Paper, 1986); according to Milanovic, the efficiency of the export-incentive policy, measured by its deviation from the optimal structure, did not show any significant improvement in the period 1980–84, but exchange-rate adjustment was correct.

[21]Rodrik, "External Debt," 161.

[22]R. Anand, S. Chhibber, and S. van Wijnbergen, "External Balance and Growth in Turkey: Can They Be Reconciled?" (Washington, D.C.: World Bank, 1988, Mimeographed), 21.

[23]Ibid.; Anand et al. go on to suggest that "[these results] show that stabilization programs relying on reductions of public sector investment will have high and permanent negative output effects. . . ." They also emphasize the fact that the key factor in this growth performance was the substantial excess capacity inherited from heavy investments made in the 1970s, which is very much in line with our discussion of the historic nature of excess capacity.

[24]For a discussion and analysis of the contractionary effects of these stabilization and liberalization policies, see, for instance, L. Taylor, *Structuralist Macroeconomics: Applicable Models for the Third World* (New York: Basic Books, 1981); R. C. Porter and S. I. Ranney, "An Eclectic Model of Recent LDC Macroeconomic Policy Analysis," *World Development* 10 (1982): 761–65; S. van Wijnbergen, "Stagflationary Effects of Monetary Stabilization Policies: A Quantitative Analysis of South Korea," *Journal of Development Economics* 10 (1982): 133–69; idem, "Exchange Rate Management and Stabilization Policies in Developing Countries," *Journal of Development Economics* 23 (1986): 227–47; E. Buffie, "Financial Repression, the New Structuralists and Stabilization Policy in Semi-Industrialized Economics," *Journal of Development Economics* 14 (1984): 305–27; idem, "The Macroeconomics of Trade Liberalization," *Journal of International Economics* 17 (1984): 121–37; P. Krugman and L. Taylor, "Contractionary Effects of Devaluation," *Journal of Development Economics* 8 (1978): 445–56.

[25]These equations are part of the 45-equation macroeconometric model estimated for the Turkish economy for the 1963–85 period, using three-stage least-square estimation techniques. For a more complete discussion of the determinants of inflation and the underlying structural rigidities, see Çeçen et al., *Türkiye'de Ekonomik Büyüme*, section 5.

[26]P. J. Conway, *Economic Shocks and Structural Adjustment: Turkey after 1973* (Amsterdam: North Holland, 1987), 199, Table 7.8.

[27]M. Celasun and D. Rodrik, "Debt, Adjustment and Growth: Turkey," in *Developing Country Debt and Economic Performance: Country Studies—Indonesia, Korea, Philippines, Turkey*, ed. J. D. Sachs and S. M. Collins (Chicago: University of Chicago Press, 1989), 3:615–808.

[28]I. Arslan and S. van Wijnbergen, *Export Incentives, Exchange Rate Policy and Export Growth in Turkey* (Washington, D.C.: World Bank Working Paper, 1989).

[29]Kopits, *Structural Reform*, Table 2.

[30]See, for instance, B. Balassa, "Exports and Economic Growth: Further Evidence," *Journal of Development Economics* 5 (1978): 181–89; G. Feder, "On Exports and Economic Growth," *Journal of Development Economics* 12 (1982): 53–73; R. Ram, "Exports and Economic Growth: Some Additional Evidence," *Economic Development and Cultural Change* 33 (1985): 415–25. Cline, Adelman, and Streeten, however, offer critical evaluations of these export-led growth strategies; W. Cline, "Can the East Asian Model of Development Be Generalized?" *World Development* 10 (1982): 81–90; I. Adelman, "Beyond Export-led Growth," *World Development* 12 (1984): 934–49; P. Streeten, "A Cool Look at 'Outward Looking' Strategies for Development," *The World Economy* 5 (1982): 159–69.

[31]A. E. Yeldan, "Turkish Economy in Transition: A General Equilibrium Analysis of Export-led versus Domestic Demand-led Strategies of Development" (Ph.D. diss., University of Minnesota, Minneapolis, 1988).

[32]M. Celasun, "Income Distribution and Domestic Terms of Trade in Turkey 1973–1983," *ODTU Gelisme Dergisi* 13 (1986): 193–216.

[33]H. Önal, "Effect of Income Distribution in Non-Agriculture on Agricultural Prices and Income: The Turkish Case," *European Review of Agricultural Economics* 14 (1987): 413–25; Önal analyzes the effects of the distribution of income in nonagriculture sectors on agricultural prices and income distribution.

[34]The relationship between income distribution, growth, and savings is debated in light of the findings of the new literature on endogenous growth. Contrary to the classical view, endogenous-growth theory maintains that more equal income distribution fosters economic growth; see P. H. Lindert and J. G. Williamson, "Growth, Equality and History," *Explorations in Economic History* 22 (1985): 341–77; T. Persson and G. Tabellini, *Growth, Distribution and Politics* (Washington, D.C.: IMF Working Paper, 1991).

[35]R. Dornbusch, "Dealing with Debt in the 1980s," *Third World Quarterly* 7 (1985): 532–51; Dornbusch argues that "Today, real wage cuts in debtor countries assure the trade surpluses and dollar earn-

ing that keep bank stockholders in the black. One might argue (or even believe) that this is essential to maintain order in the international financial system, but that raises the question of in whose interest the system works. For many who are paying the bill now, there have been few benefits before and there are no obvious ones down the road" (533).

[36]We are not claiming here that this is indeed the actual state of affairs in Turkey. This question should be empirically analyzed beyond theoretical possibility and anecdotal evidence.

[7]

THE SYRIAN ECONOMY IN THE 1980s

Volker Perthes

IN Syria, as in many other Third World countries, the 1980s will be remembered as a "lost decade for development." In the preceding decade, Syrians had become accustomed to considerable economic growth and a general, although unequal, rise in living standards. During the 1980s, however, an increasing part of the population felt its purchasing power decrease as economic development stagnated. For the first time since coming to power in 1970, President Hafiz al-Asad and his regime were threatened by a loss of legitimacy as the result of economic rather than political problems. In 1987, growing discontent and public criticism of the economic situation, and the government's apparent inability to manage the crisis, led to the sacking of several cabinet ministers and the subsequent replacement of Prime Minister Abd al-Ra'uf al-Kasm by Mahmud al-Zu'bi. Although in the following years, with promising oil finds and growing foreign financial aid, the situation seemed to improve slightly, the structural roots of the crisis were not removed.

Syria's economic problems of the 1980s resulted primarily from the development strategy and policies the Syrian leadership pursued after 1970. External factors, although exacerbating the crisis, played only a secondary role. By the end of the 1980s, Syria was still dealing with the contradictory results of the boom that took place in the 1970s.

THE BOOM YEARS: THE 1970S

Milestones on the road to Syria's rapid economic growth included the coup that brought Asad to power and the October War of 1973. Asad introduced a new

Volker Perthes currently teaches at the American University in Beirut.

MIDDLE EAST JOURNAL ■ VOLUME 46, NO. 1, WINTER 1992

economic policy—a Syrian version of *infitah*[1] —that expanded the scope of the bourgeoisie and merchant class in particular. In fact, however, compared with its Egyptian counterpart, this open-door policy remained limited. In Syria, the state retained a leading role in industry and foreign trade while, in turn, it opened the country to the world market. In essence, Syrian infitah meant a huge program of public economic investment.[2] The October War and its subsequent political and economic changes provided the financing for this program, with Syria benefiting from Arab petrodollar assistance and profiting from the rise in oil prices. In addition, cheap credit was easily available in the 1970s on the international money market.[3]

Syria's development strategy throughout these years was to achieve rapid growth and structural modernization. The objective was for the Syrian economy to move away from being an agricultural economy and catch up with "the caravan of progress,"[4] reaching the level of more advanced economies—namely that of Israel—in order to attain what was to become a central tenet of Asad's development philosophy: a "strategical balance with the enemy," meaning not just parity in armaments but also on economic, cultural, and social levels.[5] Thus, large public investments were projected in industry and communications and in the construction of dams and power stations. Advanced technology was imported, and production and consumption were geared toward Western standards. Expenses for agriculture, however, were low and amounted to less than 10 percent of the

1. In the mid-1970s, it was not uncommon to speak of *infitah* in reference to Syrian economic policy. See for example, Asad's speech on March 8, 1974, in *al-Ishtiraki*, March 11, 1974, and Arab Socialist Baath Party, "Al-Taqrir al-iqtisadi" (Economic report), *Reports and Resolutions of the Sixth Regional Conference* (Damascus, 1976), p. 84. The conference was held April 5–15, 1975, in Damascus. Syrian use of the term *infitah*, generally associated with Egypt, was dropped when Syrian-Egyptian relations became strained in the late 1970s.

2. Total investments increased from about Syrian pounds (LS) 897 million in 1970 (LS 3.2 billion in constant prices of 1980) to LS 14.1 billion in 1980. The public sector contribution was LS 638 million (LS 2.2 billion) and LS 9 billion, respectively. Central Bureau of Statistics, *Statistical Abstract*, 1988.

3. For estimates on foreign assistance and international financial credit, see David W. Carr, "Capital Flows and Development in Syria," *Middle East Journal* 34, no. 4 (Autumn 1980); Eliyahu Kanovsky, "What's Behind Syria's Current Economic Problems?" in Haim Shaked and Daniel Dishon, eds., *Middle East Contemporary Survey*, vol. VIII, 1983–84 (Tel Aviv: Dayan Center for Middle Eastern and African Studies, Shiloah Institute, Tel Aviv University, 1986), table 9, p. 332.

As for the importance of oil prices, it is notable that while the volume (tonnage) of Syria's exports of oil and oil derivates less than tripled between 1970 and 1975, the value of these exports rose from about LS 130 million in 1970 to LS 2.4 billion in 1975. Since 1974, oil and oil products have constituted Syria's main exports, contributing to the value of exports with between 58 percent in 1977 and 72 percent in 1979 and between 79 percent in 1980 and 42 percent in 1986. *Statistical Abstract*, 1975 through 1988.

4. Asad speaking to trade unionists. See General Federation of Trade Unions, *Proceedings and Resolutions of the Seventeenth Conference of the General Federation of Trade Unions in the Syrian-Arab Region* (in Arabic) (Damascus, n.d.), p. 30. The conference was held September 20–23, 1972, in Damascus.

5. See for example Asad's speech on March 8, 1986, in *al-Ba'th*, March 9, 1986.

total investments realized during the two five-year plans of 1971–75 and 1976–1980.[6]

In fact, the Syrian economy grew but structural development was limited. With few exceptions, industrialization concentrated on products for immediate consumption. Industries to develop machines or gears locally were not established. Furthermore, dependency on the outside world continued to grow with an expanding demand for foreign consumer goods as a result of changing consumer habits, a growing wage-earning middle class oriented towards Western lifestyles,[7] and easy access to foreign currency. The trade sector, fortified by a rapidly increasing number of import-export establishments, and aided by liberal import regulations, successfully satisfied consumer demand.[8] Since this policy contradicted the proclaimed aim of reducing non-essential imports (versus necessities), it can be attributed primarily to an alliance between the new political elite and the influential merchant class. Composed of both nouveau-riche elements and parts of the old commercial bourgeoisie, this merchant class, to a far greater extent than the old industrialists, had managed to survive the nationalizations and socialist measures of the 1960s.

Symptoms of Crisis

With the beginning of the 1980s, symptoms of crisis became increasingly apparent. The turning point—separating the years of growth from the years of regression—can be placed somewhere between 1979 and 1983, when inflation fluctuated at unprecedented levels around 30 percent, causing severe hardship for the majority of the population. Until 1982–83, Arab aid was comparatively plentiful, enabling Syria to cover at least half of its balance of trade deficit. From 1983 onward, however, growing political differences between Syria and her wealthier Arab brethren led to a decline in aid. A year earlier, in 1982, Syria's Commercial Bank stopped automatically allocating foreign exchange to importers once they had received permission from the Ministry of Economy to import. Thereafter, private and public importers received a foreign exchange letter of

6. State Planning Authority, "Al-Takhtit li al-tanmiyya al-iqtisadiyya wa al-ijtima'iyya fi al-Jumhuriyya al-Arabiyya al-Suriyya" (Planning for economic and social development in the Syrian Arab Republic) (unpublished, 1987), p. 23.

7. The wage-earning middle class, whose largest segment was employed in the growing state sector, increased from about 10 percent of the work force in 1970 to about 17 percent in 1981 and to an estimated 18 percent at the end of the decade. For a more detailed analysis on Syria's social structure and its development, see Volker Perthes, *Staat und Gesellschaft in Syrien, 1970–1989* (Hamburg: Schriftenreihe des Deutschen Orient-Instituts, 1990), pp. 140ff.

8. The trade sector's share of net domestic product (NDP) rose from 21 percent to 25 percent between 1970 and 1980. Imports increased from LS 1.3 billion in 1970 to LS 16.2 billion in 1980, about one-fourth of this being direct private imports. In addition, some public sector imports were made on behalf of private industry and trade, and most public sector imports were arranged by private businessmen. The number of private import-export merchants, trade agents, and middlemen rose from less than 300 in 1974 to more than 3,000 in 1981. In comparison, the number of private retailers grew more slowly, from 72,000 in 1974 to 99,000 in 1981. *Statistical Abstract*, 1975, 1980, 1983, 1986.

credit only if the bank had foreign exchange available. As early as 1981, several restrictions were imposed on the importation of goods to reduce the balance of trade deficit, and the government initiated what could be called an austere budget policy. In the productive sectors, symptoms of crisis had appeared even before these restrictions were imposed.

In industry, most plants built according to the third and fourth five-year plans (1971–1980) and which, in many cases, were not completed by the fifth five-year plan, failed to achieve intended results. The problems of turn-key projects, in particular, became obvious. Many of them did not go into operation upon completion because of the lack of local expertise.[9] The problem of technical expertise was eventually alleviated, although not solved, with the graduation of large numbers of Syrian engineers trained both in the country and abroad and by a halt in the inauguration of new industries.[10] Nonetheless, other problems remained. The new projects were capital intensive and needed a comparatively small but well-trained labor force, and they were highly dependent on imported raw materials, semi-finished products, and spare parts. Deficiencies in both fields meant that production fell short of the projects' capacities, and the resulting products were of poor quality and largely unsuitable for competition in foreign markets[11]; at the same time, costs were increasing. According the State Planning Authority's report on the results of the fifth five-year plan,

> "production costs in all sectors of converting industries—refineries excluded—have been increasing more than the value of production. . . . Large and increasing losses were a common characteristic. . . . Losses in all years of the fifth five-year plan surmounted capital consumption, thus the surplus generated was negative."[12]

Together with growing foreign exchange problems, by 1986 shortages of imported materials increasingly led to production losses and even long-term stoppages in most branches of the modern industrial sector. Not only did production of television sets come to a complete standstill but, more importantly, the production of tractors, tires, and cables dropped to less than half their previous annual

9. For example, the French-built Yuria ammonium plant took more than one and one-half years to go into operation after being completed. In 1980, the Italian-built Dayr al-Zur paper mill stopped production three months after starting and later was managed by foreign experts until Syrian engineers were able to assume control.

10. Ten years or more after they began production, some factories in the public sector still needed foreign expertise at least occasionally. See for example, Amin Habash, "Waqi' al-qita' al-amm al-sina'i wa-muhimmat al-tabaqa al-amila wa harakatiha al-niqabiyya" (The situation of the public industrial sector: The obligations of the working class and its union movement), *al-Ishtiraki,* January 12, 1987; Ahmad al-Ahmar, "Ma'mal sahr al-khurda bi-Hama" (The scrap press in Hama), *al-Thawra,* May 5, 1989.

11. See Arab Socialist Baath Party, "Al-Taqrir al-iqtisadi" (Economic report), *Reports and Resolutions of the Eighth Regional Conference* (Damascus, 1986), p. 78. The conference was held January 5–20, 1985, in Damascus.

12. State Planning Commission, "Taqrir taqwim al-khutta al-khamsiyya al-khamisa, 1981–1985: Qita' al-sina'at al-tahwiliyya" (Report on the evaluation of the fifth five-year plan, 1981–1985: Converting industries sector) (Damascus, unpublished 1986), p. 80f.

TABLE 1
Syrian Domestic Product and Output

	1970	1975	1980	1985	1987
GDP* at Market Prices (billion Syrian pounds)	20.0	39.2	51.3	58.4	52.4
Agricultural GDP (billion Syrian pounds)	3.8	6.8	10.4	10.2	9.4
Industrial GDP—Mining and Manufacturing (billion Syrian pounds)	4.5	9.5	8.4	8.1	8.4
GDP Per Capita (Syrian pounds)	3,202	5,311	5,890	5,691	4,775
Index of Agricultural Gross Output (million Syrian pounds)	40	65	100	101	96
Index of Industrial Gross Output (million Syrian pounds)	50	54	100	127	140

*Gross domestic product at constant prices of 1980 = $13 billion. Based on the official exchange rate of LS 3.95 to the US dollar.
Source: Central Bureau of Statistics, *Statistical Abstract*, 1973, 1977, 1983, 1986, 1988, 1989.

averages.[13] Production at the Hama iron and steel plant stopped completely for about two years, and partial or complete stoppages occurred in the production of fertilizer,[14] synthetic fibers,[15] cement pipes,[16] paper,[17] refrigerators, shoes, aluminium shapes, batteries,[18] and mineral water.[19] Thus, while gross industrial output continued to grow because of the completion of new plants in the first half of the 1980s and a considerable increase in crude oil production beginning in 1986, from 1980 onward the domestic industrial product remained almost stagnant, and the output of Syria's manufacturing industry decreased beginning in 1984.[20]

At the same time, although spending on agricultural production was relatively low, it was because of modernization and more intense cultivation that continuous

13. See *Statistical Abstract*, 1987 and 1989.
14. *Tishrin*, April 25, 1988.
15. *Tishrin*, February 26, 1989.
16. *Al-Ishtiraki*, March 3, 1987.
17. *Al-Thawra*, July 22, 1987.
18. *Al-Ba'th*, October 6, 1987.
19. *Al-Ba'th*, April 3, 1988.
20. Syrian statistical abstracts do not divide industrial gross domestic product figures into "mining" and "manufacturing." The official index of manufacturing industry production, based on fixed prices of 1985 (1985=100), was 109 in 1984, 99 in 1986, and 93 in 1988. The index for mining and quarrying, however, rose from 97 in 1984 to 168 in 1988. Crude oil production, ranging around 9.3 million cubic meters throughout the first half of the 1980s, increased to 15.5 million cubic meters in 1988. *Statistical Abstract*, 1986 and 1989.

growth was achieved up to 1980 when it became almost stagnant. This stagnation was partly the result of several years' low rainfall,[21] the slow pace of land reclamation in the Euphrates basin and at other irrigation projects (leaving agriculture highly dependent upon climatic variations),[22] the salination of cultivated lands, and slowed progress in the mechanization and modernization of agricultural production. The situation was further aggravated when Syrian agricultural producers shifted, where possible, from growing products over which the state had monopoly purchasing rights and had established fixed prices, to producing fruits, vegetables, and eggs which were more profitable because their sale was comparatively free of state interference. Furthermore, only wealthier landowners could afford the cost of capital-intensive fruit tree or greenhouse vegetable production. The poorer *fallahin* had to accept the prices fixed by the state—which provided little incentive to produce—or boycott state agricultural plans by not cultivating the land or by diverting harvests, or part of them, to the black market.[23]

Stagnant or declining outputs in industry and agriculture, the need to increase agricultural imports to feed a rapidly growing population,[24] and changing terms of trade made the gap in Syria's balance of trade widen sharply. In 1981, with a growing domestic demand for oil products, Syria's balance of crude oil imports and exports—crude oil being the country's most important export commodity—turned negative.[25] In addition, foreign assistance, transit fees, and remittances from Syrians working abroad tended to drop, and from 1981 onward the country was left with a negative balance of payment. Growing liquidity problems in the public treasury led to unplanned, even uncontrolled, import cuts which, as stated previously, caused production standstills and shortages of important consumer goods, particularly medical supplies. Concurrently, the black market for goods and currency flourished and the private import trade began increasingly to rely on

21. In particular in 1984, 1985, and 1989.

22. From 1970 to 1987, not more than 67,000 hectars were actually cultivated in the Euphrates basin region—about 18 percent of the area designated for cultivation during that period. See General Federation of Trade Unions, "Al-Taqrir al-amm" (General report) (Conference for National Creativity and Self-Reliance, Damascus, November 21–24, 1987), p. 336. The slow development of the Euphrates basin became a major public scandal in 1987 and led to the sacking of the ministers for public works and agriculture.

23. The Syrian press noted that state-paid agricultural prices did not support farmers' needs. See for example Khalid Rustum, "Amama mas'alat al-mazru'a" (In view of the crop situation), *al-Thawra*, March 19, 1988.

24. Population growth was estimated at more than 3.9 percent for the late 1980s. See, Hamid Mustafa Abu Jamra, "Isqatat al-sukkan wa al-quwa al-amila hasab al-umr wa al-nau' li al-Jumhuriyya al-Arabiyya al-Suriyya" (Projections on population and work force: Their age and type in the Syrian Arab Republic), *al-Iqtisad*, January 1987, pp. 9–22.

25. Syria's crude oil and oil derivates balance became positive in 1985. In 1987, Syria again achieved a surplus in its crude oil trade balance.

smuggling, so much so that it strongly influenced the accuracy of official trade statistics.[26]

The cumulative effect of low production, the balance of payment deficit, and a continual budget deficit of approximately 40 percent led to inflated prices and the devaluation of the Syrian pound in December 1987. Wages and salaries lagged far behind inflation. Industrial workers, particularly in the state sector, state employees, small farmers, and agricultural workers suffered from real income losses,[27] while merchants, brokers, and real estate speculators took home fortunes.[28] This redistribution of income, in turn, supported the economy's import tendencies: the pressure to import higher quality consumer goods, legally or illegally, while the market for mass consumer goods remained limited.

AUSTERITY MEASURES

The actions taken by the Syrian government to cope with the economic situation that developed in the 1980s did not follow a planned or effective strategy. After the political crisis of 1979–1980, with its wave of fierce clashes between the regime and Islamic opposition elements, the new government of Prime Minister Kasm took measures to tighten government control on economic development, especially foreign trade. This was partly aimed at alleviating public discontent caused to some extent by growing income disparities and, particularly, by the immense wealth gained by those who represented the so-called new class: import brokers, middlemen, and segments of the bureaucracy. Because the regime attempted to avoid hurting its social alliances and key supporters, the measures remained limited. From 1982 onward, the mixed policies adopted by the government tended to create a more liberal and capital-oriented economy. State controls on the private economy were loosened, shifting weight from the public to the private sector, while inside the private sector the role of the larger enterprises and merchants was strengthened. This, temporarily at least, increased the burden on the majority of the population.

Beginning in 1981, Syria followed a public policy that can be characterized as austere. The state budget grew slower than inflation, and in 1987, it actually decreased 5 percent in absolute terms, which—taking into account at least a 40 percent inflation rate—meant a vast cut in expenditures. These cuts affected

26. Taking into account the available data and information on consumption and production, this author estimates that smuggling constituted at least 25 percent of total non-military imports throughout the 1980s. See, Perthes, *Staat und Gesellschaft*, p. 111.

27. There was no official wage index. Taking into account available data on wages and prices, however, it can be said that from 1980 to 1989 public sector wages rose by about 300 percent whereas retail prices rose to more than 600 percent of their 1980 level. See Perthes, *Staat und Gesellschaft*, p. 168.

28. See Ilias Najmah, "Al-Mas'ala al-iqtisadiyya fi al-Qutr al-Arabi al-Suri" (The economic question in the Syrian Arab Region) (Economic Sciences Associations Fifth Economic Tuesday Symposium, Damascus, 1986), pp. 323–4.

development spending in such a way that investment expenditures, usually 50 to 60 percent of budget estimates in the 1970s, fell to almost 40 percent from 1987 onward. Real expenditures on investment usually did not reach the amounts projected because of liquidity problems or technical delays.[29] Military spending amounted to approximately one-third of total government expenditures and, therefore, remained a heavy burden on the budget and the economy.[30] The government adopted a harsh wage policy, refrained from filling vacancies in the public industrial sector, and discharged thousands of workers from construction companies.[31] Officials tried to cover unavoidable additional expenses with increases in prices and fees and with cuts in public subsidies. A gradual devaluation of the Syrian currency was also designed to lighten budget burdens.[32] On the revenue side, the importance of taxes and fees increased when transfers from the public economic sector became limited.[33]

The fifth five-year plan (1981–85)—while projecting comparatively greater expenditures in agriculture and services than its predecessors—concentrated on the completion or improvement of existing industrial enterprises rather than on new projects. A draft sixth five-year plan (1986–1990) following the same principles was not completed because financial crises led to an overhaul of state economic planning. Generally, in regard to Syria's economic policies, one should

29. From 1980 onward, investment expenditures in the final budget did not exceed 41 percent. Statistisches Bundesamt (Wiesbaden, Germany), *Statistik des Auslands: Länderbericht Syrien,* 1986 and 1988.

30. Military spending, according to the official budget as established in the annual *Statistical Abstract,* amounted to about half of the ordinary budget, or the total budget without investments. Reliable figures on arms expenditures were not available. Arms purchases were not included in foreign trade statistics, so one can assume that published budget figures for the military did not include, or only to a small extent included, military imports. Actually, arms payments did not directly affect the country's foreign exchange budget because they were mainly financed either by direct Arab aid or by Soviet loans that the Soviets probably had to partially write off. See Patrick Clawson, *Syria's Unaffordable Ambitions: Economic Consequences of the Military Build-Up* (Washington, DC: Washington Institute for Near East Policy, 1989). Syria's actual payments on its debt to the Soviet Union, which to a great extent resulted from arms purchases, were—according to Syrian Central Bank sources—made in goods rather than hard currency. Exports to the Soviet Union were paid for in local currency by the Syrian Central Bank, so monetary inflation was used to cover parts of military costs.

31. The public industrial sector work force was reduced from about 141,000 in 1985 to 139,000 in 1988 and in the public construction sector from about 155,000 to 138,000. *Statistical Abstract,* 1986 through 1989 (for industrial sector), and author's interviews with members of the Higher Council for Public Construction Companies, Damascus, December 1988.

32. The devaluation of the Syrian pound's official exchange rate from LS 3.95 to the US dollar—which had been the official rate since the early 1970s—to LS 11.95 to the dollar on December 31, 1987, meant a substantial government cut in subsidies for imports, as did the decision taken in early 1989 to price consumer goods imported by the state according to the "encouragement rate" of about LS 22 to the dollar. See *Tishrin,* February 5, 1989. As early as 1981, private imports were valued according to the "parallel rate" of LS 5.45 to the dollar instead of the official rate.

33. Taxes on income and profits amounted to about 10 percent of budget revenues in 1981 and increased to 20 percent in 1985. This may have partially been the result of modernization measures taken to improve tax surveillance and tax collection. For these measures, see Arab Socialist Baath Party, "Al-Taqrir al-iqtisadi," *Reports and Resolutions of the Eighth Regional Conference,* pp. 47ff.

be cautious when speaking of a "planned economy," since the plans—as the fifth planning period showed—lacked virtually any compulsory force.[34]

Efforts to Increase Production

Throughout the 1980s, the central element in the official policy to fight Syria's economic problems was a campaign to increase production. State, party, and mass organizations—headed by the trade unions—were to be committed to achieving this increase. On an ideological level, the campaign tried to stress the theme that a positive expression of national awareness and an appreciation for the party and the president could best be achieved through greater emphasis on production.[35] This campaign was supported by a merit-oriented wage system in the public sector that relied upon so-called production incentives: allowances granted according to individual and collective performance in production. The system had the effect of giving employees in highly productive establishments reasonable wages and, therefore, helped stabilize the work force and production.[36] In less productive establishments, however, worker turnover and the lack of competent personnel increased. In fact, in the face of shortages of spare parts and of raw materials, which lowered production levels, the incentive system—in contrast to a fixed-wage system—became a heavy burden for workers who lost bonuses to which they had become accustomed.

In addition to the production effort, another highly propagandistic campaign was launched against speculators and dishonest merchants when supply problems reached their worst in winter 1986–87. It did not take long for even the state-run press to question this campaign when, for example, small merchants who sold their parsley above the established price were arrested while wholesale and import traders were left untouched. This campaign also tended to create the impression that Syria's main problem was maldistribution rather than low production and shortages.

The efforts outlined above were accompanied by a so-called self-reliance campaign, aimed at inducing creative efforts to produce spare parts for imported machinery and develop substitutes for imported raw materials and consumer goods. However sound the idea, when put into practice it revealed the problems inherent in the years-long habit of importing technologies that did not correspond to the country's industrial potential. The campaign met with some success in traditional light industries where some spare parts for imported machinery were

34. For some critical remarks on Syrian development planning, see General Federation of Trade Unions, "Al-Taqrir al-iqtisadi" (Economic report) (Twenty-first Conference of the General Federation of Trade Unions, Damascus, November 16–20, 1986), pp. 70ff.

35. This was expressed, for example, in union activities such as unpaid "national work days" in honor of the 8 March revolution or the anniversary of President Asad's 1970 coup.

36. The system was actually introduced by Legislative Decree No. 1715/1977. In 1979, some establishments began to work according to its rules. In 1986, it was made applicable to all employed in the state and public sectors. Individual incentives could amount to 100 percent of the basic wage.

manufactured locally. In addition, in the private sector a number of new import substitution industries appeared, replacing the importation of goods which had been prohibited because of the production of similar products (which were being manufactured under foreign license and were completely dependent upon imported machinery and material). Only the very last stage of production was Syrian. The products could be brought to the market, however, with the "self-reliance" label.[37]

Despite this emphasis on self-reliance, when more sophisticated production methods were required, and when production depended on semi-finished products, Syria still had to import most of the equipment. This was true, for example, in the service sector—banking, tourism, entertainment, and state security—where there was a persistent tendency to rely on the most modern foreign technologies.

Foreign Trade and the Currency Market

Syrian plans and programs continually assumed an increase in exports and a relative decrease in imports to lighten the burden of the balance of trade deficit even though past efforts in this direction had not led to positive results. In view of the critical foreign exchange situation, particularly beginning in 1986, when Syria faced actual foreign exchange insolvency, the government persevered in trying to increase exports by all means. Priority was placed on the oil sector in order to increase production and exports to the highest possible levels, and to bring promising new oil fields in the Dayr al-Zur area into operation in record time. Efforts were also made to increase phosphate and cotton exports, and every opportunity was taken to export public sector industrial goods.

In summer 1988, the government decided to give priority to the acquisition of foreign currency. Accordingly, state sector enterprises were informed that they would not receive foreign exchange from the state treasury beyond what they obtained from their own exports. In some cases, such as the Hama iron plant, the idea of "export to the local market"—selling public sector products to private local merchants for hard currency—was promoted. Furthermore, public sector establishments were encouraged to sell their products on foreign markets at "dumping prices," because the government would subsidize the loss on such deals in local currency. Because export promotion had priority over local supply and currency stability, it resulted in shortages of locally produced consumer goods, the growth of smuggling, factories that could not export, and a further deterioration of the value of the Syrian pound. These negative effects, however,

37. Large private establishments of this kind were established to produce perfumes, biscuits, cosmetics, paper tissues, and to assemble audiotapes and air conditioners. Handwritten records of the directorates for industry, Damascus and Aleppo; author's interviews with entrepreneurs.

were considered less threatening than the complete loss of foreign exchange in the state's treasury.[38]

Despite constraints on exports from the public sector, the government tried to encourage private sector exports. Most export restrictions were abolished and the government sought to include private sector industrial or agricultural goods in barter deals it concluded with foreign partners. Above all, private sector exports were encouraged by currency policies. Beginning in 1981, policies were enacted to counteract the effects of the pound's artificially high official exchange rate by granting higher rates for foreign exchange income from certain exports and since 1986 from all exports. Because these rates still overvalued the Syrian currency, they fell short of being real incentives. Consequently, since 1987 merchants and industrialists were allowed to keep 75 percent of their total export income in hard currency in order to finance imports.[39] According to Syrian industrialists, however, the percentage was still insufficient to cover import needs, given the high share of imports in the value of products which could be sold in foreign markets with some success. In 1989, the government even began to apply the "neighboring countries' exchange rate" for the pound in the case of foreign exchange earnings changed at one of the state's banks. By doing so, the government, implicitly, recognized the black market rate.[40]

Private exports rose considerably from 1986 onward. According to the chambers of commerce, however, they included a substantial portion of exports dumped solely for the purpose of obtaining foreign exchange.[41] Another portion was what Syrian merchants called fantasy exportation. This meant that products were exported across the border but not necessarily marketed abroad. The aim of such "export" was to obtain an export document from Syrian customs which was needed to prove legal access to foreign exchange—in other words, legalizing black market foreign exchange.

At the same time, there was no effective policy to reduce the mostly private importation of high-quality or luxury consumer goods. Import bans often proved ineffective because they only served to increase the contraband trade, which damaged the national economy even more. Also, despite its socialist orientation, the government pursued a policy that was rather friendly toward private importers. Critics even spoke of an "import encouragement policy"[42] that, up to 1984, was primarily based on the overvalued exchange rate for the pound. The Syrian Commercial Bank, therefore, stopped opening foreign exchange letters of credit

---

38. Author's interviews with officials of the Ministry of Economy and Foreign Trade, November 1988.

39. Prime Minister, Decree No. 2332/1986 and 595/1987.

40. Minister of Economy and Foreign Trade, Decree No. 1048/1989 and 973/1990.

41. See "Hal tansajim ijra'at tahdir sadirat al-qita' al-khas ma'a siyasat tawhid sarf al-qata' al-ajnabi?" (Do preparations for private sector exports harmonize with the policies to unify currency exchange rates?), *Tishrin*, June 26, 1989.

42. General Federation of Trade Unions, "Al-taqrir al-iqtisadi," (Twenty-first Conference), p. 112.

for private importers unless they brought forward the foreign exchange needed.[43] Supposedly, this money was to have stemmed from commercial activities abroad, but it was made clear that its source would not be questioned. Not surprisingly, the black market for money soared.

In 1986, harsh penalties were announced for the illegal dealing in Syrian currency and foreign exchange. The result was a concentration of the black currency market in the hands of fewer traders and the restriction of legal importation to those persons who had, or could make officials believe they had, legal access to foreign exchange. This meant that small industrialists and artisans without foreign ties were forced either to join state industries in low production areas or seek the help of import-export traders to secure the raw materials they needed.

In 1989, with the similar effect of strengthening the position of private trade, merchants who had access to foreign currency were allowed to import raw materials to be converted in the Hama iron plant and the Dayr al-Zur paper mill and other public sector factories. The state enterprises were to be paid either in foreign exchange or in additional raw materials.[44] This, in fact, meant replacing some state control over private trade by giving private merchants some control over state enterprises.

If one looks at official data on foreign trade, this new orientation of foreign trade policies—or the export campaign as it was referred to in the official discourse—was successful. The private sector's contribution to foreign trade, which had decreased to some 10 percent of the total in the early 1980s, rose to more than 20 percent in 1986, to more than 30 percent in 1988, and up to 45 percent in 1989 according to preliminary figures. Also, the gap in Syria's balance of trade was gradually reduced. This, however, was because public sector imports—as a result of the acute foreign exchange shortage—had fallen to some 60 percent of their value in 1986 and had declined another 15 percent by 1988. As mentioned earlier, this led to a haphazard curtailment of industrial supplies, various shortages of government-imported consumer goods—such as medicines, meat, vegetable oil, and coffee—and an unprecedented growth of smuggling and black marketeering. Private sector imports were still rising, such that total registered imports amounted to about 60 percent of their 1985 value in 1988; exports did not increase until that year. In early 1990, however, Minister of Economy Muhammad al-Imadi announced a positive balance of trade for 1989, resulting from a further decrease of imports, a substantial rise of crude oil exports, and a more than a threefold increase in the value of private-sector exports.[45] With

43. Minister of Economy and Foreign Trade, Decree No. 47/1984 and 356/1985.

44. Minister of Economy and Foreign Trade, Decree No. 158/1989 and 160/1989.

45. See *Statistical Abstract*, 1983 through 1989. For 1989 figures, see *al-Iqtisad*, February 1990, p. 71f. According to these figures, crude oil exports rose to LS 9.1 billion (versus LS 3.7 billion in 1988). There is a remarkable rise in exports to the Soviet Union, jumping from the equivalent of some US $300 million annually until 1988 to an equivalent of about US $1 billion. Exports to the Soviet

TABLE 2
Indicators of Foreign Trade and Private Sector Contributions
(billion Syrian pounds)

	1980	1985	1986	1988*	1989
Total Imports	16.2	15.6	10.7	25.0	23.3
Private Sector	4.2	2.5	2.7	6.7	n.a.
Total Exports	8.3	6.4	5.2	15.1	33.7
Private Sector	0.6	0.5	1.6	5.5	16.2

*Foreign trade data are calculated on the basis of LS 11.20 to the US dollar from 1987 on, instead of LS 4.05 to the dollar.
Source: Statistical Abstract, various issues, 1982 through 1989. For 1989 preliminary figures, see *al-Iqtisad,* February 1990, p. 71f.

growing unregistered illegal imports on the one hand and a considerable amount of dubious exports from the private sector on the other, the significance of official figures should be treated with some caution.

PRIVATE ENTERPRISE AND FOREIGN CAPITAL

The first Syrian infitah policies encouraged private investment mainly in the commercial and service sectors. During the second half of the 1980s, and in view of the decreased share of goods production in national income, the cabinets of prime ministers Kasm and Zu'bi launched what can be called a second infitah. It was aimed at "mobilizing private sector money for investment in the productive sectors, for its own interest and in the interest of society."[46] The goal was to induce capital owners to invest in industry and agriculture instead of increasing their wealth in traditional channels, such as import trade, real estate, or investments outside Syria. Thus, exports were encouraged, facilities for new establishments were granted, and the private sector was allowed gradually to expand into several areas that previously had been restricted to the public sector. Nevertheless, the government adhered to its position that the public sector should play the leading role in industry and that industries regarded as of strategic importance should be reserved for state enterprises.[47] In response, there was a nominal increase in the private industrial sector, which was mostly small manufacturing.

Union did not contribute to Syria's foreign exchange budget because exports were partially exchanged for goods according to the Syrian-Soviet payment agreement and were partially deducted from the Syrian debt to the Soviet Union.

46. Muhammad al-Imadi, "Al-Qita'an al-mushtarak wa al-khas wa dawruhuma fi al-tanmiyya" (The mixed and the private sectors and their roles in development) (Economic Sciences Associations Fifth Economic Tuesday Symposium, Damascus, 1986), p. 34.

47. Author's interview with Minister of Industry Antun Jibran, Damascus, April 1989. The list of "strategic" industries was published in Minister of Industry, Decree No. 4343/1988.

Despite the increase, however, traditional means of becoming rich and investing in services—particularly in tourism—still seemed more attractive to private capital.[48]

This second infitah was also significant because it represented an attempt to attract foreign investments. Since the nationalizations of the 1950s, and particularly since the Baath revolution in 1963, foreign capital involvement in Syria had been insignificant although there was never a general ban on such activity. Even after 1970, foreign capital was reluctant to commit money to direct investments in Syria, apparently because of fear of instability and further nationalizations and because the competence level of the local work force was not considered sufficiently attractive. Virtually no foreign investment took place unless the Syrian government showed specific interest and endeavored to attract it. Such endeavors were in the first place aimed at attracting Arab capital and the capital of Syrian expatriates, both of which, according to the Baathist nationalist ideology, were not usually regarded as "foreign." Arab investments were subject to a different set of rules. In particular, Arabs were permitted to export their profits and reexport invested capital. Special interest was extended to any form of Syrian-Arab public or public-private joint ventures which, even if primarily state-owned, followed private enterprise patterns.

In addition, from 1974 onward, Syria granted limited drilling concessions to foreign oil companies. When oil was found, profits were to be shared between the foreign company and the Syrian state. The most successful concession holder was—and still is—a Dutch-US-German consortium that found the promising fields near Dayr al-Zur on the Euphrates. Production in these fields started in 1985 and began to exceed the output of Syria's older fields in 1990.

With Syria's second infitah of the 1980s, official interest in attracting foreign non-Arab capital to other sectors of the economy also grew. Foreign establishments in the free zones were to be allowed to leave these zones, and, generally, their right to enter the local market was broadened.[49] Syrian government officials said they welcomed and would support foreign-Syrian joint ventures, such as the Spanish-Syrian tractor company in Aleppo. These moves reflected the government's desire to attract direct foreign investments in a variety of sectors, whether in production or in tourism.[50]

New policies were also gradually developed concerning what could be called

48. For a closer look into the structure and development of the Syrian private sector, see Volker Perthes, "The Syrian Private Industrial and Commercial Sectors and the State," *International Journal of Middle East Studies*, forthcoming May 1992.

49. Prime Minister, Decree No. 792/1987. Syria established free zones in 1972. In 1981, in the context of government measures to reaffirm state control of trade, free zone activities were restricted causing several plants to close. From 1986 onward, the government tried to reattract investors to the zones.

50. See Ministry of Economy and Foreign Trade, *Qawanin wa anzima al-istithmar fi Suriya* (Laws and regulations for investments in Syria) (Damascus, 1988). It contains a list of perspective options for foreign investments in tourism.

Syrian big business. In the 1970s, after the nationalization of most of the important private companies during the early years of Baathist rule, permission was given to form so-called mixed joint-stock companies in the tourism and transport sector. "Mixed" meant that the state held a minority share while the rest was held by private Syrian and Arab capital. Because of the government's interest in the quick growth of tourism, these companies obtained special privileges and grew—in Syrian terms—into large enterprises.

Agriculture

To move private money into agriculture, in 1986 the Syrian administration permitted the establishment of mixed agricultural joint-stock companies; 25 percent of the shares were held by the Ministry of Agriculture which made its contribution by supplying land.[51] Only a year after permission was given, a dozen such companies had been established or were in the process of being founded.[52]

In the beginning, buyers' interest in the agricultural companies' shares was high, apparently because most of the founders appeared to be successful "new-class" businessmen. After a growing number of companies were established, however, public interest in the shares slackened, and it seemed that some of the companies' founders were more interested in the exceptional privileges connected with the new mixed agricultural sector than in agriculture itself. As of early 1989, only one, and by the end of that year only three, of the companies had actually started production. Their privileges included the right to transfer or retransfer profits and capital in hard currency at any time; guarantees against nationalizations; and, exemption from all import regulations, currency regulations, customs and local duties, and from all Syrian laws regarding workers' rights. The companies were an ideal instrument for disguising or quasi-legalizing obscure and questionable commercial practices, such as speculating, smuggling, and contraband trade.[53]

In principle, there was nothing wrong with the attempt to direct private money into the productive sectors. The policy of developing the Syrian countryside by means of big, private agro-companies, however, raised questions. It clearly contradicted the idea of land reform, according to which Syrian agriculture was to consist primarily of cooperative-type working private farms, thereby limiting landownership to a maximum of 200 hectars. In fact, land reform was

51. Legislative Decree No. 10/1986.

52. Ministry of Agriculture. The capital of these companies ranged between LS 25 million (Sanabil) and LS 500 million (al-Sham).

53. Ghadaq, the first of these companies to go into production and to announce (in 1989) a distribution of dividends to its shareholders, made a substantial part of its stated profits not through production but by exporting agricultural products from the Syrian market and from interest on bank deposits, trade with imported goods, and import licenses. See a recent detailed study, Hans Hopfinger, "Kapitalistisches Agro-Business in einem sozialistischen Land? Syrien versucht neue Wege in der Landwirtschaft," *Die Erde*, no. 121, 1990, pp. 157–76.

never fully implemented. Only part of the expropriated land was distributed to the fallahin, while other parts were rented to previous owners or to new agro-entrepreneurs.

Land distribution, in general, favored middle class farmers rather than those without property. As new big agricultural estates came into being, many of the smaller farmers became financially dependent upon the wealthier landowners or even lost their lands and migrated from the countryside.[54] The cooperatives, which were to be formed by newly landed peasants, proved of limited success. About one-third of Syria's agricultural land was cultivated by peasants who belonged to a cooperative but whose agricultural holdings usually remained individual small-plot family farms. The cooperative, at best, rendered services such as selling chemicals and delivering the peasants' harvest to the state agricultural marketing organizations.[55] The cooperatives' capital was weak, with only a few owning a tractor or a harvester. In addition, there were many complaints about the cooperatives being of primary benefit to their wealthier members and about the limited degree of democratic participation in their administration.[56]

Implementation of Syria's agricultural policy thus contradicted the theory of land reform. Instead of providing land to the new agro-companies, it would have made more sense to give the land and the supporting assistance—such as credits, seeds, fertilizer, and machinery—to the many deprived and unemployed fallahin. Even if it was expected that a capital flow into agriculture would cause an increase in agricultural products, much of the companies' expected production would ultimately be exported to cover the cost of imported machinery and equipment. It was, therefore, doubtful whether positive economic or social results could have been achieved in the countryside for the benefit of its population, particularly because agricultural production was to be capital intensive,[57] rather than labor intensive (as in family farming), and because ownership was concentrated in the cities and abroad.[58] It was unlikely that this approach would cause an improvement in the living conditions of the rural population and, in addition, lead to an

54. See, for example, Bu Ali Yasin, *Hikayyat al-ard wa al-fallah al-Suri, 1858–1979* (Land and the Syrian peasant, 1858–1979) (Beirut: Dar al-Haqa'iq, 1979), pp. 110ff.; idem., "Alaqat al-intaj fi al-rif al-suri ba'd tanfidh al-islah al-zira'i" (Relations of production in the Syrian countryside after the land reform) (Economic Sciences Associations Fifth Economic Tuesday Symposium), pp. 368ff.

55. Yasin, "Alaqat al-intaj fi al-rif." Only 11 out of more than 4,000 cooperatives were so-called production cooperatives (*jama'iyyat intajiyya*), that is, cooperatives where agricultural work was actually done collectively. See, *Statistical Abstract*, 1988, pp. 121f.

56. See for example A. Jaradat, "Ma huwa matlub min al-mu'tamarat al-fallahiyya?" (What is to be gained from the peasants' conferences?), *al-Thawra*, January 21, 1989.

57. Neither Ghadaq nor Barakat—the first two mixed agro-companies founded—with a capital of LS 315 million and LS 100 million, respectively, intended to employ more than 200 permanent or seasonal workers. Al-Sham, the biggest agro-company with a capital of LS 500 million, intended to employ about 1,000 largely seasonal workers. Author's interviews with Sa'ib Nahhas, Abd al-Rahman al-Attar, and Usama Daqr, chairmen of the boards of the respective companies.

58. Foreigners were allowed to buy shares in the companies. All the founders of al-Furat Agricultural Co., the third of these joint-stock companies to be established, were Arab businessmen from the Gulf.

expansion of the local market for locally produced consumer goods, as well as halt the exodus from the countryside. It was also doubtful that shareholders, living far from the areas of production, would show any great interest in ecologically protecting the land. Thus, it would seem that this new agricultural policy might lead to a replication of the same pattern of distribution whereby the urban areas accumulated rural surplus. This pattern dominated Syria before the 1958 land-reform initiative, when absentee landlords based in Aleppo, Homs, Hama, and Damascus ruled the countryside with virtually unlimited power.

POINTS OF EVALUATION

Syria's economic policies, before and during the 1980s, often seemed to contradict long-term development plans. Instead of attributing these contradictions to the absence of political or administrative skills, however, it is more useful to analyze them as expressions of conflicting interests and policy concepts which, at least partially, were quite openly discussed by the Syrian public. One of the key questions was whether the Syrian economy should be opened up further. The government in the 1980s followed a path that it promoted as pragmatic. In fact, by limiting state control of trade and currency, by encouraging domestic and foreign private capital, and by reducing the role of labor unions, it strengthened the position of private business. Some trade unionists, economists and planners, the political Left, and most of the state sector bureaucracy favored tougher state control of the economy. This position, as far as the bureaucracy was concerned, originated mainly from bureaucratic self-interest. Some members of these groups, however, also pressed for a policy that, while democratizing and decentralizing the state sector, would strengthen the role of planning institutions vis-à-vis the military and party officials. Proponents of this viewpoint also called for limitations on the private trade sector's privileges, cessation of income redistribution at the expense of the poor, and strengthening the economy's ties to Eastern European and Arab countries.[59]

Yet, because the Syrian leadership needed to preserve the loyality of the bureaucracy and mass organizations, it could not afford to relinquish its ideological claim of leading the country toward socialism. Therefore, privatization and pro-business steps had to be taken with some caution, accompanied by slogans about the leading role of the public sector in the economy, and the role of the trade and farmers' unions in society. Contradictions between policies, plans, and programs were thus unavoidable.

From a broader perspective, however, it is evident that the coming to power of Hafiz al-Asad in 1970 led to a decisive change in Syria's development strategies. It saw the end of the socialist, egalitarian approach pursued under the

59. The General Federation of Trade Unions' 1987 general report to the Conference for National Creativity and Self-Reliance contains a good exposition of this viewpoint. See note 22.

Baath from around 1964 and the introduction of new policies more friendly to both local and foreign business and basically inegalitarian.

Syria's economic crisis was caused mainly by internal factors, namely the government's development strategy. That strategy sought rapid growth and modernization centering on industry and infrastructure, while devoting less attention to agricultural development. The goals were to be achieved with the help of foreign financing and by means of an economic opening both to the West and to the local private bourgeoisie.

The new industrial structure, however, did not become the basis for sustainable growth. Large-scale importation of foreign finished technology hindered the development of local technologies compatible with the country's abilities and capacities. The new industries were capital intensive rather than labor intensive, their output never met expectations, and they were heavily dependent upon imports. Instead of expanding and diversifying Syria's exports, the new industries increased the country's dependency on foreign finance, expertise, and supply. The growing balance of trade deficit was further aggravated by an increased need to import foodstuffs as a result of the relative neglect of agriculture and the effects of liberal infitah trade policies that opened the markets to higher quality imported consumer goods. Syria's chances of increasing exports were, to a large extent, tied to oil production and world oil prices. With growing foreign exchange problems in the 1980s, and shortages of material for both industry and agriculture, the productive sectors of the economy were subject to stagnation and, sometimes, to regression.

From a societal standpoint, Syria's post-1970 development strategy was inegalitarian. The policies of infitah, the large financial capacities of the state after the 1973 October War, and the demands of a growing middle class provided great opportunities for private business. A new enriched stratum emerged which included some higher echelons of the bureaucracy, the party, and the military as well as a new commercial bourgeoisie whose top members—the so-called new class—almost exclusively owed their status to their business ties to the state, such as direct importation on behalf of state agencies and contracting. The resulting spread of corruption was hardly surprising.

The new inequalities accompanying the infitah were largely camouflaged by the expansion of public employment and public services and private consumption, and by a general rise in living standards. These inequalities became apparent, however, when symptoms of crisis emerged at the end of the 1970s. Such inequalities were sectoral as well as individual. Many peasant smallholders whose holdings did not earn them their living—including beneficiaries of the land reform—were forced to relinquish their holdings, or at least seek alternative employment while keeping their plots as an additional source of income.[60]

60. According to the agrarian censuses of 1970 and 1981, while the number of agricultural landholders remained almost the same, the portion of those landholders whose primary occupation

Migration from the countryside to the towns was continuous although somewhat alleviated in the 1970s by seasonal employment opportunities in the Arab Gulf states.[61]

With the crisis in the 1980s and continued migration, job opportunities in the state sector—whose rapid growth had provided employment for large numbers of migrants in the 1970s—became scarce. In effect, whereas in the 1970s the wage-earning middle class constituted the fastest growing stratum, in the 1980s it was the semi-proletariat whose growth exceeded that of all other social strata.[62]

Although precise data was not available on individual income distributions, it was obvious that incomes in the productive sectors generally lagged behind those in the areas of service and distribution. In the mid-1980s, the average income in the real estate sector was seven times that of industry, in trade almost three times that of industry, and in transport almost twice that of industry. In the service sector—mainly consisting of state employees—incomes were around the national average, while incomes in industry, agriculture, and the building sector were clearly below that level.[63] Neither public sector wages, nor minimum wages decreed for the private sector, nor agricultural producers' prices fixed by the government, kept pace with the rates of inflation. Consequently, workers, state employees, and small farmers, as well as small artisans dependent on imported material, suffered real income losses.[64] The decrease in mass income during the 1980s, and the strong feelings by large parts of the work force that they did not receive sufficient return for their labor, also had a dampening effect upon development efforts. It caused farmers to limit cultivation or, otherwise, sell their harvest on the black market, industrial workers to save their energy for moonlighting, and it increased corruption among civil servants. In addition, the bureaucratic authoritarian structure of the Baath Party, the mass organizations, and public sector stifled any feeling of participation in the decision-making

---

was in agriculture declined from 93.6 percent to 65 percent of all holders. See Central Bureau of Statistics, *Agricultural Census Data, 1970–1971, First Stage—Basic Data* (Damascus, 1972); idem., *Agricultural Census Data, 1981*, 14 vols. (Damascus, 1986).

61. See Khudr Zakariyya, *Al-Hijra al-dakhiliyya fi Suriya: Nushu'uha wa tatawwuruha* (Internal migration in Syria: Its emergence and development) (Tunis: Population Research Unit, League of Arab States, n.d. 1987), no. 10, pp. 50ff.

62. The semi-proletariat grew from an estimated 6.5 percent of the work force in 1970 to about 10 percent in 1981 and to about 16 percent at the end of the decade. See Perthes, *Staat und Gesellschaft*, table XII, p. 217.

63. Based on data on gross domestic product and work force in 1984; *Statistical Abstract*, 1988.

64. The minimum wages are largely set according to public sector wages. On the latter see note 27. For the development of agricultural producers' prices see, for example, General Federation of Peasants in the Syrian Arab Republic, *Proceedings of the Sixth General Conference of the Peasants* (in Arabic) (Damascus, 1986), pp. 64ff. The conference was held in Damascus on March 8, 1986. Even according to data published by the Ministry of Agriculture, in the mid-1980s producers' prices for wheat, barley, sugar beets, chick-peas, and lentils, as fixed by the government, fell short of production costs. See Ministry of Agriculture and Agrarian Reform, *Statistical Abstract*, 1985 (Damascus, n.d. 1987), tables 111ff.

process and contributed to general indifference.[65] Thus the regimes's mobilization campaigns understandably generated little enthusiasm.

Inegalitarianism and authoritarianism, of course, were not accidental. They reflected the political, social, and economic interests of the dominant social forces, namely the alliance that emerged in the 1970s linking the top of the civil and military bureaucracy with the new, and parts of the old, commercial bourgeoisie.[66] This alliance of the old and new elites helps explain why the Asad government did not pursue an active liberalization program, one that would have required political reform and greater popular participation. Instead, it engaged in a limited privatization of public resources, which favored the commercial bourgeoisie while the costs of the economic crisis were distributed throughout the society by a variety of austerity measures.

In contrast to emphasizing domestic choices and structures, some analysts attribute only minor importance to these internal factors and view Syria's economic problems as mainly the product of external factors[67]: the Lebanese civil war and the reduction of Arab aid in particular. Without denying that these factors—and others—had some effect on Syria's economic development in the 1980s, one should be careful not to overestimate them or confuse cause and effect.

Because there are no reliable data on how the Lebanese situation influenced and still influences the Syrian economy, any statements on this issue should be viewed with caution. With this in mind, however, it appears doubtful that the Lebanese war's overall effect on the Syrian economy was damaging. The deployment of Syrian forces in Lebanon definitely led to additional expenses, namely extra pay for some 30,000 troops and the cost of fuel and material. From 1976 onward, however, most of this expense was probably covered by direct Arab payments—mainly from Saudi Arabia—for the Arab Deterrent Force, essentially the Syrian army in Lebanon. In any case, Syrian budget figures do not show any significant rise in military expenditures or any shift in the budget toward the military directly corresponding to the deployment of troops to Lebanon.[68]

The Lebanese civil war also led to certain gains for the Syrian economy: new opportunities for the Syrian tourist industry to attract Arabs who otherwise would have visited Lebanon, the return of expatriate Syrian capital from Lebanon, and the diversion of naval and air traffic and trade from Beirut to the safer ports of Tartus and Latakia and to the Damascus airport. The expansion of illegal

65. Authoritarian management practices in public sector companies and in the ministries, and the apparent indifference of public employees—even "anarchy" in the bureaucracy and the public sector—were repeatedly stressed in critical trade union statements. See, for example General Federation of Trade Unions, "Al-Taqrir al-amm" (Conference for National Creativity and Self-Reliance), pp. 37ff.

66. In the words of Elizabeth Picard, we could speak of a "complexe militaro-mercantile" to characterize this dominant alliance. See "Clans militaires et pouvoir ba'thiste," *Orient* 20 (1979) (Hamburg), p. 62.

67. See Yosef Olmert, "Domestic Crisis and Foreign Policy in Syria: The Asad Regime," *Middle East Review* 20, no. 3 (Spring 1988), p. 24.

68. On the Syrian military budget, see footnote 30.

commodity imports to Syria was not the result of the Syrian army's engagement in Lebanon. With Syrian troops freely crossing the Syrian-Lebanese border, contraband trade became easier, and Syrian military personnel increasingly took over the business from border inhabitants. This, however, did not cause smuggling. Smuggling and black marketeering were economic reactions to shortages and maldistribution. To cite one example, some elements of the Syrian army began to organize the illegal importation of cigarettes in 1981—five years after their deployment—when legal cigarette imports were banned.[69]

As to Arab aid, there is no doubt that its decline from about US $1.3–1.8 billion a year between 1979 and 1983 to US $600–700 million in subsequent years significantly affected the Syrian state's scope of action and its distribution of wealth within the society.[70] Iranian assistance compensated, and even overcompensated, Syria for its loss of transit fees when it closed the trans-Syria Iraqi oil pipeline in 1982,[71] but this assistance in no way equaled the Arab countries' reduced financial support. As noted earlier, however, crisis symptoms—notably the unsatisfactory output of Syria's state industries, their high dependency on imported material, the growing need for agricultural imports, and thus an increasing gap in Syria's trade balance—began to cause serious problems in the early 1980s when Arab financial support to Syria, stipulated at the 1978 Baghdad summit, was at its highest levels. The substantial cuts in Arab payments after 1983 exacerbated Syria's tense foreign exchange situation, but it did not cause the structural deficits underlying the poor performance of the economy. The economic base established in line with the development strategy of the 1970s largely depended on—and thus made the country dependent on—foreign aid. When from 1983 on it was forced to rely partly on its own resources, Syria's economy revealed its structural deficits.

At the end of the 1980s, Syria's economic future did not look promising. To expand its room for maneuver, the Syrian government would have to expand economic privatization at home or seek to draw increased financial resources from the regional situation by convincing fellow Arabs to increase their support for Syria. In fact, Damascus has been pursuing both of these strategies. The process

69. Because Syrian cigarette factories could, at best, cover half the local demand, and because the government decision to ban the import of cigarettes proved to be most profitable for people who were able to organize illegal importation, one might ask whether the personal interest of high officers might have influenced this decision. The value of cigarette smuggling was estimated at about US $375,000 a day in the late 1980s. On the capacity of the Syrian tobacco industry see, Mustafa al-Miqdad, "Al-Mu'assasa al-amma li al-tibgh: Intaj wa su'ubat" (The general organization for tobacco: Production and difficulties), *al-Thawra,* July 30, 1988.

70. From 1987 onward, reportedly only Saudi Arabia considerably increased payments to Syria. Parallel with the decrease of Arab aid in the first half of the 1980s, remittances from Syrians working in the Arab Gulf States also declined. This, however, only minimally affected the state's foreign exchange budget because Syrian migrants to the Gulf only transferred a small part of their wages through official bank channels.

71. From 1982 to the late 1980s, Iran supplied Syria with 1 million tons of free crude oil and up to 5 million tons at a reduced rate. See Economist Intelligence Unit, *Syria Country Profile, 1989–1990,* p. 32f.

of economic liberalization continues but without any sign of an accompanying political liberalization that will bring about more than cosmetic changes.[72] Externally, Syria has benefited from its rapprochement with Egypt in 1989 and the Ta'if agreement for an Arab solution in Lebanon. The Syrian leadership has also been able to capitalize on the Gulf War. Nevertheless, even with growing foreign assistance, rising oil revenues, the sound use of local resources, and a reasonable foreign trade policy, Syria's fundamental deficiencies will not be overcome unless major changes are made in the structure of the regime, its social alliances, and its developmental approach.

72. See Volker Perthes, "Syria's Parliamentary Elections: Moving from Absolution to Corporatist Authoritarianism?" *Middle East Report*, forthcoming March 1992.

[8]

Food Security and Rural Development in North Africa

M. RIAD EL-GHONEMY

North Africa is an amalgam of six countries, having broad similarities and significant structural variations. Apart from being ruled by Europeans for a considerable period of time, the obvious common feature is cultural: Arabic, Islam and customs. Most generalizations conceal considerable structural differences in: natural resource endowment; size of population; proportion of nomadic people; average per capita income; the relative importance of agriculture in the economy and the degree of food self-sufficiency. Within agriculture, there are also great variations in density of working people on land; the area of potentially cultivable land; and the extent of reliance on rainfall for staple food production.

The region comprises countries of different economic structures: a predominantly agricultural low-income economy (Sudan); balanced middle-income economies (Algeria, Egypt, Morocco and Tunisia); and an oil-based high-income economy (Libya). The variation is so wide that in 1988 the average annual income per person in Egypt was one-eighth of that in Libya and the latter was more than 12 times the average in Sudan. The region also includes extreme degrees of agricultural land–man ratios and population density shown in Table 2. There is a land-abundant and labour-scarce country, Libya, land and labour-abundant economy, Sudan, and a high scarcity of cultivable land in Egypt.

Tables 1 and 2 reveal two striking but related regional characteristics. One is the accelerated growth of population, being overwhelmingly rural, at the average annual rate of 3.1 per cent in the 1980s, which is higher than the average rates in the African continent (3 per cent), Asia (2.3 per cent), and Latin America (2.2 per cent). The second is that all countries are dependent for feeding their people on imports and their self-sufficiency rate of cereals fell in the 1980s relative to the 1960s.

Although the importance of agriculture relative to other sectors of the economy in terms of its contribution to total GDP has declined over the last three decades, it provides employment opportunities for a considerable proportion of the labour force (except Libya). Moreover, nearly

Middle Eastern Studies, Vol. 29, No. 3, July 1993, pp. 445–466
PUBLISHED BY FRANK CASS, LONDON

one-third of total domestic income growth is determined by the performance of agriculture. As computed in Table 1, growth rates of agricultural GDP in the 1980s is responsible for 37 per cent of total gross domestic product in Sudan, 27 per cent in Morocco, 21 per cent in Algeria and nearly 9 per cent in both Egypt and Tunisia. Compared to the period 1965–80, the slowdown in agricultural growth rates during 1980–88 has held back national economic growth.

Half of the region's total population of 140 million in 1990 is concentrated in the Nile Valley (Egypt and Sudan). In the 1980s the population of all the six countries grew faster than during the preceding two, mostly due to notable progress achieved in reducing death rates. Given the slow employment expansion in other sectors of the economy, such a demographic characteristic has implications for the labour force: its growth rates in agriculture and its productive absorption; access to land; *per capita* real income; and density on agricultural land. Likewise, the fast-growing population has important effects on the demand for land and food.

With the exception of Libya, people working in agriculture range from one quarter to two-thirds of the total. They grew faster in the 1980s than in the 1970s in Algeria, Egypt and Tunisia. Their average annual rates of growth fell slowly in the other three countries, suggesting that alternative employment opportunities in the rest of their respective economies have continued to be limited. In absolute terms, the numbers of people working in agriculture have increased during the second half of the 1980s in all countries except Tunisia. Alarmingly, *per capita* real income fell during the period 1980–88 compared to the period 1965–80 (except in Morocco). Although the usage of averages conceals the size distribution of income within agriculture, this falling real value of productivity must have hit the low income groups harder than the rich farmers.

A salient feature of the population in North Africa is its mobility in three forms. The first and the oldest is pastoral nomadism on the old-established land, communally held by tribal organizations. Owing to their continued mobility in search for rainfall and to their dispersion in vast grazing areas, the pastoral nomads and their livestock are under-numerated in population census, and they are not easily reached by public services. Yet, the socio-ecological system of pastoral nomadism employs millions of the rural population and determines the value and quality of production of a considerable proportion of food (milk and meat), wool and hides. Without pastoral nomadism, a substantial part of arid and semi-arid lands in North Africa would otherwise remain un-utilized.

Pastoral nomads as a percentage of the total rural population are

TABLE 1
SOME STRUCTURAL INDICATORS OF NORTH AFRICAN COUNTRIES, 1960–88

		Algeria	*Egypt*	*Libya*	*Morocco*	*Sudan*	*Tunisia*
1. Total population million (1988)		23.8	50.2	4.2	24.0	23.8	7.8
average annual growth rate (%)	1960–70	2.4	2.5	3.9	2.6	2.2	2.0
	1980–88	3.1	2.6	4.3	2.7	3.1	2.5
2. Agricultural population as percentage of total (1989)		24.5	41	14.1	37.2	61.4	25.2
3. Rural population as percentage of total 1987		56	52	33	53	79	46
estimated pastoral-nomadic population as percentage of rural population	1976–80	3.0	0.5	10	17.0	15.0	2.0
4. Gross Natioral Product, USS per person	1988	2382	660	5420	830	480	1230
5. Agricultural Gross Domestic Product							
– as percentage of total GDP	1988	13	21	4 (1985)	17	33	14
– average annual rate of growth	1965–80	5.8	2.8	10.7	2.2	2.9	5.5
	1980–88	5.6	2.6	7.3 (80–85)	6.6	2.7	2.4
– direct contribution of agric. GDP growth to total GDP growth(%)		20.9	9.6	–	26.7	35.6	9.9
6. Agricultural Gross Domestic Product per capita labour force (USS at 1980 prices) annual growth rate (%)	1970–80	7.9	2.2	n.a	1.2	−0.05	3.5
	1980–88	1.2	1.2	n.a	3.8	0.9	0.6
7. Exports:							
– agricultural as percentage of total	1987	1	17	1	16	97	9
– oil & minerals as percentage of total	1987	97	74	99	26	6	27
8. Human development Index	1987	0.609	0.501	0.719	0.489	0.255	0.657
ranking order		(3)	(4)	(1)	(5)	(6)	(2)

Sources:

Rows 1, 3, 4, 5 and 7. *World Development Report* 1987, 1989 and 1990: World Development indicators. Rural population calculated as the balance of urban population. Estimates of pastoral-nomadic population are rough; they are taken from population census and Ian Livingstone (1984: table 2, columns 4 and 7) except Sudan: Ministry Of Agriculture, 1978.

Direct contribution of agricultural GDP growth is for the period 1980–88, calculated by multiplying the rate of growth of agricultural GDP and its percentage share in total GDP divided by the rate of growth of total GDP.

Row 2. Calculated from 1990 Country Tables – Basic data on the agricultural sector. The Agriculture Organisation of the United Nations (FAO), Rome.

Rows 3, 6. World Bank and FAO Data Base.

Row 8. *UNDP Human Development Report* 1990: The index is based on real income per capita adjusted for purchasing power parity, life expectancy at birth (years) and adult literacy rate (percentage). It lies between 0 and 1, the higher the index, the higher the level of human development.

between 8 and 17 in Libya, Sudan and Morocco, 2 to 3 per cent in Tunisia and Algeria and only 0.5 per cent in Egypt. Due to the rising conflict of interests between nomads and urban land speculators, together with large commercial farmers who have encroached on pasture land, the nomadic population is gradually restricted within smaller boundaries. Not only have grazing areas been reduced, but they have also less rainfall and are inadequate to support the nomads and their animals.[1]

The second form of rural population mobility is the steady migration to urban of those seeking higher earnings. Urban population in the six countries has more than doubled between 1960 and 1988; from 28 million to nearly 60 million. Between about 40 and 45 per cent of this growth is roughly attributed to net rural-urban migration (United Nations, 1980).[2] The centralized bureaucracy, economic activities and political institutions in capital cities and large towns have tended to expand their population. Judging from the post-1960 growth of the largest city in North Africa, Cairo, it appears that the larger the city, the faster its growth (from 3.3 million in 1960 to 6.5 million in 1986, representing 14.5 per cent of total population). The United Nations projects that by the year 2000 the population of Cairo will reach 13 million, or 21 per cent of the projected total. The frequent droughts have also forced many pastoral nomads and small farmers in rain-fed areas to migrate to cities, seeking food and jobs.

As urban populations do not produce their own food, rapid urbanization has compounded food problems. It has increased the demand for food, contributed to rising food imports and changed the pattern of food demand, especially the consumption of wheat, vegetables and meat. Rapid urban expansion has also encroached upon the already limited cultivated land and raised its price levels, which has fuelled inflation. For example, the area of the scarce cultivable land in Egypt fell by nearly 420,000 hectares between 1970 and 1986 and the purchase price of land rocketed by 800 per cent compared to only a 150 per cent rise in the crop prices index.[3]

The third type of rural population mobility is the emigration to western Europe and to the oil-rich Arab states. As in the case of rural-urban migration, the fundamental cause has been economic, i.e. high wage rate, better quality of life, and wide income gap between native and foreign countries. There was a flow of migrants to France from Algeria followed by Tunisia and Morocco, peaking in the 1970s, which slowed down in the 1980s. Starting in the 1960s, there was another wave of emigrants from Tunisia, Egypt and the Sudan to Libya, Saudi Arabia, Iraq and other Gulf countries. This outward mobility increased significantly after the sudden rise in oil prices in 1974 and 1979. The estimates of the numbers, duration and the composition (rural, urban) of the emigrants are scarce and they vary widely. Scattered information suggests that approximately 15–20 per cent of the emigrants were adult male agricultural workers. Berks and Sinclair estimated that in 1975 the inter-Arab country migration from Egypt, Morocco, Tunisia and Sudan was nearly half a million, which almost doubled in the early 1980s before the sudden collapse of the labour market in Iraq, Saudi Arabia and Kuwait, following the Gulf crisis in 1990 and the outbreak of war in January 1991.[4]

The impact of rural outmigration differs not only among countries but within rural localities in each country. Unfortunately, micro-studies and quantitative data on this critical matter are either shaky or do not exist. This is particularly so with regard to the impact on the rural labour market, distribution of income in rural areas, and land market structure. Important among the effects which have not been adequately researched (except Egypt, IFPRI, 1991) are the allocation of remittances between consumption and direct investment in agriculture and the extent to which the temporary shortage of emigrating adult male labour induces the use of farm machinery as a substitute.[5] However, household surveys and population censuses suggest that rural outmigration results in agriculture having a less educated and mostly illiterate population with a higher representation of elderly male farmers and child and female labour. The surveys also suggest the proportionate increase in non-agricultural sources of income.

Agricultural land has been viewed by most people of North Africa not only as a food-producing and labour-using asset, but also as a main source of social and political gain. This high amenity value, together with an unabated population growth in the six countries and increasing numbers of working people in agriculture, have intensified the demand for owning or leasing agricultural land. With the exception of Sudan, the aggregate supply of cultivable land is limited and the reclamation of new lands has been monopolized by over-staffed government agencies, raising the transaction cost, reducing potential social benefits, and slowing the progress in augmenting irrigated land. Such characteristics of the demand and supply of land have tended to raise land rents and to direct savings to bidding up land prices as a secure asset for holding wealth, particularly where the political future of big landowners is secure and when the rate of inflation is high. The preference for holding wealth in land and livestock has, in turn, tended to condition the allocation of private savings among alternative investment opportunities.

Not only is the present supply of agricultural land limited, but also its potential expansion.[6] Most lands with suitable soil fertility and moisture are presently used. A large part of the lands used for agricultural

TABLE 2

SUPPLY OF AGRICULTURAL LAND AND LABOUR AND FOOD AVAILABILITY, 1970–89

	Algeria	*Egypt*	*Libya*	*Morocco*	*Sudan*	*Tunisia*
Average annual rate of change (%)						
total arable land 1970–79	0.96	1.76	0.16	0.62	0.58	0.19
1980–88	0.17	0.66	0.33	1.15	0.09	0.43
irrigated land 1970–79	0.61	1.50	2.54	2.84	0.86	5.65
1980–88	4.69	0.67	0.81	0.43	0.76	7.59
Irrigated land as percentage of total arable average 1986–88	5.12	97.0	13.23	15.45	15.04	8.30
Labour force as percentage of total 1989	25.0	41.0	14.0	37.4	61.4	25.2
Average annual rate of change (%) 1980–89	1.12	1.38	1.06	0.9	1.32	−0.36
Labour density on arable land, persons/ha. 1986–88	0.20	2.38	0.08	0.34	0.38	0.21
irrigated land, persons/ha. 1986–88	3.82	2.22	0.64	2.20	2.55	2.47
Production: (average 1979–81 base period) (%)						
annual rate of change, total 1970–80	1.3	1.5	6.2	1.0	3.4	2.1
1981–88	4.3	4.1	2.5	6.4	1.4	2.7
annual rate of per capita productivity						
1970–80	−1.8	−0.9	1.7	−1.3	0.4	−0.2
1981–88	1.2	1.3	−1.7	3.6	−1.6	0.2
Food imports as percentage of total imports average 1980–86	21.0	29.0	16.0	18.0	19.5	14.2
Self-sufficiency rate of cereals including rice						
average 1969–71	74	77	25	95	97	61
1983–85	33	49	24	67	97	63

Notes: Labour force is the economically active population in agriculture. Per capital food production refers to total population. Self-sufficiency ratio is the percentage of domestic cereal production to total domestic human consumption and non-human uses such as animal feed and seeds.

Sources: Based on data given in *FAO Production Yearbook*, several issues and *FAO 1990 Country Tables*. Self-sufficiency rates: FAO Study *World Agriculture toward 2000, Belhaven Press, 1988, Table A5.*

purposes have desert soils, rocky slopes and shifting sands with nil or very low potential for supporting rain-fed agriculture (FAO, 1986). This soil texture is moisture-deficit and it dries quickly under high temperature. The length of its plant-growing period is, therefore, very limited in any one year (about 80–100 days in semi-arid areas).[7]

In 1990, of 838 million hectares (the total area of the six countries), only 10.6 per cent (about 89 million hectores) is cultivable, 45 per cent of which is already under annual and permanent crops. Out of total future cultivable land, 76 per cent is in Sudan, 10 per cent in Libya, five per cent in Egypt and between three and four per cent in Algeria, Morocco and Tunisia (FAO, Agricultural Land Use Data Base). A small portion of the potentially cultivable lands is rain-fed and most of it must be irrigated.

In the two most populated countries in North Africa, Egypt and Morocco, the potential expansion is very small. In the almost rainless, Egypt (average 0.4 inches of rain per year), the potential is only irrigable and there is no consensus on its extent. The estimates range from 0.2 million hectares (FAO, 1986) to 1.4 million hectares.[8] With regard to Morocco, the potential expansion is estimated by FAO at 0.2 million hectares under rain-fed agriculture and 0.5 million hectares irrigable. If the present trend of accelerated population growth, rapid urban expansion on agricultural land, slow industrial growth and the high rates of entrants into the agricultural labour force continues in Egypt and Morocco, the prospect for access to cultivable land is gloomy indeed. This is particularly worrying in the face of the present political environment which is not favourable to enact further land reforms. The above study forecasts that by the year 2010 potentially cultivable land per capita will be one-third its 1980 level in Egypt and half in Morocco.

Sudan, on the other hand, has the largest potential cultivable area of land; 48 million hectares rain-fed and 1.9 million hectares to be irrigated. By the year 2010 it is estimated by FAO that average cultivable land per person will be eight times that in Morocco and nearly 100 times as much in Egypt. Alas! and despite the talk about 'Arab brotherhood', current international relations are not conducive to the entry of Moroccans and Egyptians into the Sudanese agricultural land market. In ranking order, Libya comes after Sudan in proportionate terms but not in absolute quantity of potentially cultivable area. However, almost 90 per cent of Libya's total cultivable land is already in use.

Even the limited supply of irrigable land requires a long time of gestation after irrigation investment. This period is between the time of the construction of the irrigation network, land levelling and the realized output growth, i.e. increase in annual returns on investment over annual costs. The length of period is due partly to the prolonged duration caused by existing administrative weakness in coordination among the several government departments responsible for the diverse activities in irrigation, land reclamation and agricultural development. It is also due to the physical characteristics of soil which necessitate a long period for bringing land productivity to the expected level. Sandy soil requires about five to eight years, calcareous soil three to five years and clay soil five to six years.

The discussion so far suggests a serious challenge facing the governments of North Africa to realize their common development objective of food self-sufficiency from domestic production, i.e. increasing food production faster than domestic demand. The task is daunting in the face of increasing their dependency on food imports. This situation contrasts with what is known from time immemorial about the region's cereal production surplus which attracted European countries to the conquest of North Africa. Paradoxical as it may appear, and despite the twentieth century's rapid advance in yield-increasing technology, the region has, since the 1960s, been a net importer of cereals. At present, it comprises three food-deficit countries (Egypt, Morocco and Sudan) classified by the United Nations to be eligible for food aid. Ironically, Morocco's comparative advantage in wheat production was an important factor in its occupation by France in 1912 as reported by Swearengen (1988).[9] In the 1980s Morocco's wheat imports represented one quarter of its total agricultural imports and food imports represented on average 35 per cent of total domestic consumption. What is worrying is that Morocco's self-sufficiency rate of cereals and rice declined by 31 per cent between 1969 and 1971 and from 1983 to 1985 (see Table 2).

The data given in Table 2 suggest that there has been an overall disequilibrium between the demand for food and domestic supply. Only Libya was able in the 1970s to have a rate of growth per capita food production above one per cent. The other five countries had either a negative rate of change (Algeria, Egypt, Morocco and Tunisia) or a very low positive rate (Sudan). In the 1980s there was a general improvement; the rates were positive, above one per cent in Algeria, Egypt, and Morocco, but negative in Sudan and very low in Tunisia. Nevertheless, dependency on food imports is substantial and wheat imports together with cereal-aid have remained over the last two decades a permanent feature of the food situation in North Africa. In 1988 food imports as a percentage of total domestic requirements was 69 in Algeria, 47 in Egypt, 42 in Tunisia, 31 in Morocco and 12 in Sudan. Between 1980 and 1985 the percentage of aid to total cereal imports reached 41 per cent in Sudan, 19 per cent in Egypt and 13 per cent in Morocco (FAO, *Aid in Figures*, 1987). Table 3 shows that, with the exception of Libya, wheat grain and

TABLE 3
WHEAT IMPORTS IN NORTH AFRICA, 1961–1988

	Wheat grain and flour imports as percentage of total agricultural imports					
Years	*Algeria*	*Egypt*	*Libya*	*Morocco*	*Sudan*	*Tunisia*
1961	13.5	14.4	23.9	15.9	13.5	35.1
1970	12.3	12.3	11.1	13.3	20.2	30.4
1975	26.5	44.9	17.0	27.8	11.6	11.0
average 1985–88	25.0	28.0	9.0	24.1	40.0	25.8

Source:Calculated from 'Country Tables: basic data on the agricultural sector', several issues, FAO, Rome

flour wheat take up, on average, 24–28 per cent of total agricultural imports during the period 1985–88.

The hydraulic characteristics of North African agriculture continue greatly to influence the region's food production performance. Only in Egypt is all cereal-producing land almost all irrigated (95 per cent). In the rest of North Africa, most of the cereals (wheat, barley, millet and sorghum) are grown in rain-fed areas, and the wide fluctuation in cereal output is thus closely associated with sudden year-to-year variability in rainfall. Scientists and climatologists still debate whether the recent world weather changes are signals of a new trend. Politicians, on the other hand, tend to take advantage of these changes, attributing the years of good harvest to government efforts and bad years to natural events or 'God's will'. Whereas short-term variation is likely to be caused by natural events, drought does not come as a surprise in the presence of advanced techniques on rainfall measurement and forecast. Nor is climate always to blame for the problems of food supply and the frequent occurrence of famine in Sudan.[10]

There are other possible determinants of cereal production instability. Apart from investment rates in irrigation, they include: (a) government policy in pricing cereals far below world market prices; (b) the intervention of governments in the allocation of land, and irrigation water among cereals and non-food crops; (c) the threat of desert locust; (d) political upheavals and civil wars; and (e) the extent of the intensive use of yield-increasing technical inputs, particularly the drought-resistant varieties of seeds.

The cumulative effect of weather, technical and institutional deter-

TABLE 4
ESTIMATES OF TOTAL FOOD AND CEREAL PRODUCTION INSTABILITY INDICES, ALGERIA, EGYPT, MOROCCO AND TUNISIA, 1954–84

	Algeria	*Morocco*	*Tunisia*	*Egypt*
1. UNCTAD – total food production coefficient of variation				
1954–69	0.97	0.83	0.94	0.07
	(3%)	(12%)	(2%)	(95%)
1970–82	0.43	0.93	0.30	0.05
2. FAO – cereal production insatability index	(5%)	(14%)	(5%)	(97%)
1969–84	19.7	17.5	16.0	1.9

Notes: Figures between brackets are the percentage of irrigated area to total cultivated area for the last year of each period. For the definition of UNCTAD coefficient of variation and FAO instability index, see note 2 at the end of the article.

Sources: 1. 'Food Insecurity in developing countries: Causes, trends and policy options', a study prepared by Peter Svedberg, United Nations Conference on Trade and Development (UNCTAD), No. TD/B/C. 1/257, Table V–1, Geneva, 1984.

2. 'Food Security in the Near East: Review of the situation and measures to strengthen food security in the region', Document no. ESPC/NE/85/3, Table 6, Near East Regional Economic and Social Policy Commission, FAO, May 1985.

Irrigated area: *Production Yearbook*, several issues, FAO, Rome.

minants of instability is manifested in short and long-term variability in the time-series analyses of yields and total harvest.[11] Based on yearly total food and cereal output data, the deviation of which from an estimated long-term trend was calculated respectively by UNCTAD (1984) and FAO (1985). The corresponding results for four North African countries are given in Table 4.

The sets of data given in Table 4 show an inverse relationship between the magnitude of year-to-year fluctuations and the proportion of irrigated land to total agricultural land. Although Algeria, Morocco and Tunisia have recently expanded their irrigated area, the bulk of their food production is still rainfall-dependent, and their cereal production remains highly unstable. These results contrast with Egypt's low degree of fluctuation. As noted earlier, the area cultivated by food crops, especially cereals, is almost completely irrigated.

Finally, we need to highlight two facts established by the results of agricultural censuses and governments' sample surveys (Enquête). First, with the exception of Tunisia, it is small landholders of less than five hectares who are the primary growers of food grain. The proportion of food crops to total area of holdings by size is substantially higher in small holdings than larger ones. Second, there is a tendency (probably induced by governments' pricing policy) towards reducing the area under cereals and increasing the cultivation of high-value food crops (vegetables, fruits and green fodder for livestock production).

Having characterized the development issues of the interlinked population growth, limited supply of cultivable land and the region's food insecurity, the discussion turns to describe briefly the historical and institutional framework influencing these features of North African agriculture.

The independence of the six countries of North Africa as nations states is relatively recent, mostly since the 1950s.[12] All were ruled by European countries for a considerable period of time; the longest colonial rule being in Algeria. During their rule, the Ottoman Turks, the French, the British and the Italians imposed their own legal systems and forms of government upon the indigenous systems of social organization. They also linked the agricultural policy pursued in the colonized countries to their own home policies in order to serve their primary interests.[13]

The historical experience of the countries suggests that, starting in the sixteenth century and for a period of nearly three centuries, the prime interest of the Ottoman rulers was fiscal. They extracted exorbitant land taxes from the *fellaheen* through assigned local agents in exchange for granted large landholdings. Subsequently, the French and Italian rulers in the Maghreb were chiefly concerned with colonizing vast areas of the best agricultural land to settle their own individual and corporate farmers. The 'colons', using their technical knowledge and native cheap labour, grew wheat, sugar beets, and vineyards for wine-making against the Islamic principles which prohibit drinking alcohol. On the other hand, the British administration in Egypt and Sudan did not colonize lands for British farmers. Instead, the interest was in expanding cotton production and its export to the British textile industry. Another concern was the promotion of the British private sector's involvement in land development and commercial activities. Nevertheless, the French, Italian and British colonial rule introduced elements of agricultural modernization and land and credit markets: purchase, sale, charging interest for lending and the introduction of contractual arrangements for leasing and mortgaging land.

Property and usufruct rights in land were also granted by the colonial administration to certain tribal chiefs, senior officials and influential native families on whom the power of the foreign rulers depended. Both categories of large farmers (the foreign settlers and native families) held a dominant power in the land market structure. The source of foreign economic power in the rural economy of the colonized countries is revealed by official records at the time of independence. The area of foreign-owned lands (individuals and land companies) as a percentage of total cultivated lands was nearly 30 in Algeria, 20 in each of Libya and Tunisia, 10 in Egypt and 3.6 in Morocco. In Sudan, the Gezira scheme was not owned by the British. It was a triple partnership between the Sudanese government, the British management and the cultivators. Totalling 0.2 million hectares in 1956 when Sudan gained independence, the area of the scheme was irrigated, growing mostly cotton, and represented 30 per cent of total irrigated land but only two per cent of total arable land.[14]

Hence the formation of large estates was initiated and the duality in the production structure between modern and traditional sectors established. The duality was manifested in the juxtaposition of export-oriented, foreign and large native farms mostly irrigated on the one hand, and the vast area of poorly rain-fed sub-sector, producing at subsistence level and embracing the majority of farming and nomadic population, on the other hand. Thus, a wide disparity in production techniques and wage differentials prevailed, and the process of polarization in the distribution of land and income took root in most countries of the region.

This brief historical account sheds light on the post-independence increasing role of the state in the management of the rural economy within a framework of national development planning. While we appreciate the urge for initiating the process of rural development based on the repossession of foreign-owned lands and the reform of agrarian institutions inherited from colonial rule, we do not understand the continuing state control of agricultural production, marketing and trade. Invariably, there has been an extensive bureaucratization of agriculture through a wide range of government intervention, weakening the producers' incentives and motivation and increasing transaction costs. One possible explanation is that a combination of nationalism and reformation of agrarian institutions has induced further government intervention.

The second possible explanation of the centralized state authority is rooted in the form of government. The new country leadership combined legislative and executive authorities after liberation from colonial administration (Algeria, Morocco and Tunisia) or after coups d'état (Egypt, 1952 and Libya, 1969). Third, the state power in agriculture is derived from its control of the scarce irrigation water and being the largest single landowner managing state farms and deciding how much, by whom and under what terms the state-owned reclaimed land should be held. The results of agricultural censuses and 'Enquête' on the size distribution of land carried out in the early 1980s show the share of state ownership, as a percentage of total arable land, was 15 in Egypt, 12 in

Tunisia and seven in Morocco. In addition, the state owns forest lands and holds property rights in grazing areas. In Sudan, landed property is vested in the state.

The common feature of state control is the top-heavy state bureaucracy, backed by considerable police and military establishments in North African countries. Their heavy burden on the economy is reflected in the high shares of general government expenditure and services in GDP and the low shares of domestic savings.[15] However, despite the sharp rise in government expenditure, agriculture has been neglected. There is a contradiction between what agriculture actually receives and what the policy-makers declare in national development plans with regard to the realization of self-sufficiency in food production, and enhancing agricultural growth. In practice, agriculture has been crippled.

The available, incomplete, information on the share of agriculture in total public expenditure and Gross Fixed Capital Formation compared to its share in GDP and total labour force during the period 1980–85 suggests, in broad terms, that with the exception of Libya, agriculture (including irrigation and soil conservation) did not receive the needed support by governments. Further scattered information suggests also that private investment in most of the countries has been constrained by cumbersome bureaucratic procedure. As we have noted earlier, agriculture provides employment to a major section of the total labour force (between one-third and two-thirds). Likewise, it contributes between 20 and 35 per cent of total GDP. Although the governments of the region committed themselves to implement the target set by the Organization of African Unity to allocate 20–25 per cent of public investment to agriculture, this share in the 1980s is much lower, ranging from seven per cent in Morocco and nine per cent in Egypt to 13 per cent of total in Libya and Tunisia. Although the components of public expenditure on agriculture vary from country to country, most of the expenditure is allocated to irrigation and drainage, which bring about long-term benefits.[16]

The small private sector, on the other hand, concentrates on quick-return benefits from investment in: fertilizer, water-pumps, tractors, planting fruit trees, and production of poultry and livestock. Any expansion in investment in *large scale* irrigation and drainage schemes as well as agricultural research cannot be expected from the private sector. It should come from the government. Furthermore, private traders and urban businessmen cannot be relied upon to undertake the needed volume and proper pattern of investment in agriculture. With regard to direct foreign investment in agriculture, the flow of foreign capital under negotiated agreements with government enters into profitable fields of little risk: direct involvement in exportable-cum-industrial crops but not traditional food crops; the importation and trade of farm machinery; and seed breeding and distribution.

The inadequate public investment in irrigation expansion for augmenting the supply of cultivable land and its productivity towards food insecurity reduction has been compounded in the 1980s by the deepening of the countries' economic difficulties. This adverse effect has already been manifested in the sharp fall in the annual rates of expansion of both the total arable and irrigated lands, except Tunisia, during the period 1980–89 compared to the 1970s (see Table 2). The reality of neglecting agriculture is contrasted with the unaffected higher priority accorded to the non-productive sectors of government administration and military expenditure, including the purchase of arms and the armed forces' wage bill. The IMF data for the 1980s show that in the poorest country in North Africa, Sudan, military expenditure exceeds the combined public allocations for health, education and agriculture. Military expenditure relative to total central government expenditure in the other countries ranges from the low six per cent in Tunisia, to 15 per cent in Morocco, to 29 per cent in Egypt.[17]

There is a common sexual prejudice against the legitimate rights of women in access to land, credit, technical knowledge in farming and agricultural cooperatives' membership. As household heads, farm workers, producers of livestock and dairy products, their role in agriculture, in general, and their contribution to the food sector, in particular, are underestimated. This imbalance is suggested by the results of national censuses and in programming agricultural services. Rhetorical statements of ministers of agriculture at international fora, are at variance with practice in rural areas.[18]

Despite an increasing awareness among policy-makers of the importance of women in agricultural production and harvesting, processing and storing food products, they tend to be invisible to many agricultural extension agents, agricultural credit bankers and to land administrators. They are not reached because of legal discrimination but mostly due to culture-based sexual bias. For example, the 1984 National Survey of Labour Force in Egypt shows that 38 per cent were women, but their share in landholdings was only 9.2 per cent according to the 1982 Census of Agriculture (Table 4.6 of the published results).

Whereas redistributive land laws do not discriminate between men and woman as land recipients, the administrators interpret 'household head' to mean the male heads. They tend to assume that the accrued benefits reach all members of the household, irrespective of intra-family variation in the distribution of labour, production and processing responsibilities. In land settlement schemes, allocation of land units is almost totally confined to male household heads on the assumption that women do not possess the physical strength required in these schemes. Consequently, women's access to landed property is virtually limited to marriage and inheritance arrangements. In the privatization of communally held land, not only do women tend to lose their long-established equal rights in land-use under customary tenure, but they are also deprived of self-produced food crops. In most cases, the allotment of individualized rights in land are pro-male and pro-cash crops. As substitutes, cash-exportable and food crops reallocate labour to the disadvantage of women.

Most of the present agricultural extension programmes in North Africa are geared towards improving the role of women as housewives and mothers, but not as farmers. Yet the female working people represent between 20 and 40 per cent of total economically active population in agriculture.[19] Apart from the prevailing cultural and customary bias against rural women among agricultural technocrats, their under-enumeration usually rests on procedure. Husbands respond to enumerations on behalf of their household members and they tend not to classify their wives or daughters as farmers, no matter how much they are involved in farming and animal husbandry.

The post-1970 rise in male migration noted earlier has far-reaching consequences on rural womens' responsibilities as temporary heads of households, both in type and amount of work. The added tasks are in addition to all year-round domestic workload, child care and livestock husbandry. Maintaining agricultural production on their absentee husbands' farming units is difficult without adequate support by local institutions (extension service, cooperative supply of inputs, lending credit and marketing the products). Micro studies on these effects and on changes in female participation in the rural labour market in affected localities are decidedly scarce. Similarly, we know little about the impact of high rate of illiteracy among female adult farmers and working girls on agricultural production and nutritional levels of children in rural North Africa. Instead, we find unhelpful generalization. The lesson learnt from past experience is that cultural constraints in rural areas cannot be altered by laws but only from within a process of social change.

Over the last four decades, there have been fundamental changes in the distribution of land and income for the benefit of the *fellaheen*. There has also been notable improvement in the quality of life in North African rural areas which were appallingly backward before independence. Nevertheless, and despite implementing several types of land reforms and rural development programmes, inequality, landlessness, infant mortality and illiteracy rates remain high.

Sudan, which is a land-abundant country, has followed a *laissez-faire*

TABLE 5

CHANGES IN THE DISTRIBUTION OF LAND, QUALITY OF LIFE AND RURAL POVERTY LEVELS, NORTH AFRICA, 1951–87

Countries in alphabetical order	Land Distribution: redistributive scale of land reforms — years of reform Laws and area redistributed as % of total arable land	Land Distribution: land recipients as % of total agricultural households	Land Distribution: Gini Coefficient of inequality in land distribution	Quality of Life Indicators: Nutrition average annual growth rate of calorie supply 1969–71 to 1979–81 %	Quality of Life Indicators: Infant Mortality (aged 0–1) reduction 1960–85 %	Quality of Life Indicators: Life Expectancy at birth increase 1960–85 %	Quality of Life Indicators: Rural Pop. with access to safe drinking water 1985–87 %	Quality of Life Indicators: Illiteracy percentage adult population — reduction between 1960–85 %	Rural Poverty Levels estimates of rural population living in poverty and year of estimate %
	1		2	3	4	5	6	7	8
Algeria	(1962, 70) 68	n.a.	n.a.	3.6 (2)	50 (2)	30 (2)	55 (3)	41 (2)	n.a.
Egypt	(1952, 61) 10	13	0.611 (1951) 0.348 (1965) 0.432 (1985)	2.2 (3)	44 (3)	33 (1)	56 (2)	21 (4)	56.1 (1951) 23.8 (1965) 17.8 (1982)
Libya	(1970–75) 15	13	n.a.	4.7 (1)	43 (4)	29 (4)	90 (1)	49 (1)	n.a.
Morocco	(1956, 63, 73) 4	3	0.755 (1974) 0.690 (1982)	0.7 (6)	42 (5)	25 (5)	27 (5)	15 (6)	45 (1977–85)
Sudan	no land reform		no complete census	1.0 (5)	32 (6)	20 (6)	10 (6)	20 (5)	70 (1983) 85 (1987)
Tunisia	(1956, 58, 64) 57	49	0.603 (1981)	2.0 (4)	68 (1)	31 (2)	31 (4)	22 (3)	26[A] (1966) 7 (1985) 47[B] (1966) 31 (1985)

Notes: n.a.: not available. Numbers in brackets in columns 3 to 7 are the ranking order of countries.
The Gini Coefficient is a measurement of the degree of inequality in distribution. This index lies between 0 and 1, the lower the index towards 0 the less the degree of inequality, and vice versa. [A] = World Bank estimate; [B] = ILO estimate.
Sources: Columns 1 & 2 calculated by the author from countries' reports and studies on the implementation of land reform programmes and the results of agricultural surveys and censuses, respectively. Column 3: *Fifth World Food Survey*, FAO, Rome, 1985, Appendix A. Columns 4, 5, 7: *World Development Report 1979 and 1987*, Indicators, World Bank, Oxford University Press. Column 6: *Human Development Report 1990*, UNDP, New York. The percentage of change is calculated from these Reports. Column 8: *Egypt*, El-Ghonemy (1990), Table 6.11 *Morocco*, World Bank cited in UNDP, 1990, op. cit., *Sudan*, Abu-Sheikha (1983) for the 1983 estimate and the World Bank Data Base for 1987. *Tunisia*, A 1966 estimate from World Bank and 1985 estimated by Tunisia's Institut National de la Statistique. ILO estimates[A] together with estimates A are explained in Radwan *et al.* (1991), Tables 4.6 and 4.10.

land tenure policy. Its state-determined pattern of agricultural growth has widened inter-regional inequality to the disadvantage of the large traditional rain-fed sector where most of the poor cultivators and all nomadic-pastoral population live.[20] Likewise, Sudan's indicators of quality of life and its UN Human Development index are the lowest, and its absolute poverty level is the highest among the six countries (see Tables 1 and 5). In its classification of all developing countries, UNICEF places Sudan in the category of 'Very high infant mortality'. Not only is the poverty level in rural Sudan very high, but it has also increased in the 1980s from 70 per cent to 85 per cent, according to the estimates presented in Table 5.

In the other five countries, the redistributive scope of their series of land reforms varies greatly; so do results. With the exception of Algeria and Libya, the redistributive scope of agrarian reforms in Egypt, Morocco and Tunisia excluded the wage-dependent landless workers from the transfer of property rights. Available estimates made in the 1980s suggest that they were approximately 30 per cent of total agricultural households in Egypt, 33 per cent in Morocco and 20 per cent in Tunisia.[21] The vulnerability of these landless families for under-nutrition and seasonal unemployment as well as their reliance on the imperfect grain market for calorie intake remain high.

The sequence of rural development actions suggest that the impulse of agrarian reforms has created a political environment conducive to the rapid development of villages, roads and access to safe drinking water in the countryside. Considering that more than half the total population is rural, the national indicators of nutrition, education and health given in Table 5 place Morocco (with its lowest scale of land redistribution) and Sudan at the bottom of the six countries as shown by the following ranking:

	Nutrition	*Infant Mortality*	*Life expectancy*	*Literacy*
Morocco	6	5	5	6
Sudan	5	6	6	5

These poverty characteristics are consistent with the high poverty levels of the two countries during the 1980s compared to other countries for which estimates are available. Likewise, among the six countries, Morocco and Sudan are also ranked at the bottom by the UNDP Human Development Index given earlier in Table 1.

The limited availability of statistical information on the size distribution of land measured in terms of the Gini Coefficient (L) and the percentage of rural population living in absolute poverty (P) makes it difficult to relate these two important variables (see definition of the Gini

Coefficient in Table 5). Moreover, there are conceptual differences among estimators in establishing a poverty line at a point in time. These problems are evident from the wide range of estimates made for Tunisia (see column 8 in Table 5). However, there do appear to be a few broad relationships. The Egyptian and Moroccan data suggest a positive correlation between inequality index L and P i.e. the higher L is, the higher the P, and vice versa. But the data for Tunisia do not follow this relationship. They indicate that, despite a relatively high inequality index of L, poverty levels are low, which suggest the importance of rural people's earnings from non-land assets and non-agricultural activities for alleviating rural poverty.

Therefore, a generalization on the direct relation between the reduction in land concentration, through the redistribution of landed property by land reforms on the one hand, and subsequent reduction in rural poverty levels on the other, is a simplification, without considering the influence of the several dynamic determinants of changes in poverty incidence. For example, the quick reduction in Egypt's rural poverty levels from 56.1 per cent in 1951 to 17.8 per cent in 1982 cannot be solely attributed to the partial land redistributive scale of the two reforms of 1952 and 1961. They redistributed 13 per cent of cultivated land to only 10 per cent of total agricultural households.[22] But we should not overlook the gains to the tenants which have been on a larger scale. The number of tenants whose rental payment was controlled was nearly one million, representing two-thirds of total landholders in 1961. The reduction in rental values (in real terms) by land reform law has been considerable. Likewise, earnings from the widespread ownership of non-land assets (livestock) and non-farm activities were estimated in 1973–74 at 60–64 per cent of total income of household beneficiaries. The post-1970 steady rise in real wages, together with the remittances from nearly 15 per cent of total working people in agriculture, migrating to neighbouring Arab countries, have significantly contributed to poverty alleviation.

When the Gini Index of L is considered together with agricultural growth rates given earlier in Table 1, the data show a weak association, i.e. having no clear observed linear relation. This applies to the growth rates of agricultural GDP at the two levels: total agricultural GDP and per capita income of agricultural labour force. Their weak relationship to the inequality index of L is perhaps due to omitting other important factors such as climatic events, percentage of irrigated area, technological change, variation in the area and output of the production of food and non-food exportable crops, pricing policy, etc.

On considering individual countries, we find varied relations. We know that Libya and Algeria have implemented an egalitarian policy in

TABLE 6
INEQUALITY INDEX OF LAND DISTRIBUTION AND AGRICULTURAL GDP GROWTH RATES, 1954–88

	Egypt	*Tunisia*	*Morocco*
Gini Coefficient of L inequality	0.35, 0.43	0.6	0.76, 0.69
Average annual rates of growth (%)	(1965) (1984)	(1981)	(1974), (1983)
total agricultural GDP			
1965–80	2.8	5.5	2.2
1980–88	2.2	2.4	6.6
per capita agricultural labour force			
1970–80	2.2	3.5	1.2
1980–88	1.2	0.6	3.8

Sources: 1. Gini Coefficient, calculated by the writer from land distribution statistics in CAPMAS for Egypt and the published results of Ågricultural Surveys (Enquête) for 1981 in Tunisia and for 1974 and 1983 in Morocco.

2. Agricultural GDP growth rates, see Table 1.

agriculture with strong state intervention. Both countries are also endowed with a flow of public revenue from oil and natural gas exports which has enabled their governments, through central planning, to allocate sufficient resources to modernize agriculture, expand irrigated areas, and to subsidize heavily the means of production. Consequently, their agricultural growth rates were the highest among the six countries during the period 1965–80; 10.7 per cent for Libya and 5.8 per cent for Algeria.[23] Having redistributed wealth and income they, together with Egypt and Sudan, could however not sustain the rates of growth during the subsequent period of 1980–88. In fact, Morocco realized during the latter period high growth rates of agricultural GDP at 6.6 per cent and real income per working person in agriculture at 3.8 per cent per annum. In spite of its high L, Moroccan growth rates are the highest among the six countries during that period. To understand the relations between agricultural growth and L index during the whole period of 1965–88, the corresponding data for the three countries whose L index is available are presented together in Table 6.

We have elsewhere conducted a regression analysis of these two variables (poverty level as dependent variable) for a larger sample of 20 developing countries, including Egypt and Morocco. The results are not statistically significant, and the coefficient of determination being very low at 0.04 indicates that only four per cent of the variation in agricultural

GDP growth rates is 'explained' by the degree of inequality of the size distribution of land.[24]

Our discussion suggests that despite government efforts and according priority in their development plans to food self-sufficiency since the 1960s, the North African countries have failed to feed their people from domestic food production. Nor have they sustained high rates of agricultural growth and increases in the real income per person working in agriculture. Food insecurity and food production instability are likely to continue in the 1990s if agriculture continues to be denied its capital needs, particularly rain-fed areas where most of the rural poor live, and if the rates of population growth remain very high. The share of health and education in total public expenditure in most of the countries is deplorably low, resulting in illiteracy rates higher than the weighted averages of the corresponding groups of developing countries. So are the years of life expectancy which in all North African countries are lower than the averages of low and middle-income economies, according to the World Bank classification.

The discussion and analysis of empirical evidence on equity and poverty characteristics suggest that: (a) the less the inequality of land distribution, the more likely that the benefits from agricultural growth reach the poor cultivators and the faster the alleviation of poverty would be; (b) the more egalitarian the agrarian structure, the more likely the quality of life is to improve faster in terms of nutrition, health and educational opportunities; and (c) the earnings of the rural people from non-land assets, international remittances and non-agricultural activities make significant contributions to alleviating rural poverty.

How governments would tackle the problems of food security and rural development presented in this article remain to be seen. But a new dimension in policy-making is anticipated: the influence of the rising moral force induced by the Islamic fundamentalists who are gaining strength in the political power structure. Their influence cannot be underestimated in rural areas where Islamic belief is strong and the incidence of deprivation is high. Foremost among the fundamentalists' demands is the strict application of the Islamic principles on what is permitted *halal* and what is prohibited *haram* in the Quran. The latter obligations apply to human conduct (individuals, organization and government) with regard to usury *riba*, other fraudulent transactions, exploitation, widening inequality, illegitimate profit-making and corruption in bureaucracy. Time will tell how these ethical principles of social welfare will be put into action with regard to the reform of present arrangements for agricultural credit, land mortgage, property rights in land and the protection of the entitlements of the rural poor.

NOTES

1. On the problems of definition and enumeration of pastoral nomads, see Ian Livingstone, *Pastoralism*, a study prepared for The Food and Agriculture Organisation of the United Nations(FAO), Rome, 1984. For a detailed discussion on the subject in the Maghreb countries, see Sliman Bedrani *Les Pasteurs et Agro-Pasteurs au Maghreb*, a study prepared for FAO (Rome, 1987).
2. United Nations, *Patterns of Urban and Rural Population Growth*, New York, 1980.
3. These changes are analysed in M.Riad El-Ghonemy, 'The Egyptian State and the Agricultural Land Market: 1810–1986', *Journal of Agricultural Economics*, Vol.43, No.2 (May 1992).
4. J. Birks and R. Sinclair, *International Migration in the Arab Region*, International Labour Organisation [ILO] (Geneva, 1980) pp.134–5.
5. This study was carried out in three Egyptian villages in 1986–87. See Richard Adams, *The Effects of International Remittances on Poverty, Inequality and Development*, International Food Research Institute [IFPRI] (Washington, DC, 1991).
6. The estimates on potential expansion are based on soil studies on potential cultivable lands until the year 2020 carried out by FAO. See *Atlas of African Agriculture*, Tables 3.02 and 3.16, FAO (Rome, 1986).
7. Ibid.
8. For the Egyptian estimate, see Adel al-Beltagy, 'Land reclamation schemes and expanding employment opportunities' in *Proceedings of the Symposium on Development of Employment Opportunities in Egypt*, Cairo, 20–22 Dec. 1987 (in Arabic).
9. W.D. Swearingen, *Moroccan Mirages: Agrarian Dreams and Deceptions 1912–1986* (London; I.B. Tauris 1988).
10. For a survey of the determinants of 1984–85 Famine in Sudan, see A. de Waal, *Famine That Kills, 1984–1985*, (Oxford: Clarendon Press, 1989).
11. Measurment of instability is sensitive to both the accuracy of data used and the index chosen. The index or the coefficient of variation estimated by UNCTAD is, in simple terms, the sum of the square of deviations of the *actual* food production in a given year from the *trend value*, divided by the sum of the square of the deviations from the average of actual production during the number of years. On the other hand, the FAO's index is 100 multiplied by the deviations and divided by the trend value. The index of instability is useful to policy-makers in the formulation of food security programme and the assessment of food imports.
12. The independence years are: Egypt, 1923; Libya, 1951; Morocco, 1955; Sudan, 1956; Tunisia, 1956; and Algeria, 1962.
13. For a detailed account of these imposed institutional changes, see Charles Issawi, *An Economic History of the Middle East and North Africa* (London: Methuen 1982), particularly Ch.VII.
14. Estimates for Egypt and Libya are based on data on expropriated and redistributed areas given in their progress reports. Those for Algeria and Morocco are calculated from data given in M.Riad El-Ghonemy (ed.). *Land Policy in the Middle East* (Rome: FAO, 1967). Information on the Sudan are taken from Arthur Gaitskell, *Gezira: A Story of Development in Sudan* (London: Faber, 1959).
15. See *World Development Reports 1988 and 1989*, development indicators, World Bank (Oxford University Press) and *Government Finance Statistics Yearbook*, International Monetary Fund (IMF), volumes VII-IX (Washington, DC). Share of agriculture is not disaggregated.
16. M.Riad El-Ghonemy, *The Political Economy of Rural Poverty: the case for land reform (London and New York: Routledge, 1990). For the data on Tunisia, see Samir Radwan et al, Tunisia: Rural Labour & Structural Transformation* (London: Routledge, 1991).
17. See note 15 for the sources.
18. These statements were made at the 18th Regional Conference for the Near East organized by FAO and held in Istanbul, March 1986. It was attended by the ministers of

agriculture and the subject was 'the role of women in food and agriculture in the Region'.

19. Censuses and labour surveys under-estimate the time allocated by rural women for productive work in agriculture which is considered the criterion for the economically active population. There is also a wide variation in estimates within the same country. For example, the Egyptian census of population of 1986 reports female share in agriculture at 19 per cent, while the Labour Survey of 1984 indicates the share at 39 per cent.
20. This statement is based on Ahmad Abu-Sheikha, *Towards the Alleviation of Rural Poverty in Sudan*, Poverty studies series, no.1 (Rome; FAO, 1983) and 'The Sudan: A Report of the Special Programming Mission', (Rome: International Fund for agricultural Development, 1988).
21. FAO study on 'Landlessness', 1986 (mimeographed) and the Tunisian government's 'Indicateurs socio-économiques permettant de surveiller et d'évaluer la réforme agraire et le développement rural' Institut National de la Statistique, 1982).
22. See the source (El-Ghonemy, 1990) cited in note 16, p.235.
23. See text, Table 1.
24. This is the result of a regression analysis presented in El-Ghonemy, 1990, p. 175 and Appendix A, op. cit.

[9]

Int. J. Middle East Stud. 13 (1981), 409–425 *Printed in the United States of America*

Alan Richards

AGRICULTURAL MECHANIZATION IN EGYPT: HOPES AND FEARS

> The fellah has never used tractors, reapers, binders, and threshing machines, and it is unlikely that he ever will. He is too poor, and in any case feels no need of intermediaries between him and the soil . . .
>
> H. H. Ayrout, *The Egyptian Peasant*, 1963.

Father Ayrout might be surprised by the Egyptian countryside today! Agricultural mechanization has been spreading rapidly, especially since 1973. Although national tractor censuses are notoriously unreliable because of the problems of treating old machines, current official estimates place the number of four-wheeled tractors at 25,000. Over 1,000 tractors have been manufactured at the Nasr works in Helwan every year since 1973; the number of tractor imports has quadrupled in the same period (see table 1). In Sharqiyya province, land preparation and threshing are almost entirely mechanized; plowing is over 85 percent mechanized and irrigation pumping nearly 75 percent in Behera, where plans are now being made to mechanize the harvest of rice, wheat, and *birsim* (Egyptian clover).[1] Indeed, agricultural extension agents and officials at the *muhafaza* (governorate) level repeatedly emphasize that mechanization is their primary problem and principal need. In this they echo government policy: The Five Year Plan calls for the mechanization of *all* operations by 1990. Major external aid agencies, such as the World Bank and USAID are assisting this effort: the former organization, for example, has a plan to mechanize completely the agriculture of Minufiyya and Sohag provinces. Nor is the current government alone in backing mechanization: the Left opposition likewise strongly supports the diffusion of tractors, threshers, and water pumps.[2] Mechanization is central to current and alternative agricultural development plans.

Mechanization advocates have high hopes. Among the principal alleged benefits of such technical change are lower production costs, higher farm incomes, increased land yields, improved timeliness of agricultural operations, increased meat and milk production, and improved health standards in rural areas.[3] Some believe that mechanization will save water and free children from manual labor.[4] All envision a virtuous circle of rising incomes, increased social welfare, augmented savings, and economic growth as a result of mechanization. In some cases, the tractor becomes almost a symbol of the entire agricultural and rural development process, a talisman of modernity on four wheels.[5]

TABLE I *Tractor stocks, flows, 1965–1978*

Year	Tractor park	Tractor imports	Domestic tractor production
1965	14,500		
1966	15,000		
1967	15,400		895
1968	15,572	3,719	731
1969	16,962	3,182	484
1970	17,500	1,901	1,071
1971	18,500	1,632	1,050
1972	18,500	1,670	937
1973	20,036	1,500	1,143
1974	21,000	1,952	1,259
1975	21,500	2,850	1,435
1976		3,398	2,500
1977		6,061	1,000
1978	29,784		1,260

Sources: Stock (1965–75); *FAO Production Yearbook;* 1978: Calculated from imports and domestic production, assuming a 10 percent depreciation rate; Imports and Domestic Production: al-Hossari's Report (1979).

There can be no question that such technical change brings important private benefits: greater leisure for the farm family, less exhausting and debilitating work, improved local transportation, and (perhaps) increased incomes. It is not difficult for an outsider to empathize with Egyptian farmers who want these benefits, or to sympathize with the hopes of agricultural planners and policy makers. Clearly, Egypt must increase her output, her land yields, and her labor productivity in agriculture. As is well known, the land area of Egypt is not likely to expand much in the next generation, while the population will be at least 65 million, and probably closer to 75 million by the year 2000. Land yields must therefore rise if production is to keep pace with such growth. It is also obviously desirable to raise agricultural labor productivity and incomes in agriculture.

Yet one cannot help feeling a certain disquiet at both the process of agricultural mechanization and the enthusiasm of policy makers. If mechanization displaces labor, workers may simply trade one kind of low productivity job for another or, indeed, for open unemployment, unless there is a very large expansion of employment in industry. Insofar as mechanization stimulates rural to urban migration, it will exacerbate the already severe housing and transportation crises. Of course, the cost of providing social overhead capital for housing, transportation, and employment for additional urbanites is much higher than for rural inhabitants. We know that mechanization reduces labor per unit of output in agriculture. The social question then becomes: Will it raise production enough to prevent a net decline in employment? There are also some further distributional questions, since it is normally thought that mechanization will reduce grain supplies but increase milk and meat production.

The purpose of this paper is to inject a note of skepticism into the current chorus of praise for mechanization in Egypt. At the least, the potential problems which current policies may engender do not seem to have received careful scrutiny. I do not wish to suggest that current policies are necessarily wrong, although that is possible. Rather, I would like to draw the attention of Egyptian and foreign economists and policy makers to some of the potential problems so that planning to cope with them may begin *now*, while there is still time. If the adjustment costs are large, developing programs and allocating resources to cover them cannot be done overnight. I also hope to indicate some gaps in our knowledge about mechanization in Egypt, and to indicate needed further research.

Three issues dominate discussions of agricultural mechanization in Egypt: (1) the opportunity cost of land used to grow animal fodder, especially birsim; (2) the impact of mechanization on land yields; and (3) the problem of excess demand for labor when using traditional techniques – the famous ''labor shortage.'' Let us examine these questions in turn.

Two major studies of Egyptian agriculture, the Ministry of Agriculture–USDA–USAID report, *Egypt: Major Constraints to Increasing Agricultural Productivity*, and H. A. el-Tobgy, *Contemporary Egyptian Agriculture*,[6] stress the need for mechanization to release land presently planted in fodder for other uses. El-Tobgy outlines the problem, and discusses the feed requirements of buffalo in some detail, but he does not go much further. The authors of the *Constraints* volume, on the other hand, are rather more concrete. They call for the mechanization of three specific operations: (1) water pumping, (2) land preparation, and (3) grain threshing. They stress that since the point is to reduce animal numbers, these three functions should be viewed as a package. Al-Hossari's *Report* takes a very similar position.

At first glance, this argument is appealing. Roughly half the fodder fed to animals is clover; perhaps 25 percent of the cropped area is devoted to animal fodder. Clearly, such land has alternative uses. The chopped straw and other crop residues that are used to feed the animals also have a significant opportunity cost. Since birsim provides enough fodder for only about half the year, fellahin strip green leaves off maize plants and shun Mexipak wheat because of its low straw yield. These practices are assumed to reduce yields substantially. The general argument will be familiar to students of agriculture in the Indian subcontinent, where it has been advanced as an explanation for mechanization in the Punjab.[7]

There are several problems with this viewpoint. First, a recent study of the practice of stripping maize stalks found, somewhat surprisingly, no relation between such a practice and maize yields. The reason appears to be that, as usual, fellahin are clever farmers: they only strip after flowering, never take the ear or above-ear leaf, and seldom take even the next leaf.[8] Second, some authorities estimate that birsim yields could be raised by as much as 95 percent.[9] As usual, drainage appears to be the main problem here. Also, very little research on breeding higher yielding types of birsim has been done. Since it is a nitrogen-fixing crop, the task may be difficult, but it certainly does seem to be an unexplored alternative: El-Tobgy, for example, believes that "the field is wide-open for real breeding achievements" in birsim.[10] If this additional fodder could be stored, the current animal population could be fed on clover year round, thereby eliminating the need to strip maize stalks at all. Depending on the relative costs of machinery and improved storage facilities, investing in the latter plus raising birsim yields might be the optimal response to a fodder shortage.

The opportunity cost of the land planted in birsim remains, of course. But here several additional points are in order. First, since birsim is a nitrogen-fixing crop, its removal from the crop rotation could have deleterious consequences for the yields of succeeding crops, usually cotton.[11] Birsim not only supplies nitrogen to the soil, but also contributes to the formation of a tilth and to the permeability, and hence drainage, of the soil. Perhaps more importantly, at present prices birsim itself is a highly profitable crop. Several factors contribute to this profitability. The government's policies of economic liberalization have increased money in the hands of fairly well-to-do urban consumers and have increased the numbers of foreign tourists in the country. These, in turn, have raised the demand for milk and meat products because of the high-income elasticity of such goods. There is also some evidence which suggests that the domestic price of meat and milk is above international prices, primarily owing to government import quotas for meat. Given these policies and assuming a growth in real incomes for Egyptians, it is highly unlikely that there will be any substantial reduction in the birsim area.[12]

The multiple functions that water buffaloes and cattle play for small farmers further reduces the likelihood that mechanization will eliminate them and thus free clover land for other uses. Most of these animals are owned by small holders. In addition to traction power, these animals fulfill four functions for small farmers. First and most important, they provide cheese and milk for home consumption; such dairy products constitute the main (often the only) source of animal protein for the fellahin. Second, any surplus can be sold. Third, the animals constitute a kind of insurance. If farmers have a bad year, or are faced with a major financial crisis, they can sell the animals. Fourth, it is likely that owning at least a share of such animals is necessary if a farmer wishes to lease additional land. Bell and Zusman have pointed to this phenomenon for share-cropping contracts in India; a similar situation prevailed in pre-reform Egypt.[13] Clearly, peasant-owned work animals are deeply imbedded in the current social structure. This, too, militates against any large reduction in their numbers and release of fodder land.

Such a conclusion is reinforced by the lack of spare parts, skilled mechanics, and repair shops in the rural areas. There is a general shortage of adequate spare parts; local manufacturers do not maintain an inventory of parts, but rather, manufacture them on demand.[14] Further, some twenty to thirty signatures are needed for spare parts delivery. There is an acute shortage of rural repair mechanics – hardly surprising, since they can make "at least 300% more in industry or abroad." The result is that farmers often must wait three to six months for repairs.[15] In such an environment, farmers retain their work animals as "spare parts on the hoof."

Several recent studies of Egyptian farm mechanization support the view that such technical change is unlikely to release much land for other uses. Both the World Bank study of the Minufiyya-Sohag mechanization project and the ERA 2000 report argue, as I do, that any gains from released land are at best long-run gains. In the near term they see the benefits of farm mechanization coming from increased quantity/improved quality of milk and meat production if animals do little or no farm work. The World Bank estimates that animals that stop work can double their milk yields. Some other studies in progress seem less optimistic.[16] It should be pointed out here that some 80 percent of farm animals' work time is devoted to irrigation work. Since this work uses relatively little adult labor (small boys normally tend the animals turning *saqiya*s [waterwheels]), and less adult *hired* labor (*tambour* [Archimedean screw] and *shaduf* [lifting device] labor being normally a family task), the social benefits of mechanizing irrigation should be particularly high. Indeed, the fact that mechanization of irrigation would displace primarily child labor, increase milk yields, increase the precision of irrigation, and have some potential health benefits indicates that water pumps should have the highest priority in mechanization. Curiously, what one finds instead is a combination of 65 h.p. tractors and *saqiyas*. One wonders what role government policy played in generating such a pattern of mechanization. Further, some current cost-benefit analyses purport to show that the internal rate of return on mechanical pumps is substantially lower than that of threshers and tractors, precisely *because* pumps save relatively little labor.[17] This raises the crucial question of the social opportunity cost of labor, a point taken up below.

The second principal argument advanced for mechanization is that it will raise yields per unit land. These gains can be divided into three parts: (1) the grain saved by mechanical threshing, (2) the benefits of deeper plowing, and (3) the benefits of more timely planting. It might be noted that the first benefit is thought to derive not merely from the technical superiority of mechanical drum threshers over *nurags* (threshing sleds), but also from reduced transportation losses when the grain is moved by tractor-drawn trailer rather than by camels. The gains from better tillage are variously estimated at between 5 percent and 15 percent. Roger Garrett estimates that rotary tillers can raise maize yields by 13 percent, cotton yields by 27 percent and beans by 14.6 percent. He reports that chisel ploughs would raise maize yields by 5 percent.[18] In 1968 the agricultural engineer Hilmi Abdal-Ghani Sa'ad asserted that rotary ploughs would raise maize yields 8 percent, cotton yields 18.2 percent and bean yields by 6.8 percent. Yet in this same symposium, these figures were questioned by the economist Amr Mohie Eldin, who retorted that there was little hard evidence that mechanization increased crop yields.[19] However, further support for the "pro-tractor" argument may be found both in the World Bank study and in one chapter of the ERA 2000 report. Both place the yield gains from better tillage at approximately 15 percent. In a fine example of a book written by a committee, a later chapter of the ERA 2000 report contradicts its earlier assertions, claiming that neither cotton nor wheat yields are affected by deeper ploughing, that only maize showed some response.[20]

All of this evidence is based on agricultural experiment station trials. The World Bank report adds that "evidence from other countries substantiates yield increases in the range of 5 percent to 15 percent." This is highly debatable. Consider a recent summary of the Indian evidence: "For all regions combined we are at best left with five or six instances out of 118 where large yield differences remain in the absence of equally large or larger differences in fertilizer use. These studies fail to provide much support for the yield increasing effect of tractor cultivation."[21] The problems inherent in generalizing from agricultural experiment station data to the field are well known. Indeed, the World Bank report explicitly recognizes this and points to evidence which suggests that farmers use tractors just as they would buffaloes: "Tractors with chisel ploughs can cultivate without prior irrigation, and when used twice can effectively cultivate to twenty-five or thirty centimeters. In practice, however, tractor ploughing does not at present result in an improvement in work quality and only in some cases does it improve timeliness as farmers delay cultivation to await the tractor."[22] *At present farmers plough no more deeply with chisel ploughs than they do with baladi ploughs.* This means that "under existing conditions, the only advantage in using mechanical ploughs as opposed to animal ploughing is the lower cost."[23] Such a perspective reinforces the importance of determining whether or not private and social costs for various inputs (like labor) actually coincide. It also makes it essential to have studies based on samples of actually mechanized and of nonmechanized farms to see if there is any real yield difference between them.

It is possible that such problems could be remedied with time and with an adequate extension of service to diffuse the proper use of machines in rural areas.[24] But the current extension program is woefully inadequate: it is understaffed and starved of resources and materials. The system offers few incentives for agents to live in the countryside. Peasants commonly perceive agents as regulators who enforce government decrees rather than as technical experts who dispense useful information. The agents' training leaves much to be desired; very little of it takes place in the countryside. If mechanization were to spread as the government plans, then a thoroughgoing reform of the extension service would be required. This is an important area for policy action, and is recognized as such by the Ministry of Agriculture. However, the magnitude and complexity of the problems do not engender optimism.

Finally, there is the timeliness factor. It should be stressed that although increased timeliness may raise crop yields, it is unlikely to increase the cropped area itself. With a cropping intensity of about 2.0 on non-orchard lands, most authorities agree that the maximum increase in the cropped area would be to 2.1 over the next five to ten years. Perhaps mechanization will increase the cropping intensity of rich farmers. These crop less intensively than their smaller neighbors because of the problems of supervising and controlling a large hired labor force. Mechanization might increase their cropping intensity; if so, by definition, such a change will not generate any additional employment. A recent study has found no relationship between tractor use and cropping intensity in the Fayyum.[25]

Turning to the effect of timeliness on yields, the World Bank suggests that at an aggregate level crop production could increase by some 5 percent. They argue that "even a saving of a few days can be expected to increase yields by one or two percent."[26] Using unmechanized techniques, it is apparently very difficult to plant at the optimal time, in part due to a lack of labor, in part because the native plough cannot be used for soil preparation unless the land is irrigated for five to seven days before ploughing. The problem is apparently most acute for planting the summer crops of maize, cotton and rice when they are preceded by wheat or birsim. Current price policies, which favor meat and milk at the expense of field crops, probably contribute to the practice of taking extra cuts of birsim and delaying the planting of cotton; ERA 2000 estimates that some 25 percent of cotton is planted late. One wonders whether mechanization would change this much if price policies remained the same. Maize and rice, on the other hand, usually follow wheat. Here mechanization of wheat threshing and land preparation would indeed permit earlier planting. The ERA 2000 report estimates that some 50 percent of both maize and rice is planted late. As a result, total rice and maize output per unit land is some 84 percent and 92 percent, respectively, of what it would be if there were no late planting.[27]

Although these results are plausible, three caveats are in order. First, the arguments on depth of ploughing are based on agricultural experiment station data, of which the relevance to actual field conditions is questionable. Indeed, one recent study finds no effect of timeliness on maize yields when looking at the actual practices of farmers, nor did it find any evidence that farmers using tractors plant maize earlier than those not doing so.[28] Second, the ERA 2000 report implicitly assumes that there is only one optimal planting date for maize for the whole of Middle and Lower Egypt, which seems unlikely, given the temperature differences in these areas. Third, historical evidence indicates that only complete mechanization eliminates, or even ameliorates, seasonal bottlenecks. In the U.S. cotton south, for instance, the initial effect of tractor mechanization was to increase the peak season demand for labor by nearly 50 percent.[29] This is encouraging from the point of view of labor displacement owing to partial mechanization. The problem, however, is that farmers continue to press their mechanization effect forward, which then eliminates the new, sharper seasonal bottlenecks – and most of the jobs. As noted above, there are already some signs of this process in Behera province.

In summary, current studies do not support the notion that mechanization will substantially increase cropping intensity or release fodder land for other uses. The primary benefits of threshing mechanization and land preparation appear to be grain saved during threshing and transportation, increased milk and meat production, and labor savings. Although there is experimental evidence that mechanization raises yields, this finding is not supported by any actual field studies of which I am aware. In short, there is no evidence that tractor farms have higher yields or cropping intensities than unmechanized farms.

Augmented meat and milk supplies are another alleged benefit of mechanization. The increase in meat might simply be that which is gained by retaining former work animals and then holding their feed rations constant. Mechanization advocates, however, more commonly envision an enlarged cattle industry, which, in turn, would require additional resources. This raises some serious distributional questions on the commodity demand side. As the *Constraints* authors note, "Per capita supplies of maize and sorghum grains for human consumption would be reduced, but dietary levels would be improved by the projected increase in the supply of livestock products."[30] If livestock production is to be expanded, the former assertion seems likely, the latter highly improbable. Both the urban and the rural poor consume proportionally much more maize than do the urban middle classes and foreign tourists. The *Constraints* authors acknowledge that these latter are the principal consumers of meat and milk. It is not plausible that the poor will be able to substitute meat for the grain which has now become more expensive because of reduced supply. A much more likely scenario would be: (1) the reduction in grain supplies increases grain prices which (2) leads to a reduction in the poor's consumption of grain and (3) to a proportionally larger reduction in their consumption of meat because of the large income effect which an increase in grain prices represents for such consumers and the higher income elasticity of meat and milk products.[31] The high grain:meat conversion ratio makes it very likely that increased meat supplies will fail to offset such a dynamic. The problem here is especially severe if, as many experts believe, the primary nutrition problem in Egypt is undernutrition (i.e., not enough calories) rather than malnutrition (although pellagra does continue to be a problem in some areas).

Given the importance of labor savings in the sum of benefits of agricultural mechanization, it is essential to look at the conditions of labor supply. There are, of course, indications of increasingly tight labor markets. Money wages of agricultural laborers have risen some 350 percent in the last ten years. There is disagreement on the trend of real wages. If, however, we use the rural Consumer Price Index as a deflator, we find that real wages have risen some 150 percent in the last ten years. Further, impressionistic evidence suggests that workers usually stop work at around 12:00 noon or 2:00 P.M., and that they demand (and receive) such "fringes" as meals, tea, and cigarettes. All of these indicate an improved bargaining power for rural workers; they also help to explain farmers' private desires to mechanize. If the cost data in table 2 are reliable, the more rapid rise of labor costs may act as a "focusing device," inducing the shift to more mechanized techniques.

The evidence, however, is insufficient to establish that the social opportunity cost of labor has been rising relative to that of capital. Insofar as "labor shortage" means "seasonal peaks in labor demand" (which is al-Hossari's conception), we have seen that there is reason to question whether the partial mechanization envisioned for 1985 will improve matters. Further, not surprisingly,

TABLE 2 *Production costs for field crops, 1972–1976*

Year:	1972	1973	1974	1975	1976
Labor Costs as Percent of Variable Costs per Feddan for:					
Wheat	26%	27%	26%	31%	32%
Rice	33	34	36	40	43
Maize	33	35	36	41	44
Cotton	46	48	51	53	55
Rent (L.E. per feddan)					
Wheat	15.46	15.52	16.45	18.07	18.37
Rice	10.95	11.90	13.43	14.82	17.45
Maize	12.08	12.58	13.29	15.02	18.91
Cotton	25.14	25.27	26.1	26.11	32.00

Source: Calculated from *Al Iqtisad Al Zira'i*, Vol. 2, Section 35, 1978. Cairo: Ministry of Agriculture, Center for Agricultural Economic Research and Statistics.

both capital and operating costs of mechanized techniques are subsidized. A variety of loan sources and terms are available: in general the rate of interest on tractor loans does not exceed 12 percent, and may be as low as 5 percent.[32] With an inflation rate of perhaps 20 percent per year, the real rate of interest on such loans is negative. Needless to say, this does not even remotely reflect the opportunity cost of capital to the Egyptian economy or to the agricultural sector. On the other hand, the proposal to increase the percentage of locally manufactured tractors to 62 percent by 1985 works in the opposite direction. The value added of such "reassembly" factories may well be negative and a 35 percent ad valorem tariff will be imposed;[33] such policies would, of course, raise the domestic price of tractors. Operating expenses are less ambiguous: roughly 50 percent of the international price of diesel fuel is subsidized to Egyptian farmers. Since hydroelectric power is fully used, additional electric power for pumps and stationary threshers must come from the new gas- and petroleum-fired generating stations now under construction. Assuming that the opportunity cost is equal to the marginal cost of electricity at international prices, Egyptian electricity cost L.E. .093 per kilowatt hour in 1979, while users paid only L.E. .015 per kilowatt hour.[34]

Given the increases in petroleum exports, workers' remittances, and tourists' spending, it could be that capital has become increasingly abundant in the Egyptian economy. Some observers seem to think so.[35] Others believe that the reduced flow of Saudi and other Arab investment in Egypt has not been offset by concomitant inflows of Western capital.[36] Nor would it be prudent to rely on remittances for long-range capital supply, as the Turkish case illustrates. Ankara incurred substantial foreign debts to finance development projects when overseas remittances were high, and now has to try to repay them when such payments are much lower.[37] Further, the agricultural sector has numerous domestic competitors for such scarce capital. If Egypt is to accelerate her economic development, she must embark on a large-scale expansion of labor-intensive industry and on the reconstruction of her infrastructure. The capital costs here are staggering. Further, given the likely persistence of inflation in OECD countries, the prices of imported machinery (or of parts for locally assembled machines) are likely to continue their upward climb. The international price of fuel, both diesel and gasoline, may also continue to increase.

This point must be emphasized: One must base a social policy for farm mechanization not merely on present conditions (which I have argued by no means ambiguously support current policies), but also on projections of future scarcities. In addition to the problems of future capital costs, several points stand out. First, population growth will continue; under the best of assumptions, it will reach perhaps 55 million by 1990. Indeed, for all the talk of rural "labor shortages," the agricultural labor force continues to expand, albeit at a sharply diminished rate.[38] Second, the capacity of Cairo to absorb new migrants has long since been surpassed. Present rural to urban migration is stimulated by the current construction boom in Cairo, the departure of some 40 percent of construction workers for the Gulf, and the subsidized costs of urban living. The latter will presumably continue, since the urban poor could not survive without them. They do not, of course, reflect the real social opportunity costs of the resources used. The construction boom is overwhelmingly concentrated in upper middle class and luxury construction—at least 70 percent of new units fall into this category.[39] Such booms are notoriously short-lived; the United States in the 1920s provides a graphic example. Of course, there is enough construction work in Egyptian cities to occupy the urban population for many years to come. But such work would require either effective demand from the poor or a large-scale program of public construction. Neither seems likely in the near future, despite recent government pronouncements. The creation of "satellite cities" in the desert to relieve pressure on Cairo will, of course, require enormous funds.

Nor is it clear how long overseas migration, another alleged source of reduced labor supply, will persist. One recent study estimates that (1) overseas migration of Egyptians is as low as 400,000 (in 1975), and (2) that these numbers are likely to decline in the near future as the OPEC countries complete the "construction phase" of their development.[40] The current number of Egyptians abroad is almost certainly over 1 million, but the weight of the available evidence supports Birks and Sinclair's second point. To be sure, the new Saudi Five Year Plan projects very large increases in construction, which alone employs at least one-third of all Egyptians in that country.[41] However, one should not conclude that the increased spending will lead to an increase in the demand for Egyptian labor. Saudi construction methods are becoming increasingly capital intensive, and Egyptian labor in the Gulf faces severe competition from South, Southeast, and Far East Asian labor. All Saudi government construction contracts in 1979 were given to Korean firms. Further, Egypt's political relations with both Libya and Saudi Arabia are highly uncertain. Perhaps the most comprehensive study of the Gulf construction industry, based on the research of over one hundred fifty British banks with Middle Eastern branches, predicts a deceleration in construction activity in the principal labor-importing states, simply because "basic infrastructure is now well in place."[42]

The essential problem is that the growth of population and the labor force must make very heavy demands on both capital resources and overseas migration if open unemployment is to be avoided. Mechanization advocates hope that the combination of new industrial jobs, overseas migration, and the virtuous circle of higher incomes for farmers leading to increased spending on labor-intensive goods will create enough demand to absorb the growing supply.[43] Again, one may be skeptical. Clearly the manufacture of tractors will in itself create few jobs: tractor manufacture, like automobile assembly, is highly capital intensive, with very large economies of scale.[44] Indeed, al-Hossari's report estimates that the new joint-venture assembly plant with Massey-Ferguson will create a whopping 731 jobs, of which 412 are skilled or supervisory positions. Threshers seem somewhat more promising, but here too, there are some problems. Most of the axial flow threshers now spreading in the rural areas are manufactured in plants with more than fifty employees; in such plants the capital:labor ratio is somewhere near L.E. 3,000.[45] Although we have our latter-day Mandevilles like John Mellor[46] we also have our modern Marxes like Raj Krishna: Using a linear programing/input-output framework, he found that in the Indian Punjab, whose agronomy closely resembles Egypt's, mechanization would generate net unemployment, even under generous assumptions about the rate of economic growth and about the role of mechanization in stimulating that growth.[47]

Although adequate data to replicate Krishna's methodology for Egypt is as yet unavailable, some simple calculations can be illustrative. It is commonly thought that approximately 300,000 new jobs must be created annually to keep up with new additions to the labor force. It has recently been estimated that for investments under Law 43 (the "*infitah*" policy), about L.E. 14,000 of investment is required to create one job.[48] If we assume that fear of inflation would induce the government to constrain investment to under 3 billion pounds annually, and if all investments were of the infitah variety, only 21,400 jobs would be created. Taking a different approach, one can note that mechanization advocates have placed the total savings due to mechanization at approximately 150 million pounds.[49] It seems likely that this is an upper boundary, since we have seen reason to doubt the productivity gains due to mechanization upon which such a number is based. Suppose, improbably, that all of this increased income were invested. If the incremental capital:labor ratio (i.e., investment needed to create one job) were roughly L.E. 3,000, then some 46,880 jobs would be created. Only if the investment per job ratio were as low as L.E. 500 would such investment generate enough jobs to keep up with the growth of the labor force.

Of course, not all of the funds will be invested. Indeed, the current evidence suggests that the marginal propensity to save is very low.[50] Consumption spending out of additional income could generate additional employment if it is concentrated on locally produced, labor intensive goods. There is insufficient evidence to evaluate this possibility at present. It should be noted, however, that so far I have only discussed the investment needed to create jobs for additions to the labor force; I have said nothing about the problems of either rural labor displaced by mechanization or overseas Egyptians returning as a result of changed conditions in the political economy of the Oil States. The latter has been discussed above; the former is no less reasonable a fear: some estimates have the numbers of man-hours per feddan falling from sixty to less than two for wheat, and from ninety to less than four for cotton.[51] These figures are for full mechanization; even partial mechanization, however, would greatly reduce the amount of labor required per feddan.[52] And, as we have seen, there are reasons to suppose that it may be difficult to limit farmers to partial mechanization.

Obviously, these calculations are extremely crude; research is underway to obtain more rigorous estimates of the employment consequences of farm mechanization. Nevertheless, the risks of a decreasing rate of migration abroad for employment, the fairly high incremental capital:labor ratio, the labor-displacing potential of mechanization, and the inexorable growth in the domestic labor force should make one cautious about labor-displacing technical change. We also clearly need more research on (1) the extent to which planned mechanization will displace labor, (2) the structure, especially the incremental capital:labor ratios, of rural small-scale industry, and (3) the long-run potential for continuous overseas migration.

Migration is not the only commonly cited cause of the alleged "labor shortage" in agriculture. Some argue that the price policies which favor meat and milk production have led to a withdrawal of women and children from the labor market to household animal husbandry.[53] As is well known, women and children do perform a wide variety of agricultural tasks and also work as hired laborers. Usually, however, they are employed for harvesting and pest control. There is no evidence of which I am aware which suggests that such operations are the critical labor constraint. On the contrary, we have seen that wheat threshing and land preparation for maize, rice, and cotton constitute the principal bottlenecks. Such jobs are more commonly performed by men than by women and children.

The experience of military service, the guarantee of government jobs to veterans, and expanding rural education may also reduce the numbers of rural workers. Indeed, such social phenomena may be the principal force slowing the growth of the agricultural labor supply. Spreading education is obviously highly desirable and hopefully will continue and accelerate in the near future. Equally obviously, more educated young people are reluctant to engage in the back-breaking work of unmechanized agriculture. Yet, again, some skepticism is in order. Even the Ministry of Education does not claim that all rural male (much less female) children are enrolled in primary school. At best, 75 percent are enrolled, and some experts place the figure nearer to 65 percent.[54] If roughly 30 percent of male children do not attend school, with population growth the number of male illiterate entrants into the labor force will rise every year. The military picture is even clearer. The numbers of men in the armed forces have risen by almost one-third (from 298,000 to 395,000) between 1973 and 1978.[55] Since all of those who served in the October War were given government jobs, their labor was withdrawn from the private labor market. It is well known, too, that Egyptian veterans, like soldiers everywhere, are often reluctant to return to village life after a tour of duty. Although it ill behooves Americans, especially these days, to tell other countries to reduce their military spending, one might ask whether the rising trend of men under arms is either economically sustainable or politically necessary. Here again, it is not obvious that future conditions will resemble the recent past.

In any case, the important question remains: What jobs will be available for the newly educated or recently discharged youths who leave the countryside to seek their fortunes in the cities? The above calculations here indicate the magnitude of the problem for creating industrial jobs. Of course, "government services," not industry, is the fastest growing source of employment. The problem seems to be one of social organization; as education spreads people move from the fields into government offices. Although the conditions of work are infinitely superior in the latter, and although the individual is undeniably better off, a case could be made that a fellah with a hoe has higher productivity than many a government functionary. Society may experience little, if any, gain. Indeed, since the functionary has a higher level of consumption, such changes are probably not sustainable over the long run. If they are to be provided with productive work, considerable changes in work habits, expectations, and relative status ascriptions, as well as massive capital spending, will be necessary. But we have seen that such spending may not be available and would raise the opportunity cost of capital for the agricultural sector even higher. If social changes of such magnitude are contemplated, a different, equally difficult, but probably cheaper alternative might be to improve the quality and status of village life.[56]

A final consideration in agricultural mechanization is the profit squeeze argument. This view holds that wages have been rising more rapidly than prices, largely because of government policy, but also, perhaps, because of oligopsony in marketing. There is evidence which supports this hypothesis.[57] But if this problem were truly acute, we would expect to observe falling land rents and a bearish market for agricultural land. In fact, we observe the opposite.[58] And even if the profit squeeze were severe, it is not obvious that a change in price policies, rather than mechanization, might not be the appropriate response. Farmers may mechanize to farm the land themselves, and thereby get around laws guaranteeing security of tenure to tenants. Here, too, it is hardly obvious that this is in society's interest.

CONCLUSION

I have argued that there are considerable grounds for skepticism about the net social benefits of agricultural mechanization in Egypt. The evidence on land yields and crop intensification is moot, at best. The distributional consequences of increased milk and meat production at the expense of food grains are unsavory. The extent, and especially the persistence of a reduced quantity of labor supplied at a given wage are open to doubt. Insofar as the current trend toward mechanization has been induced by government policies rather than by changes in social opportunity costs, it is not obvious that further mechanization is the socially optimal response to the bottlenecks and anomalies which such decisions engender. The question must be asked: If all agricultural operations are to be mechanized by 1990, where will the people displaced by such mechanization be employed? Where will the capital come from to create their new jobs? What will happen if the overseas migrants return? Where will all of these people live?

Much of the difficulty in assessing the wisdom of current mechanization policies stems from the lack of sufficiently careful and detailed studies. The truth is, we do not know whether mechanized farms have higher yields than nonmechanized ones; we do not know what capital is worth to the agricultural sector; we do not know whether there is a "labor shortage"; we do not know how long such a shortage is likely to last, nor what has caused it. It is disturbing that vital policy decisions with long-term consequences were made in such a knowledge vacuum.

Clearly, planners are caught in a cruel dilemma. Who can deny the desirability of eliminating the exhausting work of plowing with *gamusa* (water buffalo) and *mihrat* (Egyptian plow) or of laboring with a *fas* (hoe)? Who could deny that freeing children from field labor or from tending *saqiyas* would be an enormous stride forward for rural Egypt? Who would deny that they, too, would seek work in the cities if they were given the same choices as discharged Egyptian rural soldiers? But the removal of jobs from landless, hired workers, the poorest of the poor, should give us pause, as should the other probable distributional consequences of mechanization. If agriculture does not at least retain the current number of jobs, the already horrendous difficulties of the cities will be exacerbated. Father Ayrout may have been correct to say that "to mechanize agriculture will . . . overthrow a way of life which has grown up as the only one suitable for an abundant population on a limited soil."[59] But, of course, that same way of life imposed terrible costs on the fellahin. As so often, it is the peasants who will pay the costs of policy decisions.[60]

It has not been my purpose to try to dissuade Egyptian farmers and agricultural planners from mechanizing their agriculture. The process is probably far enough advanced to be irreversible. Rather, I hope that the likely problems and possible disappointments of such a strategy are confronted immediately, so that the actual course of technical change may be designed to minimize the dislocations. Much more needs to be done to encourage the growth of rural small-scale industry – probably the only real hope for sustained growth of incomes and jobs. There is at least the hope that the tensions of such changes may provide a source of dynamism to the economy,[61] if the problems are anticipated and planned for. The future welfare of the entire country may depend upon it.

UNIVERSITY OF CALIFORNIA, SANTA CRUZ

NOTES

Author's note: Information for this paper was gathered during three trips to Egypt in 1979 and 1980, while I was working for the Agricultural Development Systems Project of the Ministry of Agriculture, University of California USAID. Neither the Project nor the sponsoring institutions bears the least responsibility for the views expressed here. I would like to thank Frank Child, Jim Fitch, Nicholas Hopkins, and Philip Martin for helpful comments on an earlier draft.

[1]Conversations with agricultural economists at Zagazig University; conversation with Abd ar-Rahman Shazli, Agricultural Director, Behera Governorate.

[2]See, e.g., Izz al-Din Kamil, *Al-Zira'at al-'Aliyya* (Cairo, 1976), passim; Fathī 'Abdel Fattāh, *Al-Qariah al-Misriyya Bayn al-Islah w'al-Thawra, 1952–1970* (Cairo, 1974), pp. 170–184.

[3]This information comes from an unpublished, untitled Arabic report prepared for the Office of the Undersecretary of Agriculture for Engineering Affairs. From the text it appears to have been done in 1979. I am indebted to Dr. Eng. A. M. al-Hossari, Undersecretary of Agriculture for Engineering Affairs, for showing me this report (hereafter al-Hossari's "Report").

[4]Izz al-Din, p. 124.

[5]Ibid., pp. 106–107.

[6]U.S. Department of Agriculture, Cooperating with the U.S. Agency for International Development and the Egyptian Ministry of Agriculture, *Egypt: Major Constraints to Increasing Agricultural Productivity*, United States Department of Agriculture Foreign Agricultural Economic Report No. 120 (Washington, D.C., 1976), hereafter *Constraints*; H. A. el-Tobgy, *Contemporary Egyptian Agriculture* (2d ed.; Cairo, 1976).

[7]C. Hanumantha Rao, "Farm Mechanization in a Labour-Abundant Economy," *Economic and Political Weekly*, Annual No., pp. A–201–211, February, 1972; Richard H. Day and Inderjit Singh, *Economic Development as an Adaptive Process: The Green Revolution in the Indian Punjab* (Cambridge, 1977).

[8]James B. Fitch, Ahmad A. Goueli, and Mohammad el-Gabely, "The Cropping System for Maize in Egypt," paper presented to the Food and Agricultural Organization workshop on "Improved Farming Systems in the Nile Valley," Cairo, May 8–14, 1979.

[9]World Bank, Report on Egyptian Agriculture (Washington, D.C., 1978), p. 35.

[10]El-Tobgy, p. 135. This is, of course, a worldwide problem. As Day and Singh argue in their study of the Indian Punjab, "When animals provide the main source of farm power, greater attention must be paid to finding the ways and means of keeping this source cost effective, at least in the short run" (p. 177).

[11]Birsim precedes about 80 percent of the cotton crop.

[12]World Bank, "Arab Republic of Egypt: Agricultural Development Project (Minufiyya-Sohag); Staff Appraisal Report, 1977," p. 40. Recent field research has found that birsim's return over variable costs is roughly 200 percent that of wheat, 800 percent that of rice, 255 percent that of maize, and 133 percent that of cotton. I am indebted to Dr. Gene Quenemeon of Montana State University for this information.

[13]Clive Bell and Pinhas Zusman, "A Bargaining-Theoretic Approach to Crop-Sharing Contracts," *American Economic Review*, 66 (Sept., 1976), pp. 578–588; Alan Richards, "Land and Labor on Egyptian Cotton Farms, 1882–1940," *Agricultural History*, 52, 4 (Oct., 1978), 503–518.

[14]ERA 2000, Inc., *Further Mechanization of Egyptian Agriculture* (Gaithersburg, Md., 1979), pp. ix–9.

[15]IBRD, 1977, A2, p. 11.

[16]Al-Hossari's "Report" places the gains at 33 percent, p. 10.

[17]IBRD, 1977, pp. 13. Diesel fuel is also subsidized (see below, p. 417).

[18]Roger Garrett, "Impressions with Respect to Mechanization," USAID mimeo, 1978. These numbers are cited repeatedly by students of Egyptian farm mechanization; they also appear, for example, in Izz al-Din, p. 115, and al-Hossari's "Report," p. 12. They all appear to have the same source: a set of trials conducted at the Cairo University experimental farm.

[19]"Debate on Egyptian Agricultural Mechanization," *L'Egypte Contemporaine*, 331 (Jan., 1968), 191–209 (in Arabic).

[20]IBRD, 1977; ERA 2000, incl. chaps. iv and x.

[21]Hans Binswanger, *The Economics of Tractors in the Indian Sub-Continent: An Analytical Review* (Hyderabad, 1978), p. 19.

[22]IBRD, 1977, A1, p. 3.

[23]IBRD, "Arab Republic of Egypt: Agricultural Development Project (Minufiyya-Sohag), Staff Appraisal Report, 1978," p. 16. Al-Hossari also recognizes this point (interview of March 1980, Cairo).

[24]A point recognized by Izz al-Din, pp. 144 ff.

[25]Preliminary data from the Ford Foundation Farm Management Survey. I am indebted to James B. Fitch for this information.

[26]IBRD (Minufiyya-Sohag), 1978, p. 38.

[27]ERA 2000, Inc., pp. x, 45, 51.

[28]Fitch et al., pp. 7, 11.

[29]Richard H. Day, "The Economics of Technological Change and the Demise of the Share-cropper," *American Economic Review*, 57, 3 (June, 1967), 427–449; Day and Singh, chap. 6.

[30]*Constraints*, p. 15.

[31]Cf. John W. Mellor, "Food Price Policy and Income Distribution in Low Income Countries," *Economic Development and Cultural Change*, 27, 1 (Oct., 1978), 1–26. Of course, the poor may be protected from such effects by government subsidies. In that case the government would have to increase its food imports, thereby reducing foreign exchange and raising the social opportunity cost of capital.

[32]ERA 2000; al-Hossari's "Report," p. 8.

[33]al-Hossari's "Report," p. 10.

[34]I am indebted to Dr. Gene Quenemeon for this information.

[35]*Business Week*, Sept. 24, 1979, p. 74. Nazli Choucri, Richard S. Eckaus, Amr Mohie-Eldine, "Migration and Employment in the Construction Sector: Critical Factors in Egyptian Development," Cairo University/Massachusetts Institute of Technology (1978).

[36]See, e.g., the report of Mahmoud Marzouk of the LINK project, in *Business Week*, Oct. 22, 1979, pp. 96, 100.

[37]See below p. 15 on possible trends in Egyptian labor migration.

[38]The agricultural labor force is reported to have changed as follows:

1971	4,056,900
1972	4,122,800
1973	4,162,800
1974	4,212,400
1975	4,218,900
1976	4,222,900

I have been unable to locate more recent figures. Source: Ministry of Agriculture, Center for Agricultural Economics Research.

[39]John Waterbury, "Urbanization and Income Distribution in Egypt," Princeton University Income Distribution Project (Princeton, N.J., 1979), draft, mimeo.

[40]J. S. Birks and C. A. Sinclair, *International Migration and Development in the Arab Region* (Geneva, 1980), p. 151. The study was based on 1975 data. It is very likely that the current number of Egyptians abroad is probably between one and one-and-one-half million.

[41]Choukri, Eckaus, and Mohie Eldine, p. 13.

[42]Economist Intelligence Unit, "Saudi Arabia," 3rd Quarter, 1979, p. 18; Gerard Castoriades, "Bouncy Contracting Market Draws Far East Challenge," *Middle East Economic Digest*, June 6, 1980, p. 11.

[43]Izz al-Din, pp. 132–135.

[44]Robert Kudrle (*Agricultural Tractors* [Lexington, Mass., 1977], chap. 2), estimates that the least cost plant size for tractor manufacture is a factory producing at least 90,000 tractors per year. He notes that the entire non-communist world could be served by no more than eight plants of such size.

[45]I am indebted to Ahmad Bahgat of the Catholic Relief Service, Cairo, for information on threshing manufacture. The capital:labor ratios are from K. M. Barbour, *The Growth, Location, and Structure of Industry in Egypt* (New York, N.Y., 1972), pp. 118 ff.

[46]Bernard de Mandeville, *The Fable of the Bees* (London, 1714); John Mellor, *The New Economics of Growth: A Strategy for India and the Developing World* (Ithaca, N.Y., 1976).

[47]Raj Krishna, "Measurement of the Direct and Indirect Employment Effects of Agricultural Growth with Technical Change," in Lloyd G. Reynolds, ed., *Agriculture in Development Theory* (New Haven, 1975), pp. 297–323. Some other studies have contradicted this finding, arguing that because tractors had promoted large increases in cropping intensity, they may have increased the demand for labor. See Shyamal Roy and Melvin G. Blase "Farm Tractorization, Productivity and Labor Employment: A Case Study of Indian Punjab," *Journal of Development Studies*, 14 (Jan., 1978), 193–209. However, as Binswanger notes (p. 16) in general in India, tractors have not led to increased cropping intensities. And we have seen that there is little likelihood that cropping intensities will increase markedly in Egypt. (The average cropping intensity in Egypt is well above the intensity achieved using tractors in the Punjab).

[48]I am indebted to Professor Henry J. Bruton of Williams College for this information.

[49]Izz al-Din, p. 140; al-Hossari's "Report," p. 9.

[50]I am indebted to Professor Henry J. Bruton for this information.

[51]Izz al-Din, pp. 110, 118.

[52]Mechanization of plowing and threshing alone and retaining hand labor for harvesting might reduce the man-hours per feddan of wheat to 18 (Izz al-Din, p. 110).

[53]Ilya Harik and Abdel-Basit Hassan, "Socio-economic Profile of Rural Egypt" (Cairo, March 15, 1979), mimeo.

[54]I am indebted to Professor Saad Gadalla of the American University in Cairo for this information.

[55]International Institute for Strategic Studies, *The Military Balance* (London, Annual Issues 1973–1979).

[56]Such changes would probably include some mechanization. The problem seems to be the classic one that the techniques need to relieve drudgery while minimizing labor displacement do not currently exist.

[57]Data from the Center for Agricultural Economics Research of the Ministry of Agriculture show that whereas the average yearly percentage rise in price for wheat, maize, rice, and cotton in 1975–1978 was 6⅔ percent, 12⅔ percent, 18⅔ percent, and 10⅔ percent, respectively, costs of the same crops rose 14⅓ percent, 20 percent, 13⅓ percent, and 14⅔ percent, respectively, during the same period (see table 2). Birks and Sinclair argue that even if migration is as low as they believe, the highly segmented labor market in Egypt magnifies shortages. This is an interesting hypothesis, and further work is underway to test it. Casual observation generates some skepticism, however. For example, it is not unusual to see large numbers of women working on construction sites and in agricultural tasks that were formerly performed only by men.

[58]Land prices and rents are controlled, of course. As usual, the market works around such controls; in some areas land rents doubled from 1978 to 1979 (cf. also table 2).

[59]H. H. Ayrout, *The Egyptian Peasant* (Boston, 1963), p. 53.

[60]As so eloquently argued by Barrington Moore, Jr., *Social Origins of Dictatorship and Democracy* (Boston, 1966).

[61]Cf. Albert Hirschman, *The Strategy of Economic Development* (New Haven, 1958).

[10]

FARMERS AND THE FAILURE OF AGRIBUSINESS IN SUDAN

Stephen Kontos

NOT more than a decade ago, Sudan was widely regarded as the future "breadbasket" of the Arab world, a vast, fertile land with abundant water from the Nile watershed. International lenders and oil-rich Arab investors poured more than $2 billion into Sudan's agricultural sector between 1975 and 1985, yet, during this period, its farm productivity stagnated and export earnings actually declined.[1] For a country in which 40 percent of the gross national product and more than 90 percent of its export revenues come from agriculture, such a failure is a bitter one indeed.

The failure of large-scale commercial agriculture in Sudan was evident even before the economic crisis, political instability, and natural disasters of the mid-1980s. Of all the major agricultural projects started in the 1970s and early 1980s, not one can be said to have been a commercial success.[2] Those still

1. Between 1974 and 1981, the period when most projects became operational, the annual volume of three major exports—cotton, groundnuts, and sesame—fell from an average of 168,000 tons, 99,000 tons, and 70,000 tons to 81,000 tons, 43,000 tons and 41,000 tons, respectively. World Bank, *Sudan: Investing for Economic Stabilization and Structural Change* (Washington, DC: World Bank, 1982), Report No. 3551a-SU. For annual production figures of the major crops during this period, see Brian D'Silva, *Sudan: Policy Reforms and Prospects for Agricultural Recovery After the Drought* (Washington, DC: US Department of Agriculture, 1985).

2. Major foreign investments in agriculture during the 1970s included the Kenana Sugar Corporation, the Arab Sudanese Blue Nile Company, the Faisal Agricultural Corporation, the Tenneco Sahara Agricultural Venture, the Seleit Food Company, the Egyptian-Sudanese Integrated Company, Damazine Corporation, along with the Suki, Junaid, and Haggar al-Salaya sugar projects. The Triad Corporation of Adnan Khashoggi had rights for 500,000 feddans of undeveloped land, and 250,000 feddans were committed to Tenneco Inc. of Houston, but neither company used the land. (A feddan equals 1.038 acres.)

Stephen Kontos is a US foreign service officer and formerly a representative of Tenneco in the Sudan from 1982 to 1986. The views expressed in this article are solely the author's and do not necessarily reflect those of the US government or the Department of State.

operating have done so at a loss, providing little, if any, return to their shareholders. Several—the $750 million Kenana Sugar Corporation estate, for example—are considered technically successful, but shortages of foreign exchange, poor transportation links, lack of skilled labor, and declining international commodity prices have made them dependent on subsidies for survival.

Most of the projects that failed did so because of economic or environmental problems. For many, the common denominator has been poor land. Because land in the vicinity of the Nile cannot be easily transferred or sold,[3] some of the largest farm projects, such as the 700,000 feddan Faisal Agricultural Corporation project, were established in remote areas on marginal land. Far from the Nile's fertile soil and dependent on erratic summer rains, these projects were handicapped from the start. Access to good soil and water for irrigation, in most cases, would have required the participation of local farmers, something that few organizations, public or private, have managed successfully. In Sudan, most projects that involved local farmers incurred heavy financial losses primarily because the farmers had little incentive to improve productivity. What is remarkable in Sudan, though, is that even the few projects that offered farmers sufficient incentives were commercial failures as well.

In this article, two examples of this phenomenon provide a useful measure of farmers' attitudes in Sudan's irrigated sector. One, a project in northern Sudan started in 1979 by Tenneco, a US multinational corporation, is a graphic example of local farmers failing in a major commercial venture. Despite incentives, which included a direct role in management and shares in the profits, the venture quickly fell apart because of the farmers' lack of commitment to their own cooperative. Their inability or reluctance to work toward the long-term objectives of the venture deprived them of long-term profits. Although they understood the rationale for the project and had already seen the benefits of the new technology introduced by the US sponsor, they had few expectations from it and even less confidence in its prospects for success. The second example is the 2.1 million feddan Gezira scheme, Sudan's largest irrigated estate. Farmers there showed a similar lack of commitment to the scheme's overall viability, notwithstanding better incentives offered by the Sudan Gezira Board (SGB) after 1980. In spite of favorable terms for cotton—Gezira's main cash crop—many farmers continued to divert their water and fertilizer rations to local market, fast return crops such as sorghum.

3. As the Anglo-Egyptian Condominium extended its rule over Sudan in the early 1900s, it divided all land into *milik* (private land) and *miyri* (government land). Any family that could prove that it had inhabited and farmed a particular plot of land received a deed formalizing its ownership. Any land that was unclaimed, or for which a claim could not be substantiated, reverted to government ownership. This, of course, meant that the bulk of the land in Sudan was under government control and remains so to this day. Conditions for leasing land are strict and forbid individuals to sell or transfer their rights (though, under current law, heirs have the right to renew a lease). The tiny amount of milik is subject to fewer restrictions under civil law, but Islamic inheritance law has led to the fragmentation of holdings and a near complete paralysis in transactions.

This seemingly self-defeating attitude is related to two major trends that have helped shape Sudan over the last 20 years. First has been the well-entrenched tendency toward government control of the economy, which climaxed in the 1970s with then-president Jaafar Numayri's nationalization of businesses, banks, and trade unions, as well as tighter control over agriculture and commerce. The second trend has been the steadily increasing rate of emigration from rural areas to Khartoum and to Arab countries.

Government efforts to micro-manage the economy have left farmers with a deep mistrust of all institutions, even of their own cooperatives, which had come to serve as instruments of state intervention. At the same time, the migration of many farmers away from their districts disrupted bonds of kinship and longstanding ties to the land. Because of a lack of commitment or sense of common purpose, those who replaced them have shown little interest in long-term improvements, not to mention innovations offered by outside investors. That these attitudes are so widespread suggests that commercial agricultural ventures in Sudan will not be viable for years to come. Economic reforms are a prerequisite for the nation's recovery, but even if introduced, it will take many years before their impact is noticeable in the fields.

THE GEZIRA MODEL AND IRRIGATED AGRICULTURE

The decline in Sudanese agriculture can be traced to two shifts in government and investors' priorities. One shift took place gradually in the years after independence, with the government asserting steadily greater control over farming on irrigated lands, thereby reducing farmers' incentives. The second occurred as undeveloped rainfed lands came to be seen as a potential source of new wealth. Together, these shifts sapped the real strength of Sudan's agricultural economy, namely irrigated farming.

The conceptual ancestor of the big agricultural investments of the 1970s was the Gezira scheme established in 1911 by the Sudan Plantation Syndicate, a private British consortium.[4] Located on the rich alluvial plain between the White Nile and the Blue Nile, Gezira is ideal for irrigated production of a wide range of crops. Under the auspices of the syndicate—and, after independence in 1956, the SGB—the scheme was devoted to producing long-staple cotton for export to Britain and other overseas markets. It also became the home for 96,000 tenant farmers, many of whom had migrated from the northern provinces. The scheme had the main ingredients of commercial success: water, good soil, a stable labor base, and (at the time) a high-value crop with an assured market. Other government estates started after independence, such as the Rahad, New Halfa,

4. The original acreage of Gezira was 1.2 million feddans irrigated from water stored behind the Sennar Dam on the Blue Nile. The completion of the Roseires Dam allowed the addition of nearly 1 million feddans of adjacent land known as the Managil extension. See Arthur Gaitskill, *Gezira: A Story of Development in the Sudan* (London: Faber & Faber, 1959).

and Agricultural Reform Corporation projects, followed the Gezira model of tenant farmers growing one or two major export crops under the management of a state-owned company. The more "successful" private projects of the 1970s were also irrigated and lay in the fertile areas adjoining the major rivers. Like the Gezira, these projects incorporated small farmers as tenants or sharecroppers.[5]

The importance of irrigated farms along the riverbanks is underlined by the fact that, even with all the investment in new areas, they still account for the bulk of Sudan's farm production and exports. For example, the Gezira scheme represented less than 11 percent of Sudan's cultivated area at the close of the 1970s, yet it alone produced 60 percent of the country's cotton, 75 percent of its wheat, and 35 percent of its groundnuts.[6] Irrigation enables farmers to take advantage of the cool (though rainless) winter in Sudan by planting temperate-zone crops such as wheat, fava beans, and many types of vegetables. In addition, control over water allows farmers to plant and harvest at optimum times, using up to three rotations a year. On the other hand, very little irrigated alluvial land is uninhabited and untended. As a result, individual farmers have—and will continue to have—a crucial role to play in the Sudanese economy. With the recurrence of drought in the region and the low productivity of the rainfed land, it is unlikely that this role will be diminished in the foreseeable future.

Rainfed Agriculture

Investments in the 1970s focused on the development of new areas, primarily rainfed lands to the east and south of Gezira. In contrast to Gezira and its counterparts, however, these projects—notably the large fully mechanized farms, such as the Faisal scheme—never lived up to expectations and certainly did not provide a viable alternative to irrigated estates. The quality of their soil was a major constraint—it was poor in nutrients and often high in salinity and mineral content. On the mechanized farms, yields of sorghum, a staple crop, averaged less than half those in the irrigated areas and below one-fifth those in developed countries.[7]

In Sudan, unless the soil is fertile, the expense of irrigation is prohibitive. Heavy use of fertilizers may improve crop performance enough to compensate for poor soil, but Sudanese farmers must import fertilizer, along with fuel, machinery, and other inputs. Given the high costs for these items, not to mention the scarcity of foreign exchange, the productivity of the rainfed lands is far too low to justify the use of fertilizer, much less major expenditures for equipment and farm infrastructure. Farm productivity is further hampered by outmoded cultivation practices and, unlike most other developing countries, an insufficient work force

5. Some notable examples are the Arab-Sudanese Fruit and Vegetable Company, the Seleit Food Company, and the Abu Nama estate of the Sarkis Ismerlian Company.

6. World Bank, *Sudan*.See also D'Silva, *Sudan: Policy Reforms*, p. 16.

7. Food and Agriculture Organization, *Production Yearbook*, (Rome: FAO, 1986).

to support the labor intensive cultivation common on rainfed as well as irrigated farmland.[8] Another constraint on rainfed farming is the short growing season—three to six months—characterized by intense heat and unpredictable rainfall. The soil and climate severely limit the variety of crops that can be grown, which in turn increases the farmer's risk, whether from market fluctuations or crop failure. Only sorghum, sesame, short-fiber cotton, and some varieties of groundnuts are suited for large-scale cultivation in the rainfed areas, but, according to Food and Agriculture Organization figures, at least 80 percent of rainfed cropping is sorghum alone. The prevalence of a sorghum monoculture merely poses the additional risk of depleting the already poor soil quality.[9]

Given the poor outlook for rainfed farming, why were investors even tempted to shift their attention away from existing irrigated estates such as the Gezira? In large part, they did so because of the (paradoxically) disappointing performance of the irrigated estates, not to mention the perceived difficulty of managing the resident farmers on the land. As events in the 1970s and 1980s were to show, each of these problems fed the other.

Gezira's Failure

The large irrigated estates in Sudan, notably the Gezira scheme, resolved the issue of land and people by incorporating local farmers as tenants. Under the tenant system, the estate management (in most cases a government corporation) controls water, provides services and inputs, dictates what is to be produced, and markets the harvested crops. The system is well suited to labor-intensive crop production, stable market conditions, and centralized management—essentially the environment of the 1920s rather than that of the 1980s.

The hallmark of the Gezira tenant farming system has been its extensive control over the activities of the tenants. This is evident in the original basic tenancy agreements between SGB and each of its tenant farmers:

8. Even most of the "mechanized" farms in the rainfed areas depend on legions of migrant workers to harvest sorghum and sesame. The common varieties of Sudanese sorghum are not combinable, so laborers must cut the grain stalks and feed them by hand into combines for threshing. Sesame harvesting must also be done by hand, otherwise the seeds will shatter. The heavy dependence on manual labor increases costs, especially during bountiful crop seasons when competition for workers is keen. Efforts to introduce combinable sorghum hybrids and varieties to rainfed areas failed according to a study commissioned by Arkel International on behalf of the US Agency for International Development. See also Morag C. Simpson, "Large-Scale Mechanized Rainfed Farming Developments in the Sudan" in *Post-Independence Sudan,* Proceedings from the seminar "Post-Independence Sudan," Centre of African Studies, University of Edinburgh, November 21–22, 1980, pp. 197–212.

9. Harold D. Nelson, ed., *Sudan: A Country Study* (Washington, DC: US Government Printing Office, 1983 [The American University Area Handbook Series]), p. 158. As early as 1975, a joint International Labor Organization and United Nations Development Programme team raised concerns about the rapid depletion of land in the rainfed areas. See International Labor Organization, *Growth, Employment and Equity: A Comprehensive Strategy for the Sudan* (Geneva: International Labor Organization, 1976), p. 47.

■ The tenant shall grow only cotton and sorghum, the latter for personal consumption only, not for sale. [Wheat and groundnuts were later added to the rotation.] All cotton shall be delivered to the SGB which will pay the farmer 40 percent of profits to be credited to a joint account.

■ The farmer must pay the SGB for water, fertilizer, mechanized farm operations [such as plowing and the application of pesticides] and other services provided by the Board. These charges are deducted from the joint account as a fixed percentage of the profits for the year.

■ The farmer is responsible for the irrigation of his plot, maintenance of feed canals, weeding, harvesting cotton [by hand], and clearing his fields of stubble left from previous crops.[10]

The joint account system, finally discontinued after the 1981–82 season after pressure from the World Bank, was the most obvious, but by no means the sole, disincentive for farmers. By charging percentages rather than fixed costs, the joint account system penalized the more productive farmers. Despite other measures to improve incentives, such as bonuses and price premiums, overall productivity in the Gezira project did not significantly improve during the 1980s. Evidently, more far-reaching changes were needed, as suggested in a 1987 US Department of Agriculture study:

> Managers presently decide on cropping patterns and input use within large irrigated schemes like Gezira and Rahad, and tenants have minimal decision-making power and operate only within a restricted economic environment. The only major decisions that tenants control are timing of weeding and harvesting and allocation of labor between hired [workers] and family for various operations. Hence, while price incentives may have been initiated, tenants do not have the freedom to allocate their resources in response to the changing structure of incentives. This suggests that effects of macroeconomic policy reforms may not be as expected and a further understanding of pricing changes on the efficiency of resource allocation is necessary.[11]

In theory, as market conditions change for the worse, other crops would become more attractive to farmers, who would then seek ways to profit from the market regardless of management policy. In Gezira, limiting the cash crops to cotton threatened farmers' incomes when prices for cotton began to fall in the 1970s. Unless the SGB increased subsidies, which it was in no position to do, farmers stood to lose money by growing cotton. In fact, however, most farmers cheated on the system by illegally allocating resources to maximize the yields of other crops, especially sorghum.

Sorghum is a particularly attractive crop for Gezira farmers because, unlike cotton, groundnuts, or wheat, there is a free market for it throughout Sudan.

10. Gaitskill, *Gezira*, appendices.

11. Regarding the joint account system, see Brian D'Silva and Kamil Hassan, *Institutional Change, Incentive Effects and Choice of Technology in Sudan's Irrigated Subsector: A Model of the Rahad Scheme* (Washington, DC: US Department of Agriculture, 1987), p. 8; D'Silva, *Sudan: Policy Reforms*, p. 35.

Many farmers therefore give extra water to their sorghum at night, though the SGB specifically prohibits watering after dark. Another common practice is for farmers to obtain a fertilizer ration from the SGB for planting cotton and then use it for sorghum or even sell it on the black market. Other examples of tenants' resourcefulness in beating the SGB were noted by a British observer in 1980:

> . . . Farmers [on the Gezira scheme] find many ways of manipulating or evading the regulations. . . . Tenant absenteeism is widespread. Cotton may be transferred from tenant to tenant either in *shayl* (loan) transactions or to avoid debt repayment. Many tenants let out their land . . . to sub-tenants on a sharecropping basis. Encroachment of livestock on cotton and other crops seems to have greatly increased. Labor-saving methods of crop watering are used instead of those officially prescribed.[12]

New incentives introduced in 1980 by the SGB had little effect and, if anything, made matters worse. The SGB offered immediate cash bonuses to farmers who obtained yields of over 3.5 kantars per feddan of long-staple cotton and above 5 kantars for medium-staple cotton. (One kantar equals 143 kilograms of seed cotton.) No sooner had these been introduced than a black market appeared in which tenants with surpluses sold cotton to less productive farmers who needed more to qualify for the bonus.[13]

Similar tenant systems exist on the other major parastatal schemes, including the Rahad, the Blue Nile Corporation, and Khasm al-Girba, all of which face comparable problems with productivity and farmer incentive. Although successful irrigated farming in Sudan will continue to depend on local farmers and laborers, the Gezira no longer suffices as a model for bringing farmers into large-scale commercial farming projects. The tenant system, therefore, will have to give way to a new model that better preserves the independence of individual farmers.

Investors considering agricultural projects in Sudan must take into account two related factors: first, that new projects on marginal land away from the Nile will probably not be cost-effective and, second, that use of the land near the river will require an accommodation with local farmers which avoids the inadequacies of the Gezira tenant system. Ideally, if there were a free economy, investors could purchase the land or develop it in joint ventures with local landowners. The Sudanese economy, however, is not free. Moreover, the privately-owned farmland still left near the river is fragmented into plots far too small to support economies of scale. A model tailored to the current political and demographic

12. I.G. Simpson, "Institutional Constraints to Agricultural Development in the Sudan" in *Post-Independence Sudan*, p. 157. See also D'Silva, *Sudan: Policy Reforms*, pp. 35–36 and D'Silva and Hassan, *Institutional Change*, pp. 9–10. In the latter report, D'Silva mentions that the management of the state-owned Rahad scheme mixed herbicides into the fertilizer to keep farmers from using it on sorghum. One can only guess the results of this misguided policy. Apart from wasting foreign exchange, any mistakes in labeling or storing the fertilizer could have led to the destruction of legitimate crops.

13. I.G. Simpson, "Institutional Constraints," p. 159.

realities of Sudan, consequently, would lie somewhere between privately-owned estates and the government-owned corporations, more along the lines of farmers' cooperatives or partnerships. The problem in Sudan is that even these have failed to improve farm productivity.

CONTRACT FARMING

In the developed countries, one model that has successfully brought small farmers into commercial production and marketing schemes is contract farming. This model involves either seasonal or long-term contracts between individual farmers and corporations that process and market the crops. Unlike developed countries, however, to be successful in Sudan contract farming would require companies to help farmers complete the transition from subsistence to market-oriented farming. They would need to modernize infrastructure and be directly involved in producing the crop, rather than merely marketing it. At the same time, they would have to preserve the incentives that motivate individual farmers.

At least one US multinational, Tenneco, did exactly this during the early 1980s, attempting to establish a contract farming venture with hundreds of local farmers who had organized their own cooperatives. Despite a conscious effort to preserve farmer incentives, the experiment failed completely. The incentives provided under the contracts were singularly effective in motivating the farmers, yet the results were disastrous, not just for the company but for the cooperatives and, ultimately, the farmers themselves.

In 1979, the company established a pilot farm in a remote area of the north. The original purpose of the project, which was called the Sahara Agricultural Venture (SAV), was to develop saline land in the desert and ultimately to use it for the export of fruit and vegetables to Saudi Arabia. After two years of operation, however, it became clear that the project would not be commercially viable. Faced with low productivity, along with the high cost of land reclamation, SAV's management devised an alternate strategy for the project. Because the pilot farm lay close to an extensive stretch of fertile, underused land adjoining the Nile, it was proposed that SAV provide technical assistance to local farmers, work with them to bring their land into full production, and market the crops. To do this, SAV opted for a system of contract farming based on a model conceived by Orville Freeman, former secretary of agriculture of the Kennedy and Johnson administrations, and Ruth Karen. As Freeman and Karen put it, both the farmers and the company would benefit from

> . . . harnessing the dynamic of the private sector, specifically by creating a symbiosis of corporate know-how, farmer devotion to the land and sound government policy. . . . . In agriculture, a private sector resolution of world problems means mobilizing smallholders . . . around a corporate core that effectively moves these farmers from subsistence agriculture into the market economy, as both producers and consumers,

with all the developmental multiplier effects this implies, socially as well as economically.[14]

Practically speaking, SAV proposed to work with local cooperative societies, which had large enough tracts of land for mechanized farming—an average of 500 feddans each—as well as the necessary pumps, canals, and labor.

Unlike Gezira and other tenant farming schemes, the cooperatives were owned and operated by local farmers and shareholders. As such, they offered an ideal combination of size, resources, and private incentives. Rather than assume the entire burden of managing and supervising hundreds of farmers, SAV intended to work jointly with the cooperative managers in carrying out the venture. The "corporate core" would comprise both the cooperative societies and SAV, thereby assuring the farmers that management would take their interests into account. With the organizational infrastructure thus established, SAV's staff would be able to devote themselves to the technical aspects of the venture, while minimizing the uncertainties of a foreign company working with local farmers.

The history of the local cooperative societies augured well for the success of the contract farming project, as they represented an example of home-grown initiative and self-sufficient rural development in Sudan. The Northern Province's first farmers' cooperative societies were formed in the 1930s, not far from the SAV site, by Sudanese who had worked in Egypt and had seen similar societies there.[15] Shareholders pooled cash and, in many instances, private land-holdings to create large farms extending into the empty government-owned land farther from the river. Share capital went toward leasing government land, as well as purchasing and installing mechanical pumps, while farmers contributed their labor to construct earthen dikes for the main irrigation canals. The societies were managed by a board elected by the farmers. The board made all decisions about expenditures, loans, and other matters, though, in practice, societies would often put major issues to a direct vote by the farmers. In addition, the boards would frequently hire or appoint a farm manager and a mechanic for maintenance of the pumps. The formula for distribution of the crops worked out by the early cooperative societies, and prevalent to this day, was a straight 50:50 division between the cooperative society and the farmers. The cooperative's 50 percent was expected to cover farm expenses such as fuel and parts for the pumps, seeds, fertilizer, and salaries for the manager and mechanic. Any surplus cash or crop production accruing to the cooperative was converted into dividends to be distributed to the shareholders. The farmers' 50 percent compensated them for

14. Orville Freeman and Ruth Karen, *The Farmer and the Money Economy: The Role of the Private Sector in the Agricultural Development of LDC's* (New York: Business International Corporation, 1981), p. 15.

15. The first society was founded in 1934 at Mushu, a village on the Nile, about 10 miles from the SAV pilot farm. Under the commercial code at the time, the societies were private "trading companies" owned by shareholders. Many still retain the "Trading Company" designation in their charters.

their labor in plowing, planting, distributing water, weeding, harvesting, and threshing.

In effect, the cooperative societies mobilized the resources of their communities with the aim of utilizing up-to-date technology (at the time, mechanical pumps) and expanding cultivation. In the early years, the Anglo-Egyptian government encouraged this trend by offering land at low rents, but, unlike the Gezira scheme, the initiative came from the farmers themselves:

> The government schemes and the private schemes did not directly promote the cooperative movement, but directly created an atmosphere which the male landholders saw as an example for cooperative efforts to start similar pump schemes for increasing production.[16]

The formation of cooperative societies also provided an innovative solution to the problem of land fragmentation resulting from Islamic inheritance law. Under Islamic law, it is mandatory for property to be divided among all offspring (though not in equal shares for sons and daughters). Unless land is sold, it is not unusual to find a five-feddan field owned by scores of people, none of whom has a viable unit for farming. According to one study, Sudan, at one point, averaged 300 co-owners for every 10 feddans of private farmland in Northern Province.[17]

Largely because of the initiative of the cooperative societies, the area under cultivation in the north increased more than fourfold between 1935 and 1960. Cooperatives now account for about 40 percent of all registered farmland in Northern Province, while the remainder belongs to government-owned tenant estates (37 percent) or is freehold (23 percent).[18]

Failure of the SAV Experiment

By 1980 cooperative societies were but a shadow of what they had been before 1960. A SAV study, completed in 1980, determined that less than half the cooperative land remained under cultivation, while the societies themselves were financially incapable of maintaining their existing pumps and canals, much less of making new investments. In the vicinity of SAV, 11 active cooperatives, holding title to 6,655 feddans, saw the number of their farmers drop by almost half—from 1,000 to 550—between 1970 and 1980. By 1983, according to a SAV estimate, less than 30 percent of cooperative land was planted each year. SAV attributed the decline of the cooperatives primarily to Sudan's economic difficulties such as high

16. W.S. Mann, *The Cooperative Movement in the Democratic Republic of the Sudan* (Khartoum: Khartoum University Press, 1978), p. 13.

17. Mohammed Hashim Awad, "The Evolution of Land Ownership in the Sudan," *Middle East Journal*, vol. 25, no. 3 (Spring 1971), pp. 212–28.

18. Figures from Ministry of Agriculture, Northern Province. In 1982, cooperatives accounted for 77,554 feddans out of the total of 195,718 feddans of registered farmland. A significant amount of cooperative acreage has been abandoned since the 1960s, however, figures are not readily available. Some observers estimate that the abandoned land represents at least half the total acreage.

production costs and low farm prices and the inability of cooperatives to modernize their production. The SAV management reasoned that, if the cooperatives could adopt modern production and marketing techniques, the decline could be reversed. SAV failed to consider, however, that no amount of technical assistance could restore the initiative that had driven the cooperatives in their early days.

SAV proposed to revitalize the cooperatives by introducing new irrigation techniques (by means of precision land leveling) and fully mechanizing their production.[19] As unused cooperative land was brought back into production, individual farmers could expect to farm much larger plots, while crop yields would improve and unit production costs would fall to competitive levels. To maintain an equitable sharing of costs (given that farm machinery owned or contracted by the cooperative societies would take over much of the farmers' manual labor), the cooperatives and the farmers needed to change their crop distribution ratio from 1:1 to 7:1—that is, rather than half for the cooperative and half for the farmers, the cooperative would receive seven-eighths and the farmers one-eighth.

Two farmers who worked on a 30-feddan plot leveled for demonstration purposes agreed that one of them could have handled twice the acreage under the new system. Assuming the cooperative societies mechanized their production, assigned farmers to larger plots, and made the corresponding changes in crop distribution, they would not only cover the costs of mechanization but also assure farmers of a higher income than under the old system. SAV calculated that one farmer working on a 60-feddan plot under the new distribution system would see at least a 700 percent increase in his income. The cooperative would earn at least a 20 percent profit after operating and capital costs, the latter mainly for land leveling. During a transitional period of up to five years, SAV offered to provide its farm machinery on a contract basis until the cooperatives could purchase their own, preferably through SAV. Similarly, SAV proposed to take responsibility for marketing the crops, thereby receiving a share of the profits from sales, particularly in export markets.

After demonstrating the benefits of the new system on the trial plot, SAV found that both the leaders and other members of the local cooperatives were enthusiastic about it, even with the change in crop distribution. The company subsequently signed contracts with four cooperatives for land leveling and mechanized services, contingent on their receiving loans from the Agricultural

19. The most labor-intensive part of Sudan's irrigated farming, especially in Northern Province, is the system of water distribution. Virtually all farmers irrigate their fields with *hiyad* (small pools or basins). A field of only a few acres may contain dozens of these small hand-made basins, hence building and maintaining the hiyad takes up a substantial part of the farmer's time. The hiyad system not only restricts the area each farmer can cultivate, it makes mechanized cultivation and harvesting nearly impossible. SAV proposed using furrows or large basins extending up to several hundred yards without a break, something relatively easy to do since the introduction of laser-calibrated land leveling in the 1970s. This simplified water distribution and allowed easy access by farm machinery.

Bank of Sudan for the leveling; the question of marketing was deferred until more land was brought under production. The bank's management was similarly impressed with the idea and agreed to three of the four loans, although only one was processed in sufficient time to coincide with the crop season. Local and national government officials, as well as members of the surrounding communities, were excited about the initiative, believing that it might attract further investment by both Sudanese and foreigners. The government was determined to see the venture succeed, and it made every effort to ensure the timely delivery of fuel and fertilizer (both state-controlled commodities) despite severe shortages.

The cooperative that signed the first contract had only about 12 active farmers at the time because it had just resumed operations after a hiatus of nearly 20 years. By the next year, more farmers from the community, as well as others from the surrounding villages, had joined the cooperative. SAV's local staff estimated that the number of farmers would rise to more than a hundred because everyone who was a cooperative member (or his sons) had the privilege of working the land if he wanted to. Although the cooperative had 750 feddans—more than enough to go around—only 100 feddans had been leveled at that point. In membership meetings, the farmers nonetheless argued that everyone who wanted should be allowed to work on the leveled land, although that would have made for individual plots of one feddan or less, defeating the whole purpose of the venture. One counterproposal called for rotating several different farmers onto the leveled land each season, while letting the others cultivate the traditional way elsewhere on the farm but, the idea was rejected. Eventually leaders and members reached a compromise solution that would allow 30 farmers each to work approximately three feddans of leveled land. The farmers, however, soon pressed the cooperative leadership for additional changes that threatened to unravel the entire initiative.

The farmers argued that given the division of land, the seven-eighths versus one-eighth division of the crop was unfair. One-eighth from three feddans was indeed minuscule, so they proposed that distribution be changed back to 50:50. Some farmers again argued against any limitation on the number permitted to work the leveled land. In addition, one group demanded that they be allowed to use the traditional method of irrigation by using small pools of water (*hiyad*) on the leveled land. Not only would this have deprived other farmers of water unless they, too, used the hiyad, it would have made impossible the use of farm machinery. At the same time, bitter arguments erupted among the farmers over who should work the best plots of land, and none would accept the solution of rotating leveled plots among them. Despite the efforts of both the cooperative leaders and SAV staff, the farmers effectively stifled the entire program by voting to return to the 50:50 distribution of the crop. The remarkable part of the farmers' decision was that it put their own cooperative in a precarious financial situation, eventually forcing it to default on its loans and, of course, forego the profits that would have enabled it to expand.

The land leveling and mechanization concept itself was not an issue among the farmers. Although a few questioned its value, dozens of others with their own private plots (usually not more than 10 feddans and, therefore, not viable units for the program) offered to pay considerably more than the going rate for land leveling. The seven-eighths to one-eighth distribution of the crop was also not the main issue, as SAV had worked with farmers on this basis to grow wheat on its own land. Each farmer at SAV had been assigned 20 feddans, and, despite SAV's distance from their villages, most had returned for subsequent seasons. What then was the issue? It was clear from the actions and statements of the farmers that they had no confidence in the cooperative society and saw no benefit in working to enhance the welfare of the whole unit. Instead, each farmer sought to maximize his own return, even at the expense of the cooperative. The objective of the new program was to raise the productivity of the cooperative over a period of several years, but, rather than commit themselves to such a distant goal, most of the farmers preferred to concentrate on the short term and get what they could, while they could. That they held shares in the cooperative and would be entitled to share its profits did not, evidently, weigh heavily in their thinking.

FARMERS AND THE STATE

The attitudes of the Gezira farmers and their counterparts in the Northern Province cooperative societies have much in common. The SGB and the cooperatives, over time, completely lost the confidence of farmers. Farmers no longer believe that either institution effectively preserves or promotes their interests. At best, the SGB and cooperative societies are considered ineffectual. At worst, they are regarded (like the Sudanese government itself) as adversaries who undercut the efforts of the individual farmer. Similarly, farmers have little faith in the management of these institutions, an attitude that hinders efforts to introduce new technology and farming methods. The evidence for this malaise lies, first, in the unusually low productivity of these farms and, second, in the large number of farmers or tenants who have left them.

Under the Numayri government, the cooperatives began to take on more of the character of parastatal farms such as the Gezira. The 1973 Cooperative Act (amended in 1977) all but nationalized cooperative societies, placing them under the direct control of the state. The general provisions of the act refer to the "right of the State to supervise the Cooperative Movement and to guide it towards its objectives."[20] Besides limiting the scope of the cooperatives' business transactions, such as distributing profits, taking out loans, and selling shares, the Cooperative Act required that members defer to the new Ministry of Cooperation

20. Democratic Republic of the Sudan, Council of Ministers, Cooperation Act of 1973, General Provisions; and Ministry of Cooperation, Commerce and Supply Cooperative Societies Bill, 1977 (in Arabic).

in questions of management. To administer the act, the government assigned local officials to participate in membership meetings and advise the cooperative boards. Along with increased government supervision, the act mandated subsidies for seeds, fertilizer, pesticides, and other farm inputs, as well as assuring the cooperatives of priority for government services, the most important being allocations of petroleum products. Cooperatives were exempt from taxes on "commercial and industrial profits," but 10 percent of their "surplus" income was to be contributed to "local development, support for the Cooperative Movement, training [and] cooperative education and social services for its members. . ."[21]

In addition, the minister of cooperation had broad powers to determine the use of all surplus funds, appoint members to the boards, and set guidelines for contracts and borrowing funds. The act was consistent with Numayri's efforts to impose central government control over a variety of institutions, ranging from banks to trade unions. Companies, cooperatives, unions, and, of course, political parties were regarded as rival bases of power, hence Numayri tightened his grip on them through legislation and, in the cases of many private firms, outright confiscation. Private companies that were not nationalized suffered through the selective allocation of state-controlled services and commodities, notably fuel, fertilizer, and credit.

Under these circumstances, farmers quickly lost confidence in the cooperative societies. Thousands of young men emigrated from the north during this period.[22] Others continued to farm, but abandoned membership in cooperatives to lease their own small plots on land farther out in the desert; water for these plots came from shallow bore wells. The regional government, short of cash, was more than willing to award leases to anyone prepared to pay both a title fee and annual rent for desert land. Despite the poor quality of the soil, many farmers preferred this land to remaining on that of the cooperatives. Savings and remittances from emigrants went increasingly to pay for their relatives' small wells and pump sets rather than to develop cooperatives. When SAV started its contract farming program, farmers on small plots besieged the company with requests for land leveling and other services. It is hard to imagine a more inefficient use of resources and capital than this. While thousands of feddans of prime farmland lay idle, individual farmers committed their money and energy to postage stamp-sized farms that could not pay for themselves in the foreseeable future.

21. Cooperation Act of 1973, Article 39, paragraph iv.

22. Migration has long been a part of Nubian life, but in the last two decades, the flow of migrants has turned into a flood. A European Community (EC) report issued in 1980 states that, between 1956 and 1973, about 35 percent of the male population left the province to work in other parts of Sudan or in Arab countries. No formal estimates exist for later years, but it is commonly believed that the figure is now more than 50 percent. See European Community, "Northern Provinces Micro-Project Programme." See also Sir M. McDonald & Partners, Ltd. (Cambridge, UK), "Reappraisal of the Northern and Nile Provinces Pump Schemes," (Prepared for the Democratic Republic of the Sudan, Ministry of National Planning, Khartoum, 1979), pp. 47–48.

Farmers who remained on the cooperatives did so with the least of expectations. Under the 1973 Cooperative Act, they found that a major benefit of cooperative membership was the privilege of obtaining seeds, fertilizer, and other inputs at subsidized prices and doing so with priority over private farmers. At the same time, cooperative farmers came to believe that the government would prop up financially strapped cooperatives in the same way that it did for the parastatal farms. Whether for this reason or because of government levies on surplus cooperative funds, it became the norm for cooperative societies to operate at a deficit or, at best, not to record profits on their books. Farmers had every reason to conceal harvested crops from the cooperative and to understate the produce from their plots.[23] They were also less inclined to devote their time to work on behalf of the cooperative. Over time, maintenance of the canals and pumps was neglected, and cooperative infrastructure deteriorated. A 1980 SAV survey of 15 cooperatives revealed that none had posted any profits during the previous five years and that most of their canals and pumps were either unusable or in serious disrepair.[24] Most cooperative farmers were interested merely in producing crops for subsistence, and so their horizons seldom extended beyond one or two crop seasons. Cash cropping was done elsewhere, usually on private plots or in household gardens. Farmers were also quick to leave the cooperatives if the work became too demanding or if production suffered for any reason such as pump breakdowns or collapse of canal banks. They might move on to another cooperative, emigrate from the area entirely, or, if they had enough savings, lease their own plots in the desert. Unlike the decades before the 1970s, they rarely opted to remain with the cooperative and to invest their labor and capital in repairs and improvements. As a result of this new mobility, farmers had little sense of responsibility to the cooperative society, much less an interest in innovations or long-term development.

The Gezira scheme has suffered from a similar lack of confidence among its tenants. Tenants have little say in what they grow or how they grow it. As market prices for cotton have declined, they have lost the incentive to do anything but grow crops for subsistence. More often tenants have quit the scheme entirely, leaving their tenancies to be farmed by sharecroppers or hired laborers. (Tenants cannot legally sell or lease their rights to the land.) SGB figures indicate that fewer than half of all tenants are still directly involved in farming, and only 15 percent

23. Growing conditions for temperate crops, such as wheat, in Northern Province are better than those in Gezira, yet posted yields are not appreciably different. Government statistics show average wheat yields in Northern Province at about 1.5 metric tons per hectare versus 1 ton in Gezira. Egypt, which has climatic and soil conditions comparable to those in Northern Province, has average wheat yields of more than 4 tons per hectare. Under-reporting of harvests in Northern Province is certainly one reason for the abnormally low figures. Another factor is the increased use of marginal desert land for private plots.

24. Two of the four cooperatives slated for the SAV land leveling program were selected largely because they had installed new pump sets bought with grants from the EC. The two others were located in areas of Northern Province with high per capita incomes. This wealth, it was hoped, could be tapped to pay for much needed maintenance of pumps and canals.

of the overall labor requirements are met by tenants and their families. It is safe to say that the majority of work on the Gezira scheme is done by migrant workers, primarily from western Sudan. In 1983, according to the World Bank, 56 percent of the work force consisted of migrant laborers, and 29 percent were resident hired laborers.[25]

KINSHIP AND AGRICULTURE

For Gezira, as for the cooperative societies, demographic changes have had a subtle but profound effect on farm productivity. As established farmers (or tenants) departed in search of better opportunities and were replaced by sharecroppers and migrant laborers or by farmers from outside the community, both family and community ties have been weakened. Until the mid-twentieth century, the basic economic and social unit in the riverain areas of northern Sudan has been the *sagiya,* which combined the labor of each extended family to cultivate an irrigated plot. The sagiya, literally, was the wooden ox-driven water wheel normally used to irrigate several feddans. In the vocabulary of the northern Sudanese, it also refers to an extended family group, which "was an independent unit in making its own decisions concerning crops, areas to be cultivated, crop rotations."[26] El-Haj Bilal Omer, a Sudanese sociologist, in his book about social changes in Northern Province, observed that a significant decline has occurred in the "corporateness and solidarity of the extended family, which has gradually given way to a nuclear family organization."[27] He argues that, as large-scale farming in the north has replaced the sagiya system of farming, extended family ties have been diluted. At the same time, "Cooperation in the production process [is] decreasing," since individuals are more self-sufficient, relying more and more on technology, not to mention other opportunities, such as wage labor.[28] Unfortunately, no credible institutions have emerged to replace the sagiya as a focus of individual loyalties and confidence.[29] In the past, cooperatives consisted primarily of farmers from a single village, most of whom had extended family relationships. Nowadays, village and family ties are still important elements of a person's identity in northern Sudan, but they are less likely to be combined with membership in a cooperative. Hence, as cooperatives replaced their original members with farmers from other villages (or even from other provinces), the

25. Interview with World Bank official.

26. El-Haj Bilal Omer, *The Danagla Traders of Northern Sudan: Rural Capitalism and Agricultural Development* (London: Ithaca Press, 1985), p. 6.

27. *Ibid.*, p. 29. Omer's thesis follows a Marxist paradigm, emphasizing that economic changes are prior to social changes: "The fact that the organization of economic production defines, in many respects, the kinship system and internal organization of the peasant families is an important proposition of this study." (Cf. p. 29.) This view belittles the role of kinship in preserving mutual confidence among participants in cooperative economic ventures.

28. *Ibid.*

29. See Brian D'Silva, *Sudan's Irrigated Subsector: Issues for Policy Analysis* (Washington, DC: US Department of Agriculture, 1986), p. 13.

thread of common identity and purpose was broken and cooperative organization began to disintegrate.

Because so many Gezira tenants are of northern Sudanese origin, the sagiya system of extended family cooperation was, in the past, important for meeting the labor needs of each 10-feddan tenancy. As in Northern Province, the migration of family members away from the Gezira scheme increased reliance on outside labor. Although the influence of tenants on SGB policy is limited, this demographic shift nonetheless widened the gap between them and the management. The importance of sorghum as payment in kind to migrant laborers illustrates this. Sorghum functions as a sort of currency in central Sudan and is widely marketable, so it is the payment of choice for outside laborers. As the demand for migrant labor has increased, tenants' and laborers' resistance to SGB curbs on growing sorghum has intensified.[30] The reliance on outside labor is now so widespread in the Gezira that the current tenant system has become outmoded and actually hinders productivity. Many tenants are no more than middlemen, living in towns and doing the minimum necessary to retain their rights to the land. Growing sorghum, by no means the most profitable crop in Sudan, at least allows them to pay laborers and have a marketable crop as well. Until the SGB allows tenants to lease or sell their rights to the land, this sort of attitude will persist and continue to hold back productivity.

Farmers, Productivity, and Progress

Throughout Sudan's irrigated sector, the trend during the 1970s and early 1980s was toward greater government control and centralization. Changing conditions in the world market merely accentuated the rigidities and disincentives of centralized farm management in Sudan. For the most part, foreign assistance programs encouraged a greater government role in agriculture insofar as they placed considerable amounts of foreign exchange and imported goods at the disposition of the central government. Also, exports of cotton and several other agricultural commodities were among the few sources of foreign exchange that accrued directly to the central treasury.

With these benefits, not to mention the huge bureaucracies spawned by government agricultural activities, it is unlikely that conditions for small farmers will change significantly in the near future. Successive governments in Sudan have apparently convinced themselves that "job security" and government supports, in the form of subsidies and services, will satisfy farmers' aspirations, but centrally managed agriculture in Sudan must confront the same questions as the

30. This reflects continuation and intensification of the decline of the sagiya system that had begun already in the mid-nineteenth century. See Anders Bjørkelo, *Prelude to the Mahdiyya: Peasants and Traders in the Shendi Region: 1821–1885* (Cambridge and New York: Cambridge University Press, 1989), especially chapter 4.

private schemes: is it possible to compensate farmers adequately for their loss of decision-making power and control over their land and crops?

Orville Freeman's concept of contract farming through a "corporate core" attempted to resolve this problem while introducing modern economies of scale. Because such initiatives depend on capital and technical expertise—crucial in Sudan, given the complexity of irrigated farming—it often necessitates a delicate balance between a large organization such as a corporation, cooperative, or government agency on the one hand and the farmer and landholder on the other. The early Sudanese cooperative societies enabled small farmers themselves to strike this balance as well as to preserve it for many years. Only in the late 1960s and the 1970s did a combination of demographic changes and government intervention weaken the cooperatives to the point that they could barely provide subsistence for their members.

The irrigated sector in Sudan will continue to depend heavily on small farmers, hence it follows that the model of the pre-1973 cooperative societies is a good one for investors. Arthur Gaitskill, a British historian and authority on Gezira, alluded to this model in his 1959 book. In his list of recommendations, "Some Cardinal Principles, Supported by the Gezira Experience, Important to the Success of Development Projects of this Nature," he hinted that Gezira itself would be better off if it were turned over to cooperatives. New projects should be started, he argued, " . . . [with] an ultimate intention to withdraw the government partner and leave the undertaking to a cooperative, and [with] adequate preparation for that objective."[31] The lesson of the SAV experience, however, is that Sudanese cooperative societies, as presently constituted and regulated, are far removed from their dynamic forerunners. Under the present system in the irrigated sector, farmers have no faith that their collective efforts will be rewarded. From the investor's perspective, tax holidays and other concessions under Sudan's investment code, however generous, will not offset the lack of motivation common among farmers and bureaucrats alike.

It appears unlikely that private investors or donor agencies will consider backing major new agricultural projects in Sudan, even if the political climate improves. Neither economic conditions nor the state of Sudan's own private sector give much reason for optimism. In any event, the key to reviving Sudan's commercial agriculture will not be so much an infusion of fresh capital as the creation of an environment that will promote its effective use. This means that private institutions, such as companies and cooperative societies, should operate free of government influence over their management. It means that they must make their own decisions about production, crop selection, marketing, use of profits, and—most of all—the sale or leasing of land. Finally, it means that farmers must themselves adapt to changes already in motion, such as technological advances, rapid shifts in world commodity markets, and the weakening of family

31. Gaitskill, *Gezira,* Appendix III, p. 355.

and community ties. If past experience has shown anything, though, it is that the government should follow the lead of the farmers rather than expect farmers to follow that of the government. The future health of Sudan depends on them.

[11]

Land Reform in Syria

Ziad Keilany

In early 1956 Syria joined Egypt in forming the United Arab Republic under the leadership of President Nasser. One of the major consequences of this union was the introduction of a land reform program in 1958. In 1970 the Syrian government announced that the land reform program was completed. This paper examines the history of the land reform in Syria and assesses its consequences as an instrument of modernization in the country.[1]

Syria, like most less-developed countries, has had two major problems in its land tenure: maldistribution of land and tenancy problems. The former refers to the possession of a large amount of agricultural land by a few people, on the one hand, and the sharing of a small, fragmented farm area by a large number of peasants on the other. The latter refers to the prevailing tenancy arrangements which impose an excessive and unreasonable burden on a vast number of cultivators.

BACKGROUND TO LAND REFORM

Land ownership in Syria was unequally distributed during the days of the Ottoman Empire. This maldistribution of land was further aggravated by the French authorities around the 1920s. They encouraged the growth of private latifundia, facilitating the private appropriation of land, especially by those who collaborated with the Mandate. Large areas, formerly the personal property of Sultan Abdul Hamid were sold, leased, or given in the mid-1920s to big landlords and influential persons at low prices.[2]

Also, ownership of state lands occupied by tribes in the Jazira and Euphrates areas was granted to tribal chieftains, who thus became great private landowners. Consequently, by the end of the 1930s big landlords owned a very substantial part of the cultivable land. In other parts of the country such as the Druze and Alawi Mountains and Hawran, where small and middle-sized properties prevailed, smallholders suffering from population pressure on the land were often as badly off as sharecroppers on big estates.

Although reliable figures on land distribution were not available, the International Bank for Reconstruction and Development (IBRD) estimated that 49 per cent of the total area of privately owned land was holdings of over 100 hectares (a hectare = 2.471 acres) and only 13 per cent in small holdings of 10 hectares and less.[3] The distribution by size of holdings is illustrated by Table 1. Furthermore, it was estimated that about 82 per cent of the rural population was either landless or owned individual holdings of less than 10 hectares.

Concomitant with uneven distribution of land was widespread absentee landownership: 'Most of the large owners do not live permanently on their land but operate through some type of sharecropper system.'[4] The sharecropper usually worked under the direction of the landlord or his agent and

TABLE 1

DISTRIBUTION OF LAND BY SIZE OF HOLDING 1952

Classification of Holdings (hectares)		*Per cent of Area*
Small holdings		
Less than 1		1
2–5		5
5–10		7
	Total	13
Medium holdings		
10–25		17
25–50		11
50–100		10
	Total	38
Large holdings		
100–500		24
500–1000		9
Over 1000		16
	Total	49
	Total all Groups	100%

Source: IBRD, pp. 354-55.

depended on him for farm supplies and operating capital. His status was more nearly that of a laborer than a tenant. The sharecropper was very much subject to the will of the landlord while a true tenant had rights of occupancy and land use that were protected under law.

In rainfed areas the sharecropper generally received about 30 per cent of the crop if he provided only his labor, and around 70 per cent if he provided working capital. On irrigated lands the sharecropper received 20–30 per cent of the crop if he furnished his labor, about one-half of the crop if he provided his working capital. Ownership of the critical factors carried with it, in fact, the ability to demand a large share of the output.

The above tenancy system suffered from many defects. Tenancy contracts were verbal and terminable at will by the landlords. Furthermore, the small peasant-owners and the sharecroppers who carried on most of the agriculture:

> wrest a bare living from the soil and are chronically in debt to the merchant, the professional moneylenders or the landlord. Unable to bring their produce to the market or to wait for better prices, they must accept the price offered to them locally for whatever they produce in excess of their own needs. They till their own land with methods hallowed by time and their equipment for the most part consists only of a pair of draft animals and a wooden, iron-tipped plow.[5]

THE LAND REFORM OF 1958

The first comprehensive land reform program was introduced by President Nasser when Syria became part of the United Arab Republic. Under the banner of Arab Socialism, The Agrarian Reform Law No. 161 was enacted on 27 September, 1958 and put immediately into effect. According to this law no person was allowed to own more than 80 hectares of irrigated land and 300 hectares of rainfed land. About 1.37 million hectares were to be expropriated.[6] Landowners were to be compensated in full for expropriated land over a period of forty years by means of negotiable bonds at 1.5 per cent interest.[7] The number of the beneficiaries from this program was estimated in 1958 at 750,000 persons which involved about 150,000 families representing 17 per cent of the population or 27 per cent of the rural population.[8] Expropriated land was to be distributed to landless peasants in plots not exceeding eight hectares of irrigated land and 30 hectares of non-irrigated land.

The land reform program was preceded, before the Union, by the Agricultural Relations Law which regulated working conditions between landowners and sharecroppers and agricultural laborers. It stipulated the limits of the landlord's share of the crop according to the nature of the land. It further prohibited life contracts and required written leases and curtailed the landlord's right to cancellation. The law laid great emphasis on the formation of agricultural labor unions. However, President Nasser did not permit the formation of these unions.

Right from the start, the execution of the land reform program encountered serious difficulties. The first was a severe three-year drought which reduced Syria's agricultural output to less than half the 1957 level and rural income to 60 per cent of that of 1957. In these circumstances the land reform did little to alleviate the lot of the peasants and thus undermined its effectiveness.

The second difficulty was that the land reform program was copied from the Egyptian law without taking into consideration the fact that Syria's agriculture is extensive and Egypt's is intensive. The law for example distinguished only between two land categories: irrigated and non-irrigated. However, there are differences in value of land irrigated by pump and by flow; between fertile land and pasture; between land in zones of maximum rainfall and arid or semi-arid land.

An example of this diversity could be found in the village of Mashrafe in the district of Homs. In 1964, an examination of the nature of land in that village and a rough calculation of the net income per hectare revealed the following:

Land Categories	*Area in Hectares*	*Net income per Hectare (Syrian Pounds)*[9]
Vineyards	784	158
Irrigated by flow	214	801
Irrigated by pump	676	636
Rainfed Category A	1484	128
Rainfed Category B	2286	62
Rainfed Category C	2041	32
Noncultivated	195	
Total	7680	

Source: Ministry of Agrarian Reform, *Land and Agrarian Reform in Syria,* (Damacus, 1966), p. 166 (in Arabic).

Another problem is the distribution of population. Population is heavily concentrated in the western part of Syria while the eastern part is sparsely populated. This disparity resulted in serious difficulty in so far as distribution of expropriated land. Because of heavy density of population in certain areas, there was not enough land to satisfy all peasants, thus resulting in the persistence of landless peasants in these areas. A survey of seven villages in different districts revealed the dilemma:

District	*Villages*	*Expropriated Land (hectares)*	*No of Beneficiaries*	*Peasants Remaining Landless (%)*
Damascus	Ayssam	576	79	75
Dara	Kanaf	233	34	80
Dara	Zeta	255	38	75
Homs	Kabi	336	14	50
Hama	Tell Sahlab	634	284	80
Hama	Akrab	857	191	90
Allepo	Khan Ahmar	258	15	50

Source: Ibid., p. 165.

Lack of recognition of these differences resulted in many inequities in the application of the law. A fourth difficulty was that Syria lacked the skilled personnel to carry out the program. Finally, the resistance put forth by landlords further hampered the execution of the program. By the end of 1961 the land which had been expropriated amounted to 670,212 hectares of which only 148,440 hectares was actually distributed. In addition the state distributed 27,070 hectares of public domain. The number of families who became owners of land as a result of this distribution were estimated at 15,000.[10]

Following Syria's break-off from the United Arab Republic in 1961, the conservative government of Marouf Dawalibi which took over revised the land reform law to correct several inequities of the 1958 law as reflected by landowners' complaints that ownership limitations were too stiff and the method of compensation too far drawn out. The amended law provided for an increase in the amount of land which landowners could retain, depending on such factors as the nature of the land and the method of irrigation. The maximum area of ownership which landowners could retain was 200 hectares of irrigated land and 600 hectares of non-irrigated land. It revalidated the distribution of land made by landowners to heirs between 1958 and 1961 which was cancelled during the Union. Other revisions also affected the period and method of reimbursement of landowners. (See Table 2.)

The subsequent government of Bashir Azmeh, however, cancelled the latter law and reinstated the original law of 1958 with minor revisions. When the revolutionary socialist government of the Ba'ath Party took over in 1963 it introduced much harsher amendments against landowners. (See Table 2.) The Ba'ath government also accelerated the pace of expropriation and distribution of land and by the end of 1966 expropriated land amounted to 994,058 hectares of which 232,050 hectares had been actually distributed.

By 1972, of the 1.37 million hectares expropriated only 239,000 remained undistributed. Most of these are being rented out on an annual basis to the private and the cooperative sectors.

RESULTS OF REFORM: ACHIEVING EQUITY AND PRODUCTIVITY

Land reforms are usually expected to achieve several, sometimes conflicting, objectives. The relationships between the changes they bring about and economic development are complex. There are two central issues often cited in any land reform program; the first is increasing productivity which means the rise of agricultural output both per unit of land and per unit of labor. The second issue is providing social justice which signifies equity, i.e. equalization of agricultural income, rights—opportunities.

It is often argued that land reform creates new economic incentives which is conducive to increasing productivity. The security felt by the peasant when he becomes a landowner encourages him to invest in land, improve cultivation practices, and adopt longer crop rotations; he is in a better position to take the long view. But the significance of these effects can be exaggerated. In Syria, the distributed land was previously owned by landlords who did not lack these incentives.[11] In fact, it appears that in Syria, the significance of land reform lies mostly not in increasing productivity but rather in its equity and other non-economic aspects.

Equity effect can best be ascertained through an examination of the impact of reform on the landholding pattern, and the productivity effect by analysis of the general trends of agricultural growth in the post-reform period.

In Syria the proportion of the total farm land that was redistributed and the proportion of the total farm families receiving land indicate the degree of change in the landholding pattern brought about by land redistribution. As Table 3 shows, 40.5 per cent of cultivated land is redistributed to peasants and 25 per cent of farm families have benefited by receiving land and other aids from the land reform program. Syria compares favorably with other countries in terms of numbers of peasant families who benefited from the land reform with the exception of Mexico and Taiwan. Syria is also contrasted quite favorably with countries such as Iran and Taiwan in terms of redistribution of land and appears less favorably when compared with Mexico.

As it aims at a more equitable landholding pattern, land reform leads to a decline in land concentration. The equity effect of reform can, therefore, also be seen in the degree of decline in land concentration. There is no doubt the land reform program has led to a profound decline in land concentration in Syria due to ownership ceiling stipulated by law. The average size of land holding has become 9.7 hectares. Table 4 illustrates the impact of land reform on the size of land holdings in the country.

There are a host of difficulties associated with isolating the impact of land reform program on production. As a United Nations report has commented: 'Time series of an aggregative type permitting comparison of agricultural output before and after land reform are rarely if ever available, while cross-section comparisons tend to be inconclusive.'[12] In addition to this

TABLE 2

TABULAR SURVEY OF SYRIAN AGRARIAN REFORM LEGISLATION

Aspect of Law	*Original 1958 Law*	*Dawalibi's Government: 20 Feb, 1962 Parliamentary Revsions*	*Azmeh's Government: 30 April, 1962 Revisions*	*23 June, 1963 Ba'ath Revolution March 1963 (Law 88)*
I. Retention of Land by Landowners				
1. Irrigated land	80 hectares	200 hectares	80 hectares	15-45 hectares depending on area.*
2. Non-irrigated	300 hectares	600 hectares	300 hectares	80-200 hectares depending upon rainfall.
3. Non-irrigated land in certain areas	450 hectares	1,200 hectares	450 hectares	300 hectares in northeast areas.
II. Limitations on Gifts to Wives and Children				
1. Gifts to wives	10 h. irrigated 40 h. non-irrigated (to *one* wife only)	1/8 of land retained by owner (to *all* wives)	10 h. irrigated 40 h. non-irrigated (to *all* wives)	8% of area allowed to landowner
2. Gifts to children	As in II.1 above, to *three* eldest children.	As in II.1 above, to *all* children.	As in II.1 above, to *all* children.	
III. Payments to landowners				
1. Length of payments period	40 years	10 years	a) compensations under L.S. 100,000 10 years b) compensations over L.S. 100,000 15 years	Equivalent to 10 times the average rent over 40 years.
2. Annual interest	1.5 per cent	2.5 per cent	1.5 per cent	1.5 per cent

continued overleaf

TABLE 2 *(continued)*

TABULAR SURVEY OF SYRIAN AGRARIAN REFORM LEGISLATION

Aspect of Law	*Original 1958 Law*	*Dawalibi's Government: 20 Feb, 1962 Parliamentary Revsions*	*Azmeh's Government: 30 April, 1962 Revisions*	*23 June, 1963 Ba'ath Revolution March 1963 (Law 88)*
IV. Distribution of Land to Peasants				
1. Irrigated land	10 hectares	10 hectares	8 hectares	8 hectares
2. Non-irrigated land	30 hectares	15 hectares	a) 30 hectares b) 45 hectares if in certain areas	30-45 hectares
V. Payments by peasants for land received				
1. Length of payments	40 years	land rec'd free	40 years	25% of value of distributed land to be paid to cooperatives
2. Cost of land received	full cost, inc. admin. fees	land rec'd free	half of full cost, inc. admin. fees	

*Some areas have abundance of water than others.

TABLE 3

COMPARATIVE AGGREGATE RESULTS OF LAND REDISTRIBUTION

Countries	*Period*	*Land Redistributed as a percentage of Total Cropland*	*Farm Families who Acquired Land as a percentage of Total Farm Families*
Iran	1952-67	30.5	18.26
Mexico	1915-60	43.3	53.09
Tawain	1951-63	26.97	43.69
Syria	1958-72	40.5*	25.00†
Egypt	1952-64	15.4	8.40
India	1951-66	2.5	4.21
Colombia	1962-69	.81	2.93
West Pakistan	1959-65	5.99	1.52
East Pakistan	1950-60	1.35	n.a.
Philippines	1954-68	2.70	n.a.

Source: Hung-Chao Tai, *Land Reform and Politics,* (Berkeley, University of California Press, 1974) pp. 308-9.
*Calculated from Syrian Arab Republic, *Statistical Abstract,* 1974, p. 221.
†Tibran, op. cit., p. 205.

TABLE 4

AVERAGE SIZE OF LAND HOLDINGS, *1972*

Governorates	*Average Size of Land Holdings*
Damascus	3.8
Aleppo	12.7
Homs	9.3
Hama	8.2
Lattakia	1.9
Deir-ez-zor	5.3
Idleb	6.0
Hasakeh	24.9
Al-Rakka	14.7
Sweida	10.2
Dar'a	9.1
Tartous	3.3
Quneitra	5.1
Average Total	9.7

Source: Syria, *Statistical Abstract,* 1974, p. 214.

problem, there is the difficulty of separating the economic effects of tenurial reform from those of non-tenurial changes. Nevertheless an attempt is made here to measure the average annual rate of growth of the agricultural sector during 1960–65 and compare it to the rate of growth during 1966–70 in which the land reform appeared to receive a definite commitment by the revolutionary Ba'ath regime.

The agricultural sector lagged far behind other sectors of the economy with an average annual growth rate of only two per cent compared to about six per cent for the industrial sector during 1956–70. Furthermore, the average annual rate started falling rapidly during the 1960s. Specifically, the average annual rate of growth in agriculture fell as low as .25 per cent during 1966–70 compared to 3.5 per cent for the period 1961–65.[13] This situation became highly undesirable, given a 3.3 per cent population growth rate.

The relatively poor performance of the agricultural sector during the second half of the 1960s may raise a serious question concerning the economic impact of the land reform. However, the picture is too complex to be dismissed by a simple conclusion, and in order to place the land reform in proper perspective, one must examine the factors which operated simultaneously with the advent of the land reform.

The agricultural sector in Syria is heavily influenced by weather conditions. The irrigated area constitutes only 18 per cent of the cultivated area under crop. Drought years have in fact adversely affected agricultural output in five years out of the decade of the 1960s, as can be seen from Table 5. Furthermore, the impressive expansion of irrigated and non-irrigated land which Syria has witnessed in the post-war period had by this time reached its limit. The irrigated portion of the land, which was about 18 per cent remained almost unchanged until the early 1970s. The reason for this stagnation was that as the areas of land readily commanded by pumps are developed, more and more powerful pumps are required to command the

TABLE 5

PRODUCTION OF MAIN CROPS AND THEIR YIELDS
(PRODUCTION IN 1,000 OF TONS; YIELD PER HECTARE IN TONS)

Year	*Wheat*	*Yield*	*Barley*	*Yield*	*Cotton*	*Yield*
1953	870	—	472	—	123	—
1954	965	—	635	—	221	—
1955	438	—	137	—	233	—
1956	1,051	0.7	462	0.7	252	0.9
1957	1,354	0.9	721	0.9	291	1.1
1958	562	0.4	228	0.3	250	0.9
1959	632	0.4	218	0.3	265	1.2
1960	555	0.3	156	0.2	279	1.3
1961	757	0.6	335	0.5	325	1.3
1962	1,374	1.0	798	1.1	404	1.3
1963	1,190	0.8	784	1.0	410	1.4
1964	1,100	0.7	637	0.8	470	1.6
1965	1,044	0.9	690	1.0	473	1.7
1966	559	0.7	202	0.6	375	1.5
1967	1,049	0.9	590	0.9	329	1.4
1968	600	0.6	512	0.8	394	1.4
1969	1,003	0.8	627	1.0	382	1.3
1970	625	0.5	235	0.2	383	1.5
1971	662	0.5	125	0.3	408	1.6
1972	1,808	1.3	710	1.2	419	1.8
1973	593	0.4	102	0.1	404	2.0

Source: Syria, *Statistical Abstracts,* 1965, 1970 and 1975.

more distant areas. The greater the height the water has to be pumped the more expensive it becomes so that the extension of pump irrigation becomes uneconomical. The expansion of the cultivation of unirrigated land (which depends upon rainfall) also tapered off in the early 1960s. Here again as the expansion moved in the direction of the south and east towards the arid Syrian desert and beyond the Euphrates, rainfall becomes less dependable, thus successful cultivation becomes unreliable.[14]

The changes of government and the accompanying political instability which plagued Syria resulted in serious delay in carrying out the reform, which in turn, brought about a prolonged period of uncertainty facing both landlords and those peasants who were the beneficiaries of the reform. The landlords stopped investing in land. In many cases they ceased to provide credit to their sharecroppers. The result was a serious decline in net capital formation in agriculture. (See Table 6). Investment in agriculture, however, appears to have recovered by early 1970s.

TABLE 6

GROSS FIXED CAPITAL FORMATION, 1963-73
(MILLIONS OF SYRIAN POUNDS AT 1963 PRICES)

	1963	1964	1965	1966	1967	1968	1969	1970	1971	1972	1973
Agriculture	96	93	67	48	51	52	131	210	228	215	197

Source: United Nations: *Yearbook of National Accounts Statistics 1974,* Vol. II, p. 590.

Another factor which seems to have influenced the rate of capital formation in agriculture is the nationalization of foreign trade in 1965. There was an abrupt drop in the number of tractors, pumps, motors, and other machinery sold to farmers, presumably due to the shortage of foreign exchange. Furthermore, most machinery available at the time had either become obsolete or beyond repair. Even when the government allowed the importation of tractors and pumps, the level of sales was low due to the fact that former buyers, mostly big landowners, either could not afford them or did not need them. The same pattern was applicable to the importation and use of insecticides and fertilizers.

In the early years of the reform, peasants who received land did not always succeed in cultivating it. In the absence of a state policy of adequately financing small peasant beneficiaries, giving them technical assistance and providing state marketing facilities, they were unable to cultivate the land. In fact there were incidents in which the peasants abandoned the land distributed to them and sought employment with former landlords to work as sharecroppers or in some instances to rent the land to the landlord and use the rent money to migrate to the cities.

By the latter part of the 1960s and early 1970s the Ba'ath revolutionary government of President Assad consolidated its grip over the country.[15] The first task facing the regime was how to prevent the land reform in particular and the agricultural sector in general from further deterioration and converting the former into a viable program. The regime's strategy has three dimensions. First the acceleration of the creation of cooperatives. Second, increasing credit and technical assistance to peasants. Third, increasing the irrigated area by harnessing the water resources in the country to lessen the dependence on rainfall.

The Land Reform Law paved the way for agricultural cooperatives for the first time in Syria. The Law stipulated the compulsory grouping of land reform beneficiaries into cooperatives. Such compulsory memberships initially 'run up against the highly individualistic character of the Syrian peasant who had no tradition of agricultural cooperation'.[16] By the early 1970s, however, Ba'ath agricultural policies achieved significant success in the cooperative movement.

Legislative Degree No. 88 (1963) exempts the beneficiaries allotted expropriated lands from paying three-fourths of the value of the land and stipulates that the remaining one-fourth is to be paid by installments over 20 years to the agricultural cooperatives of which the beneficiary is a member. The objective of the decree is to soften the impact of the mandatory participation of peasants into cooperatives. The total number of cooperatives both of land reform and public domain was 1,725 at the end of 1973.[17] (An increase from 1,089 by February 1970.) The cultivable area by them, however, constituted only 11.6 per cent of the total cultivable land in the country, and 15 per cent of the actually cultivated area in 1973.

Cooperatives can, in principle, influence agricultural productivity through the supply of credit, fertilizers, seeds and technical advice. They also provide a convenient network which the government use to promote 'new input' and diffuse new techniques. The cooperatives in Syria significantly fulfilled their basic functions, i.e. to secure loans (in cash and in kind) from the agricultural banks for their members. The interest rate charged to these cooperatives by the Agricultural Cooperative Bank is 1.5 per cent lower than that charged

TABLE 7

DISTRIBUTION OF SPECIALIZED BANK CREDIT TO THE AGRICULTURAL SECTOR
(MILLIONS OF SYRIAN POUNDS)

	AGRICULTURAL COOPERATIVE BANK		COMMERCIAL BANKS		
Year	*Amount*	*Percentage of Total Loans to Agriculture*	*Amount*	*Percentage*	*Total*
1962	120.8	66.9	59.7	33.1	180.5
1963	128.8	65.9	66.4	34.1	195.2
1964	121.6	65.7	63.3	34.3	184.9
1965	121.3	64.8	65.8	35.2	187.1
1966	144.3	67.8	68.3	32.2	212.6
1967	159.4	76.4	49.1	23.6	208.5
1968	169.2	71.8	66.4	28.2	235.6
1969	187.3	73.0	69.1	27.0	256.4
1970	209.0	75.2	68.9	24.8	277.9
1971	234.0	78.4	64.1	21.6	298.1
1972	206.0	75.7	65.8	24.2	271.8
1973	210.0	77.0	62.5	22.9	272.5

Source: Syrian Arab Republic, *Statistical Abstract, 1974*, pp. 796-97.

on individually obtained credits; furthermore, the cooperatives are granted a 5 per cent discount on the value of loans in kinds, namely fertilizers, seeds, and tools. (See Table 7.)

It should be pointed out, however, that the increase in bank and cooperative loans after the land reform exaggerated the actual expansion of rural credit. Before the reform, landlords used to supply their tenants with seeds and fertilizers and often extended them loans. Moneylenders, also, provided credit to peasants. Government financial institutions simply assumed some of the functions of private lenders after the reform.

Despite some lucrative concessions granted to cooperatives, their number and coverage remained limited compared with the needs of the agricultural sector. The peasants still must depend in many instances upon expensive sources of credit not obtained through the agricultural and commercial banks. As can be seen from Table 8, the proportion of credit granted by banks to agricultural sector remained at about 19 per cent of total credit extended to the economy for most of the 1960s and began to decline in the early 1970s.

Perhaps the most significant attempt on the part of the Syrian government to improve and expand the agricultural sector and transfer more land to landless peasants is the implementation of the Euphrates project and the fertilizer plants (nitrogenous and phosphates). Also, in 1973 a tractor assembly factory capable of producing 2,000 tractors per year was completed. This factory also assembles and manufactures pumps and agricultural implements. All of these will contribute to the vitality of the land reform program. The Euphrates project will more than double the irrigated area available for cultivation.[18] The additional reclaimed land will benefit those peasants who were not included in the distribution of land. The availability of fertilizers, whose demand has been rising very rapidly in recent years, should, when combined with other inputs, improve production significantly.

TABLE 8

DISTRIBUTION OF AGRICULTURAL CREDIT, 1962-1973
(MILLIONS OF SYRIAN POUNDS)

	Agricultural Sector	*All Sectors*	*Per cent*
1962	180.5	881.4	20.4
1963	195.2	978.5	19.9
1964	186.9	972.9	19.2
1965	187.1	894.0	19.0
1966	212.6	1096.1	19.3
1967	208.5	1095.0	19.0
1968	235.6	1162.5	20.2
1969	256.4	1317.8	19.4
1970	277.9	1391.4	19.9
1971	298.1	1535.5	19.4
1972	271.8	1895.4	14.3
1973	272.5	2322.0	11.7

Source: Syrian Arab Republic, *Statistical Abstract, 1974,* (Damascus) p. 797.

SOCIAL CONSEQUENCES: NATIONAL AND PSYCHOLOGICAL INTEGRATION

In addition to equity and productivity, land reform can have other non-economic consequences which may have far reaching impact on the process of modernization. When discussing these non-economic consequences of land reform, one is faced with two basic limitations. One relates to the inadequacy of data explicitly relevant to the social impact of land reform, and the other concerns the difficulty of devising appropriate methods to appraise such an impact. In many instances pertinent social information is often less available than the scarce economic data, and the tools for analysis even more inadequate.

With these limitations in mind, we want to find out to what extent the Syrian land reform program contributed to the integration of isolated peasant communities into a national whole. National integration may be said to consist of two dimensions: a territorial extension of the authority of the central government of a country from the capital to the periphery, and a growing psychological identification by the populace with the nation.

As land reform is generally initiated by the national government, an enforced program will create an impact on the peasants' attitude towards the nation. In countries dominated by landed gentry, a United Nations report has observed, 'the redistribution of land may represent the first occasion in which the central . . . government makes any impact on the farmer's consciousness, and this . . . can lead to the spread of a national consciousness, which is a necessary precondition for a 'popular National Government' to be possible.'[19] The degree of psychological integration of the peasantry caused by a reform program can therefore be assessed by reference to peasant perception of the program, which involves two aspects: the awareness of the program by the peasantry as a whole and the evaluation of the program by its beneficiaries. The greater the number of peasants on the program and the more favorable the evaluation of it by its beneficiaries, the greater the contribution of reform to psychological integration.

In Syria where the various governments, perhaps with the exception of M. Dawalibi's who had a lukewarm attitude toward land reform, have been strongly committed to the land reform, a 'conflicting' pattern prevailed. That is to say, in the implementation of land reform the flow of national authority was basically in conflict with the political strength of the landed class.[20]

The Ba'ath's effort to eliminate the political privileges of the big landlords was uncompromising from the beginning. With the rural power of the landlords removed, the Ba'ath party made strenuous efforts to extend its authority into the villages. In fact, the land reform program itself was used as a vehicle to establish 'political linkage extending between the revolutionary elite and the masses in their villages and neighborhoods'.[21] The induction of the peasants into the electoral process, the organization of rural cooperatives under close national supervision, the systematic integration of the rural population into local government and the Arab Socialist Party, and the establishment of a system of agrarian relations to protect peasants' rights and to provide them with credit, marketing facilities, agricultural education and technical assistance—all these measures have resulted in a new socio-economic infrastructure in Syria which broke the traditional physical and social isolation of the peasants and engendered among them some sense of national awareness, However, although the land reform program has succeeded in considerably weakening the political base of the landlords, it has not eliminated it completely. In fact, a coalition between the former landlords and traditional leadership in the villages still exists in some areas which tend to weaken the new integrative system.[22] Moreover, government blunders have often undermined this integrative process. An example of such blunders was the 1969 peasant uprising in the Ghab region.[23]

The extent to which the land-reform program of a country contributes to the peasants' psychological integration with the national community is determined by the perception of the program. The most important factor affecting peasant awareness of a program is, of course, the extent of the program's implementation. The greater the implementation, the greater the awareness. Other factors affecting awareness include the manner in which the government overcomes the resistance of the landed class, the publicity given to a program and the degree of involvement of the peasants in the process of implementation. As to the evaluation of a reform, it is seen primarily in the changes in income and well-being of the beneficiaries.

The peasantry in Syria has shown (especially in the initial stages when expectations ran high,) a great deal of awareness of and enthusiasm for the reform program. The mood was enhanced significantly by President Nasser's propaganda machine.

The beneficiaries of reform in Syria appear to have favorably evaluated their new life. The acclaim that Nasser and later Ministers of Agrarian Reform received from the villages during their extensive tours in rural areas did contain a genuine sense of peasant appreciation for their leaders' concern with peasant welfare. Available evidence—fragmentary in nature but uniform in content—shows that the beneficiaries generally experienced a rise of income and expressed some satisfaction with being new landowners.[24]According to a United Nations sponsored study which surveyed 62 villages, there seems to be an increase in the average income of peasants who benefited from the program. This increase in income is evidenced by an increase in consumption, mostly of food and other commodities and services such as clothes, medical services and prilgrimages to Mecca.[25]

CONCLUSIONS

There is no doubt that the land reform program has had an important impact on the coutryside in Syria. The extent of this impact appears to be, though slowly coming, favorable. The results include solid commitment of the government to the redistribution of income in favor of the peasants and away from landlords. Examples of this commitment include the distribution of the appropriated land to landless peasants, the emergence of the cooperative movement with its benefits to the peasants, and the reallocation of resources in favor of the agricultural sector. Examples of the latter is the establishment of fertilizer factories, the assemblying of tractors and the building of the dam on the Euphrates. Though the picture is too complex to be certain, the reform does not seem to score too highly on the productivity test, not at least during the period under investigation.

Land reform, however, appears to play a critical role in integrating the rural areas with the rest of the country. In fact, the reform program is used as a vehicle to develop a new rural socio-economic infrastructure. The Syrian peasants have, generally, been freed from the domination of the landed gentry, but have become dependent on the government; and the latter has become a centripetal force pulling together the geographically scattered peasantry into a national community.

NOTES

1. Land reform refers in this paper to public programs that seek to restructure equitably and rationally a defective land-tenure system by compulsory drastic means.
2. See League of Nations, *Proceedings of the Permanent Mandates Commission* 7th Session. 1926, p. 72.
3. International Bank for Reconstruction and Development, (IBRD) Report of a Mission, *The Economic Development of Syria*, (Johns Hopkins Press, 1955) pp. 354–355. For another and similar estimate see Samir Makdisi, *Syria: The Public Sector and Economic Growth 1945–57* (Unpublished Dissertation, Columbia University, 1961), pp. 35–36.
4. IBRD, p. 351.
5. Ibid., p. 38.
6. It was estimated that 254,700 hectares, or 43.5 per cent of irrigated land, and 1,123,500 hectares, or 27.5 per cent of dry farming land, were subject to expropriation.
7. Syrian Republic, *Official Journal*, No. 54, Laws 134 and 161. September 1958.
8. U.N., *Economic Development in the Middle East, 1959–1961*, (New York, 1962), p. 13
9. The official exchange rate for the Syrian pound is 3.82 for U.S. $1.00.
10. Eva Garzouzi, 'Land Reform in Syria', *The Middle East Journal*, Winter-Spring 1963, p. 86.
11. The big farmer entrepreneurs who were called 'merchant-tractorists' were responsible for opening up the northern part of Euphrates province and the creating of one of the most important sources of agricultural production. They were pioneer and risk-taking capitalists. Of course, they were the first to be put out of business because of the application of the land reform. See Doreen Warriner, *Land Reform and Development in the Middle East*, (Oxford University Press, 1962), pp. 89–93.
12. U.N. *Progress in Land Reform, Third Report*, p. 8. See also Eric H. Jacoby, *Evaluation of Agrarian Structures and Agrarian Reform Programs, A Methodological Study*, (Rome: FAO, 1966).
13. United Nations, *Studies on Selected Development Problems in Various Countries in the Middle East* (New York, 1971), pp. 28–29.
14. Ben Hansen, 'Economic Development of Syria' in *Economic Development and Population Growth in the Middle East*, eds. C. A. Cooper and S. S. Alexander (American Elsevier, 1972), p. 343. See also Ziad Keilany, *The Role of National Planning in Economic Development, Syria: A Case Study, 1960–1964*, (Unpublished Dissertation, Indiana University, 1968), p. 19 and p. 59.
15. For a detailed account of the emergence of President Assad and the favorable impact of his liberal policy, see Tabitha Petran, *Syria*, (Praeger, 1972), Ch. 13.
16. Petran, op. cit., p. 137.
17. Syrian Arab Republic, *Statistical Abstract, 1974* (Damascus, Syria) p. 257.
18. H. Charles Treakle, 'Syria Dams the Euphrates,' *Foreign Agriculture*, January, 1970, pp. 8–10.
19. United Nations, *Progress in Land Reform*, Fourth Report (New York, 1966), p. 161.
20. In contrast, for example, countries such as Colombia, India, Pakistan and Philippines, where 'the elites had no intention of carrying out large scale reform, a complementary pattern operated. The extension of national authority and the continuation of the political hold of the landed class in rural areas were mutually supporting'; Tai, *op. cit.*, p. 363.

21. Raymond A. Hinnesbusch, 'Local Politics in Syria: Organization and Mobilization in Four Village Cases,' *The Middle East Journal*, Winter, 1976, p. 1.
22. Ibid., p. 7.
23. Petran, op. cit., p. 208.
24. S. Hammadi, *Comments on the Result of Agrarian Reform in Syria,* Planning Institute for Economic and Social Development, (Damascus, 1967), pp. 6–14.
25. Ibid., p. 14.

[12]

ON THE RELATIONSHIP BETWEEN LAND REFORM AND RURAL-URBAN MIGRATION IN IRAN, 1966–1976

M.G. Majd

THE year 1992 marks the thirtieth anniversary of the launching of the Iranian land reform (1962–1971), possibly the most significant event in the agrarian history of modern Iran. Despite three decades of research and debate on the subject, this effort remains a source of controversy. Until recently, much of the debate centered around the "rural destruction and destitution thesis." It was argued that land reform in Iran excluded a large number of peasants and gave insufficient land to the remainder. The subsequent agricultural neglect and anti-rural policies resulted in peasant impoverishment, rural destitution, and mass migration to the cities that contributed directly to the revolution.[1]

Those who challenge this view maintain that land reform had been extensive and that Iran's post-reform agricultural growth was superior when judged by international standards.[2] Moreover, they argued, contrary to a widespread view,

1. A large number of authors can be cited. The following is a partial list: Eric Hooglund, *Land and Revolution in Iran, 1960–1980* (Austin: University of Texas Press, 1982); Nikki R. Keddie, *Roots of Revolution: An Interpretive History of Modern Iran* (New Haven, CT: Yale University Press, 1981); Homa Katouzian, *The Political Economy of Modern Iran, 1926–1979* (New York: New York University Press, 1981); Ali Farazmand, *The State, Bureaucracy, and Revolution in Modern Iran: Agrarian Reform and Regime Politics* (New York: Praeger, 1989); Robert E. Looney, *The Economic Origins of the Iranian Revolution* (Oxford: Pergamon Press, 1982); Fred Halliday, *Iran: Dictatorship and Development* (Harmondworth: Penguin Books, 1979).

2. Ahmad Ashraf, "State and Agrarian Relations before and after the Iranian Revolution, 1960–1990," in Farhad Kazemi and John Waterbury, eds., *Peasants and Politics in the Modern Middle East* (Miami: Florida International University Press, 1991), pp. 277–311; Shaul Bakhash, "Iran," *American Historical Review* 96 (1991); Jahangir Amuzegar, *The Dynamics of the Iranian Revolution: The Pahlavis' Triumph and Tragedy* (Albany: SUNY Press, 1991); Massoud Karshenas, *Oil, State, and Industrialization in Iran* (Cambridge and New York: Cambridge University Press, 1990); Elias

Mohammad Gholi Majd is a fellow of the Middle East Center and a visiting lecturer in the Department of Regional Science, University of Pennsylvania. He is also an adjunct assistant professor at the Hagop Kevorkian Center for Near Eastern Studies at New York University.

Iran's agricultural economy had been a beneficiary of substantial protection and public investment. Because the available data now demonstrates that there was a combination of rising agricultural production by peasants, expanding nonagricultural employment, and rising consumer expenditures in rural areas, the rural destruction thesis is not as widely held as it was previously. Nevertheless, discussion of the nature and consequences of land reform continues with vigor.

A current debate centers on the historical role of land reform in the promotion of capitalism and industrialization. Iran's land reform is viewed by Marxist scholars in the same context as the eighteenth-century English enclosure movements that resulted in dispossession of the peasantry, their conversion to wage labor, subsequent migration, and proletarization.[3] In this paradigm, enclosure-type land reforms that result in peasant dispossession appear necessary for the development of industrial capitalism. While the relevance of such an approach to Iran's land reform has been questioned by some scholars, it has been used by others as a basis for explaining rural-urban migration in Iran during 1956–1976.[4] In comparing land reform in Iran with the English enclosures, it has been argued that land reform resulted in large-scale peasant dispossession and that the ensuing development of capital-intensive agriculture led to rural unemployment, rising inequality, and created an environment in which the push factor was dominant over the pull factor in the decision to migrate. The push factor is thus seen to originate from land reform and the resulting inequality rather than from Malthusian pressures associated with rapid population growth. Describing the level of migration as a "massive migratory exodus," it is said that the presence of the "masses of migrant labor in the cities . . . provided the crucial momentum for the revolution of 1979."[5] In short, so the argument goes, dispossession and the proletarization of the peasantry in Iran ultimately resulted in revolution.

In contrast to the above, other studies have concluded that the level of rural-urban migration during 1966–1976 was considerably smaller. After studying the causes of urbanization and the growth of the urban population, Nima Nattagh concluded that rural-urban migration accounted for only 35 percent of the

Tuma, Economic and Political Change in the Middle East (Palo Alto, CA: Pacific Book Publishers, 1987); Hassan Hakimian, "The Impact of the 1970s Oil Boom on Iranian Agriculture," *Journal of Peasant Studies* 15 (1988); Hossein Mahdavy, "Thirty Years of Change in a Village on the Ghazvin Plain," *Agah Book on Land and Rural Issues* (Tehran: Agah, 1361 [1982/83]), pp. 50–74, in Persian; M.G. Majd, "Land Reform Policies in Iran," *American Journal of Agricultural Economics* 69 (1987); M.G. Majd, "The Political Economy of Land Reform in Iran," *Land Use Policy* 8 (1991).

3. Bagher Momeni, *Land Question and Class Struggle in Iran* (Tehran: Peyvand, 1359 [1980/81]), in Persian; Afsaneh Najmabadi, *Land Reform and Social Change in Iran* (Salt Lake City: University of Utah Press, 1987); Mohammad Javad Amid, *Agriculture, Poverty and Reform in Iran* (London and New York: Routledge, 1990); Hamid Mohtadi, "Rural Inequality and Rural-Push Versus Urban-Pull Migration: The Case of Iran, 1956–1976," *World Development* 18 (1990).

4. Ahmad Ashraf is a proponent of the former theory. Hamid Mohtadi is a proponent of the latter.

5. Mohtadi, "Rural Inequality," p. 837. Likewise, Katouzian portrays a moving picture of the proletarized, impoverished, and noble peasant arriving "at the gates of the city, dispossessed of his land, deprived of his cultural identity. . . . " Homa Katouzian, "Oil Versus Agriculture: A Case of Dual Resource Depletion in Iran," *Journal of Peasant Studies* 15, p. 367.

increase, and that, "contrary to what many observers believe, [migration] has not been the most important source [of urbanization]."[6] Similarly, an examination of the level of rural-urban migration by Massoud Karshenas concluded that "the commonly held view of associating the high degree of rural/urban migration during the latter half of the 1960s and early 1970s with the effects of the land reform programme, may be mistaken."[7]

In the debate on the size and causes of rural-urban migration, two issues need to be addressed. The first concerns the nature and consequences of land reform. For Iran's land reform to be comparable to the English enclosures, it must be shown that it resulted in widespread peasant expropriation. This article will first review the overall results of land reform and examine the findings of a micro-level study and the effects of land reform in six provinces. These studies reveal no empirical basis for the view that land reform resulted in peasant expropriation. Of particular interest are the results of land reform at the provincial level. Detailed studies published by the Islamic republic during the 1980s confirm that land reform was not only extensive in terms of the number of peasants receiving land, but also show that the amount of land received by the peasants was considerably greater than estimated, even by those who argued that land reform had been comprehensive. Moreover, the statistics show that the size of the landless population (*khoshneshin,* those who neither rented nor owned land) before land reform was considerably smaller than it has been indicated in much of the literature.

The economic consequences of land reform and the principal indicators of the rural economy, namely, the growth of the agricultural sector and the level of rural employment will next be examined. Since the growth of agricultural output and agricultural development policy are important determinants of rural conditions and have been neglected in the current debate on migration, an examination of Iran's post-reform agricultural policy and performance will follow. The growth of agricultural output, high by international standards, resulted in substantial productivity gains. Moreover, the statistics on rural and agricultural employment show that the rise in rural employment exceeded the combined increase in the labor force and the decline in agricultural employment and resulted in a decline in the unemployment rate.

A second issue concerns the actual level of rural-urban migration during the decade prior to the revolution. Given sharp disagreement over the magnitude of the rural exodus, an examination of these estimates and some of the sources of error that have led to an exaggeration of the level of rural-urban migration is essential. Finally, the age composition of rural migrants and the changing structure of rural settlements will be analyzed in the context of the origin of

6. Nima Nattagh, *Agriculture and Regional Development in Iran, 1962–1978* (Wisbech, UK: Middle East and North African Studies Press, 1986), p. 61.

7. Karshenas, *Oil, State, and Industrialization in Iran,* p. 283.

rural-urban migration. Two important characteristics are identified: First, by far the largest migrant groups consisted of males aged 10–24 years. Second, rural-urban migrants after 1966 originated primarily from small and medium-sized villages, often located in semi-arid or mountainous regions. Both economic and educational opportunities were limited in these small settlements, hence an exodus of the young. Given the concentration of migrants from such villages and their youth, it follows that rising migration had little to do with land reform or the increase in rural inequality that is supposed to have followed land reform. Moreover, in contrast to the previous decade, post-1966 migration was small from larger villages, where the majority of the rural population lived—an indication that land reform may, in fact, have reduced the overall migration.

THE RESULTS OF LAND REFORM: SOME NEW EVIDENCE

Since there appears to be agreement among scholars that one million peasants received land under phases 1 and 2 of the Iranian land reform, the discussion of the aggregate results here is mostly concerned with phase 3, the final stage. The basic argument of the dispossessionist school is that under phase 3 nearly 1.2 million peasant households did not receive any land and were subsequently evicted. Unable to make a living in rural areas, it is argued, a large portion of this population migrated to the cities and played a crucial role in the overthrow of the *ancien régime*. Given the lack of solid empirical evidence to support this view and incontrovertible evidence to the contrary, the persistence of this view would seem to be due to a continued reliance on secondary sources and a disregard of primary sources. Some of the secondary sources, on which much of the analysis by the dispossessionist school is based, were written in the 1960s and early 1970s—before the final results of the reform were published (in the mid-1970s). For some time, however, detailed information on the results of land reform has been readily available.

More by accident than by design, research on the nature and extent of land reform in Iran is greatly aided by the agricultural censuses that preceded the beginning and followed the end of land reform—namely, the 1960 inaugural census of agriculture, the 1974 census of agriculture, and the 1975 rural survey. The strength of the official land reform statistics lies in the fact that such data is consistent with census results, despite often confusing definitions and several misclassifications under the 1960 census, one of the earliest of such undertakings in a developing country. Moreover, by the standards of the Third World, as noted by several writers, Iran's social, economic, and rural statistics are extensive and reliable.[8] Also, as indicated above, detailed results of land reform in several

8. See Wolfgang Lautenschlager, "The Effects of an Overvalued Exchange Rate on the Iranian Economy, 1979–84," *International Journal of Middle East Studies* 18 (1986), p. 31. Karshenas, *Oil, State, and Industrialization in Iran,* also concluded that the agricultural sector statistics were

provinces have been published by the Islamic government, and these provincial results are fully consistent with the overall results.

The 1960 census of agriculture counted 2.44 million agricultural households, of which 1.8 million were sharecroppers or tenants and were thus potential beneficiaries of the land reform that sought to transfer ownership of land cultivated by tenants to the tenants. The remainder were primarily peasant proprietors and would not be included in such a land reform since they already owned the land they cultivated. The final result of land reform, based on adding the number of beneficiaries reported to have received land under each phase, showed that 2.214 million peasants received land, which exceeded the figure derived from the 1960 census. Adding the number of peasant proprietors who owned land before reform brought the total to 3 million, a number exceeding the 2.48 million agricultural holdings reported in the 1974 census.

The key to these discrepancies was found in a large-scale micro-level study of land reform by Cyrus Salmanzadeh and Gwyn Jones, a contribution of lasting value.[9] The study found that at least 97 percent of the 6,927 eligible peasants residing in the 169 villages studied had received land. The study also reported that one-third of those receiving land under phase 3 had also received land under phase 1. Thus, the number of first-time recipients of land under phase 3 was not 1.2 million, which was the total number of beneficiaries under that phase, but 800,000. When this was added to the recipients of land under phases 1 and 2, the sum of 1.814 million was entirely consistent with the census results and indicated that all eligible peasants received land. It was also estimated that land reform transferred the ownership of at least 60 percent of the agricultural land to peasants.[10] A similar result was obtained by Ahmad Ashraf and Mohammad Javad Amid.[11] When added to landholdings already peasant owned, it follows that at least 85 percent of the agricultural land was in peasant hands by the completion of land reform in 1971.

These estimates are fully supported by the results of land reform in the six provinces to be discussed here—Bakhtaran (formerly Kermanshahan), Fars, Hamedan, Isfahan, Lorestan, and Markazi (Central). The information in these

consistent with the other sectoral and overall macroeconomic data. If anything, the agricultural growth statistics were on the conservative side. It is noteworthy that the prerevolutionary statistics on agricultural output have been revised upward by the Islamic government. In addition to the overall consistency of the land reform statistics with the 1960 and 1974 agricultural censuses, a study of the sugar industry found that the microeconomic and regional statistics on the sugar farmers were highly consistent with the findings of the 1975 survey of agriculture. M.G. Majd, "The Oil Boom and Structural Transformation in the Sugar Industry of Iran," *Journal of Rural Studies* 7 (1991).

9. Cyrus Salmanzadeh and Gwyn Jones, "An Approach to the Micro Analysis of the Land Reform Program in Southwestern Iran," *Land Economics* 55 (1979).

10. See Majd, "Land Reform Policies in Iran," p. 845.

11. Ashraf, "State and Agrarian Relations," p. 285, states that between 52 and 62 percent of the agricultural land was transferred to peasants. In a study that was highly critical of land reform, *Agriculture, Poverty, and Reform*, p. 107, Amid readily concedes that the available data show "that by the end of land reform *all* sharecroppers and fixed-rent tenants must have become peasant proprietors. . . . and that about 60% of all villages were redistributed among peasants."

TABLE 1

A. *Results of Land Reform in Six Provinces of Iran (in Hectares)*

Province	Peasants	Land Received	Average Holding
Central	146,714	985,604	6.7
Isfahan	69,680	176,042	2.5
Fars	141,931	586,765	4.1
Lorestan	62,633	331,330	5.3
Bakhtaran	78,073	629,292	8.1
Hamedan	86,971	773,334	8.9
TOTAL	586,002	3,482,367	5.9

B. *Landowners Able to Maintain Land in Six Provinces (in Hectares)*

Province	Landowners	Land Received	Average Holding
Central	3,451	67,568	19.6
Isfahan	7,741	44,343	5.9
Fars	12,966	162,972	12.6
Lorestan	1,996	21,060	10.6
Bakhtaran	4,023	54,778	13.6
Hamedan	2,068	38,492	18.6
TOTAL	31,975	389,213	12.2

Source: Islamic Republic of Iran, Ministry of Agriculture, "Investigation of the Amount of Land Received by Peasants and Landlords due to the Implementation of Land Reform Laws," cited in K. Khosravi, *A Statistical Investigation of the State of Landownership in Six Provinces of Iran* (Tehran: Center for University Publications, 1367 [1988/89]), in Persian.

reports on the number of peasants and the amount of land received by them, or maintained by landlords, is based on files pertaining to each village. Recognizing the problem of multiple counting because of the inclusion of many peasants in more than one phase of land reform, a special effort was made to avoid it by identifying each recipient as listed in the files. According to the 1966 population census, Iran's 3,068,619 settled rural households resided in 66,438 villages.[12] The 1966 settled rural population of these six provinces consisted of 949,956 households and the number of villages was 21,767. Thus, the population share of the six was 31 percent of the total and the number of rural settlements was 32 percent. The number of peasants who received land under the three phases of land reform was 586,002, which is 32.3 percent of the 1.814 million peasant beneficiaries of land reform. (See table 1.)

12. Iran Statistical Center, *Yearbook of Statistics, 1352* (Tehran, 1353 [1974/75]), pp. 33–5, in Persian.

TABLE 2
Scope of Land Reform in Six Provinces of Iran

	Central	Isfahan	Fars	Lorestan	Bakhtaran	Hamedan	Total
Total Villages	6,588	3,336	5,520	2,309	2,726	1,288	21,767
Reform Implemented	4,226	1,421	3,656	1,607	2,664	1,270	14,844
Percentage	64.1	42.6	66.2	69.6	97.7	98.6	68.2
Not Affected	2,362	1,915	1,864	702	62	18	6,923
Reasons for Exclusion from Land Reform							
Peasant Owned	1,608	1,526	1,287	698	12	16	5,147
Percentage	68.0	79.7	68.5	99.4	19.4	88.9	74.3
No Agriculture	439	322	432	—	—	—	1,193
Percentage	19.0	16.8	23.2	—	—	—	17.2
Orchards, Other	315	67	145	4	50	2	583
Percentage	13.0	3.5	8.3	0.6	80.6	10.1	8.5

Source: Islamic Republic of Iran, Ministry of Agriculture, "Investigation of the Amount of Land Received by Peasants and Landlords due to the Implementation of Land Reform Laws," cited in K. Khosravi, *A Statistical Investigation of the State of Landownership in Six Provinces of Iran* (Tehran: Center for University Publications, 1367 [1988/89]), in Persian.

Of the 3.87 million hectares of land affected by the program, 90 percent was transferred to peasants. The data also shows that land reform was implemented in 68.2 percent of the villages and 72 percent of the agricultural villages. (See table 2.) Of the 6,923 villages where land reform was not implemented, nearly three-fourths (5,147) were already owned by peasants and were thus exempt. A large number (1,193) were without agriculture. Of the remaining 583 villages not subject to land reform, 212 consisted of nationalized pastures or solely of orchards; 210 were declared part of urban areas; 82 villages were declared "mechanized," since the owners used wage labor and machinery to cultivate the land. In only 68 villages—a minute fraction of the 21,767 villages)—were landlords able to purchase the cultivation rights of peasants which would result in the "dispossession" of the peasants.

The magnitude of this radical transformation in landownership can be seen by the following statistics. With 25 percent of the 20,574 agricultural villages before land reform owned by peasants, private (excluding peasant proprietors), religious, and public landownership constituted 75 percent of the total. Because 90 percent of this land was distributed to peasants, it follows that land reform transferred some 67.5 percent of total agricultural land to the sharecroppers and tenants. When land previously owned by peasants is added to this, fully 92 percent of the agricultural land consisted of peasant holdings by the completion of land reform in 1971. This result is consistent with the 1974 agricultural census finding that 90.6

percent of agricultural land was owner-occupied. Applying El Ghonemy's criteria that a complete land reform is one in which at least 50 percent of the agricultural land is transferred to peasants,[13] Iran's land reform qualifies as "complete," and appears to be the most radical land reform implemented by a non-Marxist state during the twentieth century.

The Landless

Households that neither rented nor owned land were not included in the provisions of land reform. The size of this group has been variously estimated at 1–1.5 million households, or 30–50 percent of the rural population. These households are said to have been an important source of migration. The origin of this inflated number of landless households can be traced to two misclassifications under the 1960 agricultural census. First, in contrast to the practice under the 1956 population census when settlements under 5,000 were designated as rural, the 1960 agricultural census included all settlements under 10,000. Thus, some 400,000 urban households were misclassified as rural landless. Second, up to 600,000 tenant farmers performing wage labor were also misclassified by being included in the ranks of the landless.[14] Thus, in reality, the size of the landless was much smaller than cited in the literature.

As noted, the number of settled rural households in 1966 was 3.068 million. The number of households with land rights—cultivators and fruit growers—was 2.464 million. The difference of 604,000 households constituted the landless population. This was 19.7 percent of the rural population. In terms of the overall average of 46 households per village, 9 households were landless. Not all of these, however, were employed in agriculture; many were rural traders, professionals, or craftsmen. The actual size of the agricultural khoshneshin can be estimated using the 1966 census. That census enumerated 368,000 seasonal rural workers of which 86 percent were classified as agricultural wage earners. (See table 3.) Thus, some 320,000 rural landless households, 10.3 percent or 5 households per village, relied on agricultural wage employment. The remaining 287,000 (an average of 4 households per village) were rural traders or craftsmen who did not rely on agriculture. A more egalitarian land reform could have given land to some additional 320,000 households by expropriating much of the 1 million hectares that remained in the possession of 69,800 landlords. Aside from issues of equity—landlords had already lost heavily—this amounted to 2.5 hectares per household. Given the scarcity of water and arable land, a meaningful solution was to find alternative productive employment for this population.

13. M. Riad El Ghonemy, *The Political Economy of Rural Poverty: The Case for Land Reform* (London: Routledge, 1990), p. 255.

14. Majd, "Land Reform Policies in Iran," p. 844.

TABLE 3
Indicators of Rural Employment, 1956, 1966, 1976 (millions)

	1956	1966	1976
Rural Labor Force	4.173	5.073	5.460
Regularly Employed	4.100	4.505	4.687
Seasonally Employed	N.A.	0.368	0.596
Unemployed	0.073	0.200	0.177
Unemployment Rate (%)	1.7	3.9	3.2
Agricultural Employment	3.108	3.550	3.357
Nonfarm Employment	0.992	1.323	1.926
Rural Agricultural Employment (%)	75.6	72.9	63.5

Source: Rural and Agricultural Statistics of Iran, *Agah Book on Land and Rural Issues* (Tehran: Agah, 1361 [1982/83]), pp. 176–7, in Persian.

POST-REFORM AGRICULTURAL PRODUCTION AND POLICY

The performance of the agricultural sector is a crucial determinant of rural welfare because agriculture is the major source of employment and income in rural areas. Its neglect in the current debate on the causes of rural-urban migration is, therefore surprising. The rapid increase in agricultural output and productivity during 1966–1976 was probably unprecedented in Iran's recorded economic history. According to the data published by the Islamic republic,[15] the agricultural growth rate during 1966–1976 was 5.6 percent, a very high rate by international standards, according to the World Bank,[16] and contrasted with a weak growth rate of 2.2 percent during 1959–1966. Particularly strong growth was recorded in the production of cash crops such as sugarbeets, cotton, oilseeds, fruits, and vegetables, products whose production was dominated by small farmers who grew the crops on small plots.[17] With declining agricultural employment, productivity rose by nearly 7 percent per year. While the pre-1966 decade was one of declining per capita food production, the trend during 1966–1976 was completely reversed, and per capita food production rose by 2.9 percent per year, justifying the argument that land reform removed one of the main obstacles to industrial growth, namely the slow growth of agricultural output reported for the 1950s and early 1960s.[18]

15. Bank Markazi, *National Accounts of Iran 1338–1356* (Tehran, 1360 [1981/82]), pp. 112–113, in Persian.

16. See Amuzegar, *Dynamics of the Iranian Revolution*, p. 61.

17. M.G. Majd, "The Oil Boom and Agricultural Development: A Reconsideration of Agricultural Policy in Iran," *Journal of Energy and Development* 15 (1989).

18. Karshenas, *Oil, State, and Industrialization in Iran*, p. 162.

Iran's agriculture also benefited from substantial protection and government investment. Reportedly, the improvement in the terms of trade for farm products during the 1950s, which resulted from the slow growth of agriculture and strict import controls, continued during the 1960s and 1970s because of import controls and tariffs on industrial crops, price supports for grains, and the near 10 percent increase in demand for food.[19] Indirect protection consisted of providing a wide array of producers with subsidized chemical inputs and credit. Such programs were effective in helping small farmers cultivate resource-intensive cash crops, such as sugarbeets and cotton, and resulted in a large increase in the use of fertilizers by peasants.[20]

In addition to improvements in the terms of trade, government development expenditure and subsidized long-term loans resulted in a substantial transfer of resources into the agricultural sector. Total government capital expenditure during 1963–1977 (354.2 billion rials) and credit provided by specialized state banks (357.5 billion rials) amounted to 711.7 billion rials, or $10 billion, excluding interest rate and input subsidies. This exceeded the corresponding sum of 663.1 billion rials provided to manufacturing.[21] Thus, unlike the experience of most developing countries, and contrary to a widely held view, agriculture was a beneficiary of substantial protection. When loans from commercial banks and other private sources of finance are added to state funds allocated to agriculture during the 1970s, the resulting yearly sum of $2.6 billion amounted to 5 percent of the GDP, a formidable sum given that the contribution of agriculture to the GDP had fallen to 8.7 percent by 1977. This expenditure was also well in excess of corresponding figures in such oil-producing countries as Mexico and Nigeria.[22]

RURAL AND AGRICULTURAL EMPLOYMENT, 1956–1976

Iran's population census is conducted during the month of November when agricultural activity is at its lowest, and the level of unemployment among seasonal agricultural and construction workers is at its peak. Consequently, the population census figures have tended to overstate the true level of unemployment. In recognition of this factor, the census definition of the seasonally unemployed as "all persons who were unemployed due to the effects of the seasonal nature of their work. . . . (and who) had neither received wages or salaries in cash or in kind nor had been seeking work," makes it clear that the seasonally unemployed are not to be counted as unemployed when computing the

19. Ibid.

20. "Rural and Agricultural Statistics of Iran," *Agah Book on Land and Rural Issues* (Tehran: Agah, 1360 [1981/82]), p. 185, in Persian; Majd, "The Oil Boom and Structural Transformation in the Sugar Industry of Iran."

21. Karshenas, *Oil, State, and Industrialization,* p. 107.

22. Majd, "The Oil Boom and Agricultural Development," p. 135.

rural unemployment rate.[23] To treat seasonal workers—of which 86 percent in 1966 and 96 percent in 1976 consisted of agricultural workers—as "unemployed," as has been done in the literature,[24] is an inappropriate use of the rural employment statistics. In the 1956 population census, those classified as "seasonally unemployed" were specifically treated as employed. In order to maintain consistency between the three census results, the seasonally unemployed have been treated as employed when computing the unemployment rate.[25] The unemployment rate reported in table 3 is based on the census definition of unemployed as "all persons who have never been employed or have been previously employed but were not employed and were seeking work during the seven days preceding the census enumeration." An alternative measure of the unemployment rate can be derived by including the nonagricultural seasonal workers in the ranks of the unemployed. This alternative measure of the unemployment rate was 4.9 percent and 3.7 percent for 1966 and 1976, respectively.

Several other features are of interest. First, while seasonal agricultural employment rose sharply by 256,000 (81 percent), full-time agricultural employment fell by 421,000 (13.2 percent), resulting in a net decline of 193,000 (5.4 percent). Second, there was a sizable expansion in nonagricultural employment during 1966–1976, which grew by 603,000—655,000 when non-farm seasonal workers in 1966 are excluded. Third, the rural construction industry accounted for 62.7 percent of the increase in nonagricultural employment. Employment in that industry rose from 248,000 in 1966 to 626,000 in 1976, an indication that rural Iran experienced a construction boom in this period.[26]

THE MAGNITUDE AND ORIGIN OF RURAL-URBAN MIGRATION, 1956–1976

Although data on population and migration prior to 1956 is sketchy, the evidence indicates that rural-urban migration had been underway at least since the early 1900s, at the onset of an increasing rate of population growth, and that the urban population growth had exceeded the overall population growth at least since 1935. The population of Tehran, grew from 0.5 million in 1940 to 1.5 million in 1956, an annual growth rate of 7 percent.[27] During the 1956–1976 period, population and labor force grew by 78 percent and 62 percent, respectively. Agricultural employment and the rural labor force grew by 8 percent and 30 percent, respectively. Despite the slower growth of the rural labor force, due to migration and stagnant employment in agriculture, and the substantial increases in

23. Iran Statistical Center, *National Census of Population and Housing, November 1976: Total Country* (Tehran: Plan and Budget Organization), b-c.
24. Mohtadi, "Rural Inequality."
25. Rural and Agricultural Statistics of Iran, pp. 157–59.
26. Ibid, p. 158.
27. Ashraf, *State and Agrarian Relations*, p. 289; Nattagh, *Agriculture and Regional Development*, p. 61.

TABLE 4
Rural and Urban Population, 1956, 1966, 1976 (millions)

Year	Rural	Urban	Total
1956	13.001	5.954	18.955
1966	15.994	9.795	25.789
1976	17.854	15.855	33.709

Source: Rural and Agricultural Statistics of Iran, *Agah Book on Land and Rural Issues* (Tehran: Agah Publishers, 1361 [1982/83]), p. 175, in Persian.

productivity during the 1960s and 1970s, there remained a large gap between the rural-urban per capita income and productivity.[28] This gap was indicative of a large reserve of surplus labor in the rural sector. Given the limited scope of agriculture as a source of additional employment and income, the real solution to the problems of rural poverty and underemployment consisted of creating nonfarm employment in rural areas or of migration. Describing conditions in some of the remote highland villages, one observer painted a bleak picture of overpopulation and Malthusian pressures that could only be alleviated by migration.[29]

Reliable data on Iran's population in this period is provided by the population censuses of 1956, 1966, and 1976. (See table 4.) The compound annual population growth rate during 1956–66 was 3.1 percent; during 1966–1976, it declined to 2.71 percent; during 1956–1976 span the rate was 2.92 percent. Urban population growth was a steady 5 percent per year during this 20-year period and does not indicate a sudden upsurge in rural-urban migration. In the absence of data covering the entire period, migration has to be estimated. The estimates, however, differ considerably.

Using the demographic survival ratio method, which measures the difference between the actual population in the "end year" and the population that would have survived based on the natural growth rate and the population in the base year, Mohtadi arrived at 3.5 million rural-urban migrants during 1966–1976.[30] In contrast, using the vital statistics on births and deaths, Karshenas arrived at an

28. Karshenas, *Oil, State, and Industrialization in Iran,* p. 275.

29. See Bowen-Jones's observation in V.F. Costello, *Urbanization in the Middle East* (Cambridge and New York: Cambridge University Press, 1977), p. 46.

30. As pointed out by Mohtadi (p. 841), the census years (1956, 1966, 1976) do not correspond with the land reform period (1962–1971). The practice of using the pre-1966 and the post-1966 years as pre- and post-land reform years can be justified on at least three grounds. First, the censuses provide the only source of reliable and extensive data on population. Second, although land reform was launched in 1962, because of a shortage of trained personnel it did not proceed simultaneously in all provinces, and, especially during the initial phase, it took place in one province at a time. Third, in 1966 the second phase was far from completion, and phase 3 (1969–71), the most important stage in terms of peasants and landlords affected, was some years away. The 1966–1976 period accurately reflects the period of land reform and beyond.

estimate of 2.34 million. Similarly, a study by the Iran Statistical Center (ISC) estimated that migration was 2.26 million during 1966–1976.[31]

The figure of 3.5 million noted by Mohtadi substantially overestimates the actual level of migration, but the other estimates, are relatively accurate. The first problem with Mohtadi's estimate is that it is based on an assumed natural rural population growth rate of 3.5 percent and an urban population growth rate of 2.4 percent. Given the rural-urban population share, this amounts to an overall growth rate of 3.1 percent during 1966–1976. The population census, however, indicated that the growth rate was 2.71 percent. The second problem concerns the definition of urban and rural settlements. In accordance with the United Nations definition, in the three prerevolution population censuses, an urban settlement (*abadi-e shahri*) consists of a population site of 5,000 and above. Exceptions are few and insignificant.[32] A rural settlement (*abadi-e roostai*) is one with less than 5,000. When the population of a rural settlement surpassed 5,000, it would be reclassified as "urban" in the next census. This resulted in an exaggerated growth of the urban population and an underestimation of the growth of rural population. Census data show that the number of towns with populations of 5,000 and above was 186 in 1956, 263 in 1966, and 373 in 1976. Since the doubling in the number of towns during 1956–1976 was due to reclassification of those rural settlements whose population reached 5,000, the reclassification was considerable. Specifically, the 1976 population of the 110 "new" towns was 666,083. The corresponding figure for the 77 new towns in 1966 was at least 385,000 and more probably 462,000.

The third problem concerns the inclusion of nonsedentary groups consisting of tribal (*ashayer*) and nomadic (*moteharek*) populations in the rural population figures reported in table 4. The nonsettled population in the 1966 census was reported to be 709,799. (The tribal component was 462,146, and the nomadic component was 247,653.) The figure for the 1976 nonsettled population shows an astonishing drop to 347,812 (337,176 for tribal and only 10,636 for nomadic). Thus, the nomadic all but disappeared. Assuming a normal population growth for these groups, it appears that 313,000 nomadic and 267,000 tribal members (580,000 total) had left the ranks of the nonsedentary population by joining the settled rural population, or more likely, by migration to urban areas, or by emigration.[33] While

31. Iran Statistical Center, "An Investigation on the Extent of Overall Rural-Urban Migration," n.d., in Persian, cited in Nattagh, *Agriculture and Regional Development*, p. 86.

32. The number of towns with less than 5,000 was 22 under the 1966 census, little changed from that of 1956. The number had seemingly declined to 6 by 1976. Iran Statistical Center, *National Census of Population and Housing, 1966: Total Country Settled Population*, vol. 168 (Tehran: Plan and Budget Organization, August 1969); Iran Statistical Center, *Yearbook of Statistics, 1360* (Tehran, 1361 [1982/83]), p. 68, in Persian.

33. Iran Statistical Center, *Yearbook of Statistics, 1360*, p. 58. Examples are provided by the Bakhtiari and the Baluchi tribes. The trend for the Bakhtiaris was to become wage laborers in the oil industry in Khuzestan. The Baluchis, in contrast, emigrated to the Arab side of the Persian Gulf. (The author is grateful to Brian Spooner for these examples.) The exodus of the nonsettled population from the rural areas during 1966–1976 is indicated by the jump in the number of empty or abandoned *abadis*,

TABLE 5
Structure of Rural Settlements by Population Size, 1956, 1966, 1976

	1956		1966		1976	
Size	Settlements	Population	Settlements	Population	Settlements	Population
4,999–2,500	256	868,739	308	1,024,855	484	1,612,000
2,499–1,000	1,682	2,414,516	2,087	3,011,208	2,735	3,990,000
999–500	4,314	2,937,366	5,314	3,635,593	6,442	4,306,000
499–100	24,427	5,637,654	27,351	6,441,030	26,680	6,428,000
99–50	8,420	622,511	10,528	766,266	9,758	706,000
49–25	4,688	173,801	7,884	286,051	7,500	272,000
24–1	5,267	66,757	12,966	148,735	11,654	135,000
TOTAL	49,054	12,757,344	66,438	15,313,738	65,253	17,449,000

Source: Iran Statistical Center, *Yearbook of Statistics, 1349* (Tehran, 1350 [1971/72]), p. 38, in Persian. Iran Statistical Center, *Yearbook of Statistics, 1362* (Tehran, 1363 [1984/85]), p. 41, in Persian.

this remarkable decline in the nonsettled population during 1966–1976 merits investigation, the change in the status of the nonsedentary population cannot be treated as regular rural-urban migration. Moreover, since the debate concerns the magnitude of the rural-urban migration that is said to have resulted from land reform and agricultural policy, the population of interest is the settled one, the size of which is given in table 5.

Subtracting the reclassified, nomadic, and tribal components from 3.5 million, the resulting 2.2 million is very close to the estimates provided by Karshenas and the ISC. Thus, on average, rural-urban migration during 1966–1976 amounted to 220,000 to 230,000 per year compared to 152,000 during the previous decade. Annual rural-urban migration during 1956–1966 amounted to some 1.2 percent of the rural population, and the corresponding figure for 1966–1976 was 1.5 percent. This hardly qualifies for the description of a "massive migratory exodus." Migration accounted for at most 35–40 percent of the increase in the urban population. Moreover, the growth of the urban population that resulted from migration in Iran was lower than that of many other countries of the Middle East and North Africa.[34] In addition to employment considerations, a principal reason for rural-urban migration appears to have included educational opportunities for young males and marriage by young females.

which rose from 15,929 in 1966 to 26,952. These abadis frequently served as seasonal residences for the migrating tribes. This contrasted with a decline of 1,185 in the number of settled villages. (See table 5.) Iran Statistical Center, *Yearbook of Statistics, 1362* (Tehran, 1363 [1984/85]), p. 41, in Persian.

34. Of the 17 other countries in the region, rural-urban migration during 1965-1980 accounted for more than 40 percent of the increase in the urban population in 8 countries; it was 36–40 percent in 3 countries; it was under 35 percent in ther remaining 6 countries, which included Kuwait and the United Arab Emirates. See Alan Richards and John Waterbury, *A Political Economy of the Middle East* (Boulder, CO: Westview Press, 1990), p. 266.

A demographic study by the ISC during 1973–76 documented the importance of educational needs and noneconomic factors in rural-urban migration. In particular, the study found that the highest migration rates for any age category were for boys 15–19 years of age. This prompted the study to conclude that "heavy migration, undoubtedly because of school, begins in rural areas around age 10 but in the cities only by age 15, boys moving in much larger numbers than girls. . . . The migration of women of 15–24 years is to a large extent caused by marriage."[35] Economic migrants were mostly men 20–24 years of age. After 25, migration fell steeply and the population 35 and over was almost sedentary. These results are also contrary to the statement that the Iranian "land reform appears to have played a crucial role in the subsequent migratory process."[36] The tendency for the offspring of farmers to leave their rural homes for the cities is a worldwide phenomena. It cannot be blamed on land reform. Moreover, the young age structure of the migrants indicates that migration consisted of some of the natural population growth of rural areas. This clearly points to Malthusian pressures noted above: young men left to seek an education and a better livelihood than the one available in rural areas. Data in table 5 on the changing structure of rural settlements derived from the three censuses highlights this point.

During the period 1956–1966, the population of the larger villages (500 inhabitants and above) grew an average of 2.1 percent per year, and that of medium settlements (100–499 inhabitants) increased by 1.3 percent per year. Considering that the overall population growth in this period was 3.1 percent (natural rural population growth was likely 3.5 percent), and that more than 90 percent of the rural population resided in villages of 100 or more inhabitants, the slow growth of these settlements is indicative of substantial migration from medium and, to a lesser extent, from larger villages. The population of small villages (under 100 inhabitants) increased by 2.9 percent per year. This increase, however, appears in part to be the result of undercounting in the 1956 census of villages with less than 50 inhabitants. The sharp rise in the number of these villages from 9,955 to 20,850 in the 1966 census is not plausible and points to an undercount in the 1956 census.

There were some interesting changes in the structure of rural settlements and in the migration pattern during 1966–1976. First, the population of small villages (under 100 inhabitants) fell by 7.3 percent and some 1,000 were abandoned. Next, the population of settlements with 100–499 inhabitants, by far the largest category in terms of population and settlements, was unchanged, an indication that the bulk of the natural increase had migrated. In contrast to the 1956–1966 period, the population of villages with 500 and above grew by 2.6 percent per year, only slightly less than the overall 2.7 percent growth during 1966–1976, an indication of

35. Iran Statistical Center, "Population Survey of Iran, Final Report, 1973–1976" (Tehran), June 1978, pp. 106–8.

36. Mohtadi, "Rural Inequality," p. 842

a much lower migration rate than in the earlier decade. Moreover, the population of settlements in the 1,000–4,999 range increased by 3.1 percent, well above the 2.7 percent overall population increase. Thus, by giving the ownership of land cultivated by peasants to the peasants, land reform appears to have reduced migration. By 1976, 58 percent of the rural population resided in settlements in excess of 500 inhabitants, up from 48 percent in the previous decade.

To sum up, in contrast to 1956–1966, when rural migration originated primarily from large and medium settlements (100 inhabitants and above), rural migration during 1966–1976 originated mostly from medium and small settlements (under 500 inhabitants). In particular, much of the migration came from villages of 100 to 499 inhabitants, with an average of 235 (or 47 households), and from villages with under 100 people (average of 39 persons or 8 households). Often located in mountainous or semi-arid regions, these villages could neither provide an adequate standard of living for the rising population nor meet the educational needs of the young, thus leaving migration as a way out. This is clearly demonstrated in the case of villages in the 100–499 person group. In contrast, there was little pressure to leave the larger villages. In addition to greater educational and social amenities, a rapidly rising agricultural productivity benefited most the areas where enhanced production took place, namely, larger villages located in well-watered fertile regions and not the marginal villages found in mountainous and semi-arid parts. Moreover, the expanding nonagricultural employment (in particular the rural construction boom) occurred mostly in these larger rural population centers.

CONCLUSION

As already stated, land reform in Iran has been possibly the most radical non-Marxist land reform of the twentieth century. It gave land to all of Iran's tenant cultivators and did not result in peasant dispossession and destitution. Nor did it result in a "massive migratory exodus." The analogy with the English enclosures is, thus, entirely inappropriate. In terms of agricultural growth and productivity, land reform was a huge success. Thirty years later, and with much research in between, the persistence of so much myth and misinformation on the subject is remarkable. Much of the problem can be attributed to a continued attempt to analyze Iran's land reform within a neo-Marxist paradigm with its emphasis on class struggle, the predicted proletarization, and the eventual disappearance of the peasantry. The salient features of Iran's land reform, however, do not fit this theory. The continued use of early secondary sources, written years before the final results of land reform were known, and the disregard of the primary sources, have also contributed to the confusion and misinformation.

[13]

Pergamon

World Development, Vol. 22, No. 3, pp. 369–380, 1994
Elsevier Science Ltd
Printed in Great Britain.
0305–750X/94 $7.00 + 0.00

Unskilled Urban Migrant Women and Disguised Employment: Home-working Women in Istanbul, Turkey

E. MINE CINAR*
Loyola University of Chicago

Summary. — Formal and informal labor market opportunities for women are examined for Turkey. Data collected from three surveys are used to describe types of home work and hourly wages are imputed for home work to compare with formal sector wages. The number of migrant women who take home work in the city of Istanbul is estimated.

1. INTRODUCTION

Home working has recently reemerged, in both less-developed and developed countries. In developed countries, home working is observed in both unskilled and highly skilled work. In less-developed countries, home working involves unskilled or semi-skilled labor, usually migrant labor. In general, there are no estimates of the number of women who take work in their homes, for this is part of disguised employment and the shadow economy. Most of this type of employment is hidden in official statistics.[1]

The economic development literature has studied mass migrations and changes in urban, unskilled male labor markets in developing countries since the introduction of dual economic development models. Attention has also been drawn to self-selection and migrant earnings in developed and developing countries (Borjas, 1987) and to the gender–wage gap in development (Ashraf and Ashraf, 1993). Changes in the urban, unskilled female labor force and in job opportunities for this group have escaped attention in economics.[2] The jobs open to unskilled females vary from the formal sector where the women work in factories, receive wages and social insurance benefits, to informal home production where jobs are subcontracted to women. Formal sector jobs are defined in this study as those in the organized sectors which are subject to minimum wage legislation and which come with health insurance and retirement benefits.[3]

Whether home working in developing countries has appeared because international competition dictates cost efficiency (i.e. demand driven) or because it is a by-product of the supply of migrant women in urban centers (i.e. supply driven) is a valid question. As a proxy for internal cost efficiency, one purpose of this study was to find out whether formal factory or workshop production was being switched to homes due to cost advantages.

Studies of developed countries show that home working comes in many forms. One study using data from a national random sample in Britain (Hakim, 1987) found that home workers were not exclusively women and only 10% of home workers had manufacturing jobs. In general, they were more educated than the rest of the labor force, more qualified for the jobs and less likely to be from ethnic minorities. Some were also very highly paid compared to the rest of the labor force.

For developing countries, studies have examined the issues of informal job markets, marginality, dependency and gender. In general, gender studies

*This study was partially funded by Loyola University of Chicago and by a postdoctoral grant from the Joint Committee on the Near and Middle East of the Social Science Research Council and American council of Learned Societies with funds provided by the Ford Foundation and the National Endowment for the Humanities. T. Belgesan assisted the study in Bursa. A. Okten of Yildiz University, Istanbul and her students in urban planning made the surveys possible. Turkish State Institute of Statistics provided the 1987 sampling base of small-scale industrial firms in Istanbul. Bursa and Istanbul Chambers of Commerce provided their member registration records. B. Cinar helped with data organization. Anonymous referees made suggestions regarding literature in gender studies. I thank them all. Final revision accepted: September 30, 1993.

have examined the impact of industrialization on the female labor force in terms of either integration, marginalization or exploitation.[4] Since the extent of home working is not known in developing countries, these studies had to rely on exploratory samples where they examined home working in unskilled or semi skilled jobs. Beneria and Roldan (1987) studied 140 women home workers and 67 subcontracting firms in Mexico City and examined gender, class and division of labor within the family. Benton (1989) found that restructuring in the Spanish shoe industry led to both female and male home work. Her first sample of 2,085 households interviews led to a second sample of home workers and 25 industry participants. She found that women's home work included managerial aspects such as reorganizing production with different shoe models. She also noted that as decentralized shoe production turned to home work, it lost quality and became overdependent on low wages. The industry lost international competitiveness by not upgrading quality.

Using data from three surveys conducted in Turkey, this study tries to answer the following questions: who prefers to do home working in Istanbul today? What kind of jobs are assigned to home work? Why do employers prefer to give out home work? Is there any switching from formal factory/workshop production to home work production? Are the wages in home working substantially less than formal sector wages? What is a minimum estimate of women who take home work?

Istanbul is a good case study because it has been a major target for industrialization and has had an urban population explosion through internal migration. In 1985, 77% of the females aged 12 or above (18% of which were illiterate; SIS, 1987) in the city had at best a grade school diploma.[5] Taking work into the home has become an important part of production involving female migrant labor in the city. Shops and exporters which market their products have flourished.

Section 2 describes the data sources. Section 3 examines formal sector employment for women. Section 4 examines informal sector employment, the type of work given out to homes and the characteristics of the home-working women. Section 5 imputes home work wages and section 6 approximates the number of women who actually work in their homes in Istanbul. The last section gives the conclusions.

2. DATA

The data are based on three different surveys, one on women taking work into their homes, one on small-scale textile firms (both conducted in Turkey during July and August 1987) and one on subcontracting shops in Istanbul (conducted during the summer of 1989). Two surveys were conducted simultaneously during the summer of 1987. The first was the subcontracting survey where a multistage sampling was conducted. In the first stage subcontracting employers/shops were contacted and interviewed. The second stage of the subcontracting survey involved the home working women. They were either selected randomly from the neighborhoods, from addresses supplied by the shop, or were among the women who brought their finished work to the shop that day to get their payment. A total of 52 women were surveyed. Even though considerable attention was paid to the sampling base from which these observations were drawn, no assertions can be made about the representativeness of this sample because the total population of women who work from home was not known in 1987. In general, the samples in a particular area were representative of the sampling population of the area; in almost all cases, the shop owner's informal description of a typical subcontractor was confirmed by descriptive sample statistics later. A follow up study, survey of 1989, was done to determine the total population of women who work from home.

The second survey conducted in Bursa and Istanbul was an industrial survey, with stratified random sampling of all the small-scale textile firms employing 1–25 people. In Bursa, a stratified random area sampling was done with a sampling fraction of 5%, using the sampling frame developed by Mentes (1984) and updated by Cinar, Kaytaz and Eucimen (1988).

In Istanbul, the Turkish State Institute of Statistics provided the 1987 sampling base of their Industrial Survey, which included all of textile firms employing 10–24 people and a 15% random sample of all firms employing 1–9 people. A multistage sampling was used for Istanbul which included proportional stratified and systematic sampling techniques, with a sampling fraction of 2%. A total of 287 firms were surveyed, with 156 firms in Bursa and 131 firms in Istanbul. This survey was designed to examine capital and labor usage in the firm, as well as to determine the export orientation and survival potential of the small-scale firms.

A third survey on subcontracting shops was conducted in the summer of 1989 in Istanbul with 128 firms/shops in major districts of Istanbul. Out of these 128 shops, 57 were found to be actually using home-working women as laborers. The rest were subcontracting their orders to organized workshops. Using the data from the 57 shops, an estimate was made of the number of women taking work to their homes.

In the surveys, we found no evidence of production switching from factories or workshops to informal home work. Employers stated that large volume domestic and export orders had to be filled in a timely fashion with uniform quality and that home working was unreliable both in terms of time and quality control. T-shirts, leather jackets, coats, etc. were all done in formal workplaces. The type of production that developed around home work was that of one-of-a-kind hand-designed items (the employers created the design), knitted sweaters, embroidery, etc., with flexible delivery schedules.

3. WHY NOT WORK IN THE FORMAL SECTOR?

(a) *Home workers' perspective*

The women we interviewed in this study did not regard home work as "work." Almost all women viewed their work as temporary and their knitting as a hobby, even though some had done this for over 10 years. Consequently, this type of work may suffer from declaration bias in household surveys because the women may not declare themselves in the national or urban censuses. One important advantage of home work is flexible work hours which is important to mothers of young children. On the other hand, the major advantage of formal sector employment is social security and medical benefits.

There are several other reasons why unskilled migrant women do not work in the formal sector in Turkey. First of all, formal sector job openings at the unskilled level are usually announced by word of mouth within the firm. Newspaper advertisements are rare. Another avenue for formal sector job searching is through the public Labor Placement Office (LPO). Among the applicants to this office by educational backgrounds, the lowest usage rate (18%) is for women who are illiterate or who have no educational diplomas. The remaining 82% search for jobs through other means, that is, through informal information networks.

Second, in all educational background categories, the unemployment rate for females is higher than the unemployment rate for males (SIS, 1985, p. 200). Even if they find jobs in the formal markets, women in general have longer unemployment spells. Unemployment duration differences by gender in urban areas in 1982 are given in Table 1. The number and percentage of unemployed males decline in the first 10 months (columns 1, 4) but remain steady for females (columns 2, 5). In fact, the male to female unemployment ratio over time has a declining trend (column 3). This indicates that unemployed men can find jobs more easily than women. Hence, females may be "last in, first out" and have a bigger challenge in finding jobs when they are unemployed. The overall official unemployment rate itself is also higher for women at 22.36% than for men at 9.09%, roughly 2.4 times the male unemployment rate.

Another reason for women to prefer home work is the low potential for salary increase and career advancement compared to male workers. There were no observed wage differences between males and females at entry level jobs. Both unskilled males and females in the formal sectors entered the work force at minimum wage. Yet, there were substantial differences in positions within the firm and therefore earnings by the end of five years. Men learned on the job and looked for promotion opportunities within and outside the firm. Women were firm-dependent and did not change jobs as frequently as men did in the small-scale textile firms covered in this study. Most of the women preferred to stay in the same firm because finding a safe place to work is of paramount importance to women who work in the organized sector. This is also one of the reasons why female neighbors/relatives clustered around the same workplace. This gave them safety in numbers and protected their

Table 1. *Gender differences in unemployment duration, urban areas only, 1982**

Job search duration	Number of males	Number of females	Male/female ratio	% of unemployed males as % of economically active males	% of unemployed females as % of economically active females
1 month	42,545	7,307	5.82	0.84 %	0.84 %
2 months	30,302	7,746	3.92	0.60 %	0.89 %
3 months	26,127	7,794	3.35	0.52 %	0.90 %
4 months	29,326	11,426	2.57	0.58 %	1.32 %
5 months l	18,009	5,477	3.29	0.36 %	0.63 %
6 months	31,054	11,778	2.64	0.61 %	1.36 %
7 months	9,147	1,806	5.06	0.18 %	0.21 %
8 months	15,266	7,989	1.91	0.30 %	0.93 %
9 months	6,666	2,202	3.03	0.13 %	0.25 %
10 months	14,626	8,252	1.77	0.29 %	0.95 %
12 months and over	233,172	121,894	1.91	4.61 %	14.07 %
Totals	460,043	193,673	—	9.09 %	22.36 %

*The unemployment statistics are measured with respect to economically active populations.
Source: Calculated from SIS, *1985 Statistical Yearbook*, No. 1150, p. 200.

reputations in the neighborhood. This lack of job mobility helped keep female wages lower than men in the long run, even if both entered the firm at the same minimum wage scale.

This study found yet another deterrent that kept the unskilled women out of the formal markets — the lack of husbands' permission. This issue was closely related to real or perceived sexual harassment that took place in work outside the home. This restriction will be discussed with survey findings in section 4.

(b) *Employer's perspective*

Interviewed employers stated that the presence of "severance pay," a lump sum of money the worker receives if she or he gets fired after five years in the firm, causes them to prefer women workers with short time horizons. Employers said that a young, single, unskilled female's work horizon is limited,[6] stating that the young, single women primarily work to accumulate household assets and durable goods during her premarital years, i.e., to prepare a trousseau, and to help out with the household budget. Therefore, they are willing to take entry-level jobs at minimum wages and on the average, they are in the workforce for three to five years. Employers stated that severance pay leads employers to exclude married women who want to reenter work with a longer time horizon. Consequently, home work becomes a realistic choice to married women seeking work.

Employers also liked the flexibility for overtime production since singles could work longer hours on short notice. In addition, there are no paid maternity leaves or erratic attendance due to sick children. Therefore, single women are cheaper than married ones and are preferred especially in sectors where competition is high such as textiles, export-oriented shops and retail sales and profit margins are low.

4. INFORMAL SECTOR EMPLOYMENT: HOME WORKING

Married, unskilled women who want to reenter work could only find jobs in the informal sector as seamstresses, knitters or embroiderers where merchants or shop owners subcontract the work out. This seems to be the dominant mode of work, especially in the labor-intensive industries such as knitwear and embroidery. The advantages to employers for subcontracting work are numerous; first of all, in the survey, payment per satisfactory piece produced (and converted to hourly wages) was less than employer's cost of minimum wage, for the employer did not have to pay the employer's contribution to social security. Hence, the shop had cost advantages by subcontracting.

The employer kept the workforce flexible through subcontracting and matched seasonal and fluctuating export demand by changes in the workforce. The subcontracting arrangement also saved on space in the shop. In some cases, successful shops were operated from the home of the employer who ran the operation and exported the sweaters to European Community countries.

Many risks were cited by employers for farming work out to homes. Among these were complaints about first-time workers taking material and never showing up again.[7] Employers also complained about being unable to control and speed up individual production. An employer in Bursa complained that he would train the knitters with respect to patterns, hand-knitting gauge and design, and then lose both the knitter and the design to competition. In addition, the women could exit and enter the market anytime, causing some employers to complain about the large labor turnover. One employer in Bursa cited a 30% turnover rate in a year, causing him in most cases to lose the design and the yarn. A problem cited by male employers in both cities was the fact that sometimes they had to have a female go-between, for some women were afraid of gossip and of husbands' disapproval. Most of the women in Istanbul considered home work to be a hobby to get extra pocket money and almost all had their husband's permission and approval for doing this type of work. In Bursa, however, some of the women worked without their husband's permission and required a female go-between for transacting with the wholesaler. They took work home to help with food, shelter costs in the household, because their husbands could not provide enough for the house or were alcoholics. There were a number of females who were embarrassed and refused to see us in Bursa for they did not want their neighbors to know that they took in work. In contrast, females in migrant settlements in Istanbul were extremely helpful in every single case since most neighbors also took in home work.

(a) *Characteristics of the sample of home-working women from the 1987 surveys*

A priori, scarcity of jobs open to unskilled, married females in formal job market leads us to expect mostly married females in our sample of women who take work at home. Survey findings confirm this; of the total sample, 90.38% of females were married[8] and the average number of children was 3.5. The number of children in the household ranged between zero and nine. The ages of respondents were 18–60 years, with an average age of 34.2. The Pearson correlation coefficient between the age of the respondent and the number of children was high and positive (0.63); the older women in the survey had larger families. The smaller families of younger women can be associated with

Table 2. *1987 Survey results: Causes of migration to urban centers (percentage responses)*

A. *Financial reasons*		
— Husband needed a job	53.33 %	
— Children needed jobs, family followed	2.22 %	
— Financial hardship at place of origin	13.33 %	
— Share from inheritance insufficient at place of origin	2.22 %	
Subtotal		71.10 %
B. *Other reasons*		
— Got married into the city	11.11 %	
— Husband got transferred	4.44 %	
— Wanted better education for children	4.44 %	
— Wanted city comforts	2.22 %	
— Her family came when she was a minor	4.44 %	
— Family migrated from Bulgaria	2.22 %	
Subtotal		28.87 %

more access to birth control as well as the higher implicit costs of raising children in urban areas (SIS, 1982b; Cinar, 1980). The number of years spent in the large city, i.e., the date of migration was not correlated with home working.

Among the women in the sample, there were very few extended families, and all the women in the survey were taking care of their own children. The nature of the job, which allowed women to set their own pace and work hours, was not an impediment to child care. In households where the female worked long hours in take-home production, the eldest daughter was in charge of babysitting and kitchen work.

The households in the sample had migrated and settled in the urban centers, most owning the squatters' homes they lived in. All the husbands in the sample were employed, either as salaried workers or were working for themselves in the informal markets, such as push-cart peddlers. The husbands' average monthly salary was US$ 183.33 (165,000 TL at the current exchange rate during the survey, US$ 1 = 900 TL[9]) or slightly more than three times the monthly minimum wage.

Average hours of home work per week were 22.15. Earnings per month ranged from $6.22 to $54.44 (5,600 TL to 49,000 TL), with a sample average of $25.09 (22,582 TL). The payments per piece differed between $0.67 and $6.67 (600 TL to 6000 TL), depending on the work and the difficulty of execution. The work consisted of machine-embroidering bed linens, sewing (bathrobes, towel seams) and knitting projects of all kinds, using wool, cotton, silk thread or leather strips and bead work. The materials and design were provided by the shop or the wholesaler. The women took the materials home and returned with the finished piece(s) to get their payment for labor. The pay per piece, based on difficulty of execution, was fixed throughout the city, and the women were price takers.

Average years of home work was found to be 3.9 years. The majority of respondents had been doing this type of work for four years or less (78.4%). Roughly one out of five women had been in home production for over five years and 9.8% had worked from home for 11–22 years. Yet, none of the females interviewed in this study took their work seriously or considered themselves as working. Their perception was that this was transitory income and they were grateful for such an opportunity to "earn money in their spare time."

Almost 51% of women who did this type of work were uneducated, with no school attendance, 2% were grade school drop-outs, and 39.21% had finished grade school. In total, 92% of the women in the sample had a grade school education or less. The high school graduates who did subcontracting viewed the job as transitory; they were still searching for jobs in the formal sector while they did work at home for "pocket money."

Causes of urban migration are given in Table 2. Financial causes were cited by 71.10%, with the major reason being that the husband needed a job. Only 4.44% migrated to give the children a better education. In fact, most of the female children of the women we interviewed were not getting any more education than their mothers; they seemed to follow in their mothers' footsteps.

A woman's education was positively correlated with her parents' education, years spent in the city, husband's education, and negatively correlated with age of the respondent and husband's age. Only 19.14% of the respondents in our sample had worked previously. Of those who worked, 40% had worked in sewing jobs, 30% had worked as factory workers, 20% as salesclerks and 10% as janitors. Average number of years of previous work was 2.86 and only 60% of the respondents had social insurance benefits when they had jobs outside the home before marriage.

Table 3. *1987 survey results: Reasons for not working outside the home before marriage and at present (percentage responses among home working women)*

Reasons	Before marriage (percentage)	At present (percentage)
— Father/husband did/does not permit work	64.28 %	54.35 %
— Because of children		23.91 %
— "Too old"		4.35 %
— Large family, has to do housework	26.18 %	4.35 %
— They do not need the money		2.17 %
— Already retired, has pension		2.17 %
— Does not want to work		4.35 %
— Would not look good to others if worked	7.14 %	
— Still searching for work, unsuccessful	2.38 %	4.35 %

(b) *Husband's permission as an obstacle*

Among those who previously worked, 54% said they had to quit when they got married for their husbands did not permit them to continue work. Among those who never worked, the majority did not work before marriage due to lack of father's permission (Table 3). When they married, they did not look for jobs outside the home due to lack of their husband's permission. Most of the women were proud of the fact that their husbands would not let them work outside the home.

This is a labor supply restriction among the unskilled female migrant laborers. Permission of the male household head is necessary before any attempt can be made to search for jobs in the market. This is contrary to findings in other developing and industrialized countries around the world in which there are higher female labor force participation rates and where taking care of children is the primary reason for abstaining from labor markets (Moskoff, 1982; Youssef, 1972). Wilson (1991, p. 161) also reports that husbands' agreement was an important obstacle to work for Mexican women in workshop production. A study of 518 Turkish female university students in Bursa (Mordoglu, 1987) found that the planned duration of work after graduation for a minority of 8.1% of respondents actually "depended on their husband's approval" after marriage, even for this educated group. In our survey, the presence of children at home is definitely of lesser importance, when compared to lack of permission from the male head of household.

Eighty four percent of those surveyed responded[10] when asked what jobs they would desire if they could search for a job and the remaining 15.69% said they did not want to work outside the home (Table 4). Since only 19.14% of respondents had worked previously and since only 4.35% were actively searching for jobs now, this left a vast majority of females in this group who could not work outside the home because they did not have their husband's permission. Various statistical estimates for the exact determinants of husband's permission in this study failed to give any meaningful results, suggesting that withholding permission is probably sociocultural rather than economically determined for this group.[11]

The women were also realistic about their job prospects. While 84.31% showed a preference for a job, only 56.86% thought they would get one (Table 4). The highest percentages in both the desired and feasible job categories were for work as a maid. Even though this job did not have any social security that a formal sector job would have, it was easy to find and it paid the most.[12] Thirty six percent of the respondents

Table 4. *1987 survey results: Desired job versus feasible job (percentage responses)*

	Desired job (percentage)	Feasible job (percentage)
— Seamstress in a factory or a shop	20.93 %	17.24 %
— Knitting	9.30 %	10.34 %
— Lace work, embroidery	2.32 %	—
— Cleaning woman, maid, maid-babysitter	39.53 %	44.83 %
— Factory worker	13.95 %	17.24 %
— Entry level civil servant	4.65 %	—
— Sales clerk	4.65 %	3.45 %
— Secretary*	2.32 %	3.45 %
— Janitor	2.32 %	3.45 %
% of respondents	84.31 %	56.86 %

*The respondents were recent high school graduates, searching for jobs at the time of the survey.

were aware that they would receive minimum wages or less if they worked outside the home. While 38% had no idea about their market opportunity wage, 26% thought they would get more than the monthly minimum wage. It should be noted here that the only job that consistently paid more than the minimum wage was that of a maid. While shop clerks made less than or equal to minimum wage, maids in Istanbul during the time of the survey were making almost four times the monthly minimum wage.

5. IMPUTED HOME WORKING WAGES VERSUS THE MINIMUM WAGE

The hourly wage earned by women working from home has been calculated and compared with alternative hourly wages they could potentially earn (Table 5). The results from the subcontracting survey showed an average of 22.15 hours of work from home per week with a mean monthly income of $25.09 (22,582.05 TL), resulting in an hourly wage of $0.28 (254.23 TL). During the time of the survey, the minimum wage was raised; the new gross monthly minimum wage was raised to $82.50 (74,250 TL) on June 6, 1987 from $46.00 (41,400 TL), previously established on November 10, 1985. Assuming 21 work days per month with eight hours a day, the minimum hourly formal sector and informal sector wages have been calculated in Table 5.

With the old minimum wage in effect before June 30, 1987, the subcontracting wage as of July 1987 (28 cents or 254.23 TL) was on par with the gross formal sector wage (27 cents or 246.42 TL). It should be noted, though, that formal sector wages are accompanied by health, pregnancy, vacation and retirement benefits which are nonexistent with home employment. In addition, one has to be cautious in interpreting the old minimum wage. The minimum wage in Turkey had not changed for some time, and it's purchasing power had eroded due to inflation by the summer of 1987.

With the new minimum wage, the hourly wages of working from home are less than both the gross and net hourly minimum wage for this period. Employers had to pay out 28 cents (254.53 TL) for home work rather than 33 cents (294.48 TL) before July 1, 1987 and 59 cents (528.14 TL) afterward.

As for the women, being a cleaning maid paid as much as four times the other wages among all alternatives. This observation is not confirmed in other studies. Bunster and Chaney (1985, p. 49) report that, on the average, wages as maids were less than formal sector minimum wages in Peru.

A purpose of this study was to find out whether formal factory or workshop production was being switched to homes due to cost advantages. We did not observe any switching from assembly line or workshop production to home work. To calculate cost advantages, hourly wages received by the

Table 5. *1987 survey results: Hourly wages in home work and in formal, informal sector work*

I. Estimated hourly wage in home work	$0.28 (254.23 TL)
II. Minimum hourly wage in formal sectors*	
A. (between 10/85 to 7/87)	
1. Cost to employers (49,473 TL/168 hrs)	$0.33 (294.48 TL)
2. Gross min. hourly wage (41,400 TL/168 hrs)	$0.27 (246.42 TL)
3. Net min. hourly wage (34,698 TL/168 hrs)	$0.23 (206.53 TL)
B. (after 7/87)	
1. Cost to employers (88,728 TL/168 hrs)	$0.59 (528.14 TL)
2. Gross min. hourly wage (74,250 TL/168 hrs)	$0.49 (441.96 TL)
3. Net min. hourly wage (49,094 TL/168 hrs)	$0.32 (292.23 TL)
III. Hourly wage in informal sector (wages of a cleaning maid)† (180,000 TL/168 hrs)	$1.19 (1,071.43TL)

Sources: Calculated from our survey and SIS, *Memur, Isci ve Emeklilerin Nominal Ucret Serileri (1963–1987)* (1963–1987 Nominal Wage Series of Public Employees, Workers and Retirees), Devlet Planlama Teskilati, DPT 2119, Mart 1988, p. 33.
*Cost to employers include employers contributions such as social security and reflect the true cost of hiring under minimum wage legislation. Gross wages are the base from which contributions, premiums and tax rebates are calculated. Net wages are what the workers receive.

All the minimum wage legislation in Turkey is based on monthly wages. Assuming 21 work days with eight hours each (total of 168 hours), the monthly wages have been converted into hourly wages. Alternately, one could convert home work earnings into potential full time monthly earnings by multiplying $0.28 or 254.23 TL by 168 hours. This would result in potential $47.04 or 42,710.64 TL in net pay for full time home work, with no social security health or retirement.
†Number of hours as a cleaning maid are probably longer than 168 hours. Since there are no data on the exact number of hours worked, however, 168 hours were used as the conversion factor. Yet even if one used 200 hours per month based on a six-day work week, the hourly wage from working as a cleaning maid is still greater than any of the alternatives ($1 or 900 TL per hour).

Table 6. *1989 survey: Sample of firms (number of home working women employed per firm by type of business)*

Type of business	Employment per firm	Number of firms
Ready-made apparel	50	9
Fur and leather clothing (includes embroidery and beadwork on leather)	3	5
Knit goods	205	19
Bridal gowns and accessories	15	17
Linens, lacework and trousseau (hand or machine embroidered)	8	4
Embroidered patches (machine embroidered)	3	2
Children's wear	1	1
Total		57

women were imputed for home work and were found to be close to minimum wages. While the expectation in the existing literature seems to be that home work wages were substantially cheaper than formal sector wages, we did not observe important differences with respect to what the women received as net wages.

6. ESTIMATES OF HOME WORKING WOMEN FROM THE 1989 SURVEY

On a national level, the female labor force participation rate in formal or organized sectors in Turkey has declined from 33.4% to 31.4% while the male labor force participation rate has increased from 52.6% to 54.0% during 1965–80 (SIS, 1985, p. 184). In general, the data do not include disguised employment of women producing marketable output at home. In 1982, 7.58% of Turkish females in urban areas were classified by the Turkish State Institute of Statistics as unpaid family workers.[13]

The perception by women that home work is not "work" and the present tax code for part-time workers result in an underdeclaration of the number of women who work from home. The tax code in Turkey is also in need of a major overhaul. It is cumbersome for small firms who employ nonregular part-time workers (firms in home working, marketing, sales, etc.). Tax accounting requires that several monthly status reports be filed for each employee even if they work for two weeks a year. Therefore, firms tend to underreport nonregular part time employees. They make up for the costs by buying inflated bills of sale for inputs at a premium or by substituting their family members as full time employees. Hence, home working does not show up in employment statistics.

An attempt was made to calculate the number of women who work from home in Istanbul during the summer of 1989. The sampling base for the survey design was the member registration records of small firms from the Istanbul Chamber of Commerce (ICC) for 1988. There were 2,564 firms were listed as members of ICC, most of which were concentrated in the export business. This was because membership in ICC was prerequisite to getting export tax rebates during this time period. This gave the sampling frame a selectivity bias. Even though a 5% overall ratio was achieved with the survey, some districts in Istanbul which were primarily serving the domestic markets were oversampled, such as Uskudar, Eminonu, Kartal and Kadikoy, since these firms were under-represented in the ICC sample.[14] One hundred and twenty-eight shops which subcontracted work out were surveyed in the city and 57 were found to employ home-working women as their labor force. The survey collected information on costs, products, and employment for the firms. Only the information on home-working women is employed here for the purpose of estimating their number.

Table 6 reports the number of home-working women employed by shops in the different types of business. Since the number of shops of embroidered patches and of children's wear were insignificant both in the total firms and in those that were found to give work out to women, they were taken out for the rest of the analysis. This effectively left a sample size of 54 shops.

Shops selling or exporting knitted goods employed the most women, 205 per shop, who worked out of home hand-knitting sweaters. On the other hand, shops selling fur and leather clothing, bridal wear beadwork, lacework and linens employed a smaller number of women. These shopkeepers stated that they picked their workers on the basis of excellence of work. The data in Table 6 were further broken down for each type of shop in each district (see Table 7). The variation in the number of employed women was large among the shops in different districts, where the firms which were geared toward domestic markets employ more women than the exporters.

The table also gives the distribution of firms as reflected by the registration records of ICC as well as the percentage of firms which gave out work to women as found in the 1989 survey. Combining the data from Table 7, the estimates of home-working women can be found by type of business and by district (See Table 8). It is approximated that 88,000

Table 7. *Average number of home working women per firm (a), distribution of small scale firms registered by the Istanbul Chamber of Commerce (b), and percentage of firms who give work out to home working women (c), by district and by type of business*

District	Type of business*					
	Ready-made apparel	Fur and leather	Knit goods	Bridal wear	Linens, trousseau	Total
BAKIRKOY						
(a)	51.66	2	17	3	463.25	
(b)	351	53	29	3	21	457
(c) %	75.00	80.00	75.00	100.00	100.00	
BESIKTAS						
(a)			40	56		
(b)	55	3	4		4	66
(c) %			100.00	100.00		
EMINONU (MERCAN)						
(a)						
(b)	108	2	17		3	130
(c) %					100.00	
KADIKOY						
(a)	130	20	400	6.25		
(b)	184	23	7	3	16	233
(c) %	100.00	12.5	100.00	100.00		
KARTAL						
(a)			50	1.50		
(b)	63	5	7		2	77
(c) %			100.00	100.00		
SISLI						
(a)	66	6	112.09	2.00		
(b)	1266	82	147	13	28	1536
(c) %	30.00	20.00	68.75	100.00		
USKUDAR						
(a)	15			7.00		
(b)	47	3	8	1	3	62
(c) %	25.00			100.00	33.33	
TOTAL						
(b)	2074	171	219	20	77	2561
SURVEY AVERAGE						
(c)	37.93%	33.33%	73.91%	100.00%	40.00%	

Sources: (a) and (c), 1989 Survey; (b), Member registration records of Istanbul Chamber of Commerce.
*Shops specializing in children's wear or embroidered patches have been excluded due to small sample size.

women work from home, taking piece work. Most employment seems to be generated by the ready-made apparel industry.

This is a crude estimate, yet it gives an idea of the number of women who are employed by taking work at home. It is also biased downward since not all shops registered with the Istanbul Chamber of Commerce. Yet there are no other corresponding estimates which quantify the number of home-working migrant women in urban centers.

The number estimated here corresponds to 3.10% of the total female population in Istanbul. It is also 23.38% of the uneducated/illiterate female population aged 18–64 in the city. That means at least one in four migrant women take in home work. This is a sizable workforce.

7. CONCLUSIONS

Given the mass migrations into urban centers and the number of unskilled migrant women in developing nations around the world, our estimates indicate a sizable percentage of them take work at home and are engaged in disguised employment.

There was no evidence to support the hypothesis that mass production in factories or workshops is being switched to home production. Timing and quality control factors in large-scale production demanded work under supervision and was not conducive to home production. For Spain, in which switching was observed for the shoe industry, the differentials between formal sector and home-work wages must have been large enough and variations in quality

Table 8. *Estimates of demand for home working women, by district and by type of business, 1988–1989*

District	Number of home working				
	Ready-made apparel	Fur and leather	Knit goods	Bridal	Linens, trousseau
Bakirkoy	13599.49	84.8	369.75	9.09	9728.25
Besiktas			160.00	0.0	
Eminonu					0.0
Kadikoy	23920.00	57.5	2800.00	18.75	
Kartal			350.00	0.0	
Sisli	25066.80	98.4	11327.12	26.0	
Uskudar	176.25			7.00	0.0
Subtotal	62762.54	240.7	15007.57	34.75	9728.25
Total 87,799.805 or 88,000 women.					

between different "homes" negligible or unimportant for this switching to occur. In this study, work given out to homes required individual handwork such as "one of a kind" products. As such, this type of output was entirely different and smaller in scope than that which could be found in the formal sector textile industry.

In the formal markets, an important dilemma was presented by the mandatory "severance pay." This gave long-time workers job security but led to demand for women workers with short work horizons. This meant that the employers made distinctions between married and single females, preferring the latter for they offered a more flexible and sometimes cheaper input in the production process. This severely limited the job opportunities available for married women in the organized or formal sector. On the other hand, paid work at home was well organized in the low-income migrant neighborhoods and work was plentiful. Adjustable working hours and productivity according to the workers' convenience and competitive earnings with formal wages made home working appealing. Before July 1, 1987, home workers received the rough equivalent of formal sector's gross hourly minimum wage with the exception of social security benefits.

Women regarded their home-working income as transitory and were grateful for the opportunity to earn "pocket money" while at home. They did not think of their activity as "work." They chose the number of hours they worked by choosing the number of pieces to complete in a week. Home working gave them an alternative to being cleaning maids which was their only other feasible job. The presence of small children is usually cited for the primary reason why women stay at home and/or work out of home. Our survey did not confirm this widely held belief.

Frequently, the decision to work from home was less of choice than of necessity. Some had been looking for jobs in the organized sector for up to five years. Moreover, the majority of these women were not allowed to work outside the home by the head of the household. Women were also proud of this fact. One of the main reasons cited by women for this lack of permission was the potential of harassment in formal sector jobs. A safe place to work was important to women who worked in the organized sector and was partly responsible for neighbors and relatives working in the same firm. The concern of women and their families for a safe work environment is again one of the important reasons why women did not change jobs as frequently as men did in the small-scale textile firms covered in this study. This lack of job mobility helped keep female wages lower than the men in the long run, even if both entered the firm at the minimum wage.

NOTES

1. Disguised employment is used here to denote the type of employment which is completely disguised from official statistics as well as national accounts.

The attribute "unskilled" used here is in the context of the market valuation of services. All of the women surveyed were very skilled in knitting and embroidery as well as household services. In the Middle East, skills such as sewing, knitting, and embroidery are still generally distributed among the female population. Machines have also been able to duplicate these services at low costs. Therefore, the services these women offered are plentiful in supply and, at the same time, employers' demand elasticity for these services is high, due to the degree of substitution between inputs.

The desirable "skills" required by employers were bookkeeping, typing, foreign languages, i.e. professional or semi-professional services. These skills are not generally distributed among the female population. In fact, their distribution is highly skewed even among the educated urban female population.

2. The fast growth of the unskilled females in megaurban centers in the developing countries have also marked the

clear distinctions between the educated female urban elite and the unskilled migrants and between formal and informal markets. Due to the concentration of the infrastructure and the educational opportunities in large urban centers, public education and training at all levels are easily available to the city born in large urban centers in Turkey. This leads to urban citizens having considerably better education than rural citizens who have close to none. While job markets for skilled professional women in the urban centers, especially those with English and computer skills, resemble their counterparts in the more developed countries, job markets for migrants is entirely different. Women's movements by the educated urban elite have also been unable to address the problems faced by the unskilled female migrants which now make up the majority of females in large urban centers.

3. For a more detailed description of formal, informal markets, see Perlman (1976), Tinker (1987), Cinar, Kaytaz and Evcimen (1988), Evcimen, Kaytaz and Cinar (1991), Portes, Castells and Benton (1989).

4. The integration thesis states that industrialization eventually leads to gender equality by involving women in the market economy and politics. The marginalization thesis has four different interpretations. One version examines job roles within the family and gender-related unpaid work at home. Another version defines marginalization as women being pushed into the informal sector as development occurs. Other versions interpret female marginalization as the concentration of women in low-paying formal sector jobs, such as bank tellers, or as wage inequality between males and females for equal work. The exploitation hypothesis studies the international division of labor and draws from dependency theory to state that industrialization needs and develops a cheap army of female laborers who are exploited by the system. For more information, see Tiano (1986); Wilson (1993), (1991); Schoenberg Rozen (1979): Bunster and Chaney (1985); Chaney and Castro (1989); Tripp (1992).

5. Among the Islamic countries in the Middle East, Turkey was the first to "Westernize" and to remove almost all legal barriers against women. The government granted them equal political and legal rights in the 1920s and early 1930s. Provided the family is willing, there are no limits to urban women's education and there are numerous urban families with third generation professional women in urban areas such as Istanbul, Ankara, Izmir and Bursa today. Even though primary education has been mandatory for half a century, however, 62.84% of all females, aged 12 or over, were still either illiterate or had never finished grade school in 1980, 29.70% had primary, 5.74% had secondary and 1.04% had higher education (SIS, 1985, p. 184). Istanbul has higher rates of female literacy than the national average, even though they are skewed by internal migration. In 1985, 34% of all females, aged 12 or over, were still either illiterate or had never finished grade school (43% had primary, 20% had secondary and 3% had higher education (SIS, 1987, pp. 23–41)). For more on the education and gender gap, see Ozbay (1979).

During 1975–80, the number of illiterate or non degree-holding women increased by 3.24%. The increase may be due to the late resurgence of Orthodox Islam in urban Turkey where Koranic schools, taught in Arabic with Arabic script, are preferred over state schools for female children. This is one of the problems faced by non-Arab Islamic countries who have a different language and use Latin or other scripts. While sending girls to Koranic schools in Egypt teaches them a more classical Arabic grammar than in public schools, the same action results in female illiteracy in non-Arab Moslem countries such as Turkey. Beside the resurgence in Islam, though, the politicization of students and the resulting confrontations with the establishment in the 1970s has led to severe, sometimes fatal, campus conflicts, which has also been instrumental in degrading the value of education in public opinion.

It should also be noted that the results of the 1980 Census are thought to have larger errors of estimation compared to earlier censuses. Hence, the changes in the figures during 1975–80 may also be due to census estimation errors.

6. Yet, employers in the organized sectors will not employ unskilled young men who have not done their mandatory military service for the opposite reason. In the case of men, the employers are looking for a longer work horizon and a commitment to the firm.

One of the serious complaints by small-scale employers during interviews was "job hopping" of skilled male employees which they disliked. Women employees were thought to have more allegiance to the firm, but in almost all the firms/shops in the sample, women were in unskilled positions and were not promoted to skilled or managerial positions.

7. This was a problem in Bursa where knitters were scattered around the neighborhoods, but in Istanbul, since the knitting operations were organized around the squatters' settlements and the wholesaler/employer and workers knew each other and had regional or kinship relationships. In Bursa, the knitters were dispersed within the city and the shopkeepers did not have the degree of control over the workers of their counterparts in Istanbul did.

8. The single females were high school graduates and had been searching for jobs in the formal sectors. In the interim, they were taking work into the home.

9. The exchange rate is valid for the last part of the survey. The 1987–88 inflation rate in Turkey was around 70%. The Turkish currency itself was devalued, on a daily basis, by 18.75% during the three months during which the survey was taking place.

10. This 84.31% includes those who preferred taking knitting at home (9.30%) and were happy doing their present job. The remainder 75.01% desired jobs which are different from what they were presently doing.

11. Various statistical models were tried, using a binary dependent variable (permission/no permission) and independent variables such as education levels, income shares, earnings of wives and husbands, number of children, previous work outside the home before marriage, and husband's type of job. They all failed to explain statistically the permission variable.

Papps (1992, p. 607) discounts the idea that Islamic religion directly results in low female labor force participation. She notes that it is difficult to separate the influence of Islam from other cultural factors and high correlations between variables result in murky statistical results.

12. For Latin America, Chaney and Castro (1989) found that for women the transition was from working as a domestic servant to street vending. While there are numerous male migrant street vendors in Istanbul, some very successful, there are few women street vendors.

13. In SIS's urban household survey (1982a), "unpaid family workers" is a broad category that includes women who take work at home as well as family members who work in their family businesses. In this group 89% neither had education or only primary school diplomas. "Unpaid family workers" constitute the major labor pool that subcontracting employers recruit for home work.

14. The percentage sampling ratios of shops from the different districts of Istanbul are as follows: Bakirkoy 4.60%, Besiktas 4.55%, Sisli 3.44%, Uskudar 20.97%, Kadikoy 6.01%, Eminonu 10.77% and Kartal 12.99%. The overall total sampling ratio from the ICC membership lists were 5.00% or 128/2464.

REFERENCES

Ashraf, J., and B. Ashraf, "Estimating the gender wage gap in Rawalpindi City," *Journal of Development Studies*, Vol. 29, No. 2 (1993), pp. 365–376.

Beneria, L., and M. Roldan, *The Crossroads of Class and Gender: Industrial, Subcontracting and Household Dynamics in Mexico City* (Chicago: University of Chicago Press, 1987).

Benton, L. A., "Homework and industrial development: Gender roles and restructuring in the Spanish shoe industry," *World Development*, Vol. 17, No. 2 (1989), pp. 255–265.

Borjas, G. J., "Self-selection and earnings of migrants," *American Economic Review*, Vol. 77, No. 4 (1987), pp. 531–553.

Bunster, X., and E. M. Chaney, *Sellers and Servants: Working Women in Lima, Peru* New York: Praeger Pub., 1985).

Chaney, E. M., and M. G. Castro, *Muchachas No More* (Philadelphia: Temple University Press, 1989).

Cinar, M. E., *1973–1974 Kirsal Kesim Hanehalklari Tuketim Harcamalarinin Ekonometrik Analizi*, Dozent Thesis (Istanbul: Bogazici University, 1980).

Cinar, M. E., M. Kaytaz and G. Evcimen, "The present status of small scale industries (Sanatkar) in Bursa, Turkey,"*International Journal of Middle East Studies*, (1988), pp. 287–301.

Evcimen, G., M. Kaytaz and M. Cinar, "Subcontracting, growth and capital accumulation in small-scale firms in the textile industry in Turkey," *The Journal of Development Studies*, Vol. 28, No. 1 (1991), pp. 130–149.

Hakim, C., "Home-based work in Britain: A Report on the National Homeworking Survey and the DE Research Program on Home Work," Paper No. 60 (London: Department of Employment Research, 1987).

Mentes, G., *Location and Site Selection of Petty Production in Bursa*, Research Reports 1, 2 and 3, (Ankara, Turkey: Middle East Technical University, Department of City and Regional Planning, 1984).

Moskoff, W., "Women and work in Israel and the Islamic Middle East," *Quarterly Review of Economics and Business*, Vol. 22 (1982), pp. 4–89.

Mordoglu, K., "Yuksek Egitim Goren Kadin Isgucu Adaylari ve Calisma Egilimleri," *METU Studies in Development*, Vol. 14, No. 4 (1987), p. 226.

Ozbay, F., "Turkiye'de Kirsal/Kentsel Kesimde Egitimin Kadinlar Uzerinde Etkisi" in N. Abadan-Unat (Ed.), *Turk Toplumunda Kadin (Women in Turkish Society)*, (Ankara, Turkey: Middle East Technical University, 1979), p. 192.

Papps, I., "Women, work and well-being in the Middle East: An outline of the relevant literature," *The Journal of Development Studies*, Vol. 28, No. 4 (1992), pp. 595–615.

Perlman, J. E., *The Myth of Marginality* (Berkeley, CA: University of California Press, 1976).

Portes, A., M. Castells and L. A. Benton, *The Informal Economy: Studies in Advanced and Less Developed Countries* (Baltimore: John Hopkins Press, 1989).

Schoenberg Rozen, F., "Women in the work force: The interaction of myth and reality" in E. C. Snyder (Ed.), *The Study of Women: Enlarging Perspectives of Social Reality* (Harper and Row: New York, 1979).

State Institute of Statistics (SIS), *20.10.1985 Census of Population: Istanbul* (Ankara, Turkey: SIS, 1987).

State Institute of Statistics (SIS), *1985 Statistical Yearbook of Turkey*, Publication No. 11 (Ankara, Turkey: SIS, 1985).

State Institute of Statistics (SIS), *Urban Household Survey*, Publication No. 2356 (Ankara, Turkey: SIS, 1982a).

State Institute of Statistics (SIS), *1978–1979 Urban Places Household Income and Consumption Expenditures Survey Results*, Publication No. 999 (Ankara, Turkey: SIS, 1982b).

State Planning Organization, *Memur, Isci ve Emeklilerin Nominal Ucret Serileri (1963–1987)* (1963–1987 Nominal Wage Series of Public Employees, Workers and Retirees), DPT 2119 (Ankara, Turkey: SIS, 1988).

Tiano, S., "Women and industrial development in Latin America," *Latin American Research Review*, Vol. 21, No. 3 (1986), pp. 157–170.

Tinker, I., "Street foods: Testing assumptions about informal sector activity by women and men," *Current Sociology*, Vol. 35, No. 3 (1987), pp. 1–110.

Tripp, A. M., "Crisis, Islam and gender in Bangladesh: The social construction of a female labor force" in L. Beneria, and S. Feldman (Eds.), *Unequal Burden* (Boulder, Co: Westview Press, 1992).

Wilson, F., "Workshops as domestic domains: Reflections on small-scale industry in Mexico," *World Development*, Vol. 21, No. 1 (1993), pp. 67–80.

Wilson, F., *Sweaters: Gender, Class and Workshop-based Industry in Mexico* (New York: St. Martin's Press, 1991).

Youssef, N. H., "Differential labor force participation of women in Latin American and Middle Eastern countries: The influence of family characteristics," *Social Forces*, Vol. 51 (1972) pp. 135–153.

[14]

PALESTINIAN EMPLOYMENT PROSPECTS

Gil Feiler

In recent years, social scientists have exerted much effort investigating the economic and social problems of Palestinian society. Research has focused on prevailing physical and economic difficulties and on the integration of the refugee population in various host countries.[1] No significant research, however, has been undertaken with respect to future employment options for the Palestinians.[2] The employment of Palestinian refugees and non-refugees is one of the central issues that must be addressed in order to insure stability in the region. This matter is of particular importance in the context of the negotiations for autonomy in the Israeli-occupied territories—set in motion at the 1991 Madrid conference—and in light of almost non-existent local labor infrastructures there. An analysis of

1. See, for example, Laurie A. Brand, *Palestinians in the Arab World: Institution Building and the Search for State* (New York: Columbia University Press, 1988); Ishaq Y. Al-Qutub, "Refugee Camp Cities in the Middle East: A Challenge for Urban Development Policies," *International Sociology* 4, no. 1 (March 1989); and George T. Abed, ed., *The Palestinian Economy* (London and New York: Routledge, 1988).

2. On employment trends and labor organization generally, see Moshe Semyonov and Noah Lewin-Epstein, *Hewers of Wood and Drawers of Water: Noncitizen Arabs in the Israeli Labor Market* (Ithaca, NY: ILR Press, New York State School of Industrial and Labor Relations, Cornell University, 1987); International Labor Organization, *Report on the Situation of Arab Workers in the Occupied Arab Territories* (Geneva, 1990, 1991, 1992); Salim Tamari, "Building Other People's Home: The Palestinian Peasant's Household and Work in Israel," *Journal of Palestine Studies* 11, no. 1 (Autumn 1981).

Gil Feiler is a lecturer in Middle Eastern economics at the Bar Ilan University and a senior researcher at the Bar Ilan Center for Strategic Studies. He is also a consultant to Info-Prod Research Ltd., which provides investment advice to firms dealing in the Middle East, including the West Bank and Gaza Strip. *He would like to express his deep gratitude to Rahel Rimon of the Israeli and English bar associations for her support and assistance in preparing this article. Although this article was written before the Israeli government's closure of the West Bank and Gaza Strip in April 1993, the author feels recent events in the occupied territories strengthen the conclusions reached here.*

demographic changes among Palestinians,[3] particularly as a result of emigration,[4] is basic to an understanding of future employment possibilities.

This article examines the employment options of Palestinians in Israel, in Arab countries, and in the West Bank and Gaza Strip. Employment trends and political conditions in Arab countries and in Israel indicate that, in the medium and long term, Palestinian workers will be replaced either by other Arab laborers or by cheaper imported labor from Asia or, in the case of Israel, by new immigrants, primarily from the former Soviet Union.[5] The creation of jobs and industry in the occupied territories is, therefore, the only viable solution to the Palestinian unemployment problem.

In the context of an overall peace treaty in the region, cooperation between Israel and Arab states could lead to a unified labor market that would be of benefit to all parties concerned. Migration in search of work is easier to countries that are geographically close. To the extent that restrictions on movement are lessened, it becomes simpler to achieve the merger of separate employment markets into a more unified unit. Such a merger occurred on a small scale after 1967 with regard to the labor markets of Israel, the West Bank, and the Gaza Strip; a major contributing factor was the overland access that enabled movement on a daily basis.

During the 1970s and 1980s, Palestinians dominated the labor force in the Persian Gulf.[6] In the current economic-political state of the region, however, cooperation in the employment sphere, with the principal purpose of finding a solution to the employment crisis of the Palestinians, seems unrealistic. Temporary solutions, at least on the micro level, must be sought. Successful planning on that level is likely to encourage the parties involved to search for solutions on the macro level.

3. The most accurate demographic statistics are available from the Israeli Central Bureau of Statistics. The vast majority of reference works, including those compiled by international bodies and Arab researchers, rely on data provided by this body. See, for example, United Nations Conference on Trade and Development, *Selected Statistical Tables on the Economy of the Occupied Palestinian Territory* (New York, 1989).

4. In respect to migration trends, see Nabil Badran, "Palestinian Migration: Trends and Socio-Economic Consequences," *Conference on International Migration in the Arab World* (Nicosia: Economic Commission for Western Asia, 1981); Stuart A. Gabriel and Eitan F. Sabatello, "Palestinian Migration from the West Bank and Gaza: Economic and Demographic Analyses," *Economic Development and Cultural Change* 34, no. 2 (January 1986); Joost Hiltermann, "Seasoned Migrants to the North," *Middle East Report*, May-June 1987, pp. 19–22.

5. For example, about 470,000 Jews arrived in Israel from the former Soviet Union between late 1989 and July 1993, straining the country's already sluggish economy. Unemployment among these immigrants has exceeded 35 percent. Figures supplied by Israeli Ministry of Interior, July 1993.

6. On the Palestinians in the Persian Gulf, see Bilal al-Hasan, *Al-Filastiniyun fi al-Kuwayt* (Palestinians in Kuwait) (Beirut: Palestine Liberation Organization Research Center, 1974); Eric Rouleau, "The Palestinian Diaspora of the Gulf," *MERIP Reports*, May 1985, pp. 13–15.

WORKER MIGRATION IN THE MIDDLE EAST: AN OVERVIEW

Until the 1970s, most migrations from Arab countries were to areas outside the Middle East. The number of Arab migrant workers in the Middle East did not exceed a few hundred thousand. The oil boom following the October 1973 War, however, led to a new era in Middle Eastern migration.[7] The increase in revenues of the oil-producing states brought with it extensive investment programs and an increase in consumption, which in turn entailed expansion of service sectors.[8] The demand for goods was met with imports, but other services required human resources. Most of the citizens of the oil-producing states lacked the necessary skills and were too few in number to meet the demands created by the flow of oil income.

By 1975, about 2 million foreign workers resided in the six principal oil-producing states of Bahrain, Kuwait, Oman, Qatar, Saudi Arabia, and the United Arab Emirates. Of these workers, 68 percent came from Arab countries and most of the rest were from Asia.[9] Tens of thousands of Europeans and Americans were also employed in the oil states.[10] Five years later in 1980, there were 3 million foreign workers in the Persian Gulf, 65 percent of whom came from Arab countries. The number of foreign workers increased by two-thirds in the early 1980s, in part because the Iran-Iraq War created openings in the Iraqi labor market. By 1983 in the six Arab monarchies and Iraq, there were about 5 million foreign workers, 55 percent of whom came from other Arab countries.[11] In 1985, according to the Arab League, 3–4 million foreign workers resided in the Persian Gulf states, excluding foreign workers in Iraq[12]; of those in Iraq, at least 1.25 million were from Egypt alone. In 1985, 55 percent of the foreign workers in the Persian Gulf states and Iraq were still from Arab countries. According to a report issued by the International Gulf Bank, out of a total population of 15.7 million in

7. For bibliographies on migration in the Middle East, see Gilbert Beauge and A. Bendiab, *Migrations internationales au Moyen-Orient: 1975–1986* (Aix-en-Provence: Institut de recherches et d'études sur le monde arabe et musulman, 1987); Ian Seccombe, *International Migration for Employment in the Middle East: An Introductory Bibliography* (Durham, UK: Center for Middle Eastern and Islamic Studies, 1984).

8. In the decade following the 1973 war, the oil-producing countries invested $323 billion in extensive development projects. See *Arab Oil and Gas,* July 1984, p. 4.

9. Asian workers primarily came from Bangladesh, India, Korea, Pakistan, the Philippines, Sri Lanka, and Thailand. In general, Asians were paid less than Arab foreign workers, and their work conditions were worse. See, for example, *Arabia,* May 1985, pp. 72–3; and Mostafa H. Nagi, "Migration of Asia Workers to the Arab Gulf: Policy Determinants and Consequences," *Journal of South Asian and Middle Eastern Studies* 9, no. 3 (Spring 1986).

10. For British workers, the Middle East became their second most important foreign destination in the 1970s; most were highly skilled workers on lucrative short-term contracts. See A. Findley and A. Stewart, "Migrations des travailleurs qualifiés britanniques sous contract au Moyen-Orient," *Revue européenne des migrations internationales* 2, no. 1 (September 1986).

11. Gil Feiler, "The Decrease in Oil Prices and Its Effect on the Foreign Labour Force in the Middle East," *Middle East Focus* (Ontario) 9, no. 7 (Summer/Fall 1987), p. 13.

12. *Al-Madina* (Jiddah), June 28, 1987, p. 8.

the six gulf monarchies at the beginning of 1988, foreigners accounted for 6.9 million, or 44 percent.[13]

Iraq and Saudi Arabia were the principal labor-importing countries during the 1980s. Together they accounted for about 65 percent of the total foreign work force in the region in 1983. The other labor-importing countries included Jordan, Kuwait, Libya, Oman, Qatar, and the UAE.[14] The principal Arab countries supplying workers have been Egypt—which accounted for 60 percent of the foreign Arab labor force—Jordan, Sudan, and Yemen. The number of Egyptian workers in the Arab oil-producing countries rose from 200,000 at the beginning of 1973 to 500,000 in 1975, to 1.25 million in 1978 and to about 2.9 million in 1983.[15] To the south of Egypt, Sudan supplied about 46,000 workers to Arab states in 1975; by 1982, this number had risen to between 200,000 and 450,000.[16] A study presented at a 1987 conference on the economy of Sudan claimed that 350,000 Sudanese were working in the Arab oil states at that time.[17] In 1974, about 150,000 Jordanians were employed in other Arab countries; by the early 1980s their number had risen to 250,000, and in 1985 to 325,000, most of them Palestinians.[18] This figure is remarkably large in view of the fact that the entire Jordanian labor force in 1985 totaled only 592,000.[19]

Labor migration figures for other Arab countries are estimates rather than documented statistics. For example, some 290,000 North Yemeni nationals worked in the oil states in 1975, about 500,000 in 1979, and between 600,000 and 740,000 in 1982.[20] Information on Syrian migration to the Arab oil states is limited. Some 70,000 Syrians were estimated to be working in the oil states in 1975, their number rising to an estimated 250,000 in 1982.[21] About 267,000 Lebanese emigrated in 1975–1980, 47 percent of them to other Arab states and 53 percent to the Americas. In Lebanon's case, the civil war was the main reason for emigration

13. *Ila al-Amam* (Damascus), August 12, 1988, p. 25.

14. Jordan is also a labor-exporting country. See Ian Seccombe, "Immigrant Workers in an Emigrant Economy: An Examination of Replacement Migration in the Middle East," *International Migration* 24, no. 2 (June 1986).

15. Gil Feiler, *The Number of Egyptian Workers in the Arab Oil Countries, 1974–1983: A Critical Discussion,* Occasional Papers Series no. 96 (Tel Aviv: Dayan Center for Middle Eastern and African Studies, 1986), p. 20.

16. Eliyahu Kanovsky, *Migration from the Poor to the Rich Arab Countries,* Occasional Papers Series no. 85 (Tel Aviv: Dayan Center for Middle Eastern and African Studies, 1984), p. 63. Compare Uthman al-Hasan Muhammad Nur, "Hijrat al-Sudaniyyin li al-aqtar al-naftiyya" (Sudanese migration to the oil states), *al-Mustaqbal al-Arabi* 9, no. 87 (May 1987).

17. *Al-Siyasa* (Khartoum), January 30, 1987, claimed that more than 60 percent of the Sudanese migrants were technicians and skilled workers.

18. Gil Feiler, "Migration and Recession: Arab Labour Mobility in the Middle East, 1982–1989," *Population and Development Review* 17, no. 1 (March 1991), pp. 135–7.

19. *Al-Dustur* (Amman), July 24, 1985.

20. Kanovsky, *Migration,* p. 61. Compare B.R. Pridham, ed., *The Impact of Emigration on Social Structure in the Yemen Arab Republic* (London: Croom Helm, 1985).

21. Kanovsky, *Migration,* p. 60.

in contrast to the principally economic factors that motivated emigration from the other Arab labor-exporting countries.[22]

The governments of labor-exporting countries have participated in this massive migration by encouraging the movement of their workers to the Persian Gulf states to increase foreign currency remittances. Little effort is made to protect these nationals from exploitation by domestic recruiting officers or gulf employers. Similarly, little is done to protect the local economy from the drain of skilled labor.[23] Although the composition of the migrant worker pool varies from one labor-exporting country to another, in all countries the vast majority are young adult males. By contrast, the educational and occupational composition of migrants varies markedly, from the usually illiterate unskilled workers from Yemen to the relatively skilled non-Arab Asian laborers.[24]

With the decrease in oil revenues that began in 1985, the oil-producing countries began to tap their reserve funds and retain only those foreign workers deemed essential to the development of their respective economies. Asians and illegal workers were the first foreign workers sent back to their countries of origin. Arab laborers were dismissed at a later stage. Within the class of Arab workers, the oil-producing countries initially dismissed groups they perceived as potentially subversive, such as Lebanese Shi'a and Palestinians.[25] Special measures were adopted to restrict the size of immigrant families, and new labor laws discriminated against foreigners, who could not become citizens or permanent residents of the country in which they worked, did not enjoy equal rights, and were isolated socially. Foreigners were also prohibited from marrying local residents and from owning land.[26]

THE OIL STATES AND PALESTINIAN MIGRATION

The past history of migratory labor trends among Palestinians and current political and economic conditions would indicate that the work force in the occupied territories cannot expect the Arab states of the Persian Gulf or Jordan to solve their employment problems. In contrast to the purely economic reasons for the migration of some Arab and Asian workers to the gulf states, the migration of Palestinian workers is also due, in part, to political reasons. In particular,

22. Hadi Zurayq, "Hijrat al-amala al-Arabiyya: Dirasat halat. Amaliyyat san' al-qarar fi al-hijra, al-mua'aqqata wa al-da'ima min Lubnan" (Migration of Arab workers: Case Study. The workers' decision to emigrate temporarily and permanently from Lebanon), *al-Mustaqbal al-Arabi* 9, no. 87 (May 1986).

23. Roger Owen, *Migrant Workers in the Gulf* (London: Minority Rights Group, 1985), p. 9.

24. Alan Richards and John Waterbury, *A Political Economy of the Middle East* (Boulder, CO: Westview Press, 1990), pp. 382, 384.

25. Feiler, *Migration and Recession*, p. 150.

26. See for example, *al-Ahram al-Iqtisadi*, August 5, 1985, pp. 18–19; Owen, *Migrant Workers in the Gulf*, pp. 11–13.

substantial numbers of people migrated to, and subsequently from, the West Bank and Gaza Strip in the wake of the 1948 and 1967 wars.[27]

In the early 1970s economic expansion in Israel was decisive in stemming the migratory tide.[28] Superior earning potential drew Palestinians into the Israeli sector, while the sizable growth rate of the Israeli economy created a strong demand for the employment of Palestinian labor. In the mid-1970s, however, a slowdown in Israel's growth, combined with the opportunities available in the Persian Gulf, resulted in a sharp increase in Palestinian migration to the gulf. Counterbalancing this migratory trend, the diminished demand for labor in Israel, coupled with previously accumulated savings by residents of the occupied territories, precipitated a rise in construction in the West Bank and Gaza Strip, which sometimes was financed by external Arab sources as a means of discouraging potential migrants.[29]

Continued Israeli settlement in the occupied territories could have a variety of political and economic effects on the Palestinian propensity to migrate. An increased Israeli presence in the West Bank and Gaza Strip, political conflict, and uncertainty regarding the eventual status of this region may result in accelerated Palestinian migration.[30] On the other hand, the same phenomenon may result in an increased desire on the part of the Palestinians to remain; indeed, it seems clear that, in addition to its negative aspects from a Palestinian perspective, increased Israeli activity in the occupied territories also provides greater employment opportunities for Palestinians, thereby diminishing migratory desires.[31] Monetary donations from various states and international bodies have also helped to improve local conditions and reduce the number of Palestinian emigrants.[32] This fact also conforms to the political purposes of the Arab donors, who prefer to encourage Palestinians to develop economically within the occupied territories than to settle permanently in the gulf states.

When the rate of worker-related migration in the Middle East peaked in the early 1980s, the Palestinian share of migration had reached its nadir[33]; propor-

27. Gabriel and Sabatello, *Palestinian Migration,* p. 245–62; see also Fawzi A. Gharaibeh, *The Economies of the West Bank and Gaza Strip* (Boulder, CO, and London: Westview Press, 1985), pp. 29–30; Dan Zakai, *Economic Development in Judea, Samaria, and the Gaza District, 1983–4* (Jerusalem: Bank of Israel, 1986), pp. 30–1.

28. Gabriel and Sabatello, *Palestinian Migration,* p. 247.

29. Ibid., p. 256.

30. According to figures provided in a 1991 study by the US Department of State and reported in an International Labor Organization report, more than 200,000 Israelis live in the West Bank, East Jerusalem, Gaza Strip, and the Golan Heights, representing approximately 13 percent of the population of these territories. As a result of the Israeli government's decision to freeze new settlements in 1992, these figures are still valid. See International Labor Organization, *Report of the Director-General,* vol. 2 (Geneva, 1991), p. 21, appendices.

31. Gabriel and Sabatello, *Palestinian Migration,* p. 257.

32. See, for example, Leopold Yehuda Laufer, *Western Europe and the Palestinians: The Socio-Economic Dimension,* Policy Studies no. 39 (Jerusalem: Leonard Davis Institute for International Relations, 1990), pp. 3–20.

33. In 1983, only 4,000 Palestinians left the occupied territories in search of work. See Zakai, *Economic Development,* p. 30.

tionally far fewer Palestinians left the occupied territories in search of work than was potentially possible from the Palestinian labor export market. The reason lay in the preference of the oil states to engage workers from Arab states they considered relatively moderate, and whose citizens they regarded as less politically volatile. This also explains why Syria exported fewer workers than its potential. Even after the outbreak of the Iran-Iraq War, the Iraqis—rather than employ Syrians—preferred to employ Egyptians, despite the Arabs' severance of diplomatic relations with Egypt because of its signing of the Camp David accords.[34]

Few Palestinians have ever been granted citizenship in any of the gulf states, even though some Palestinians have resided in them since 1948.[35] Kuwait and the UAE took steps in the early 1980s to ensure that their already large Palestinian populations would not increase. One restrictive measure implemented in both states—directed primarily at Palestinians from the West Bank and Gaza Strip—prohibited migrant workers from changing jobs without first leaving the country. It was not unusual for Palestinian tourists visiting gulf states to be detained and prohibited entry. Kuwait sometimes refused Palestinian researchers permission to participate in academic projects there. The Kuwaiti government even obtained a computer program from a Scandinavian company that compares the passport details of persons entering the country with a list of Palestinian names and determines if the place and date of birth have been altered. The Kuwaitis used it as part of their policy of restricting the number of Palestinians entering the country irrespective of their citizenship.[36]

Apart from actions taken as a result of fears of potential Palestinian political extremism, the Arab states also attempted to prevent what they described as an Israeli effort to push the Palestinian population out of the West Bank and Gaza Strip. Thus, the Jordanian government adopted a policy of stopping Palestinians from crossing into Jordan from the West Bank if their travel documents showed that they would not be allowed to return to the West Bank.

These matters gained added importance as a consequence of the Iraqi invasion of Kuwait. The decrease in both the price of oil and oil revenues, the development of local labor forces that reduced the need for foreign workers, and vocal Palestinian and Palestine Liberation Organization (PLO) support of Iraq during the gulf crisis and war were all factors that adversely affected employment prospects for Palestinians. At the beginning of August 1990, Kuwaiti amir Jabir al-Ahmad al-Sabah practically provided official sanction to anti-Palestinian attitudes when he referred to an alleged "plot" by Iraq, the PLO, and Jordan to bring

34. Gil Feiler, "Peace and Egyptian Labor Migration to the Arab Oil Countries," *New Outlook*, November-December 1987, pp. 22–3.

35. United Nations, Department of International Economic and Social Affairs, *National Experience in the Formulation and Implementation of Population Policy, 1958–1979, Saudi Arabia* (New York, 1981), pp. 40–2; *al-Jazirah* (Saudi Arabia), October 23, 1979; "Gulf Limits on Palestinians," *Foreign Report* (London), July 21, 1983, p. 5.

36. "Gulf Limits on Palestinians," p. 5.

about the emigration of Palestinians from Lebanon, the West Bank and Gaza Strip, and Jordan and their resettlement in Kuwait.[37]

After the war, Kuwait deported Palestinians, including those who had played key roles in the country's civil service and private sector. Many more left on their own accord. The Kuwaiti government committed itself to wholesale Palestinian replacement even, in some cases, with Soviet and Nigerian workers.[38] The Palestinian community in Kuwait dwindled to less than 85,000 by the end of 1992—down from 350,000 before the Iraqi invasion—and, subsequently has decreased even more as the result of a reregistration policy of the Kuwaiti government. Many remaining Palestinians were born or have lived most of their lives in Kuwait and have nowhere else to go.[39]

Apart from the considerable employment difficulties as a result of their expulsion from Kuwait and other Persian Gulf countries, Palestinians have had to contend with the sudden loss of a traditional source of income. Remittances from Palestinian workers in Kuwait and the gulf states constituted a significant proportion of earnings entering the occupied territories. In 1989, remittances from the gulf totaled $270 million, 70 percent of which originated in Kuwait and 20 percent in Saudi Arabia.[40] One suggested solution to the problem of Palestinians expelled from Kuwait has been employment in Libya. Diplomatic sources have said that Tripoli is waiving visa restrictions to holders of Arab *laissez-passer* documents, including Gazans holding Egyptian papers. Libya seems to be offering the same kind of arrangement that Kuwait provided—a place to work and reside temporarily pending the resolution of the Palestinian-Israeli conflict.[41]

Employment opportunities for Palestinians in Jordan are restricted. That country exported as many as 40 percent of its own work force during the 1980s. Since the mid-1980s, however, the gulf states have provided fewer work oppor-

37. Quoted by *Sabah al-Khayr* (Beirut), August 11, 1990.

38. There are prospects for the former Soviet republics to supply up to 150,000 potential workers every year to the Near East, in particular to Bahrain, Kuwait, and Saudi Arabia. See *Megapolis Ekspres,* August 17, 1991, as quoted by "BBC Monitoring Service: Soviet Union," August 23, 1991. For Nigerian manpower, see *Middle East Economic Digest,* October 4, 1991, p. 6.

39. See Lawyers Committee for Human Rights, "The Treatment of Alleged Collaborators and Other Security Detainees in Kuwait," August 9, 1991; "Kuwait: Project to Reduce the Population by Half Under Way," *Middle East Economic Digest,* October 4, 1991, p. 6; "Middle East: Migrants Come Home to Roost," ibid., October 4, 1991.

40. Nabil Kukali, "Ta'thir azmat al-khalij fi al-iqtisad al-Filastin (Qira'a awwaliyya) (The impact of the gulf war on the Palestinian economy [Preliminary review]), *Shu'un Filastiniyya,* December 1990/January 1991, p. 21. According to Sara Roy, in 1987 total remittances from the gulf countries amounted to $250 million. See Roy, "The Political Economy of Despair: Changing Political and Economic Realities in the Gaza Strip," *Journal of Palestine Studies* 20, no. 3 (1991), p. 62. Some Palestinian economists estimated the level of remittances to be about $150 million per year. See Joel Bainerman, "The Cost of Complicity," *Middle East,* March 1991, p. 36. For the economic costs to the Palestinians of the invasion of Kuwait, see George T. Abed, "The Palestinians and the Gulf Crisis," *Journal of Palestine Studies* 20, no. 2 (1991), pp. 35–8.

41. P.V. Vivekanand, "Gazans Holding Jordanian Documents Off to Libya," *Jordan Times,* February 26, 1991, p. 2.

tunities for Jordanians.[42] Indeed, beginning in 1985 Jordan has had to cope with a modest return of its citizens from the Persian Gulf and increasing unemployment at home. Between 1985 and 1986, about 70,000 Jordanians returned home as a result of an economic recession in the gulf.[43]

Regarding Palestinians, the Jordanian policy has been to limit their migration from the occupied territories into Jordan. Within the framework of the Jordanian Five-Year Plan (1981–85), restrictions initially imposed in 1983 resulted in a decrease in the net rate of migration from the occupied territories to Jordan to about 1,000 persons a year.[44] The effects of this policy, however, were negated by the results of the Persian Gulf War, because most of the Palestinians deported from Kuwait went to Jordan.[45] Jordan also bore the brunt of the exodus of other expatriate workers from Iraq and Kuwait. According to one report, about 750,000 refugees—mainly Asian, Egyptian, and Palestinian workers fleeing Kuwait—entered Jordan during the first six months following the Iraqi invasion. Most of them subsequently returned to their countries of origin, but between 250,000–300,000 Palestinians and Jordanians remained.[46]

The returning Palestinians represented a 10 percent increase to Jordan's total population of 3.2 million.[47] Of the returnees, 80 percent settled in Amman and Zarka, the second largest city. Such concentrations of people placed great pressure on resources, water, housing, medical services, and education. The flow of refugees also increased Jordan's already high rate of unemployment to about 25 percent.[48] In addition, Jordan's natural rate of population growth—about 3.7 percent per year—means that even greater numbers of new workers will be entering the labor force in future years.[49]

Some of the Palestinians deported from Kuwait had hoped to reach the occupied territories, but a number of obstacles stood in their way. Israeli policy is that Israel is responsible only for those people who lived in the occupied territories in June 1967 and those who hold valid Israeli identity cards and satisfy the conditions imposed by Israel, such as maintaining connections with the area when absent for a few years. In Gaza and the West Bank, hundreds of Palestinians can be found with tourist visas, or with one-, two-, or three-month permits; they must leave when their permits expire and reapply for new temporary permits.

42. Allan M. Findlay, *The Jordanian Migration System in Transition* (Geneva: International Labor Organization, 1987).

43. *Al-Ra'y al-Amm* (Amman), November 25, 1986.

44. Zakai, *Economic Development*, pp. 30–1.

45. "Migrants Come Home to Roost," pp. 4–6.

46. Martha Wenger, "Who Are the Refugees?" *Middle East Report*, January-February 1991, p. 32. See also Jane Araf, "Jordan Asks West to Intervene on Behalf of Departing Jordanians," Reuter wire report, August 14, 1991; "Over 10,000 Jordanians Return from Kuwait over Three Weeks," ibid., August 27, 1991. One report stated that more than 15,000 Jordanians returned home during a three-week period in August 1991. See, "One-Third Unemployed," *Insight/Middle East Update*, September 6, 1991.

47. "Over 10,000 Jordanians Return."

48. "Migrants Come Home to Roost," pp. 4–6.

49. See United Nations, *Demographic Yearbook* (New York, various issues, 1980–1990).

THE PALESTINIAN LABOR FORCE

The Palestinian population of the occupied territories at the end of 1991 was estimated at 1,682,000—about 1,005,600 in the West Bank and 676,100 in the Gaza Strip.[50] The population continues to increase rapidly because of high birth rates (ranging in the years 1985–1990 between 37.8 and 41.3 per thousand in the West Bank and 47.3 and 52.1 per thousand in the Gaza Strip) and reduced infant, child, and crude mortality rates (infant mortality rates, for example, dropping in the years 1970–1990 from 38.1 to 22.0 per thousand in the West Bank and 86.0 to 26.1 per thousand in the Gaza Strip.[51] The growth in population is also affected by the changing migration patterns of the residents of the occupied territories. The population is young, with some 47 percent of Palestinians being between the ages of 0 and 14 years of age.[52] The labor force in the occupied territories averaged 312,000 in 1991—200,000 in the West Bank and 112,000 in the Gaza Strip—an increase of 1.4 percent compared to 1990. In 1991, there was an increase of 3.7 percent in the population over the age of 15—their numbers reaching 834,000—compared with 1990. In 1991, the labor force comprised 37.4 percent of the entire population compared with 38.3 percent in 1990.[53]

In 1991, the number of persons employed in the occupied territories decreased by 3 percent to about 287,000. A 7 percent reduction occurred in the West Bank, with 180,000 workers, while a rise in employment of 4 percent occurred in the Gaza Strip, with an average of 107,000 workers on a weekly basis. During 1991, the rate of unemployment in the occupied territories reached 7.9 percent, compared with 3.7 percent in 1990 and a similar figure in 1989.[54] The numbers of unemployed in the West Bank trebled in 1991: 10.3 percent in 1991 compared with 3.6 percent in 1990. In the Gaza Strip the rate of unemployment remained constant at 4.1 percent.[55] Every sector of Palestinian society was affected by unemployment.[56]

Palestinian sources, particularly the Federation of Palestinian Trade Unions of West Bank Workers, have claimed that the official Israeli statistics indicating relatively low levels of unemployment, are inaccurate. These Palestinian sources, based on sample surveys and field observations, claim a much higher rate of unemployment—about 50 percent in 1990.[57] A 1991 United Nations Conference on Trade and Development (UNCTAD) report presents various explanations for

50. Israel, Central Bureau of Statistics, *Statistical Abstract of Israel, 1992* (Jerusalem, 1992), p. 732.
51. Israel, Ministry of Health, *Health in Judea, Samaria, and Gaza, 1990–1992* (Jerusalem, 1991), pp. 7, 25.
52. Israel, Ministry of Health, *Health in Judea Samaria and Gaza, 1991–1992* (Jerusalem, 1992), p. 3.
53. Israel, Central Bureau of Statistics, "Memo 45," April 14, 1992.
54. Ibid.
55. Ibid.
56. For unemployment of academics, see Peter Newman, "Palestinian Education: A Road to Nowhere?" *Middle East International*, September 28, 1984, pp. 12–13; *Sawt al-Bilad* (Cyprus), July 28, 1987; *al-Fajr*, July 26, 1987.
57. Quoted by International Labor Organization, *Report of the Director-General*, p. 55.

the discrepancies between official Israeli figures and Palestinian claims, including differences in definitions.[58]

The *intifada,* which began in December 1987, has resulted in significant changes to the labor force employed in the occupied territories. Mainly due to strike actions, these changes have included an increase in unemployment, a reduction in the number of hours worked per day, and a reduction in the number of days worked per month. In 1991, the number of persons who worked full time in the West Bank comprised 83 percent of the total number of employed, a figure similar to that in 1990; in 1989, that number had been 74.5 percent; in 1987, it had been 93 percent. In 1991, the number of persons who worked part time—34 hours per week or less—was about 12 percent of the total employed, compared to 14 percent in 1990, 18.5 percent in 1989, and 4 percent in 1987.[59]

In the Gaza Strip, the number of persons who worked full time in 1991 comprised 84 percent of the total number employed, compared with 72 percent in 1990. In comparison, the rate of full-time workers was 90 percent in 1987. The number of persons who worked part time rose from 3.3 percent in 1987 to about 14.5 percent in 1989, to 19.5 percent in 1990, and fell to 8.5 percent in 1991.[60] Most of those workers from the West Bank who lost their jobs tended either to cease to be part of the labor force or emigrated. In contrast, those workers from the Gaza Strip who lost their jobs tended to find alternative work rather than emigrate. Indeed, it is more difficult for Gaza inhabitants to emigrate because they do not hold Jordanian or other citizenship.[61]

West Bank and Gaza Palestinians Working in Israel

The Israeli economy has been going through a recession since the late 1980s, but there were signs of recovery during 1992. Among other effects, the recession brought with it a large reduction in the demand for workers and a rate of unemployment that exceeded 11.6 percent by the first quarter of 1992, compared to 11 percent in the last quarter of 1991 and 10 percent in the first quarter of 1991.[62] Despite this, the current economic difficulties in Israel have not affected the modernization trend of the economy. The Israeli economy is based increasingly on technology and advanced financial and organizational systems. Underpinning the economy is a stable social infrastructure that is expressed, inter alia, by rising levels of education among the work force and rising numbers of women joining the work force.

Many sectors of the economy, however, still rely on manual labor. In the Jewish sector, manual labor is considered inferior work that many, including the

58. United Nations Conference on Trade and Development, *Recent Economic Developments in the Occupied Palestinian Territory* (Geneva, August 9, 1991), pp. 23–4.
59. Israel, Central Bureau of Statistics, "Memo 45."
60. Ibid.
61. Gharaibeh, *Economies of the West Bank and Gaza Strip,* pp. 34–5.
62. Israel, Central Bureau of Statistics, "Unemployment Statistics," June 1992.

TABLE 1
Total Number of Palestinian Employees Working in Israel by Selected Economic Branches
(in thousands)

Year	Agriculture	Industry	Construction	Other	Total
1980	10.1	15.6	35.1	12.4	73.2
1985	13.8	15.7	41.4	15.2	86.1
1988	16.3	16.5	52.1	19.0	104.3*
1990	12.4	11.1	62.7	17.5	103.7

Source: Central Bureau of Statistics, *Statistical Yearbook, 1991*, p. 736, table 27.25.
*Although the figures total 103.9 thousand, the Central Bureau of Statistics cites the total as 104.3 thousand.

unemployed, refuse. Unemployed Israelis also shun night-shift positions, such as in the printing industry. There exists in Israel, therefore, a phenomenon of "employment objectors," creating employment polarization. This is the main explanation for the inability of an economy suffering from unemployment to fill thousands of job vacancies.[63]

Until 1967, Palestinians with Israeli citizenship filled positions that Jews were reluctant to take. After 1967, these vacancies were taken by Palestinians from the occupied territories,[64] a phenomenon not unlike situations in Europe and the United States in which foreigners have taken jobs with the least social status and the lowest salaries. They also have been the last to receive services, and they suffer from discrimination and prejudice.[65] Workers from the West Bank and Gaza Strip—whose numbers in 1987, before the outbreak of the intifada, reached a weekly average of 109,000 (legal and illegal)—comprised 8 percent of the labor force in Israel.[66] The largest number—49,700—were employed in the construction sector, and their representation in this industry increased annually, reaching 42 percent in 1987.[67] About 19,700 were employed

63. "Din ve heshbon hodshi shel sar ha'avodah ve harevaha" (Monthly report of minister of welfare and labor), February 20, 1989, p. 37, and July 20, 1989, p. 37. Many contractors have expressed their anger to labor bureau staff after a lack of laborers prevented them from completing work that they had undertaken to perform. See Baruch Haklai, "Baayot ha'taasukah be medinat Israel" (Employment problems in the State of Israel), *Hamiphal*, June 1984, p. 14.

64. Semyonov and Lewin-Epstein, *Hewers of Wood and Drawers of Water*, pp. 62–3.

65. See, for example, the research on the immigration of workers to France, Switzerland, and West Germany following World War II. Stephen Castles and Godula Kosack, *Immigrant Workers and Class Structure in Western Europe* (Oxford: Oxford University Press, 1979).

66. Israel, Department of Trade, "Statistical Monthly of Israel," supplement no. 4, April 1988, p. 175; idem, "Statistical Monthly of Judea, Samaria, and the Gaza Strip" March 1988, p. 35, table 6/E.

67. In 1987, the number of employees in the building sector in Israel totaled 117,400; of these, 67,700 were from Israel and 49,700 from the occupied territories. Compared with the 1987 figure of 42 percent, in 1977 Palestinians comprised only 25 percent of construction workers. See Israel, Ministry of Housing and Construction, Center for Data and Economic Analysis, "Data on the Development of the Construction Sector and the Activities of the Ministry of Housing in the Last Month," May 16, 1989, table 1.E.

in industry—particularly food, textiles, and metallurgy; 15,800 in agriculture—mainly gathering fruit—forestry, and fishing. The remaining 23,700 were employed in services and other sectors.[68]

In addition to workers from the occupied territories, Israel imports labor from abroad. The majority come from Portugal, South Lebanon, and Turkey as well as Africa, Eastern Europe, and the Far East. Their numbers have been increasing, and at the end of 1988 were at 14,000, legal and illegal. According to figures supplied by the Israeli Ministry of Labor, based on the number of valid work permits granted in January 1989, 1,805 workers from South Lebanon and 3,662 other foreign workers were employed legally in Israel, whereas the remaining 8,500 worked illegally.[69]

In terms of Israel's economy, 1987 was the most prosperous in a decade: gross domestic product (GDP) increased by 5.2 percent, investments by 13 percent, exports by 17 percent; unemployment stabilized at 6.1 percent and inflation at 16.1 percent. The immediate effects of the intifada were the partial separation of the West Bank and Gaza Strip from Israel in terms of providing a market for Israeli products, as well as a source of labor. Estimates have put the damage to the Israeli economy in 1988 at 3–4 percent of its GDP, in 1989 at 2–3 percent, and in 1990 at 1–2 percent. By the end of 1988, the consumer markets had basically adjusted to the changed circumstances. This was not the case, however, with regard to employment. In spite of the relatively small number of workers from the occupied territories—officially 109,000 in 1987 out of 1.4 million—the lack of workers from the West Bank and Gaza Strip resulted in direct and indirect damage.[70]

As a result of Gaza's greater dependence on the Israeli economy, the intifada had less of an impact on the movement of laborers from Gaza to Israel than was the case with respect to the West Bank.[71] Throughout the intifada, more than 45 percent of the Palestinian labor force from the Gaza Strip continued to work in Israel; their earnings accounted for some 55 percent of the total income of the strip.[72] Even during periods when general strikes were called, many workers from the occupied territories came to work in Israel. For example, data provided by the civil administration of the occupied territories indicate that almost half the laborers reported for work during the general strike of October 8–9, 1991.

68. Israel, Department of Trade, "Statistics of Judea, Samaria, and the Gaza Strip," March 1988, p. 35, table 6/E.

69. "Din ve heshbon hodshi," p. 49. See also *Ma'ariv*, December 17, 1991, business section.

70. Gideon Fishelson, *Forming (1970–87) and Destroying (1988–1990) a Common Labor Market* (Tel Aviv: Tel Aviv University, Armand Hammer Fund for Economic Cooperation in the Middle East, 1992), pp. 24–5.

71. Fishelson, *Forming and Destroying a Common Labor Market*, p. 26. For Gazan workers in Israel, see Paul Cossali and Clive Robson, "The People of Gaza Speak: Part 2, A Labourer in Israel," *Middle East International*, January 11, 1985, pp. 13–14.

72. Ghasan Shihabi, "The Working Class and the Trade Unions in the Gaza Strip," *Samid al-Iqtisadi*, April-June 1991, pp. 78–9.

Since the outbreak of the intifada, both the Israeli and local markets have adjusted, but another factor was introduced at the end of 1989—the massive immigration to Israel of Soviet Jews. Given the high unemployment rate in Israel and the desperate need of these new immigrants for a source of income, the immigrants are likely in the medium term to replace workers from the occupied territories.[73] In the long run, in a normal, full employment market, workers from the occupied territories would complement the new immigrant labor.[74] In particular, it seems likely that Palestinian workers will still be required in sectors in which they have developed expertise, such as construction. In the event of a political settlement, moreover, Palestinian laborers will have to continue to work in Israel, a fact that has been recognized by senior Palestinian economists and representatives.[75]

Palestinian laborers are major contributors to the current construction boom in Israel aimed at housing immigrants and strengthening the settlements. In a national-political context, of course, the Palestinians are against immigration and settlement, but this contradiction is easily explained by the economic difficulties in the occupied territories. Traditionally, the income from Palestinian work in Israel has been a central component of the local economy. The difficult state of the local economy thus gave this component added importance because the building boom in Israel helped a large percentage of the population living in poverty. Against this background, it is possible to understand the attitude of some Palestinian activists in not making all-out efforts to prevent Palestinian workers from building houses and infrastructures for Soviet immigrants and settlers. Apparently, they are aware that such efforts could not succeed. Indeed, there have been incidents in which Palestinian workers have fought back against masked men who tried to prevent them from going to work in Israel.

Two striking changes may be noted in the nature of the employment of Palestinians in Israel over the years. First, the majority of Palestinians are now provided with work permits issued by the civil administration, whereas previously the majority of laborers worked outside the control of official labor offices. The number of licensed workers rose from 35,000 at the beginning of 1991 to about 77,000 by the end of 1991.[76] Second, the type of labor performed by workers from the occupied territories has changed. Many workers who were employed in the past in the industrial and services sector—such as restaurants and petrol stations—have been replaced by immigrants, particularly from the former Soviet

73. According to figures released in an internal memo by the Central Bureau of Statistics in December 1991, since late 1989 only 68,000 of some 350,000 Soviet immigrants have found employment. That leaves 44,000 registered as unemployed and thousands more in language and other training programs.

74. Fishelson, *Forming and Destroying a Common Labor Market*, pp. 27–8.

75. See Hisham Awartani, professor of economics at al-Najah University, as quoted in *Globes*, January 17, 1992, p. 13, and comments by Labib Terazi, PLO representative to the United Nations, as quoted in *Ha'aretz*, December 20, 1988.

76. Israel, Central Bureau of Statistics, "Labor Market in Israel," February 1992.

Union. In contrast, the sharp rise in the demand for construction workers in Israel has been met by Palestinian laborers from the occupied territories.

It seems likely that the freeze on the building of settlements in the occupied territories—ordered by the Labor Party government following the general election in June 1992—will have a significant effect on Palestinian labor. After the completion of the housing units presently under construction, the settlement boom will end, and there will be a decline in Palestinian employment. Should Palestinian construction workers, however, participate in the building of a new infrastructure within an autonomous entity, this would have the effect of compensating for the loss of employment in Israel and, indeed, might create even more employment opportunities in the long term.

The Persian Gulf War and ensuing events did not affect the size of the Palestinian work force in Israel, but did inhibit its expansion, and, in addition, led to a significant reduction in the number of days and hours worked. Thus, during 1991, Palestinians from the West Bank worked an average of 18.6 days a month, whereas Palestinians from the Gaza Strip worked an average of only 15.8 days a month. In 1991,[77] the number of Palestinians employed in Israel totaled 98,000, a reduction of 9 percent compared with 1990; they comprised 34 percent of the number of persons employed from the occupied territories.

If one takes into account subcontractors in the occupied territories supplying Israeli demands, however, the figure for direct and indirect reliance on the Israeli market is closer to 50 percent. These figures emphasize the total dependence of the occupied territories on the Israeli economy. During January-March 1991, some 80,000 workers entered Israel to work, and thereafter a gradual rise took place, with some 118,000 workers entering Israel in the last quarter of 1991 compared with 105,000 in the same period in 1990. Palestinian residents working in Israel worked 8 percent fewer hours per week in 1991 than in 1990.[78]

All sectors of the Israeli economy, including the construction sector, were affected by the impact of the gulf war and intifada on Palestinian labor in Israel. The main reduction in the number of Palestinians employed in Israel took place in industry, where the numbers dropped from 11,200 in 1990 to 7,500 in 1991, a drop of about 33 percent. In the construction sector, a slight rise was recorded, from 64,000 to 67,000. In 1991, 68.5 percent of Palestinian workers employed in Israel worked in construction,[79] about 12 percent worked in agriculture, 7.7 percent in industry, and 12 percent in other sectors.

---

77. Gil Feiler, "The Labor Market in the Territories," expert report supplied to the District Court of Jerusalem in C.A. 316/92, Taysir Atiya Mahmud Amor v. Karnit (Israel Insurance Company), Ltd., (1993).

78. Robby Nathanzon, "Shuk ha'avodah be Israel" (The labor market in Israel), Histadrut, Institute for Economic and Social Research, June 1992.

79. The importance of the Palestinian construction workers to the Israeli economy is reflected by the extensive losses caused to this sector by the closure of the occupied territories following incidents either inside or outside the territories. See, for example, *Globes*, June 9, 1992.

The above figures indicate that the number of Palestinian workers in Israel is influenced directly by both political factors and the Israeli GDP.[80] There are two factors influencing the export of labor services to destinations other than Israel. The first is the development of the GDP in the occupied territories: When there is economic growth, emigration in search of employment lessens. The second factor is the economic situation in the countries of destination of the labor export, especially Jordan and the Persian Gulf states. Prior to the gulf war, the growth factor in these countries had a positive impact on the demand for workers from the occupied territories.[81]

According to one view, in a situation where half of the labor force is employed outside its residential region—as a minority complementing, and partly substituting for, the larger region's inputs, mainly of labor—and where the complementary labor force has low skills—as well as low prestige, low earnings and little opportunity, if any, for advancement—the need to invest in the creation of jobs in the local region is imperative. Encouraging the creation of such opportunities in the occupied territories is also likely to benefit Israel in the long run and lead to beneficial cooperation in both Palestinian and Israeli labor markets. Economic separation of the two areas would cause negligible damage to the Israeli economy, apart from requiring adjustment in the technology of production in those sectors where workers from the occupied territories are most heavily employed. In the occupied territories, however, such economic separation would cause unemployment to rise by 50 percent, bringing with it economic and social disaster—unless huge investments were made to create a minimum of 130,000 new jobs.[82]

Israel has become an essential source of work and thus income for the Palestinians because there are no longer such opportunities for the Palestinians in the oil states of the Persian Gulf and there is no longer money coming in from relatives in Kuwait. Amman, seemingly the most viable alternative labor market, is overpopulated as a result of the influx of refugees from Kuwait, and also suffers from high unemployment. Added to these difficulties for Palestinians, is the dwindling flow of money from the PLO, Jordan, and other Arab states. The decrease in money from these various sources is felt sharply in the occupied territories. These factors have led to mutual dependence, linking the economic fates of Israel and the occupied territories, and indicate the substantial political, practical, economic, and social advantages to be gained by a program of regional cooperation.

80. Fishelson, *Forming and Destroying a Common Labor Market*, p. 18.
81. Ibid., p. 20; see also Gharaibeh, *Economies of the West Bank and Gaza Strip*, pp. 33–5.
82. Fishelson, *Forming and Destroying a Common Labor Market*, pp. 29–30.

CONCLUSION

Although the intifada and the Persian Gulf War have not had a significant impact on the number of Palestinian workers employed in Israel, both events have resulted in a complete metamorphosis in Palestinian employment patterns in the Persian Gulf states, Jordan, and the occupied territories. In the long term, high unemployment rates within Israel, shorter hours worked by the Palestinians within Israel, the substitution of Palestinian laborers with Soviet immigrants, and the anticipation of further massive immigration to Israel of Jews from the former Soviet republics will each reduce the availability of work in Israel for the Palestinians. In addition, voices have been heard in Israel calling on the Israeli government to place high on the agenda of the autonomy talks the separation of the Israeli labor market from that of the occupied territories. For example, it is argued that if such a step is not taken, hostility between Palestinians and Israelis not only will increase, but also technological progress in Israel will be hampered by continued dependency on cheap labor from the occupied territories.[83]

After more than two decades, the period of a single labor market between Israel and the occupied territories may be coming to an end. Unemployment has soared and living standards are dropping. The United Nations Relief and Works Agency (UNRWA) is now distributing basic food supplies to the entire Palestinian population. Given that one of the demographic features of the occupied territories is the high rate of young persons who will join the ranks of those seeking work in the next few years, it appears that the situation is likely to become worse. Moreover, a decrease in emigration has an effect on the structure of age and gender of the population. If, in the past, the male population of work age tended to emigrate, causing a shortage of men, the reduction in rates of emigration may lead to higher birth rates and a greater degree of destitution and poverty. This is particularly applicable to the refugee camps, where people live without hope and without natural resources, thus fueling the frustration that sometimes leads to violence.

Significant changes in the occupied territories can be achieved only through massive injections of foreign capital and preparation of a comprehensive Marshall-type plan. Among the Palestinians of the occupied territories there is a strata of entrepreneurs capable of absorbing foreign capital. Cooperation with Israel would greatly assist in working cost effectively, which, in turn, would create an opening for reconciliation, and a new and more healthy relationship between Israelis and Palestinians.

Israel has taken some steps to help develop the economy of the occupied territories. In 1991, for example, the civil administration issued more than 100 permits for new businesses, reflecting an 85 percent approval rating, compared to

83. See for example *Ha'aretz*, July 6, 1992, p. C1.

less than 10 per year in the 1980s.[84] The Sadan Committee, appointed by the Ministry of Defense and whose recommendations were adopted by the Israeli government in 1991, called for the cancellation of administrative restrictions on investors and for the end of harassment on tax issues. Private foreign investors, however, are reluctant to invest in the occupied territories because of the political situation, and Palestinians themselves are unwilling to invest in local projects because of uncertainty about the future. In the Gaza Strip, where there is little available land and the price of land rises yearly, landowners attempt to maximize their profits by waiting and not appropriating their land, for example, for building factories. This reluctance to invest heavily in local enterprises halts the proper development of marketing and employment opportunities.

In the absence of an established local basis of production, the Palestinian work force, both in Gaza and the West Bank, will continue to seek employment in the Israeli labor market and in Jordan and the Persian Gulf states. It has been shown, however, that neither the oil economies nor the Jordanian economy can guarantee Palestinians employment. The best hope, in the short term, lies in the Israeli labor market. In the medium and long term, other solutions have to be found. In light of the political situation by the middle of 1993, it would seem that longlasting solutions to indigenous economic and social problems—such as the creation of a local basis of production and of a significant number of employment opportunities—will become possible only in a framework of comprehensive regional cooperation.

The labor market in Israel cannot, under any circumstances, provide by itself a solution to the unemployment crisis of the Palestinians, and the economy of the occupied territories cannot provide a solution to the employment problems of the sizable population of Palestinians living on a permanent basis outside the occupied territories. In the event that autonomy or other political arrangements are established in the occupied territories, it may be anticipated that diaspora Palestinians, in particular those who reside in refugee camps and have failed to become integrated into their host countries, will wish to return and work in the area, thus aggravating an already difficult employment situation. One source estimated that between 750,000 and 1 million Palestinians could be expected to enter the occupied territories following autonomy.[85]

There is no choice, therefore, but to encourage massive foreign investment in

---

84. Interviews with Palestinian businessmen and employees of the civil administration, Jerusalem, 1992.

85. Sari Nusseibeh and Mark Heller, *Bli tupim, ve hazozrot* (No trumpets, no drums) (Tel Aviv and Jerusalem: Shoken Press, 1991), p. 72. For figures for refugees compiled by UNRWA, see *Report of the Commission General of the United Nations Relief and Works Agency for Palestine Refugees in the Near East, 1 July 1990–30 June 1991* (New York, 1991), pp. 31–2; for demographic figures for Palestinians worldwide and forecasts to the year 2010, see "Ihsa'at wa istiqsa'at: Tawaqqu'at adad al-sukkan al-filastiniyyin fi sitt ashra dawla/mintaqa, 1990–2010" (Statistics and analysis: The estimated number of Palestinian inhabitants of sixteen countries/territories of the world, 1990–2010) *Majalat al-dirasat al-Filastiniyya*, no. 7 (Summer 1991), pp. 220–2.

the occupied territories, and to remove restrictions on marketing from the West Bank and Gaza to Jordan, Israel, Egypt, and Europe. A framework of peace and thoroughly planned regional cooperation would support efforts to improve employment opportunities for the Palestinians to the benefit of all the states and societies in the region.

[15]

THE CORPORATIZATION OF THE EGYPTIAN LABOR MOVEMENT

Robert Bianchi

This essay seeks to illustrate three important aspects of the development of the Egyptian labor movement and its changing relations with the state. First, since World War II, Egypt's ruling elites have gradually restructured the union movement from pluralist to corporatist forms of organization.[1] Second, although the particular variety of corporatism that has arisen in this sector can be described as an example of "state corporatism," the long-term consequence of corporatist policies has been to strengthen and selectively coopt working class organizations rather than to smash them and exclude them from the policy-making process.[2] Third, this process of corporatization is by no means irreversible; indeed, it already has generated new tensions throughout the union hierarchy which may help to promote the reemergence of pluralism both in the labor movement and in the political system as a whole.[3]

These issues will be examined from three different perspectives, each of

1. "Corporatism can be defined as a system of interest representation in which the constituent units are organized into a limited number of singular, compulsory, non-competitive, hierarchically ordered and functionally differentiated categories, recognized or licensed (if not created) by the state and granted a deliberate representational monopoly within their respective categories in exchange for observing certain controls on their selection of leaders and articulation of demands and supports." Philippe C. Schmitter, "Still the Century of Corporatism?" *Review of Politics*, 36, no. 1 (January 1974): 85–131.

2. Efforts to distinguish between more cooptive and more coercive varieties of state corporatism can be seen in O'Donnell's notions of "populist authoritarianism" versus "bureaucratic authoritarianism," in Stepan's concepts of "inclusionary corporatism" versus "exclusionary corporatism," and in the Colliers' distinction between "inducements-oriented" and "constraints-oriented" varieties of corporatism. Guillermo O'Donnell, *Modernization and Bureaucratic-Authoritarianism* (Berkeley: University of California Institute of International Studies, 1973); Alfred Stepan, *State and Society: Peru in Comparative Perspective* (Princeton: Princeton University Press, 1978); and David Collier and Ruth Berens Collier, "Inducements versus Constraints: Disaggregating 'Corporatism,' " *American Political Science Review*, 73, no. 4 (December 1979): 967–986.

3. For other examples of corporatist policies which have had the unintended consequence of promoting pluralism see Robert Bianchi, *Interest Groups and Political Development in Turkey* (Princeton: Princeton University Press, 1984); and "Interest Group Politics in the Third World," *Third World Quarterly*, 8, no. 2 (April 1986).

Robert Bianchi is Associate Professor, Department of Political Science, University of Chicago.

which highlights a particular dimension of the corporatization process—changes in public policy toward union organization; a brief history of the Egyptian Confederation of Labor (al-Ittihad al-Amm li-Niqabat Ummal Misr), including its increasing interconnections with governmental, legislative, and party structures; and, finally, the appearance of several types of cleavage within the confederation and its affiliates that seriously threaten the future of corporatist unionism and the stability of the current regime.

CHANGES IN UNION LEGISLATION

The gradual restructuring of the Egyptian labor movement along corporatist lines is observable in the evolution of public policy regulating the coverage, organization, activities, and leadership selection of trade unions.[4] The state has sought to promote and control unionization through four major statutes—the trade union laws of 1942, 1952, 1959 (amended in 1964), and 1976 (amended in 1981).[5] A comparison of these statutes reveals a steady shift by successive governments from pluralism to corporatism as the preferred strategy for molding and coopting the emerging associations of the working class.

The first union law passed by the Wafdist government during World War II provided the Egyptian labor movement with its closest approximation to a pluralist model of organization even though the variety of pluralism selected clearly was intended to be highly restrictive and debilitating for union leaders. Labor unions were legally defined as private, voluntary, competitive organizations with no hierarchical or federative structure and no official status or sponsorship. However, despite the new freedom and recognition accorded to unions, several features of the statute indicated the government's desire to preserve a small, fragmented, and vulnerable labor movement.

For example, unionization was prohibited among agricultural workers, civil servants, and health workers. The minimum size of a local union was set at 50 members. No provision was made for dues check-offs or union shops. Multiple

4. On the history of the Egyptian labor movement preceeding the period covered in this essay see Amin Izz al-Din, *Tarikh al-Tabaqa al-Amila al-Misriya* (The History of the Egyptian Working Class) 3 vols. (Cairo: Dar al-Katib al-Arabi and Dar al-Shaab, 1967, 1970, and 1972); Rauf Abbas, *al-Haraka al Ummaliya fi Misr, 1899–1952* (The Workers' Movement in Egypt, 1899–1952) (Cairo: Dar al-Katib al-Arabi lil-Taba'a wa al-Nashr, 1967); Marius Deeb, "Labour and Politics in Egypt, 1919–1939," *International Journal of Middle East Studies*, 10, no. 2 (May 1979): 187–203; and Jacques Couland, "Regards sur L'Histoire Syndicale et Ouvriere Egyptienne (1899–1952)," in Rene Gallissot, ed., *Mouvement Ouvrier, Communisme et Nationalismes dans le Monde Arabe* (Paris: Les Editions Ouvrieres, 1978).

5. Law no. 85 for 1942, *al-Waqāi' al-Misriya* 171 (September 10, 1942), pp. 8–11; Law no. 319 for 1952, *al-Waqāi' al-Misriya* 157 (December 8, 1952), pp. 15–19; Law no. 91 for 1959, *al-Jarida al-Rasmiya*, n.d.; Ministry of Labour, Law no. 62 for 1964 together with the Ministerial Executive Orders (May 1964); Law no. 35 for 1976, *al-Jarida al-Rasmiya* 22 (May 27, 1976); and Law no. 1 for 1981, *al-Jarida al-Rasmiya* 2 (January 8, 1981).

federations were allowed to organize in identical workbranches and regions. Although no reference was made to the establishment of a union confederation, this was interpreted by the Wafd and succeeding governments as an implicit prohibition against forming a nationwide "peak association" to coordinate union activity. Unions were specifically forbidden to engage in political and religious activities or to invest in business and profit-making enterprises. The formation of a new union required approval by the Ministry of Social Affairs which also was empowered to close down unions accused of illegal activities, even in the absence of a court order.

The 1952 union law reflected a similar ambivalence toward organized labor among the Free Officers who attempted more urgently than their predecessors to devise techniques that would simultaneously expand and strengthen unions while providing greater state controls over their leadership selection and expression of demands. The 1952 statute was the most "mixed" of all the Egyptian union laws in terms of combining both pluralist and corporatist provisions in an interesting, though short-lived, hybrid formula. On one hand, the law encouraged the rapid proliferation of new unions. Union membership was extended to agricultural workers. Check-offs were permitted and in enterprises where three-fifths of the workforce was unionized, union shops were required. The establishment of new unions required only registration with but not approval from the Ministry of Social Affairs, and the power to close down existing unions was transferred from the executive to the judiciary.

On the other hand, the principle of singular, non-competitive, hierarchical organization was introduced and clearly sanctioned by the authority of the state. At the regional level no more than one union federation was to be permitted in each occupational category. At the national level a single labor confederation was to enjoy a monopoly of representation for the union movement as a whole. The government had not yet specified the categories in which federations were to be organized, and it agreed to postpone the establishment of the Egyptian Confederation of Labor until 1957. Nevertheless, a monistic, hierarchical, and semi-official model of union organization was adopted and codified by the authoritarian regime less than five months after the July revolution.

The transformation of the unions from pluralist to corporatist structures was completed between 1959 and 1964. The Unified Labor Code of 1959 and the Trade Unions Law of 1964 were landmark pieces of corporatist legislation comparable in many ways to the labor code of the Brazilian Estado Novo. They laid down elaborate regulations encompassing all aspects of employment, including sweeping provisions for centralized union organization around a small number of nationwide industrial federations under the supervision of a unitary confederation and a new Ministry of Labor. In 1960 an official list of 64 occupational categories was issued and by 1962 new federations had been established for 59 of these groups. In 1964 the government sharply increased union centralization by reducing the number of federations to 27.

Compared to their fragmented and regionally based predecessors, the new industrial federations possessed much larger memberships, vastly expanded finances and authority, and officially guaranteed monopoly status. The size of the labor movement was rapidly increased by permitting the unionization of civil servants and encouraging organization drives among agricultural workers. Federations were empowerd to negotiate and ratify all collective work contracts and were responsible for collecting and disbursing the lion's share of union dues according to government issued guidelines. To facilitate organized labor's contribution to building the new socialist society the traditional legal bans on union political, religious, and entrepreneurial activities were abolished and were never again reinstated.

However, the socialist union laws of the Nasser era introduced several new prohibitions such as bans against inciting class antagonisms, organizing work stoppages, trying to overthrow the political system, and using force to recruit union members. In exchange for such pledges of loyalty and self-restraint union leaders were provided with highly attractive and unprecedented legal guarantees concerning job security, promotions, and retirement benefits. Thus the corporatization of the labor movement also involved the selective cooptation of a collaborative, powerful, and handsomely rewarded segment of the non-communist union leadership.

During the Sadat regime the corporatist union structure was further tightened and centralized. The top union leadership became increasingly self-recruiting, rendering it even more insulated than before from the threat of rank and file protests. Moreover, the national labor confederation broadened its power of consultation in economic policy-making and acquired important new resources for direct investment in profit-making enterprises.

The most recent union laws of 1976 and 1981 substantially strengthened the administrative and financial controls of the Egyptian Confederation of Labor over the federations and of the federations over their local affiliates, producing an organizational structure that is sharply hierarchical, or as the statutes themselves put it, "pyramid-shaped". Soon after Sadat came to power he purged the leadership of the labor confederation and reduced the number of federations to 16. By 1976 a new cadre of unionists was firmly in power and the number of federations has been allowed slowly to increase again under their control.

A new system of indirect elections has insured the tenure of top union officials and greatly reduced their accountability to their constituents. Elected positions at all levels of the union hierarchy are filled nearly simultaneously, with higher echelon leaders being chosen by lower echelon leaders after a screening of all candidates by the Socialist Prosecutor's office. The term of elected leaders has been lengthened gradually, from two years to three years after 1976 and to four years since 1981. Since 1973, turnover in the federation and confederation leaderships has fallen steadily and was virtually nil in the most recent union elections during 1983.

As confederation leaders have become more secure they also have become more prominent political and economic figures. The confederation president is now an ex-officio member of the cabinet, serving as head of the new Ministry of Manpower and Professional Training. Most members of the confederation's executive committee are leaders in the ruling National Democratic Party, three are deputies in the People's Assembly, and three others are representatives in the Consultative Assembly (*Majlis al-Shūra*). Confederation leaders are ubiquitous and often statutorily designated members of countless economic planning councils, parliamentary committees, public sector management boards, and ministerial consultative bodies.[6]

Since 1981 the Confederation's powers have been expanded in two important areas. It has been granted exclusive control over a new Workers' University designed to integrate a multitude of union leadership training programs formerly run by rival state and party agencies with conflicting goals and programs. In addition, the Confederation has been allowed to join in the widening movement of "syndical capitalism" initiated by the many corporatist professional associations and business chambers that have used pension funds and state subsidies to establish independent economic enterprises, including joint ventures with foreign investors. The newly established Workers' Bank now occupies a prominent area of the Confederation's headquarters, symbolizing the expansion of organized labor's economic role beyond the traditional limits of public sector industry.[7]

THE EVOLUTION OF THE EGYPTIAN CONFEDERATION OF LABOR AS AN INTEREST GROUP

Efforts to establish and manipulate a single representative association for the entire working class have been a recurrent source of intra-elite conflict and a key element in the ruling calculus of Egyptian governments since the beginning of World War II. Over time there has been a gradual, but quite remarkable change in the strategies of Egypt's political elites in dealing with the leaders of the labor movement. Since 1942 the range of state-union relations has included 1) early government suppression of all independent initiatives to build union federations, 2) Nasser's ambitious efforts to win working class support with redistributive

6. Muhammad Muhammad Ali, "al-Qiyadat al-Niqabiya li-Ummal Misr" (Union Leaders of the Egyptian Workers), *al-Amal*, 247 (December 1983), pp. 36–39 and 248 (January 1984), pp. 54–56.

7. Asam Abd al-Jawad, "al-Manahij al-Dirasiya li-Kulliyat al-Jami'a al-Ummaliya" (The Curricula in the Faculties of the Workers' University), *al-Amal*, 248 (January 1984); and Adal al-Mashad, "al-Ghazw al-Istithmari lil-Niqabat al-Mihniya wa al-Ummaliya" (The Entrepreneurial Invasion of Professional and Labor Syndicates), *al-Shaab* (January 1983).

reforms that directly benefited union members without the mediation of union representatives, 3) Sadat's more selective cooptation of collaborative union leaders through increasingly generous grants of privilege to their corporatist organizations, and, most recently, 4) Mubarak's informal acceptance of sharing power and responsibility with the Egyptian Confederation of Labor in many areas of economic policy-making.

The Confederation has been a central part of the authoritarian state's efforts to fashion effective corporatist controls over the union movement. Gradually, however, union leaders also have learned to use it as their principal instrument for penetrating administrative, legislative, and party structures in order to carve out a key role for themselves in the shaping of economic policy. Power relations between successive governments and the Confederation have become less unilateral and more reciprocal, indicating that the corporatization of the Egyptian labor movement has not been a simple matter of subordinating the working class to the authoritarian order. Rather, it appears that corporatism has, in time, provided union leaders with new means for defending workers' interests and, ironically, for limiting the decisional autonomy of the authoritarian regime in certain critical issues.

The Wafdist government that passed the first trade union statute of 1942 claimed that no legal protection had been given for the establishment of a national labor confederation. Nevertheless, that same government also encouraged Wafd Party leaders to enroll public employees in an inter-union "congress" that was designed to recapture control of organized labor from Prince Abbas Halim, who was interned for the duration of World War II. Soon after the war, the left sought to consolidate its leadership over the increasingly radical labor movement by coordinating the establishment of a national confederation (*Mu'tamar Niqābāt 'Ummāl Mişr*). Although leftist union leaders were on the verge of forming a highly inclusive peak association in June and July of 1946, their plans were thwarted by the last minute defection of the conservative transport workers' unions and by Ismail Sidqi's mass imprisonment of congress members.[8]

Six more years passed before unionists overcame government repression and internal rivalries to organize another attempt at confederation. Twice during 1952 "preparatory committees" scheduled founding conventions for an Egyptian Confederation of Labor only to see both meetings cancelled by frightened governments that had just been jolted by spectacular examples of mass protest. The first founding convention was scheduled for the day after the Great Cairo Fire of January 26, 1952, and the second was to take place within a few weeks of the new revolutionary government's bloody suppression of labor unrest at Kafr al-Dawwar the following August.[9]

8. Rauf Abbas, pp. 118–120, 122–132.
9. Abd al-Mughni Said, "Safahat Majhula min Tarikh al-Haraka al-Niqabiya" (Unknown

The Free Officers feared that a union confederation would be manipulated by partisans of the Wafd, the communists, and the Muslim Brotherhood, but the new regime also was eager to build a mass constituency for the revolution in the labor movement. Accordingly, the junta adopted many liberal labor and union reforms precisely at the time that it abolished all pre-revolutionary political parties. Moreover, the Free Officers soon reached a compromise with non-communist union leaders that permitted the formation of an unofficial "permanent congress" in lieu of the unitary confederation that had been endorsed in principle in the new trade union law of 1952.[10]

This "gentlemen's agreement" allowed both sides to justify an indefinite postponement of the revolution's promise to build stronger union structures. Meanwhile, daily contact between the junta and the labor movement was in fact channelled through the Workers' Bureau of the Liberation Rally under Major Abdallah Tu'ayma. It was Tu'ayma who later orchestrated the famous transport workers' demonstrations that provided decisive support for Nasser during the "March crisis" of 1954, when Naguib led a broad coalition against him demanding the return to parliamentary democracy. Even after Nasser had consolidated power within Egypt he was reluctant to permit a national confederation, preferring instead to promote the International Confederation of Arab Trade Unions in order to expand his regional influence during the Suez crisis of 1956. Thus, four years after the revolution Egyptian unionists were in the anomolous position of hosting and providing the vanguard for a pan-Arab labor movement while still possessing no peak association in their own country.[11]

Not surprisingly, Nasser's belated and ambivalent agreement in 1957 to permit the establishment of the Egyptian Confederation of Labor was closely connected with his desire to build means of administrative penetration into Syria. The Unified Labor Code was adopted about one year after the formation of the United Arab Republic. It was generally assumed at the time that the new statute's sweeping provisions for corporatist union organization would be implemented quickly in the Egyptian region where many labor leaders had been demanding greater centralization for years. Conversely, it also was assumed that the same measures would be bitterly resisted in the Syrian region, where autonomous local unions formed a key part of the Baath's provincial party organizations. In fact, the opposite occurred—corporatization was accomplished quite swiftly in Syria, but delayed and nearly abandoned in Egypt when Nasser was confronted with strong police and military objections to the sudden concentration of union power.

Pages from the History of the Union Movement) *al-Amal* 236 (January 1983), pp. 11–13.

10. Ibid, pp. 24–25.

11. Abd al-Azim Ramadan, *Al-Sira' al-Ijtima'i wa al-Siyasi fi Misr* (Social and Political Struggle in Egypt) (Cairo: Ruz al Yusuf, 1975), ch. 11 and appendixes; and Willard A. Beling, *Pan-Arabism and Labor* (Cambridge: Harvard University Press, 1961), ch. 2.

The project to reorganize the Egyptian labor movement was deadlocked for nearly two years due to the conflicting demands of union leaders and Hussein al-Shafai, the Minister of Social Affairs and Labor, on one hand, and Zakariya Muhieddin, the Minister of Interior, on the other hand. When Nasser realized how much dissension the proposal had created among his colleagues, he considered scrapping it altogether. Finally, the president was persuaded to proceed despite Muhieddin's opposition, but not because of any enthusiasm on his part for the notion that union-party relations had to be shaped into a more equal alliance that was free of military tutelage. Rather, Nasser was much more impressed by the "expert opinion" of the Syrian region's new anti-Baathist police chief who assured the Egyptians that the surveillance of potential troublemakers was far easier in the new unitary and centralized laboı movement than it had been in the previously dispersed and provincially based set of structures.[12]

After 1964, when the Confederation finally had completed the construction of new industrial federations, union leaders found themselves engaged in bureaucratic rivalries with some of the most powerful figures of the Nasserist era. On one hand, Aziz Sidqi, the Minister of Industry, led a strong technocratic resistance to the new socialist laws requiring the participation of elected worker representatives in the management of industrial enterprises. On the other hand, Ali Sabri and the radical Workers' Bureau of the Arab Socialist Union (ASU) applied great pressure for direct party control of union elections and of leadership training programs for union officials.

During these power struggles the leaders of the Confederation relied heavily on the patronage of Kamal Rifaat, who served simultaneously not only as Minister of Labor, but also as director of ideological development within the ASU and the government publishing houses and as director of the "modernization" program at al-Azhar. Rifaat's support was instrumental in preserving the industrial co-determination schemes against managers' demands for their abolition. He also endorsed union demands for greater autonomy from the ASU directorate, arguing that labor-party relations in a socialist society should be shaped according to the more flexible Yugoslavian model rather than the more totalitarian Soviet model.[13]

Finally, Rifaat's opposition to doctrinaire notions of "scientific socialism" and his efforts to reconcile "Arab socialism" with "Islamic socialism" were perfectly in tune with the eclectic and moderate view of the confederation leadership. With his aid the Confederation was able to resist the ASU's plans to take over leadership training programs for union officials and to transform them into "schools for social revolution" resembling the party-dominated training centers for leaders of the youth organizations and agricultural cooperatives. Rifaat

12. Said, pp. 14–23.

13. Ibid, pp. 24–38; and Anouar Abdel-Malek, *Egypt: Military Society* (New York: Random House, 1968), pp. 294–296 and 304.

and his union allies succeeded in preserving a degree of continuity in the labor movement's leadership training institutes that was quite extraordinary during the turbulent years of Egypt's "socialist transformation." These institutes continued to provide (as they do today) an unusual combination of technical knowledge with liberal socialist and Islamic principles. In this sense the programs of the union institutes reflect the enduring influence of their early directors such as Hilmi Murad, Abd al-Mughni Said, and Jamal al-Banna, all of whom have descended from what might be termed the "left-wing" or Misr al-Fatat and the Muslim Brotherhood.[14]

During the period of crisis that followed the military defeat of 1967 it appeared that Nasser was prepared to make important concessions to union leaders in order to insure their support for the weakened regime. During the mass demonstrations of February 1968 Nasser personally went to Hilwan to make a direct appeal for industrial workers to disengage from the escalating marches organized by radical university students. Shortly thereafter he also held an unusual series of meetings with the Confederation's executive committee in which each federation president rose in turn to present a list of long-ignored demands for greater union authority and autonomy. The gradual acquiescence of the labor movement in the promises of reform contained in Nasser's Declaration of March 30, 1968, allowed the regime to isolate and suppress the more persistent and violent student movement in the months ahead. Just as during his confrontation with Naguib and Khalid Muhieddin some years earlier, Nasser had to rely on labor leaders to provide a decisive display of mass support at a time when his power was threatened and while the military was divided and unreliable.[15]

Nasser continued in his final years, however, to deny union leaders anything more than a subordinate and symbolic position in the ruling coalition, just as he had after the 1954 crisis. To be sure, there were notable increases in the representation of workers and union officials in many party and administrative bodies, but no new elections were allowed at any level of the union hierarchy between the time of the 1967 war and Nasser's death three years later. Nor did the president satisfy Confederation demands that the unions be allowed to select or at least to screen the elected worker representatives in industrial management committees. Instead, Nasser encouraged still greater organizational rivalry and diffusion of authority in the workplace by assigning overlapping tasks to managers, unionists, elected worker representatives, and party-led production teams.[16]

14. Jamal al-Banna, *Buhuth fi al-Thaqafa al-Ummaliya* (Studies in Worker Education) (Cairo: Matbaa Hassan, 1977), ch. 8.

15. Muhammad Khalid, *al-Haraka al-Niqabiya Bayna al-Madi wa al-Hadar* (The Union Movement Between Past and Present) (Cairo: Akhbar al-Yawm, 1975); and Mahmoud Hussein, *Class Conflict in Egypt: 1945–1970* (New York: Monthly Review Press, 1973), ch. 8.

16. Salah al-Sayed, *Workers' Participation in Management: The Egyptian Experience* (Cairo: American University in Cairo Press, 1978), ch. 5; and Raymond William Baker, *Egypt's Uncertain Revolution under Nasser and Sadat* (Cambridge: Harvard University Press, 1978), ch. 7.

Anwar Sadat was much more forthcoming in his relations with the leaders of the labor confederation than Nasser had been, even though they commonly regarded his administration as being anti-labor and in some areas virtually counter-revolutionary when compared to the Nasser era. In fact, by the mid-1970s Sadat already had made good on most of the pledges to augment the Confederation's powers and resources that his predecessor had given in principle after the 1968 demonstrations, but never implemented. By the time of Sadat's assassination in 1981 the Confederation had become the largest, wealthiest, and most influential representative association in Egyptian society.

Especially during the earlier years of his presidency, several factors made Sadat far more dependent than Nasser had been on the political support of a strong and reliable union elite. First, Sadat still lacked the broad popular sympathy that would have allowed him to continue the Nasserist practice of ignoring the mediation of representative groups and appealing directly to the working class through personal addresses and redistributive reforms. Second, Sadat's plans to promote a multi-party system aroused considerable resistance from union officials who perceived the dismantling of the ASU as an attempt to repeal the inadequate yet substantial influence of the labor movement in the "coalition of popular working forces." Labor leaders displayed little enthusiasm for pluralist reforms of the party system until the government endorsed modifications of the corporatist union structure that created sinecures at the top of the labor movement that were even more attractive than the party posts that were abolished with the ASU.

Finally, Sadat's policies of economic liberalization were bound to generate greater working class discontent by reversing earlier trends toward social equity and exposing the economy to greater international competition. It was against the backdrop of mounting labor unrest, including the violent strikes in Mahalla al-Kubra in 1975 and culminating in the "bread riots" of January 1977, that Sadat enacted several reforms designed to strengthen the union confederation, to alienate its leaders from the rank and file, and to coopt them more effectively as junior members of the authoritarian elite and privileged partners in the new capitalist economic order.

Most recently, the Mubarak regime has tacitly recognized the Confederation as a veto group whose prior consent is indispensible to the success of any major policy initiative in such key areas as reform of public sector industries, reduction of consumer goods subsidies, and the anti-inflationary indexing of wage and price increases. Mubarak has been careful to reassure union leaders that his efforts to promote a mixed economy and to implement mild austerity measures do not constitute an assault on basic working class gains from Egypt's socialist revolution. Accordingly, he has, in effect, agreed to a partial surrender of state autonomy in many areas of economic policy-making in exchange for the cooperation of confederation leaders in implementing necessary, but painful and highly unpopular economic reforms.

As the Confederation has acquired more authority and resources its leaders have become less firmly based upon the independent support of affiliated unions and much less accountable to the general union membership. Confederation presidents, in particular, have assumed an increasingly dualistic and contradictory role of trying to represnt both the government and the union movement at the same time. The tendency of the Confederation leadership to become more encapsulated by the state bureaucracy and more insulated from rank and file pressures can be illustrated by comparing briefly the five men who have occupied its presidency and by examining long-term changes in the rates of re-election to the confederation's executive committee.

The first president of the confederation, Anwar Salama (1957–62), was the leader of the petroleum workers' federation. He had played a key role in organizing the workers' boycott of British installations in the canal zone and in aiding the guerrilla campaign of the Muslim Brotherhood after the abrogation of the Anglo-Egyptian treaty in 1951–52. Later he helped to instigate strikes and sabotage by petroleum workers in other Arab countries to protest the tripartite aggression of 1956. In 1962 Salama was appointed Minister of Labor to preside over the corporatist reorganization of the unions, but he resigned his position as Confederation president, arguing that the two offices should not be occupied by the same person simultaneously.

His successor, Ahmad Fahīm (1962–69), was the president of the textile workers' federation, the largest and best organized union in the country. He had been one of the major figures urging the Free Officers to sponsor the early establishment of a labor confederation and he was the principal author of the report on union reorganization that eventually became the basis for the corporatization of the labor movement. As with Salama before him, Fahīm also was offered the Ministry of Labor, but he declined the position preferring to remain as confederation president. His tenure was extended by the suspension of union elections after the 1967 war, and he died in office in 1969.

The third president, Abd al-Latif Bultiya (1969–71), was a transitional figure who was appointed to fill out Fahīm's already overdrawn term and then was cashiered in Sadat's purge of the Confederation shortly after the "Corrective Revolution" of 1971. Bultiya was notable solely because he was the first confederation president who agreed to serve simultaneously as a member of the cabinet. Union officials who have served under all five Confederation presidents point to Bultiya's brief term as a turning point after which the organization began to lose much of its original independence and vigor.

When Sadat ordered the first union elections in seven years his candidate for confederation president was Salah Gharib (1971–76), another leader of the textile workers' federation. Gharib was chosen, however, not because he represented a large and powerful center in the union movement, but because of his close association with Mamduh Salim, the Alexandria governor and police chief who provided Sadat with timely support in his countercoup against the Ali Sabri clique and who later became Minister of Interior and Prime Minister. In fact, Gharib was quite notorious for his unpopularity among workers in many federations, especially the strongly pro-Nasserist defense and metal workers in Hilwan, who taunted him as a government stooge and held him captive overnight during one of their factory occupations. Gharib made a serious effort to intervene in such incidents of worker protest, but when it became clear that his presence tended to aggravate rather than soothe labor unrest, he was retired from the Confederation leadership after the expiration of his second term.

The fifth and current president, Saad Muhammad Ahmad (1976–present), is the leader of the food workers' federation. In and out of the Confederation's executive committee during the 1960s, he was barred from the elections of 1971, "rehabilitated" and elected as Salah Gharib's vice-president in 1973, and then elected to three consecutive terms as president beginning in 1976. Ahmad has served longer than any of his predecessors, presiding for nearly a decade over a steady expansion of the Confederation's political influence and economic activities as well as its linkages with the state bureaucracy and the ruling party. In addition to his role as head of the union movement Ahmad also directs the Ministry of Manpower and Professional Training (formerly the Ministry of Labor), the Workers' Bank, the Workers' University, and several interministerial committees concerned with the state economic enterprises, emigrant workers and their remittances, and economic planning.

One of the most important characteristics of the Confederation presidency is that its now considerable powers are attributable primarily to the nature of the office rather than the personality of the officeholder. Saad Muhammad Ahmad is certainly conscientious, affable, and prudent. Yet he appears to be a thoroughly unextraordinary man who can be replaced by any of several rivals who also rose to prominent positions in the union hierarchy during the Sadat era. Nearly a decade and a half after its only real purge, the Confederation's executive committee now contains a rather embarrassing surplus of experienced and ambitious union leaders, many of whom feel more than prepared for higher posts.

Turnover of the top union leadership has fallen dramatically since the early 1970s (Table 1).[17] The union elite has become virtually self-recruiting with new faces appearing only as a result of the death or voluntary retirement of incumbent federation presidents and almost never because of electoral challenges or pressures from the shop floor. Of the 23 current presidents of union federations, 13

17. Al-Ittihad al-Amm li Niqabat Ummal Misr fi Ishrina 'Aman (The Egyptian Confederation of Trade Unions in Twenty Years) (Cairo: Mataba' al-Ahram al Tijari, 1977), pp. 86–91; and Muhammad Muhammad Ali, pp. 36–39 and 54–56.

Table 1. *Turnover of Confederation Executive Committee Members, 1961–1983*

Year	1961	1964	1971	1973	1976	1979	1983
Percent of members with experience in previous executive committees	28	24	14	44	48	76	92

have been in office ten years or more and four have managed to survive for at least 19 years.

NEW PRESSURES FOR PLURALISM

Competition for presidential succession is by no means the only important source of conflict within the Confederation. As the unions have grown in size and influence several lines of cleavage have emerged to crack the formal façade of corporatism and generate new pressures for pluralism both in the labor movement and in the larger political system. There are at least five dimensions of growing conflict within the labor confederation that make the preservation of its current corporatist framework highly problematic.

First, the enhanced authority and prestige of the Confederation presidency has elicited resistance from many federation leaders who are eager to demonstrate their independence from central union bodies and their separate lines of political influence. This conflict is most evident among the several federation presidents who have sought to embarrass Saad Muhammad Ahmad by openly defying the Confederation's official ban on unapproved affiliations with international union organizations. Ahmad has tried to impose an official policy of "neutrality" concerning foreign affiliations in order to dampen partisan conflicts over invitations to Egypt to join the pro-Western International Confederation of Free Trade Unions (ICFTU) which most Arab unionists regard as biased in favor of Israel. At least half a dozen federation presidents have nevertheless joined ICFTU affiliates not only to display their enthusiastic endorsement of the ruling party's pro-Western foreign policy, but also to show that their own political resources allow them to challenge the Confederation president with impunity, especially when he seeks to assuage union factions that are close to the political opposition.[18]

18. "Niqabat Ummal al-Zira' a Tunadim lil-Ittihad al-Hurr" (The Agricultural Workers' Union Joins the Free Confederation), *al-Ahali* (August 17, 1983); and "Ba'ada Khibrat Thalathin Sana ma' al-Ittihad al-Hurr" (After Thirty Years' Experience with the Free Confederation), *al-Ahali* (February 23, 1983).

Second, as the composition of the union membership has diversified it has become more difficult for the conflicting interests of all federations to be represented adequately by a unitary structure. Pronounced and growing differences separate Egypt's 23 union federations—differences in size and heterogeneity, in industrial, white collar or agricultural membership, and in public, private or foreign employers. Such inter-federation rivalries are aggravated by the government's arbitrary determination and frequent reclassification of the occupational categories within each organization's jurisdiction. The number, size, and composition of federations commonly are reshuffled by bureaucratic fiat in order to promote or inhibit the fortunes of particular union leaders. Although Confederation leaders argue that the establishment of a single peak association ended the historical fragmentation of the Egyptian labor movement, there are growing doubts within many affiliates that the interests of all workers can be served any longer by one association, especially one whose shape and character are molded more from above than from below.

Third, relations between the summit and base of the union movement have become increasingly strained by the self-perpetuating nature of the current leadership and by the widespread intervention of the police in union elections. Candidates excluded from union office by government objection are overwhelmingly young, active in local union committees, and connected with one of the opposition parties. Confederation leaders realize that their ability to contain labor unrest is seriously jeopardized when union elections lose their credibility due to open government interference. They have tried to persuade the government to stop nullifying unacceptable candidates and instead to invest greater resources in the socialization of a younger generation of "responsible" union officials in the Confederation's newly established Workers' University. In the meantime, however, workers in many enterprises are supporting a dualistic system of union representation in which informal groups arise and coexist alongside of official union structures. The importance and organizational strength of such extra-legal groups is evident in many wildcat strikes and especially in factory occupations during which workers occasionally implement obviously well-planned schemes to continue and even increase production while regular union officials are barred from entering the worksites along with the plant managers.[19]

Fourth, several Confederation leaders who belong to the ruling National Democratic Party (NDP) are openly expressing dissatisfaction with what they perceive as the party's increasing favoritism toward private business interests over the interests of organized labor. Many unionists are members of the government party by default more than by design. They are routinely enrolled by

19. "Ittihad al-Ummal Ya'tarid ala Ard Murashshahi al-Niqabat ala al-Muda'i al-Amm al-Ishtiraki" (The Labor Confederation Objects to Submission of Union Candidates to the Socialist Prosecutors), *al-Shaab* (June 6, 1983).

NDP officials who did not bother to inquire into their real partisan preferences. Many Confederation leaders hope that the government eventually will permit the establishment of a separate Labor Party in which unionists will be the dominant force. In the absence of such permission most of them prudently choose to remain in the NDP to avoid the embarrassment and possible retaliation that would accompany an open break with the government party. In the months preceding the 1984 parliamentary elections, however, some of the most powerful federation presidents resigned from the NDP, protesting the second-rate positions that were offered to union leaders by the party's slatemakers. These defectors included the head of the engineering, metal, and electrical workers' federation, representing about 100,000 public sector manufacturing workers, as well as the head of the construction workers' federation, Egypt's largest union, claiming over 400,000 members, primarily in the fast growing private sector.[20]

Fifth, three of the major opposition parties already have demonstrated their ability to draw support away from the NDP, both among top level union leaders and among voters in working class constituencies. The New Wafd, for example, has no members in the labor confederation's executive committee, yet during the 1984 elections its candidates ran extremely well in many working class districts such as Sayyida Zaynab (33 per cent of all votes cast), Imbaba (35 per cent), Bab al-Sharqi (30 per cent), Mahalla al-Kubra (29 per cent), and Kafr al-Dawwar (25 per cent). The Socialist Action Party (Hizb al-Amal al-Ishtiraki) received a share of the vote that was more than twice its national average in Damietta (17 per cent) and Kafr al-Dawwar (14 per cent). Among the opposition parties the Socialist Action Party has the most extensive overlap between its current leadership and the leadership of the union movement. Hilmi Murad and Abd al-Mughni Said both were directors of the Workers' Cultural Institute during the 1960s; Hamid Zaydan, former editor of the party newspaper (*al-Shaab*), was the editor of the labor confederation's newspaper (*al-'Ummāl*) during the early 1970s. Party members include presidents and vice-presidents of three major unions—the construction, defense, and printing federations. Finally, the leftist Hizb al-Tajammu' enjoys strong pockets of support in Hilwan and Aswan and in particular organizations such as the commercial, metal, and petroleum workers' federations.[21]

The overall political implications of these recent developments in the labor movement are not encouraging for Egypt's current rulers. If one examines the relationship in each province between the strength of the union movement and the degree of electoral support for the governing party, there are clear signs of deterioration between 1976 and 1984. In both elections provincial levels of union

20. "Said Juma Yastaqil min Hizb al-Hukuma" (Said Jumaa Resigns from the Government Party), *al-Ahali* (May 18, 1983); and "al-Hajj Muhammad Ahmad Umar: 'Istaqaltu min al-Hizb al-Watani' " (al-Hajj Muhammad Ahmad Umar: "I resigned from the National Party"), *al-Shaab* (May 1, 1984).

21. Final results of the 1984 elections appeared in *al-Ahram* (June 1, 1984).

membership are negatively correlated with support for the semi-official party; moreover, the strength of the negative relationship appears to be increasing with time and with further advances in unionization (r = −.442 in 1976 and −.652 in 1984). A clearly contrasting pattern appears, however, regarding the agricultural cooperative movement. In this instance, a mild negative correlation between cooperative membership and support for the government in 1976 (r = −.210) becomes a very strong positive correlation by 1984 (r = .788).[22]

These findings suggest a growing polarization between rural middle class constituencies that have benefited from the regime's economic policies and urban working class constituencies that have not. However, these findings also suggest that the government's pursuit of different *associational* policies toward the union and cooperative movements may have contributed to divergent political outcomes. Shortly before the 1976 elections Sadat imposed major reorganizations on both the labor unions and the agricultural cooperatives because he feared that the largest corporatist occupational associations inherited from the Nasserist period might be used by his opponents to mobilize voters against him. But Sadat did not employ the same strategy toward the two groups. In the case of the more powerful and cohesive labor movement, he strenthened the Confederation, coopted its leaders, and expanded their roles in economic policy-making. In the case of the weaker and dispersed cooperatives, he abolished the Confederation, encouraged local elites to oust centrally appointed directors, and established a new set of rural associations (the "village banks") that channelled public resources to local supporters of the regime.

Thus one reason that Mubarak has enjoyed such strong endorsement from the countryside is that Sadat moved swiftly to emasculate the agricultural cooperatives and put them under the control of groups that were opposed to many of their original purposes. Alternatively, one reason that Mubarak has had so much difficulty with the labor movement (and is nearly certain to have more in the future) is that Sadat substantially enhanced the power and resources of the top union leadership, thereby allowing them to bargain more effectively with a weak president.

22. Data on membership in unions and cooperatives were obtained from annual reports of the Ministry of Manpower and Professional Training and the General Agency for Agricultural Cooperatives.

[16]

Educational Policy and Human Resource Development in Jordan

DELWIN A. ROY and WILLIAM T. IRELAN

Jordan has one of the most advanced and sophisticated educational systems in the Middle East region. With serious limitations in natural resources, Jordanian development planners have consistently viewed the education of the country's human resources as a leading priority.

The education/training system is now quite mature as a result of the priority given to it. By 1983, enrollment ratios in the compulsory portion of education (primary and intermediate, that is, grades 1–9) were in excess of 90 per cent. Secondary education (grades 10–12) reported a 66 per cent enrollment and higher education almost 25 per cent.

The success of the system has in recent years become somewhat of a weakness. The Jordanian economy is dependent on the export of manpower, primarily to the Gulf. Remittances, even with a decline in the demand for expatriate labor, have accounted for approximately one-third of the GNP of the country. But the demand has stabilized (or may possibly be declining). Yet, the educational system designed not only to fill the internal manpower needs but also to meet what were thought to be the unlimited needs of the oil rich economies continues to turn out graduates – and more and more of these graduates are from the higher educational level.

The Jordanian economy cannot possibly absorb the increasing number of higher education graduates. It is equally unlikely that if and when the external demand picks up, these graduates will be in demand. The Gulf states and Saudi Arabia have found it much less costly to hire Egyptians, Indians and Pakistanis for those positions requiring a general secondary or college education.

What is in short supply, internally and externally, is highly qualified technicians and skilled workers. In an effort to capitalize on this present and prospective demand, education authorities and government officials are attempting to redirect more Jordanian students away from the general secondary and higher education levels to the technical/vocational education streams. While modest success is being attained, there is growing public resistance to de-emphasizing general and higher education and stronger emphasis on vocational and technical training and education. The public, long-steeped in a tradition of attaining social

Middle Eastern Studies, Vol.28, No.1, January 1992, pp.178–215
PUBLISHED BY FRANK CASS, LONDON

and economic mobility through higher education is increasingly unwilling to see children directed to what is viewed as manual labor.

The government can no longer afford to finance what one official calls 'the insatiable appetite for education to achieve social status'. Government planners are banking on an internal industrial development strategy that will make Jordan the technology production and service center of the Middle East. They also anticipate a revitalized oil economy to boost demand for the technically qualified. To this end, government policy is designed to reallocate public financial support away from the academic to the pragmatic and is telling the public that if it wants to continue the higher education tradition, then it must find its own means of paying for it.

This move away from the general education tradition to the specialized has significant consequences for the military as the new emphasis on the technological and scientific is of direct interest to it. The links between the civilian education sector and the military are extensive. While in general civilian educators view those destined for the ranks of military leadership to be somewhat academically inferior to students with other career aspirations, it is clear that a main function of secondary education and universities is to satisfy military manpower needs.

Jordan's fighting forces need technical manpower. The recent shift to restructuring the educational system to turn out more and better qualified technicians does not, at its core, have an apparent military intent. However, the military stands to benefit and this is no doubt one of several major considerations.

The public, particularly the opinion-setting elites have countered government initiatives to redirect the system by contending that education quality is weak. The system is vulnerable to this contention, but the present academic quality of education is not the real issue. While the government is responding to the charge that quality is lacking, it has not, nevertheless, been dissuaded from pursuing its revised educational policy.

The long-term political ramifications of education policy are potentially two-fold. First and somewhat less important, it is conceivable that present political tensions could lead to compromises that, in effect, will lead the government to continue to try to do both, that is, serve the traditional education appetite of the public *and* partially redirect financial and manpower resources to technical education. This could result in sufficient ambiguity of purpose to undermine both objectives. At a time when the government would need to act decisively to ward off serious unemployment, it would continue to be saddled with a 'half-baked' policy initiative.

The more worrisome political backlash will come if the government largely proves incorrect in the development strategy it has set for itself or if the time it takes to realize its benefits is protracted. Jordan exercises little control over factors external to the economy that nevertheless affect internal economic fortunes. If external labor demand doesn't revive and if the industrial development strategy calling for exports of high-tech products and services doesn't work, then unemployment of a highly educated labor force is going to become quite serious.

Jordan has confronted many crises and there is an inclination to regard the looming employment crisis as but one more difficulty that it will, ultimately, overcome. This attitude is both a strength and a weakness. Coupled with the major political problems which already beset the Kingdom, a serious employment crisis can only bode ill for political stability. Much will depend upon the pace and extent of a recovery in oil prices and on employment opportunities in the Gulf following the Kuwait war. Failing this, the government will have no choice but to become repressive in the interest of maintaining internal security; this would come at a time when the public appetite for political liberalization is at an all time high.

DEVELOPMENT OF THE EDUCATIONAL SYSTEM IN JORDAN

The development and improvement of the educational system at all levels have been important objectives of the government of Jordan since the early 1950s. The orientation of the government in this regard has consistently reflected a widespread interest in education and imparting a basic education to as large a part of the general population as feasible. That interest has kept the educational system under public scrutiny and official review. This review process has, in turn, resulted in periodic reforms and a gradual evolution of the system from one skewed toward providing basic knowledge, literacy and skills to one increasingly oriented toward academic achievement and high quality instruction.

That Jordan retains a serious commitment to the development of an objective and high quality educational system is exemplified by a statement made by King Hussein (on the occasion of Independence Day, 1984):

> In our determination to preserve and update our culture and identity to cope with future challenges, we trust our educational institution to launch the qualitative innovation in a dynamic educational process to promote analysis, pragmatism and objectivity

in its activities, and to introduce change in its content, in order to promote teaching, learning situations, depth in knowledge, criticism in learning, open-mindedness in discussion, rather than preserving the educational process in its static form, shallow knowledge, passive and narrow mindedness.

Prior to and during the 1950s the emphasis on education in Jordan was essentially quantitative; the objectives were to provide enough schools to serve the entire population and to eliminate illiteracy. As a general rule, schools were established wherever ten or more students needed one.

In the 1960s, major education reforms were instituted under the Education Act (No.16 of 1964), including the introduction of vocational education at the compulsory education stage, the extension of compulsory education to nine years and the division of the secondary stage into academic and vocational/technical streams. This represented the earliest sign of Jordan's intention to educate its population not only for Jordan's labor market needs but for those needs of other countries (Kuwait was by this time drawing heavily on Jordano–Palestinian manpower).

In the 1970s, the Ministry of Education was concerned with linking programs to the requirements of the government's general development plans and objectives. Secondary vocational education was diversified, new vocational education institutions were established and educational innovations introduced. Vocational education was diversified by adding nursing education (in direct response to the growing demand for health professions in the Gulf and Saudi Arabia), postal education and hotel management to the curriculum. Comprehensive schools, technical colleges and trade training centers were established. Educational innovations included the division of the academic year into two semesters, the revision of curricula and text books and the reduction of class periods for all schools. (See Figure 1).

By the beginning of the 1980s Jordan had one of the most impressive and well-organized educational infrastructures to be found in the Middle East. This solid base established, concern shifted to improving the quality of education. That concern was expressed initially in a specially organized conference, 'The Educational Process in a Changing Jordanian Society' (held in 1980) which delineated the responsibilities of all formal and non-formal bodies, the government and the private sector for the improvement of the quality of education.

This shift in emphasis was occasioned in part by the economic slowdown in the neighboring countries (beginning in 1982) which was having its impact on Jordanian economic fortunes. It led to a

FIGURE 1
THE JORDANIAN EDUCATION SYSTEM

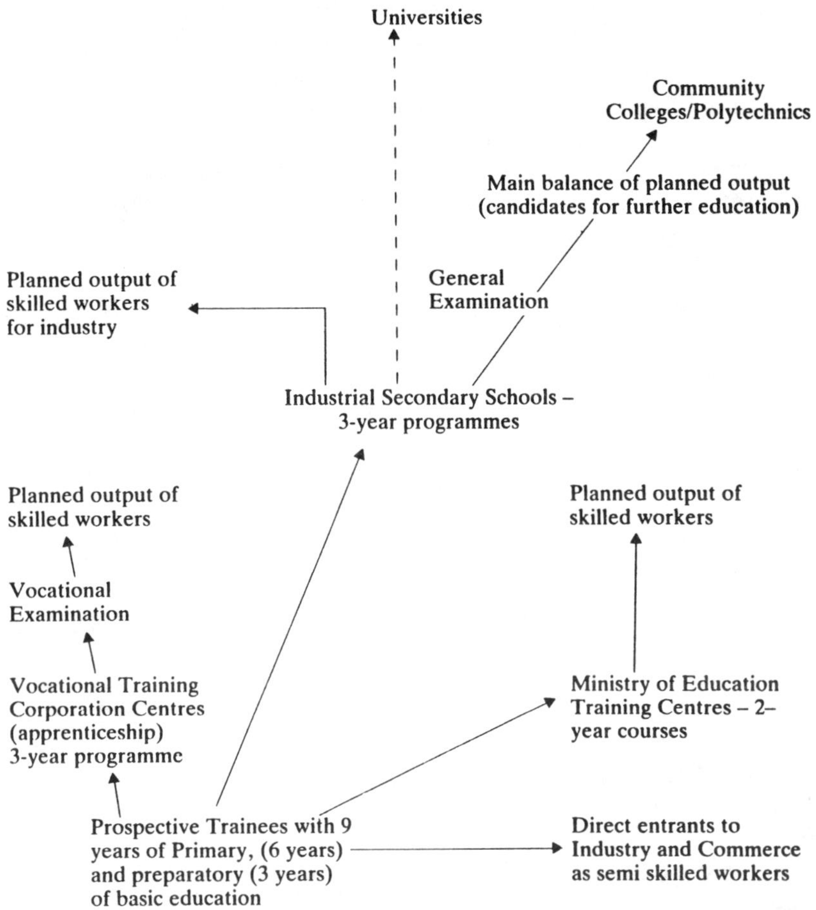

--------- The dotted line reflects the fact that relatively few industrial secondary graduates achieve university entrance

slowdown of domestic economic activity and a reduction of inflow of external resources. One immediate impact was to substantially weaken the domestic and external demand for Jordanian labor.

Simultaneously, there was a major qualitative shift taking place in the demand for Jordanian manpower. Foreign demand was concentrating more and more on the highly skilled worker and experienced professional. At the same time, the rapid increase in the Jordanian labor force (expected to continue for some years to come), fuelled by a continuing high population growth rate and by a spectacular increase in enrollment in the formal education system – particularly of women – created mounting government concern lest unemployment reach politically unacceptable dimensions. The manpower problem was shifting from one of selective shortages that through the early 1980s had triggered a substantial inflow of non-Jordanian labor to one of finding employment for a rapidly increasing domestic workforce.

To achieve the goal of improving the quality of education, the government introduced a number of changes in policy and procedures:

- the decentralization of the administrative system of the Ministry of Education.
- the emphasizing of practical linkages between the educational system and the demands of adult life, that is, life-oriented education.
- the provision of practical training during both the academic year and the summer vacation period.
- the implementation of a general examination for the community colleges to improve the quality of their graduates.
- the emphasizing of vocational counseling and guidance.
- the emphasizing of self-education.

In addition to these general policy and procedural changes, the government undertook a number of major reforms during 1982–83, including the establishment of a special directorate for educational technology to introduce modern technologies into the educational process, particularly the computer and the application of data processing tools to education, and the improvement of testing and examination.

With regard to the latter, one important innovation involved the introduction of a Secondary School Admission Test in 1984 for all students in the ninth grade. The test was designed to meet the following objectives:

- identifying student abilities in acquiring knowledge, concepts and basic skills required for secondary education.
- identifying student attitudes toward academic and educational studies.
- forecasting the type of secondary education appropriate to the needs of the student.
- classifying and chaneling the students toward the stream of secondary education for which they are most suited.

Of those who pass this Admissions Test, 60 per cent of males and 70 per cent of females are allowed to continue in general secondary education with the remainder entering vocational education. This reform, in particular, occasioned much controversy, a point discussed at length below.

In 1985 the government established the Ministry of Higher Education to assume responsibility for the development and direction of the three national universities, Jordan University, Yarmouk University and Mu'tah University. These three universities had developed independently over the years, with their own rules, procedures, governance and policies. Consequently, the government decided in the interest of uniformity to bring the three under a single institutional umbrella. The new ministry is responsible for administering all post-secondary education, including both the universities and the entire community college system.

Also in 1985 the government created the Council on Higher Education with a mandate to develop policies to raise the quality of university graduates. This Council's responsibilities are limited to the university system; it is not responsible for community colleges. The Council has, however, recently taken the decision in principle to recommend that community college graduates be permitted to enter universities.

In a period of about 30 years, Jordan's education system has in orderly fashion moved from an abiding concern for 'bricks and mortar' to intensified concern regarding the ability of Jordanians to compete for jobs abroad, particularly in the Gulf and Saudi Arabia. Up until the 1980s, the government was relatively content to let individuals select both the type and functional or disciplinary content of their education (within the standards imposed by the education system). Most recently, certainly since 1982, the government has found that it cannot afford individual choice to prevail as much as in this past. Hence, it has turned to the issue of quality of education, both as a means of increasing the competitive character of human resources and to redirect a considerably larger number of Jordanians into technical and vocational education and away from a university education.

It is not possible fully to understand the recent controversy over the future of Jordanian education without consideration of the manpower imbalance problem. The primary objective of the education and training system is to generate the human resources needed to sustain Jordan's ambitious industrial development policy and to reduce dependence on foreign labor. According to the World Bank and the Ministry of Labor, present labor force requirement forecasts show large surpluses of white collar workers and large shortages of blue collar workers. Hence, a major adjustment in educational policy – one emphasizing the expansion of the vocational/technical training component and a diminution of the emphasis on formal and higher education is the crux of the political economy of education.

The Jordanian labor force is presently growing at an annual rate of 6.5 per cent, a rate expected to continue well into the 1990s. The high natural population growth rate (3.5 per cent), the young age structure of the population and a rapid increase in the female participation rate have all contributed and will continue to contribute to this trend.

At present and for the foreseeable future, the Jordanian economy is only able to generate an increase in the demand for labor at about 2.5 per cent per annum. At that rate and given present projections *and* assuming that far-reaching policy and institutional changes would reduce the current mismatch between graduates of the education system and actual labor market demand, a surplus of manpower of the order of 76,000 (or about 11 per cent of the labor force) would ensue by 1990. If the policy changes are not made, or ineffectively implemented if made, then a much higher rate of surplus can be anticipated. Given the present absorptive capacity of the Jordanian economy, this rate of unemployment will in no event likely be less than 11 per cent.

For the first time in Jordan's experience, large surpluses are projected among the major professional categories: teachers, scientists and other professionals (the bulk of whom are liberal arts graduates). The rate of unemployment here is projected to be over 35 per cent within the next 5 years with the primary incidence most likely to fall on females. At present, women contribute 75 per cent of the entrants in the largest professional category, teachers. A considerably worse situation is projected for white-collar workers. Present forecasts place the unemployment rate at potentially over 70 per cent within the next five years. Conversely, shortages in labor supply are significant in semi-skilled manual workers (a 33 per cent shortfall) and qualified engineers and technicians.

Within the context of the situation only very briefly outlined above, one finds a rather unique situation developing in Jordan. On the one hand, the government – cognizant of the very real difficulties ahead in employment of a growing labor force – is trying to restructure its educational priorities, both as a means of shifting manpower resources away from an education that ultimately will lead them into professional and career fields that are already glutted *and* as a means generating manpower resources that will be in demand externally (that is, in the Gulf and elsewhere). On the other, parents and students seem bent on resisting this shift in government policy and are seemingly indifferent to the employment implications of continuing to over-emphasize college and university education.

Thus, despite the various reforms that have occurred in the past, Jordanians have continued to express dissatisfaction with key aspects of the educational system. One private group, the Arab Thought Forum, even submitted its own recommendations to the government on how to improve education in Jordan. Previous efforts at improving the system have not satisfied the critics. All the many improvements in books, buildings and teacher training appear to have failed to produce the quality of output expected. New reforms are, however, under consideration, particularly in the area of teacher training.

Teacher education and training, on the whole, has been of sufficient quality in the past to enable solid development of the education system. There are indeed pockets of the truly unqualified, but these represent a small minority. The basic problem with present teacher preparation is that their community college or university education has inadequately referenced teaching as a pedagogical exercise. At the compulsory level, (grades 1 through 9), teachers are required to have a 2-year community college teaching certificate. At the secondary level, teachers must hold a BA and a 1-year diploma and indeed most teachers at the secondary level have fulfilled this requirement. However, there is no requirement that pedagogical coursework be taken.

Although teachers are generally well-qualified within the limitation noted above, there is at present no method for providing special training for them. There is no requirement for career development planning and teachers who opt for additional training inevitably choose to receive it by returning to the university, which remains inadequately prepared to provide the type of further training that would enhance teaching ability.

One reform afoot, to be applied to the civil service in general, is that those civil servants who take 192-hours of additional training can receive a two-step increase in grade (and a correspondingly higher salary). There is a move to have this apply to teachers as well, who then might be more highly motivated to seek appropriate training rather than simply taking more university courses. If this is accomplished, then the intent would be clearly to specify the type of additional training that would count toward fulfilling the 192-hour requirement, said specification emphasizing pedagogical and special teacher training needs.

As a result of the general sense of unhappiness over the education system – brought to a head by the recent government decision to introduce an admissions test at the preparatory (9th grade) level – the government established (in 1985) a special 'Committee to Study the Development of the Jordanian Educational System'. This committee, composed of educators, officials and private citizens, is chaired by Crown Prince Hassan. It was given a comprehensive mandate to evaluate all aspects of the system and the results it achieves; it is to chart a course for the future development of the Jordanian education system and will form the basis for amending the present education law of 1964.

A Draft Report of the Commission has been completed and is currently under review by the various ministries concerned and other government organizations. The specific content of this Draft Report, dealing as it does with a complete review of the Jordanian educational system from top to bottom, is as of December, 1986, confidential. Ultimately, the report will set forth a comprehensive set of recommendations which will be rather more evolutionary than revolutionary.

The final report will in all likelihood be submitted to the king for approval. Although the contents of the draft are confidential, some things are known:

- Compulsory education is to be extended from the current 9 years to 10 (through the 10th grade or first year of secondary school). The intent is to get a higher proportion of students who will complete their full secondary education (that is, through the 12th grade). The premise is that if required to complete the first year of secondary education, most students and parents of students will see the wisdom of completing the final two years.
- The last two years of secondary education would, in addition to the core courses required, offer 'option clusters'. These option clusters would be in the arts, sciences, maths, the humanities, vocational arts, etc. and the entire curriculum, core courses and clusters, would approximate to a cross between a diversified secondary school (as opposed to the present comprehensive model of secondary education) and the American elective course system. The intent of this proposed revision is to get Jordanian students away from pursuing a narrowly defined course of instruction and to broaden slightly the core curriculum.
- The teacher training institutes would be closed down and the government would no longer recognize 2-year community college graduates holding a teaching certificate as qualified to enter the teaching profession. All teachers would henceforth have to hold a Bachelor of Arts degree.

There appears to be a number of specific concerns that have led to the appointment of the study committee. Above all there is generalized concern about the quality of education being provided by the system. For example, one group believes that the system is not producing the 'educated elite' required to fill positions of leadership in the society. This view holds that while the system is reaching its avowed quantitative targets, that is, providing universal education, it is not producing out of the crowd those gifted intellectuals society needs to lead it. With respect to this 'elitist' question, comparison of the present situation is made to the days of the past when the Victoria College in Egypt, the Arab College in Jerusalem and other private schools produced a class of highly sophisticated individuals who now occupy the leadership strata of Jordanian society.

Aside from the elitist issue, the concern over quality has a practical orientation behind it. The Jordanian economy depends substantially on the human resources of the country, particularly the export of trained manpower to the oil-rich Arab states in the Gulf. Jordanians must be able to compete successfully for the positions available there because, as noted, the domestic economy cannot provide the employment necessary. Reportedly, more than half the university graduates are currently unable to find work. Here, the public in general seems to be aware of the situation but is proving most unreceptive to the government's response to it.

This difference of opinion is nowhere more clear than when one considers the issue whether the government should allocate students between academic and vocational streams (as is done in most European systems). Parents typically want to see their children stay in the academic stream through the secondary level, largely as a matter of social status. Parents and students alike seem more interested in the question of the status an academic education brings compared to a vocational rather than in the question whether the education will serve a useful purpose.

As one university professor puts it, 'everyone seems to think the government owes them a university degree whether the private economy has a job to match it or not'. In his view, the government only owes an individual a basic education and it only owes society as many engineers, doctors and teachers as the society requires. It does not 'owe an individual an education to help him (her) gain status'.

The government first faced this issue squarely in 1972 when it attempted to institute an examination at the end of the compulsory (preparatory or primary) cycle to allocate students between the academic and vocational systems. The purpose of the policy was to train skilled labor for the many development projects that the government proposed to undertake in the First Development Plan (1970–75). The public outcry and objection to that policy, however, was so intense that the exam was canceled in 1973. Nonetheless, the government has over the years succeeded in directing a gradually increasing number of students into the vocational system. According to the Ministry of Education and the Vocational Training Corporation, in 1973, 8 per cent of graduates of the compulsory cycle entered vocational training; subsequently, it was raised to 25 per cent in 1980 and is now estimated to be about 30 per cent.

It is this same policy first tried in 1972 that has in 1985 led to yet one more round of intense public debate over the future course of Jordanian education. The motivation for the policy this time is somewhat different; it is as much to reduce the oversupply of general education graduates as it is to produce much needed skilled labor. Nonetheless, the new policy has created as much controversy as did the earlier one.

When the above noted Secondary School Admissions Test was introduced in 1984 many parents objected to it forcefully. When their sons and daughters were channeled to the vocational stream many brought their objections directly to the Ministry of Education and secured a reversal of the decision. Indeed, many educators themselves disapprove of the new policy, the professional objection being that the exam does not adequately do what the government claims it should, that is, effectively sort out students by aptitude. Actually, students with high marks may be channeled to the academic stream even though they may have shown high aptitudes for certain vocations.

Although the new exam now appears to have been accepted, there continues to be objections to it and parents continue to attempt to have decisions reversed. Opinion is divided about its likely permanence. The Ministry of Education has set an internal target of a 60/40 split between the graduates of the compulsory cycle going into general education and vocational training (it is at present about 70/30). It professes officially the view that the exam is limited to measuring aptitude, but at least unofficially it plans to use it as a means of raising the percentage of compulsory cycle graduates entering vocational training schools.

One developing trend may influence the course of the vocational training issue. Secondary education is not compulsory in Jordan, but is *de facto* becoming so. Currently, 70 per cent of the compulsory education students continue on to secondary school, a trend that continues upward. Because of this, the Ministry has proposed in the current Five-Year Plan (1986–1990) to unify the secondary school system, to make all students have both general education and vocational training. Students would be permitted to specialize in one field.

EDUCATION POLICY AND THE LABOR MARKET

As a resource-poor country Jordan depends largely on the earning capacity of its human resources. The great oil boom in the Arab Gulf countries in the 1970s provided unexpected opportunities for the educated manpower of Jordan. Prior to that time, Jordan had faced a chronic unemployment problem – a situation that is clearly destined to revisit the country in the late 1980s. Total expatriate employment reached some 400,000 with opportunities constantly expanding. Based on data from the Ministry of Labor, net out-migration reached 8–10,000 per annum in the late 1970s. By some estimates, remittances of Jordanian workers abroad reached a total of one-third of GNP.

The recent decline of the international oil economy has abruptly changed all of this. Growth in employment opportunities abroad has essentially ceased and demand seems to have stabilized or is moderately declining. To this must be added the effects of the Iran–Iraq war, and now the Gulf War. Much of the economic expansion of the past 10 years was predicated on expected Iraqi economic growth. The war effectively interrupted that growth with the result that Jordan's internal rate of economic growth slowed considerably, reducing the capacity of the economy to generate employment opportunities. Recently, unemployment has been estimated at some 8–9 per cent (about 50–60,000) and as noted, is rising.

Internally, the supply of doctors, engineers and other professionals greatly exceeds demand. High school and community college graduates also face great difficulty in finding work upon graduation. Demand for skilled and semi-skilled workers, however, exists and remains unsatisfied, particularly in rural areas. Labor shortages have been documented in construction, agriculture and in industry located outside the Greater Amman area. (See Table 1)

The Ministry of Labor notes that skilled workers are often paid substantial wages. The government hopes that this fact will persuade compulsory education graduates to enter vocation schools in greater numbers. Some 150,000 agricultural and construction jobs appear to be permanently filled by Egyptian and Yemeni expatriate workers. No lateral job movement (that is, from one occupation to an entirely different one) of any significance is expected as Jordanians have no interest in doing the type of work being provided by these expatriates. Inexplicably, Jordanians seem indifferent to wage levels in skilled and semi-skilled work to the extent that it is doubtful that wage movements alone will rectify the labor supply structural problems.

In general, the government appears concerned but far from overwrought about the changed circumstances. It is recognized that the boom days are over and that the demand abroad for Jordanian labor has stabilized. But the general posture seems to be that Jordan can ride out the storm. Officials believe that Jordanians have a favored position in the Arab Gulf market from which they cannot easily be dislodged.

TABLE 1
PROJECTED MANPOWER SURPLUSES AND SHORTAGES OF JORDANIANS BY OCCUPATIONAL POOLS IN 1990

			Labor Balances	
POOLS	National Labor Supply	National Labor Demand	Shortage of National Labor	Surplus of National Labor
1. Scientists and Mathematicians	9,592	6,825		2,767
2. Architects and Engineers	8,074	10,772	2,698	
3. Health Professionals And Technicians	13,044	16,931	3,887	
4. Teachers	73,677	44,034		29,643
5. Other Professionals	34,386	23,769		10,617
7. Managers	21,663	24,588	2,925	
8. White Collar Supervisors	54,856	23,063		31,793
9. Science Technicians	10,585	8,072		2,513
10. Blue Collar Supervisors And Foremen	13,721	21,415	7,694	
11. Skilled Office Workers	108,591	35,792		72,799
6. Skilled Farm Workers	14,208	24,637	10,429	
12. Skilled Manual Workers[1]	53,152	62,317	9,165	
13. Semi-Skilled Non-Manual Workers	190,923	64,696		126,227
14. Semi-Skilled Manual Workers	93,763	149,754	55,991	
15. Unskilled Workers	83,950	86,272	2,322	
Total	784,185	507,826	95,111	276,359

1. Except agriculture.

Source: World Bank estimates based on Ministry of Labor data.

Attention has thus turned to making whatever modifications in policy are necessary to ensure that when demand once again rises in the Gulf, Jordanians will be well placed to compete.

Nonetheless, the government has in various ways begun to develop policies to deal with the employment problems manifested in both the domestic and regional markets. The Ministry of Labor has established new policies and procedures limiting the importation of foreign labor. Licenses are given to employers only where they can demonstrate that no Jordanian with appropriate qualifications is available and willing to work in the particular position.

The Ministry of Industry has recently begun to promote the policy of labor-intensive industry in its industrial development planning. In 1982, the Ministry of Higher Education attempted in a modest way to survey the regional labor market to determine what types of labor will be required by the Gulf countries in the future so that the education system can prepare to produce the needed manpower.

The Ministry of Planning, however, still officially assumes that the regional labor situation is short-run in nature and that employment opportunities will pick up in the near future. The current Saudi Development plan (1986–1990), for example, calls for a reduction in foreign workers by some 500,000. The Ministry of Planning does not consider this a realistic target (current evidence would support this view), but the Saudis have shown an inclination increasingly to substitute low-paid labor for higher paid, often irrespective of the consequences for productivity and efficiency. Jordanians are often the higher paid and are losing out, increasingly, to Indians, Egyptians and Pakistanis.

Constrained by a meager natural resource base, Jordanian planners have had little choice but to place a high priority on development of the country's human resources. This emphasis on education and training has facilitated substantial expansion of the industrial base and exploitation to almost the maximum potential of the rich irrigated agricultural zone in the Jordan valley.

Jordan's education/training system is now quite mature as a result of sustained priority having been given to development of the education system. Gross enrollment rations in 1982/83, for example, were: Primary – 99.4; Intermediate – 90.8; Secondary – 65.8; and Higher Education – 23.1. In addition to these very impressive statistics, considerable progress has been made over the past 10 years in extending coverage of the education system to females as well as males and to rural as well as urban areas.

From 1973 to 1983, the number of students at all levels of education grew at an average rate of 5.8 per cent per annum (males, 5.3 per cent and females, 7.0 per cent). Enrollments in Ministry of Education (MOE) schools grew at an even faster rate, averaging 6.8 per cent per annum (males, 5.8 per cent and females, 8.1 per cent).

Despite this rapid growth, the MOE share of the national budget (capital and recurrent) has remained fairly stable, fluctuating between 6.7 per cent and 7.2 per cent from 1974–1979 and increasing to 7.5 per cent in 1980 and slightly higher thereafter (through 1985). However, this growth has not been without costs.

Although nearly all Jordanian youth are now enrolled in compulsory (basic) level schools, many facilities are often of poor quality. Over 90 per cent of urban primary MOE schools are rented, often ill-adapted, facilities which the Government, if it had the financial resources, would like to replace with permanent facilities. Furthermore, rapid population growth and more constrained government budgets are requiring reassessment of the affordability of education norms and standards (this includes the quality of education issue). This reassessment involves a review of the financing and allocation of scarce resources among the various levels of education in order to ensure sustainability of delivery of the highest affordable quality of basic education to all Jordanian children as a priority educational objective. Of particular import in the context of this education financing review is the reassessment of the current practice of supporting Jordan's universities with earmarked customs duties. Also, the government is considering new ways of generating additional financial resources through encouragement of private education (for example, at the secondary level and for community colleges) and through cost recovery, especially at the higher education level (adjustment of tuition fees and scholarship programs, for instance). The latter issue was, in part, a factor figuring in the student outbreak at Yarmouk University in May, 1986 (after which 20 faculty members were summarily dismissed).

The Ministry of Education, under the guidance of the Education Council, is responsible for formal education and training which includes primary, preparatory, general and vocational secondary and post-secondary polytechnics and community colleges (the latter will be dealt with under a separate heading in this paper). Under present law, attendance by boys and girls is compulsory through the 9th grade.

It is the government's intention to continue to provide an equitable (that is, by sex and region) basic education (currently defined as the 9 years of compulsory primary and intermediate level schooling) at the highest possible affordable level of quality. Although there are sound social and political reasons for continuing to invest in basic education, the fact is that this level of education is the key to preparing *trainable* entrants to the domestic and external labor forces. Of even greater importance is that the provision for female education is a key element in the eventual reduction of population growth. Current Ministry of Education data show that in comparison with uneducated women, educated ones have, on average, nearly 0.4 fewer children *per year* of education completed.

The government's commitment to human resource development has been manifested through the striking progress achieved in improving access to education since 1975. As of 1985, enrollments had increased by about 30 per cent at the primary level (grades 1–6), 88 per cent at the preparatory level (grades 7–9) and 178 per cent at the secondary level (grades 10–12).

Female enrollment, already high by 1975 (in comparison with other Arab countries), has continued to rise. Since 1975, female enrollment (as a percentage of total enrollment) has risen from 46 per cent to 48 per cent at the primary level, from 43 per cent to 46 per cent at the preparatory level and from 37 per cent to 46 per cent at the secondary level. Total enrollment in MOE schools was in excess of 550,000 by 1982 with elementary, preparatory and secondary schools reaching 341,000, 128,500 and 82,500 respectively.

The MOE has placed increased emphasis on more frequent use of testing and examinations for both diagnostic and evaluation purposes. Specific measures taken in the past 3 years include:

1. promotion of primary school students will not be 'automatic' but will be based on some form of evaluating the learning outcomes, such as oral tests, direct teacher observations, homework and written tests;
2. norm-referenced standardized achievement tests are being developed to measure achievement in all subjects that can be used nationally as both diagnostic and evaluative measures (grades 3 and 6);
3. aptitude tests to help with educational and vocational guidance (ninth grade level) are to be developed;
4. a national examination has been introduced at the end of the ninth grade (Secondary School Admission Test), whereby of those who pass, 60 per cent of males and 70 per cent of females will be allowed to continue in general secondary education with the remainder entering vocational education (as discussed earlier); and
5. the development of a test data bank to help test writers and teachers construct their own tests.

The MOE is the dominant provider of education in Jordan. However, schools operated by the United Nations Relief and Works Administration (UNWRA) and private schools account for about one-fourth of enrollments at the primary and intermediate levels of education.

There are three main sets of resources which together constituted the basis of Jordan's strategy for training skilled workers. These include Industrial Secondary Schools (operated by the Ministry of Education and offering 3-year courses); Training Centers (also operated by the MOE and offering 2-year courses); and, Vocational Training Centers (operated by the Vocational Training Corporation (VTC), an autonomous government agency that also administers the National Apprenticeship System).

The Industrial Secondary Schools have a dual role in producing graduates who may either enter industry in the higher craft jobs or enter the post-secondary education system, (either the community colleges or polytechnics) with a view to ultimately qualifying as technicians or technologists in electronics, telecommunications, electro-mechanical machinery and industrial design. Both the Training Centers operated by the MOE and those of the Vocational Training Corporation concentrate mainly on producing candidates for jobs as skilled workers for either the local or regional labor markets. Only a very small number of these find entry into full-time higher education.

Skilled workers turned out by the vocational/technical education system are in effect of two types: *craftsmen*, that is, the more versatile skilled workers for such activities as plant maintenance and *other skilled* work, i.e., those workers that are more narrowly skilled-based (welders, for example). The industrial secondaries are generally perceived as the main source of craftsmen and the Training Centers of the MOE and the VTC as the main source of other skilled and semi-skilled workers.

At present, about 30 per cent of those completing the compulsory stage of education are enrolling in the vocational/technical streams of skill education. In 1983, this would have amounted to about 63,000 students.

Both the vocational and technical sub-systems of the educational system are expanding rapidly and it is intended that this continues to be the case (referring once again to the new aptitude test designed to steer more students in this direction). The industrial training system as a whole has displayed a considerable amount of flexibility in responding to the demand for training places. Double-shifts are used to obtain maximum utilization of training facilities and employer plant facilities are increasingly being used via the apprenticeship system.

Neither the industrial secondaries nor the training centers have very much choice about the type and capability of students they will accept. Basically, the secondaries and centers are confined to determining how many trainees in total can be absorbed. Exams given at the end of the ninth grade largely determine who goes where in the industrial system, the least academically qualified going to the Training Centers and the somewhat more successful going to the Industrial Secondaries. On balance, it is often the least proficient student who winds up in these non-academic streams with the result that these streams are not attractive. Students complain that there is no status attached to this kind of education and seem visibly to suffer from what they perceive to be the attitude of society toward them.

Although the Jordanian system of industrial education is clearly one of the most advanced in the Middle East, the same problems arise for it as elsewhere. Students and parents alike consider this kind of education inferior and to be avoided if at all possible. A study prepared by the authors for the World Bank on technical education and vocational training has shown that even those who go through this type of education are not really permanently committed to the idea of pursuing skilled labor as a career. As several students put it, it is 'something one does while waiting to see if something better comes along'. Employers note that the industrial schools and training centers are 'not imparting the right kind of work attitudes' to students. Many employers choose to train their own skilled labor or if they do hire graduates of the technical/vocational system, undertake considerable retraining to ensure that they have the requisite skills.

To alleviate effectively the present and prospective large shortages of manual labor and technicians, the VTC and industrial technician training will have to adjust its course program to the changing technologies required for the more sophisticated manufacturing structure that development planners have in mind. It is also important that sufficient financial resources are redirected to vocational/technical training.

The higher education system in Jordan comprises three national universities and 52 community colleges. The Higher Education Council, established in 1982, was assigned broad authority to direct and develop the system of higher education (the Council has recently [1985] been abolished and a new Ministry of Higher Education established.) The universities are governed by their own boards which are responsible for establishing general policy guidelines and determining each year the number of students to be admitted to the different faculties.

In 1983, a total of 49,416 students were enrolled in higher education institutions (of whom 42 per cent were females). More than one-half (54.9 per cent) of enrollments was in community colleges with the remaining (45.1 per cent) in the three public universities.

In the same year, almost 60 per cent of the 34,000 students gaining the general secondary school certificates were admitted to higher education institutions within Jordan. The majority of the remainder not accepted by the higher education system within Jordan seemed to manage to enroll in universities and other higher education institutions abroad.

In 1985, Law No.28 was enacted, giving the Ministry of Education even broader administrative responsibilities. Within this so-called 'Law of Higher Education', the Ministry is entrusted with the carrying out of 'the government's educational, instructional, cultural and scientific policy in institutions of higher education . . .'. Among the principal responsibilities of the new ministry are the following:

- to promote integrated scientific planning of higher education according to the needs of society, including planning for establishing higher education institutions, determining the size, type, standard, degrees, and

- to support the autonomy of the universities through their boards and staff, and achieving coordination among them in various fields;
- to direct the supervision of non-university higher education to prepare technically trained manpower necessary for the development plans and cooperation with the other ministries, organizations, and institutions which have similar tasks;
- to support institutions of higher education with human and technical resources to raise the standard of scientific research;
- prepare studies and projects and undertake initiatives concerning higher education and its development in the country;
- to recognize foreign universities and institutions of higher education and the equivalency of their degrees.

Along with the new ministry, Law No.28 also established a 'Council of Higher Education' headed by the Prime Minister, with the Minister of Higher Education as the Vice President and, *inter alia*, as members the Commander-in-Chief of the Armed Forces, the Ministers of Education and Planning, the Presidents of universities and one representative each for both the public and private community colleges. Among others, the Council is entrusted with the following powers:

- approval of the establishment of all institutions of higher learning and the types of studies of each;
- approval of the plans of all higher education institutions, prioritizing of such plans and the integration of each into a general plan;
- approval of the criteria of admission of students in all institutions of higher learning;
- determining the number of students accepted annually in each field of specialization in institutions of higher education;
- determining tuition fees for students;
- approval of the holding of qualifying examinations;
- approval of the annual budgets of the universities.

Perhaps of greatest import in the new law with respect to the organization and administration of the university system is the provision found in Article 9, Section (b). That provision of the law provides that:

> The powers of the board of trustees of the University of Jordan, Yarmouk University and Mu'tah University, cited in the respective

> Laws and By-Laws issued accordingly, shall be transferred to the Council, regardless whether those powers are entrusted directly to the board of trustees, or whether a royal committee, formed for that purpose, practices them in deputation. The Council shall replace those boards of trustees, regulations and decisions issued by them shall stay valid until they are canceled or changed.

In this single provision the previously independent and rather pluralistic university system in Jordan has apparently been transformed into something approximating the state-run university systems more typically seen throughout the Middle East.

The new law also has a substantial impact on the community college system (discussed below). Article 9, Section (a) provides for the complete transfer of authority for the community college system from the Ministry of Education to the Ministry of Higher Education. The directorates of the community colleges and the civil servants who worked in them are all being transferred.

In any event, signs point toward an expansion of the local facilities for university level training. There is much discussion about the desirability of a privately owned and run university and of the possible need for yet another public university. The community colleges, particularly those privately run are said to be at a crossroads. The government must decide whether to allow them to expand, be upgraded and ultimately meld into the university system, or to keep them at their current level.

Clearly, the continuing rapid rise in higher education enrollments runs way ahead of likely demand. The Higher Education Council had the legal responsibility until recently to plan for the development of higher level manpower in the country and to decide on admission policy for higher education institutions. However, it did not fully exercise its mandate and it was questioned whether it could exercise it effectively without some control over scholarships and public funds allocated to the universities. Obviously, the Government has little control over the large number of Jordanians studying abroad. It is still too early to assess the role and the responsibility of the newly-created Ministry of Higher Education.

As previously noted, quality is an important issue in education in Jordan, perhaps more so than in any other Arab country. This seems particularly true with regard to the field of higher education.

One of the sub-committees of the current study group examining the future of the education system is reviewing the quality of the university system. The views of committee members coincide at least on three points: (a) graduates are poor in languages; (b) they need a better grounding in research techniques (problem solving); and c) in general, the university system does not distinguish itself from the secondary educational process, but merely represents a perpetuation of that process.

One committee member (a banker) complained that the universities are not sufficiently oriented to the needs of the economy, that they produce graduates without any practical notion of job opportunity or placement. In his view, university authorities are too much wed to the traditional concept of the university as an ivory tower in which

TABLE 2

FEMALES' SHARES OF ENROLLMENTS, BY LEVEL, URBAN/RURAL, 1971/72–1979/80

	1971/72	*1972/73*	*1973/74*	*1974/75*	*1975/76*	*1976/77*	*1977/78*	*1978/79*	*1979/80*
Primary – Total	44.5	45.2	45.7	46.1	46.5	46.7	46.8	47.2	47.5
Urban	46.8	47.3	47.4	47.6	48.2	47.8	47.9	48.1	48.2
Rural	40.9	41.8	42.8	43.7	43.9	45.0	45.2	45.8	46.5
Preparatory – Total	38.6	39.5	40.2	41.2	41.7	42.6	43.4	44.6	45.5
Urban	42.5	43.2	43.4	44.2	44.2	45.6	45.9	47.0	47.3
Rural	29.9	31.1	33.0	34.5	36.7	37.2	39.0	40.6	42.5
(Compulsory Cycle: Primary Preparatory– Total)	43.4	44.1	44.6	45.0	45.4	45.7	46.0	46.5	47.0
Urban	45.9	46.5	46.5	46.8	47.2	47.2	47.3	47.8	48.0
Rural	39.1	40.0	41.2	42.0	42.5	43.4	43.8	44.6	45.5
Secondary Total	30.9	31.9	34.2	36.7	38.4	39.2	39.5	40.7	42.3
Urban	33.3	34.1	36.1	38.2	39.7	40.4	40.5	41.4	42.9
Rural	14.9	17.3	21.4	27.1	31.0	34.0	35.2	37.7	40.3
Post-Secondary Institutes	31.8	33.5	36.3	38.1	34.6	35.1	38.3	43.3	45.7
University–Bachelors Level	32.3	31.2	30.6	31.3	33.5	37.3	37.2	40.4	42.0
University–Post-Bachelors	11.5	14.5	14.3	15.4	19.8	24.3	15.8	14.1	14.8
(Total Higher Education Institutions in Jordan)	31.7	31.9	32.4	33.5	33.4	35.5	37.0	40.9	43.3
Jordanian Higher Education Enrollments Abroad	N.A.	12.4	10.1	14.4	10.6	9.6	11.8	13.3	10.7

intellectual pursuit is encouraged for its own sake. In his view, Jordan cannot afford such a luxury. He asks, 'Of what value is an education if you cannot use it?'

Despite such criticism, several sub-committee members interviewed claim that on the whole Jordanian universities are now much better than the American University of Beirut (with reference to the standard of education that AUB had been able to provide through the mid-1970s, not since then). Respondents note that AUB students will in general be more worldly than the Jordanian university student, and will make a 'better presentation' of themselves, but that the Jordanian students' basic academic skills are higher.

Not every member of the committee agrees with the point of view that the university system is not producing graduates with skills relevant to the real world. One member, a Vice President of ALIA, the largest corporation and industrial employer in Jordan, maintained that the Jordanian educational system provided the great bulk of the manpower the company required, as much as 95 per cent (ALIA employs 4,600). According to this individual, the system produces nearly every type of employee the company requires – executives, pilots, ticketing agents, clerical staff, etc.

The departments of medicine, engineering, computer science and architecture, both at Yarmouk and Jordan universities have a reputation for excellence. These schools are all entered by competitive exam; a student may not simply choose a department or faculty. At the same time, there are some rather poor faculties, including social sciences, literature and law. These faculties receive the poorly prepared students who are unable to gain admission to the other faculties.

The student composition in the universities presents some interesting contrasts (See Table II). Many of the best male students from families of means are sent abroad. The bright females left behind tend to dominate the local universities. The best male students from poorer family backgrounds make up a sizeable proportion of the enrollment. They are inevitably not as motivated or hardworking as the female students in general, and the female upperclass students in particular, resulting in a situation where the girls are consistently the highest achievers. The balance of the student population is comprised of the 20 per cent of places reserved for the military. These students are of a generally lower quality and pull down the level of excellence at the universities.

The Jordanian woman is well-integrated into the education system. The girls now outnumber boys in the compulsory stage of the system, 49,000 to 47,000. In vocational training programs female students number 12,000 of the 18,000 total. In 1983, a total of 49,416 students were enrolled in higher education institutions of whom 42 per cent were females.

The integration of women into the labor force, however, is less comprehensive. According to a report by the Ministry of Social Development in 1985, two-thirds of women with university degrees think men are preferred in recruitment and in promotion. In a survey of three occupational groups (directors, researchers and social workers), the majority of women respondents (83 per cent) indicated that they believe such a preference exists.

It is not surprising then that currently 60 per cent of the teachers in the general education system (grades 1–9) are women. The women choose this professional avenue; the men do not seem as interested. Because there appears to be a social preference in the matter, the government cannot easily affect or influence this trend by planning. The preference has created a problem, however, because a surplus of teachers has resulted. By steadfastly preparing themselves for this profession, women are rapidly coming to bear the brunt of the current unemployment problem.

A policy currently under consideration regarding the teaching profession may worsen the plight of women in the labor force. The proposal calls for reclassifying teaching from a service to a trade, which would allow the government to raise the wages and benefits of teachers. The idea behind this may be to attract more currently unemployable men into teaching. If so, the result will obviously increase unemployment among women.

The community college system has an interesting history behind its development and evolution in Jordan. The first such institution was established in 1950 as a public teacher-training college. The model was replicated frequently during the next three decades, although specialized institutes were created in addition to the traditional teacher-training colleges.

By the 1980s, there were 52 such institutions with a total enrollment of 27,000, roughly equal to that of the university system. Although teacher-training appears to continue to predominate, many colleges specialize in other fields such as commerce, para-medical training, vocational training and the social sciences. The so-called institutes are run by the ministries and specialize in telecommunications, civil aviation, nursing, computer applications and statistics.

As of 1980, the government began to call all of these disparate institutes and colleges 'community' colleges (patterned somewhat after the American use of the term). Of the 52 colleges, 12 are run by the

Ministry of Higher Education, 22 are private and the rest are run by other ministries.

The community colleges all offer diplomas. If the graduate also sits for the comprehensive exam given by the Ministry of Higher Education, he or she can earn a recognized degree from the Ministry as well. This degree can be very important; for example, no aspiring teacher can get a job without holding the Ministry degree.

The community college courses are typically two years in duration. Unlike their US counterparts, community college graduates are not permitted to enter universities and complete their education. Consequently, many community college graduates have traditionally gone abroad to finish their education.

This situation may be about to change. In 1985, the new Council on Higher Education approved in principle the right of the community college graduate to admission in the university. There are other indications that the government is preparing the way for an upgrading and expansion of the community college system. A revision of the credit hours system has been carried out to give the course a value more closely approximate to its actual academic value. Schools will also soon have the flexibility to determine whether to give one, two or three-year programs. Perhaps most important, an attempt has been made to upgrade the content of community college courses to the level of those being offered in the university. Finally, a practical side has been added to the Ministry's comprehensive exam this year in an attempt to ensure that the community college graduate has skills that can be put to practical use. Along with the existing comprehensive exam an additional section is given to test whether the student has developed skills in his particular field (nursing, computer science, commerce, etc.). The test is designed to ascertain whether the student can indeed apply his knowledge to his intended profession.

Data on the number of Jordanians studying abroad vary considerably. The Ministry of Education put the number at 60,288 for the year 1983 (in 1984 this number dropped, inexplicably, to about 46,000 and in 1985, to about 38,000). These figures include a large but unknown number of students with limited attachment to the East Bank – students of Palestinian origin who have grown up mostly outside Jordan and who might not plan ever to settle in Jordan. In 1983, students abroad were studying in some 42 countries with the largest concentration in the US (15,000), Lebanon (almost 10,000), Egypt (8,350) and the USSR (4,500). More than 15,000 were studying engineering; about 11,000 were in the humanities, 8,500 in business or commerce and 7,600 in medicine.

There have been several major reasons for this substantial outflow of university-level students. There has been a lack of places for them in local universities; the government has placed no restrictions on studying abroad; there has been virtually complete convertibility of the Jordanian dinar against all other major currencies; and, as a matter of social status, many parents believe that the education received at a foreign institution is far superior to that of a local institution.

There are discrepancies in the various figures reported on students abroad and a degree of controversy as to just how many are out of the country. Jordanian educational authorities have tended to over-estimate the number in the United States (for example the government in 1983 put the number at 15,000 but the Institute of International Education in New York put it only at 7,500). A high degree of accuracy in the data is not vital; whatever the actual number, there is a student body of significant size pursuing higher education elsewhere.

The geographical distribution of those reported abroad in 1985 is as follows:

TABLE 3

Jordanian higher education at home and abroad, 1985

(Estimated)

Country	Number	Percentage
Jordan	53,895	58.6
Arab countries	15,547	16.9
Islamic countries	1,227	1.3
Western countries	14,478	15.7
Socialist countries (GDR, Poland, Yugoslavia)	5,732	6.2
Other Eastern countries (India, Pakistan)	1.055	1.3
Total	91,944	100.0

Source: Ministry of Planning

It is also of interest to note the breakdown of the programs of study of Jordanian students abroad (a full accounting of the majors of all those abroad is not possible; results listed before are therefore partial). Engineering and medicine by far attract the largest number of students. The natural sciences and economics also account for a sizeable percentage of enrollment. Conversely, the fine arts and education show a small representation.

The private sector has always played a significant role in Jordanian education. All kindergarten or pre-school classes are organized and offered by private agencies.

TABLE 4
Majors of students abroad, by discipline; 1985
(Estimated)

Subject	Number	Percentage
Natural sciences	2226	11.0
Engineering	7232	37.0
Medicine	4658	24.0
Agriculture	711	4.0
Humanities	1278	6.5
Economics	1689	8.6
Social sciences	396	2.0
Fine arts	65	0.1
Education	151	1.0
Law & shariah	1085	5.5
Miscellaneous	229	0.3
Total	19,720	100.0

Source: Ministry of Planning

The private sector grip on kindergarten may be loosening because of a proposal now under serious consideration at the MOE to have the state provide kindergarten classes. Private schools also provide facilities for students in the compulsory and secondary levels. Typically such private schools may have a religious or purely commercial orientation. They are not generally considered by most Jordanians to be better than state schools, but they do provide parents with particular interests the opportunity to satisfy those interests for their children. These private schools are particularly noted for their foreign language courses which are considered to be of better quality than those offered in the state schools. Otherwise the curriculum followed is the same as that followed in the state schools. Schools of commercial orientation are considered to be of a lower quality than the state schools; they tend to take anyone who can pay their fees.

As noted above, private community colleges now comprise 22 of the 52 in existence. These colleges, with a current enrollment of 27,000, have become increasingly important within the community college system. Begun primarily as teacher training institutes, they now include such courses as commerce, para-medical, vocational and social services. The diploma received is considered a terminal degree – students would not be admitted for additional studies at the 4-year universities. For this reason, many of these students go abroad for university studies in private college and universities such as the American University in Beirut.

Of current interest is the concept of creating a private university in Jordan. The government has already received 20 applications to organize such an institution, principally from private community colleges wishing to become full-fledged universities. The government appears to look favorably on the concept, perhaps because of its general intent to expand university enrollment to respond to the many students who are now turned away for lack of places.

In recent years, there has been a substantial evolution in the institutional base for and the environment of military training and education. The most striking example of change has been the establishment of Mu'tah University (in the south of Jordan). It opened in 1983 with an enrollment of 30 students.

Mu'tah is the third university to be established, the apparent motive being to provide university-level comprehensive educational and training facilities for the military and internal security forces. It combines the activities of two institutions, the Royal Military Academy and the Police Institute, which were abolished after Mu'tah came on line. It is not uncommon to hear Mu'tah referred to as 'the West Point' or 'Sandhurst' of Jordan.

Prior to its establishment there was considerable debate over the question of whether to permit civilian students to attend the new university. In the end, it was decided to restrict enrolment to members of the military and police. This decision apparently did not obviate the need for the civilian higher education institutions to continue to provide education for military manpower – they must still provide 20 per cent of the available places for students destined for the military. Although a young institution, Mu'tah has a fairly good reputation among educators. Its president is highly respected. The teaching staff at Mu'tah is, on average, much younger than one finds in the other two universities; again, among educators, this teaching staff has a reputation for sound intellectual skills and is thought to be of high quality.

The quality of the student body (at Mu'tah) is, on the other hand, rather difficult to determine. It is doubtful if it is as high as at the other universities (and there, students in the military are thought, generally, to be of lower quality than their civilian counterparts). Because Mu'tah has only a very few female students and, in general, since it is female students who are setting the academic norms for performance at Jordan and Yarmouk University, one can deduce that academic standards may be lower. Again, many of the brighter male students study abroad. Although such a conclusion must be tentatively rendered, it is likely that a military career is not attracting the highest caliber of student.

To appreciate developments with respect to the links between current civilian educational policy and its possible impact on military capability, it is necessary to address the government's interest in becoming *the* technology center in the Middle East. Jordan clearly sees itself as the principal supplier of high-level technological manpower to the oil-rich Arab Gulf states. To achieve this, the government is contemplating several innovative incentive programs to encourage the formation of consulting firms to service the technical requirements of the region (which in the past have been largely provided by Western expatriates).

At the basic education level, there are now programs which introduce children to all types of machinery and mechanical devices, teaching them how to take them apart and reassemble them. Computers are also being introduced at an early stage in education in both private and public schools. Correspondingly, there is growing emphasis on science and technology in the universities. (it may be worth noting that the Royal Scientific Society has recently developed a working prototype of the 'first Arab mini-computer').

A new concept in education is the Jubilee School, which has recently been established for gifted Jordanian students (grades 7–12). To give it added publicity and recognition, the school was officially opened in November 1985 on the King's 50th birthday. The Jubilee school is largely based on the American model for gifted and talented students. It has strong financial support from the palace through a royal endowment and receives no public funds. As a private school, it is governed by a law that states that a succeeding class can be no larger than the one that precedes it; hence, a student can only enter in the first (that is, 7th) grade level. The school has an approximate enrollment of 200, and though not yet fully completed, the building design and equipment are elaborate.

A similar private school for gifted children is the Salt School. This pilot program was begun about 1984, established and wholly funded by the Salt Community and Development Corporation.

The government has also given new emphasis to a policy of directing 60 per cent of 11th grade students (at the secondary level) into the scientific stream of the general education program. This policy has been in effect for 10 years but has, to date, only succeeded in obtaining about a 40–45 per cent level of enrollment in science.

This strong emphasis on science and technology and the attempt to redirect an ever-increasing portion of the academically qualified to the related fields has both military and civilian implications. It is precisely in the areas of computer applications, aeronautical (including missile) and other specialized engineering fields and telecommunications and information sciences where the military lacks adequate manpower. Although at present the intent does not appear to be directed at the military *vis-à-vis* the civilian applications of technology, the very strong links between the civilian education sector and the military will surely mean that improvements in the quality and quantity of scientific manpower will redound directly to the benefit of the military.

Education is so integral to Jordanian society and individual mobility (career and social), that the country has developed education and training initiatives in every quarter. Post-formal education training activity in the form of adult courses, seminars, training conferences and correspondence courses is readily available and routinely offered. Of this genre, management education and training is perhaps the most important.

Management education and training is offered by two autonomous institutions: the Jordan Institute of Public Administration (JIPA) and the Jordan Institute of Management (JIM). In addition, the University of Jordan and Yarmouk University are establishing MBA and MPA programs to train middle-level managers.

JIPA, like similar institutes of public administration in other Arab countries, is the major institution providing in-service training for civil servants and public sector employees. Since its establishment in 1968 (through a Ford Foundation grant) and through 1983, it has offered 200 courses and seminars attended by over 6,000 participants. The training offered covers various levels of management and operations and professional/technical subjects such as accounting and financial analysis and work-flow analysis.

JIM is by far the more superior institution of the two. It is an affiliate of the Industrial Development Bank, established in 1979, offering training to middle-level managers from the private sector (in such fields as marketing, accounting and financial management and production management).

Through 1983, JIM had offered 90 programs attended by approximately 2,000 participants. JIM has progressed sufficiently to begin to attract the attention of major international and bi-lateral donor agencies. At the present time, both the World Bank and the Agency for International Development are considering major support funding for expansion of its activities.

Overall, one must conclude that the Jordanian education system is doing an adequate and in many instances, an excellent job in educating the population. This is a major accomplishment given the nature and extent of the country's resources and the political, economic and social tumult of the region. This accomplishment is not diminished significantly by the problems now besetting that system. The most serious problem – the excess of highly qualified and trained university graduates who, increasingly, find no employment opportunities – is symptomatic of poor manpower planning but not attributable to shortcomings of the educational system. If anything, that system is doing its job too well.

There are three areas in which the educational system is experiencing difficulty: shifting students away from pursuit of the higher levels (secondary and post-secondary) of a general academic education to vocational/technical and polytechnical education and training; instilling and inspiring career and professional commitment to the pursuit of technical skill enhancement and quality job performance; and, shifting a greater incidence of the cost of education to the public. These problems are in addition to the problem already mentioned of the quality of education and the more minor technical problems of teacher salaries and teaching loads.

Although the Jordanian educational system is well advanced, it suffers from an over-emphasis on attaining higher levels of general education. This over-emphasis does not stem from any particular characteristic intrinsic to that system, save possibly that increasing investment has been made in higher education facilities making it possible for a higher proportion of the eligible population to attend. Rather, it stems from the government's heavy and sustained emphasis on formal education as the primary means of developing the country.

That much of the actual economic development Jordan has experienced can be traced to this investment in human resources is not at issue. What has changed, as the economy has matured, is the kind of human resources required, both for further internal economic growth and to continue to capture much needed capital from sources external to the country (see Table 5). As noted, an increasingly important source of this external capital flow has been accounted for by remittances.

The government is now confronted with the task of shifting the emphasis away from the pursuit of a higher education to the pursuit of a technical or vocational education. In addition, it seeks to shift a greater proportion of students pursuing the more traditional higher education to scientific and technological fields. Its efforts to accomplish this are meeting with solid resistance from the population.

Interestingly, the elites in Jordanian society have led the attack against proposed government educational policy changes by raising questions of 'quality' of that system overall. While the quality of education can stand improvement, it really isn't the issue at hand. Students and parents, long-steeped in the pursuit of higher education as a means of attaining social and economic mobility are not readily going to concede that the future lies elsewhere – especially if this is associated with performing essentially manual or blue-collar jobs.

TABLES 5
PROJECTED GRADUATES AND DROPOUTS FROM THE EDUCATIONAL SYSTEM IN JORDAN, 1980–90

	GRADUATES		DROPOUTS		TOTAL	
POOLS	Produced	Entering Labor Force	Produced	Entering Labor Force	Produced	Entering Labor Force
1. Scientists and Mathematicians	20,988	13,910	0	0	20,988	13,910
2. Architects and Engineers	20,753	11,799	0	0	20,753	11,799
3. Health Professionals And Technicians	17,797	13,946	7,409	4,107	25,206	18,053
4. Teachers	79,679	73,396	951	596	80,630	73,992
5. Other Professionals	49,939	31,793	1,994	1,073	51,933	32,866
7. Managers	27,591	18,164	0	0	27,591	18,164
8. White Collar Supervisors	27,541	26,701	31,526	16,798	59,067	43,499
9. Science Technicians	6,643	6,475	7,918	4,026	14,561	10,501
10. Blue Collar Supervisors And Foremen	8,044	7,860	323	311	8,367	8,171
11. Skilled Office Workers	29,921	21,720	116,960	70,300	146,881	92,020
6. Skilled Farm Workers[1]	1,397	1,370	3,561	1,907	4,958	3,277
12. Skilled Manual Workers	35,155	33,195	6,020	3,925	41,175	37,120
13. Semi-Skilled Non-Manual Workers	21,974	11,956	269,170	151,936	291,144	163,892
14. Semi-Skilled Manual Workers	8,081	7,760	12,443	8,780	20,524	16,540
15. Unskilled Workers	0	0	55,673	26,248	55,673	26,248
TOTAL	355,503	280,045	513,948	290,007	869,451	570,052

* Office, services, agriculture.
1. Includes 3–4% farm managers.
Source: World Bank estimates.

Education is a means of bringing about changes in attitude leading to a redirection of human resources; the educational system is merely the process by which the message is delivered. The pedagogical question, that is, what changes in the education now imparted are necessary to create new kinds of human resources for a changed economic future, is producing a public reaction that in turn is raising a system question: the quality of education being delivered. These are really two different issues and the government so far has not managed to separate them.

In fact, despite public opposition to present educational policy, substantial progress has been made in the past 10 years in expanding the vocational/technical education and training capacity of the educational system. A higher percentage of students are attending such programs. But, the quality of the student who is entering this vocational/technical stream is quite low. More important, the average vocational/technical student suffers from a perception of having 'failed', both in the eyes of his parents as well as of society in general.

This pattern of siphoning off the less able and academically qualified to the vocational/technical stream is not unique to Jordan. However, as the government is prone to see that in the main, it is Jordanian technical and skilled manpower that will be in demand in the Gulf and is required for Jordan to meet its internal industrial growth plans, it is clear that a continuing perception of vocational/technical education as a 'booby prize' cannot be allowed to continue.

In a recent survey conducted by these authors, 250 graduates of the vocational and technical education streams were interviewed to determine their success rate on the job and their view of the relevance of the education they had received. In addition, interviews with 50 employers of such graduates were also conducted (the survey was completed in the late fall of 1985). The results give evidence of the low esteem with which graduates view themselves, indicate inappropriate work attitudes to the job, and, in general pinpoint the inadequacies of the training received:

- the majority (75 per cent) aspire to pursuing higher education and continue to view their present circumstances as temporary;
- a minority (20 per cent) aspire to achieving a high degree of competency in their chosen vocational or technical education field;
- over 60 per cent of those in technical education (Industrial Secondary Schools) indicate that their education did not sufficiently prepare them for their first job;
- the majority (80 per cent) of technical education graduates

in the survey had only average or below-average scholastic performance and vocational training graduates simply are never 'failed' – a trainee can drop out of the program of his own volition but is never sent down because of inadequate performance; and,
- the majority of employers (33 of the 50 firms responding) note that the technical schools and training centers are 'not imparting the right work ethic, craft or skill standards to their graduates.'

The government is faced with a serious problem. It cannot expect to upgrade the quality of the student entering the vocational/technical stream without upgrading the societal perception of, and status accorded to, performing skilled or technical work. The government is trying to do this by administrative fiat and it is not working.

Conversely, the government cannot allow individual student or parental choice to be the primary means by which decisions regarding the level and type of education (and disciplinary majors therein) are made, at least not to the degree that is currently in practice. It is clear that this is the most serious dilemma that Jordan faces in terms of the future direction of its educational system.

The means by which the government has set about producing these substantive changes in the system (aside from issuing controversial policy decisions) includes the attempt to redirect financial resources away from the general secondary and higher education levels to the technical and vocational. In addition, within the general secondary and higher education levels the government seeks to shift the bulk of the funding to the scientific and technological disciplines and away from the social sciences, humanities and the arts. If it cannot accomplish this, then it is unlikely that the policy shift can succeed.

This issue of shifting educational priorities via redirecting the funding has become enmeshed in the public-private responsibility question. The government is saying in essence: 'We cannot do everything and are only going to fund that type of education we deem appropriate to the economic needs of the country.' If private citizens want a different type of education, then this is a matter for the private sector to provide – privatize education, and let market demand and supply work itself out.

To this end, the government is reconsidering present methods of financing education. Jordanian universities are now financially supported by earmarked customs revenues. As a matter of public finance principle, this is undesirable because it bypasses the normal procedures (parliamentary debate, for example) for allocating public funds, *including allocation among* the various levels of education. There are tuition fees at the universities and it is intended to raise them. The government will also try to offset adverse responses by creating alternative mechanisms such as scholarship and loan schemes (which can be tied to specific fields of study).

The Jordanian experience in generally allowing private community colleges to develop in response to market demand has proven to be a very effective means of mobilizing private resources for the provision of higher education. Unresolved problems with the private community colleges relate to the issues of quality and the relevance of their curricula. An appropriate accreditation system would resolve the quality issue, and development of a sound labor market information system (an admittedly long and complex task) would enable the clientele of community colleges to make informal (private) choices in keeping with the free market philosophy which underpins the private college concept.

Politically, orchestrating this major restructuring is a minefield: decreasing the importance of higher education and increasing that of vocational/technical, redirecting public funds to state educational priorities and shifting the incidence of costs to the private sector and diminishing the onus that attaches to pursuing a technical education. It is all the more so, given the degree to which educational attainment has assumed an extremely important symbolism for the dispossessed generations of Palestinians. Perhaps irrationally, it has become the 'leveling force' for those without a true homeland. As a result, the quest for peace, and ultimately, the settling of the Palestinian question are related to the more particular question of educational reform. The finding of gainful employment has always been viewed by the Jordanian public as a function of one's level of education. If employment opportunities in spite of that level of attainment are denied, and if an acceptable political resolution to the much larger question of Palestinian conflict is not forthcoming, then the potential for significant political change rises sharply.

There are more minor problems in the education system, that is, minor in comparison to those noted above, but of direct relevance to the quality of education. These relate to teaching loads and teacher salaries.

Student/teacher ratios have generally fallen over the past decade as has the average number of students per class unit. As a matter of cost minimization, it would appear that the government has the opportunity to increase class size without necessarily decreasing the quality of education. The student/teacher ratios are considerably lower than average class size at the intermediate and secondary levels of education. Presumably, this is due to the deployment patterns of specialized teachers. The task for the administrators of the education system is efficiently to 'fine tune' present load patterns so that cost savings result and the public's concern for education quality is not further exacerbated.

Average salaries for teachers are relatively low in comparison with other countries with the same per capita income range. In 1983, the ratio of primary school teachers' salaries to per capita GNP was 2.0 in Jordan, 2.5 in the OECD countries, 2.4 in Latin America, 2.6 in Asia, and 10.8 in West Africa (and 5.5 in East Africa). Teacher salaries in Jordan are also low in comparison with pay scales in industry (in 1982, average monthly wages in industry were JD 158; MOE teacher salaries were: primary, JD 94; intermediate, JD 107; and secondary, JD 108).

Here too, the government must move cautiously. As emphasis shifts to the vocational/technical education area, teachers in these areas are going to have to be upgraded and paid more. The demand for good technical and vocational teachers is increasing in industry. For the government to allow pay scales to reflect a growing disparity between vocational teaching staff and teachers in academic areas, there will have to be adequate attention paid in order to prevent a serious backlash.

These are the problems of a relatively well-advanced and sophisticated educational system. During the 1970s, significant improvements were registered in the internal efficiency of the general education system. Using promotion, repetition and dropout rates, various efficiency indicators calculated for males and females in primary, intermediate and general secondary levels of education clearly show the Jordanian system to be well in advance of other Arab countries.

However, this system is now entering a new stage. It is difficult to assess accurately the government's future economic strategy. This strategy calls for the development of skill and labor-intensive small and medium scale manufacturing and technical services *and* a human resource development approach that gives Jordanians a competitive edge in providing technical and skilled labor to the Gulf and Saudi Arabia. Even the industrial strategy has a substantial external market component to it. Given the small size of the domestic market, most of the product and services will have to be destined for export markets. Export oriented manufacturing has the added advantage of being relatively labor intensive. For planners, then, the speed with which Jordan can develop external market-oriented manufacturing industries will decide to a large extent the rate of overall economic growth and of future demand for labor. If the planners are wrong, or if the transition is not effected in a timely and efficient manner, then Jordan will simply be trading one set of labor market problems for another, that is, high unemployment of college graduates will be joined by high unemployment of technicians and skilled labor.

Large-scale unemployment of the highly educated is by far the more serious with potentially destabilizing effects. These effects have now two dimensions: effects that stem from trying to change society's expectations regarding educational choice and attainment and effects that stem from an incorrect government interpretation of Jordan's economic future. Both present serious timing difficulties.

The attempt to steer education in certain directions seems to be running foul of the public's growing appetite for a more liberal political atmosphere. The government is partly culpable here (possibly by design, possibly not): it has essentially signaled to the public that it no longer wishes to or can provide education for everyone irrespective of cost or consequence. Public opinion leaders note that 'we are tired of being told what to do or what to want by the government, the police and the army'. Educational change and redirection seems thus to have coincided with an awakened desire for a more liberal society. Political tensions are increasing as a consequence of the government's attempt to shift more of the onus (psychologically and financially) to the private sector while continuing to try to manhandle the education system into a position that reflects its economic prognosis of future development.

Far more serious problems can be anticipated if the rate of unemployment of the highly educated does not abate in the near term. Of particular concern has to be the growing number of highly educated women who find no employment outlet internally and are largely precluded from active participation in external labor markets (which will continue to be the case until and unless the Gulf, Saudi Arabia and the Arab world more generally accept the need for equality of opportunity). Nothing is likely to be more politically explosive that to continue to educate people for whom there is nothing to do.

Again, the government is inclined to take the 'we're all in the same boat' approach to the possible longer-term labor displacement question. Jordan, it is argued, simply has to export labor and Jordan has no control over the external demand for that labor. There can be no denying this truism.

The educational system expanded in order to meet the growing external demand for Jordanian manpower and is now faced with the need to contract and redirect this system. External labor demand has fallen and therefore the resources to continue (and, indeed the wisdom of continuing) in the same vein are not there.

Jordan has weathered far more serious problems than it now confronts; there is a strength and resolve to persevere that is evident both in the government and in society. This may permit the country to overcome the current economic and political problem.

On the other hand, the time it takes to overcome it is not entirely in the hands of Jordanian planners and government officials. The future of oil prices, the hiring practices of the Arab oil economies, the internal development priorities and strategies of those oil economies, the rate of development of educational systems in those oil economies and world economic trends all have a direct bearing on Jordan's economic future.

These are matters that go well beyond a purely technical evaluation of the present character and quality of the Jordanian educational system. In view of the limited resources with which the country has had to work, that system has performed remarkably. That it now is becoming the focal point of the much more important and more complex geo-political tensions that permeate the region in no way diminishes that accomplishment.

[17]

Patterns of Human Resource Development in Saudi Arabia

Robert E. Looney

Demographic change in Saudi Arabia may be one of the main determinants not only of political stability, but economic as well. In particular, the ability of the country to develop its human assets will, in the long run, determine the kingdom's ultimate success in diversifying its economy away from oil.

The purpose of this paper is to survey recent demographic trends in the Kingdom, especially as they affect the development of the nation's human resources. Based on this assessment several future scenarios are outlined.

MAJOR DEMOGRAPHIC PATTERNS

Saudi Arabia has by far the largest percentage of nationals in its labor force. Demographic trends in the Kingdom indicate that more than 720,000 Saudi Arabians, representing almost 9 per cent of the population, will reach the age of 20 during the period 1988 to 1992 (Table 1). In the same period, the total number of Saudis in the labor force is projected to rise by just over 220,000. The shortfall is of course, due to the fact that only 120,000 women or about 6 per cent of Saudi women aged 15–60 are projected to be working in 1992 (Table 2).

As a result of these demographic trends and the country's anticipated manpower requirements as its productive structure becomes more sophisticated, the foreign workforce will be increasingly crucial in filling certain specific occupations. The country now employs about 100,000 Europeans and North Americans in managerial and technical jobs.[1] However, this source may be endangered by the social trends taking place in advanced economies. In the early 1990s the number of young people entering the West European labor market will fall by 25 per cent. The result will be a growing shortage of appropriately qualified people, particularly information technology specialists and service company managers. The net effect will be that Arabian companies will find it increasingly hard to hire European managerial and senior technical staff.[2]

> Analysts anticipate expatriate pay levels will increase in real terms over the next several years as western skilled labor supply shrinks. The trend will be compounded by the weakness of Gulf currencies on foreign exchange markets.[3]

What is certain is that the private sector will have to step up efforts to develop the pool of nationals capable of running large, modern enterprises as employees, rather than proprietors.

TABLE 1
SAUDI ARABIA: NATIONAL POPULATION BY AGE, 1987 AND 1992

	1987		1992	
Age	*Number*	*Per cent*	*Number*	*Per cent*
0–4	1,386,300	20.1	1,673,400	20.5
5–9	1,077,100	15.6	1,300,500	15.9
10–14	868,200	12.6	1,027,600	12.6
15–19	722,600	10.5	854,700	10.5
20–24	614,300	8.9	721,100	8.8
25–29	500,000	7.2	589,200	7.2
30–34	391,600	5.7	456,300	5.6
35–39	317,000	4.6	366,500	4.5
40–44	251,200	3.6	288,600	3.5
45–49	200,300	2.9	231,000	2.8
50–54	158,300	2.3	182,500	2.2
55–59	138,600	2.0	160,900	2.0
60–64	115,000	1.7	136,400	1.7
65+	164,100	2.4	192,700	2.4
Total	6,905,000	100.0	8,181,400	100.0

Source: J.S. Birks and C.A. Sinclair, *Saudi Arabia into the 90s* (University of Durham: Mountjoy Research Centre, 1988).

TABLE 2
SAUDI ARABIA: NATIONAL WORKFORCE, 1978–1992

	Males		Females		Total	
	Number	*Increase(%)*	*Number*	*Increase(%)*	*Number*	*Increase(%)*
1987	1,343,100	–	101,600	–	1,444,700	–
1988	1,384,000	3.0	105,200	3.6	1,489,200	3.1
1989	1,424,500	2.9	108,700	3.4	1,533,200	3.0
1990	1,464,600	2.8	112,300	3.2	1,576,900	2.8
1991	1,505,400	2.8	115,900	3.3	1,621,300	2.8
1992	1,548,600	2.9	120,000	3.5	1,668,600	2.9

Source: J.S. Birks and C.A. Sinclair, *Saudi Arabia into the 90s* (University of Durham: Mountjoy Research Centre, 1988).

MANPOWER PROBLEMS

Statistics on population and the labor force clearly reveal the degree of dependency on foreign labor. The number of economically active nationals is fewer than might be expected for several reasons:

(1) The population is very youthful.
(2) Widespread expansion of secondary and university education has taken place in the past decade.
(3) The labor force participation has been reduced because only a small proportion of women are engaged in wage employment.

The large importation of foreign workers has raised a number of issues related to the country's manpower strategy.

(1) *Unemployment of Productive Nationals*. A major issue is whether such a level of immigration is actually causing unemployment amongst the national population. It is possible that the large numbers of cheaply and easily available expatriates are slowing down the transfer of nationals from the traditional to the modern sector. Furthermore, Saudis are becoming less inclined toward production and related occupations. This development implies a continued heavy dependence on foreigners to fill such jobs.
(2) *Underdevelopment of Human Resources*. A more profound aspect of the importation of so much labor has been the stunted development of their indigenous human resources. The widespread usc of migrant labor combined with the high level of wealth, has led to a proliferation of luxury employment for Saudis, which amounts to their withdrawal from the productive workforce. In fact, the educational system has become geared towards preparing nationals for this luxury employment rather than for productive employment. Thus migration has distorted the development of human capital in the Kingdom. Labor migration has led to native dependency on foreign manpower not only in quantitative, but also qualitative terms.

The relatively open employment policy of the government, coupled with a civil service system that minimizes competition and ignores an objective system of evaluation, has in all likelihood produced this low level of job commitment and low productivity. Continued dependency on imported labor may intensify this trend. More government efforts towards the localization of the labor force have, in general, brought about a clear mismatch between the job requirements, and the nationals available to fill them. Such a trend has resulted in the low productivity of the Saudis who make up the labor force.

LABOR MARKET DISTORTIONS

The above patterns have arisen in large part from the presence of labor market distortions in at least three areas:[4]

(1) Rural/urban population distribution.
(2) Distortions between the tradeable and non-tradeable sectors, and
(3) Skill mismatches in the labor force.

Rapid rural-urban migration has characterized most developing countries, particularly the Gulf states. However it appears to have occurred to a much larger scale in the Kingdom. While the higher urban percentage in it may be the result of geography, the higher growth in urban populations experienced over the last decade is more likely to be due to other factors.

The negative effects on development of a too rapid rural-urban migration are well documented. It can lead to shortages of labor in the agricultural sector, large-scale urban unemployment/under-employment, urban bias in the government's economic policy, large external dis-economies in urban areas and so on.

The government expenditure patterns explain much of the additional migration observed in the Kingdom. In fact the Kingdom has experienced rapid growth in government employment (predominantly in the urban areas). Apparently the heads of government bureaux seek to maximize the size of their ministries by maximizing budget allocations and hence employment. Oil revenues accruing to the government increase the ability of all bureaux to maximize their size. In addition, government employment is often used as an unemployment benefit substitute. Increased employment by the government would explain the faster migration either in terms of increasing the rural wage differential or by increasing the probability of urban unemployment.

The second area of distortion is that too high a proportion of the labor force moves into sectors that do not face international competition. Damage to development arises as the move away from tradeables undermines the resource base to produce directly productive activities. The net result is a relatively high proportion of the labor force in services in the oil producing countries, and a relatively low proportion in manufacturing.

Several factors probably contribute to this employment pattern:

(1) Government programs to reduce unemployment through public sector hiring.
(2) A cultural preference for white collar jobs which tend to be more common in non-tradeables.
(3) Dutch Disease factors whereby the relative profitability of services improves *vis-à-vis* manufacturing.

The final area of labor market distortion is that of skill mismatches. This is essentially the problem of too many PhDs and two few mechanics. The symptom of this would be relatively high levels of disguised unemployment among the highly educated coupled with a shortage of artisans. The damage arising from these skill mismatches lies in the way the various economic sectors are likely to expand while faced by labor constraints.

Two elements of the change in government behavior may provide a transmission mechanism for skill mismatches.

(1) There has been very rapid decision-making involving education. This is part of the general problem of the pressure on governments to spend quickly. This has resulted in a very rapid expansion in the tertiary education sector (including sending students abroad) with only limited consideration for the implications of this on the primary and secondary sectors, together with a neglect of technical education. In effect, education policy has developed as a by-product of spending decisions rather than as the result of any carefully laid out education policy.

(2) Once the mismatches have begun to appear the government has been willing (via its revenue access) to absorb these mismatches by its employment policies – over development of bureaucracy to provide employment for nationals returning from education abroad who would otherwise be employed below their desired status. The willingness to absorb the skill mismatches thus tends to disguise the appearance of signals warning against the development of even greater mismatches.

HUMAN RECOURCE DEVELOPMENT STRATEGIES

As noted above, in order to deal with its labor problems, the Saudi Government is attempting to develop and implement a human resource development strategy. This involves not only upgrading the skills of the local workforce, but also entail the opening up of positions for women in the labor force.

While it is true that the large number of expatriate construction workers brought in to implement the physical development of the Kingdom may no longer be needed, workers skilled in more sophisticated technology will be required to accomplish the Kingdom's new objectives. Moreover, even within the construction industry there are indications that suburban development, manufacturing construction, hospital construction and other projects to complete the country's economic base will continue to give rise to a large number of construction projects. Agricultural development plans also suggest new construction needs as does the new emphasis on the development of solar energy and the Kingdom's vast mineral resources.

Setting construction needs aside, however, the ten principal manpower implications of the current development strategy are:[5]

(1) Diversification of the Kingdom's revenue resources through the development of industry, mining, agriculture and solar energy potentials will be giving rise to new demands for technically skilled manpower. Many of these skills lie in areas in which Saudi nationals have yet to be trained.

(2) Saudization priorities by economic sector will have to be determined and then implemented if emphasis is to be placed on the employment of Saudis 'in important permanently productive sectors including those slated for predominance in the govern-

ment's investment and expenditure decisions', for example water, natural resources, petrochemical, and refined petroleum products.

(3) Operation and maintenance of the Kingdom's vast infrastructure will require a large force of Saudi nationals trained in maintenance, machine operation and other vocational skills, as well as those capable of operating capital-intensive, peak-technology modes of production.

(4) The private sector will be asked to play a major role in the education and training of Saudi nationals as part of this increased responsibility for the overall development of the Saudi economy. This will further decentralize the Kingdom's training efforts.

(5) The proposed 'dual standard' immigration criterion for Moslem expatriates versus non-Moslem expatriates will give rise to serious questions of ethnic control of specified job skills and or labor pools.

(6) Political instability in the Gulf region, together with the defense obligations incurred by the Kingdom as a member of the Gulf Cooperation Council, will result in increased pressure to Saudize the Kingdom's military forces. The introduction of compulsory military service will assist in this objective, but it will also drain the total labor pool and create new training needs.

(7) The new emphasis on human services and cultural enhancement programs will necessitate the development of Saudi manpower to manage programs for the handicapped: to deliver health service and health education to urban and rural patients, and to staff libraries and other cultural centers being proposed.

(8) A renewed emphasis on teacher education also will be required when elementary education is made compulsory, anti-illiteracy and adult programs are expanded, military education introduced at the secondary level and computer science is introduced into secondary and vocational training institutions for both girls and boys.

(9) The limitation of university positions to capable students and to those enrolled in fields of study relevant to the Kingdom's needs will necessitate a realignment of university resources, including teaching staff. Redundancy of humanities faculty may permit a reduction of expatriate staff as well as foster new career options for others.

(10) A reassessment of 'appropriate' jobs for Saudi women will need to be followed by specific government directives to assure the enactment of measures designed to facilitate entry of women into new sectors of the labor force.

It is unrealistic to believe that all ten areas can be 'Saudized' within the next decade. Saudization priorities will most likely be established and for the immediate future all other manpower needs temporarily relegated to expatriate personnel. When compulsory primary education has gained a toehold and when military training has augmented the skills of Saudi males, Saudization efforts will be possible in a wider variety of fields.

For the present however Saudization will most likely focus on those segments of the labor force that only Saudis can serve best – national security and the preservation and enrichment of the Kingdom's cultural traditions. Specifically these would include the Saudization of all natural resource development, Saudization of the military, Saudization of all ministries (enhanced by the use of Saudi women as support staff) and the Saudization of certain human services and cultural enhancement programs. The latter might also be administered in large part by Saudi women and by 'redundant' Saudi academics currently teaching in university facilities unrelated to priority national development needs.

PROBLEMS IN SAUDI HUMAN RESOURCE DEVELOPMENT

In recent years Saudi educational programs have run into a number of difficulties:[6]

(1) Education even at the primary level has not been compulsory, leaving many of the government's educational goals devoid of the means of enforcement.
(2) Rural and agriculturally oriented families do not have a tradition which places high value on education beyond the study of religion and perhaps some basic literacy skills. They are unable to perceive the long-term economic value of pursuing an education.
(3) Students are dropping out of elementary and secondary education as soon as their literacy or basic skills are adequate to permit them immediate employment. Once out of school and without benefit of reinforced learning, even those rudimentary skills are often lost.
(4) Mobility, particularly from rural to urban areas, is fostering the student drop-out rate and encouraging young men to seek employment in factories, in the military, and in various vocational fields.
(5) There is an abundance of means by which young people can make money without high levels of education. The economic incentive to remain in school is therefore greatly weakened.
(6) Wealthy parents may destroy a student's motivation to pursue education by giving a youth all the economic privileges that regularly accrue to those who have worked to attain them.

The net result has been a significant economic loss as well as a human resource loss for the Kingdom as a whole and for the individual. Were one to assess the situation from a purely economic viewpoint, it could be suggested that the government might concede all clerical, craft, trade and similar skills to expatriates, encouraging the Saudis either to remain in agricultural pursuits, or to pursue professional skills.

The main problem is that the large working middle class that stands as a backbone of most developed societies have yet to emerge in Saudi Arabia, and it is not likely to develop until education is made compulsory at both the elementary and secondary levels and truancy laws are enforced.

Current statistics indicate that male Saudis now require an average of 11.34 years to complete 6 years of primary education and female students require an average of 8.67 years to complete their primary education.

Until all sectors of society, public and private, progress beyond the current practices of putting an immediate need for Saudis in the labor market ahead of the long-term educational development of the population, the problem is likely to persist. While the opening of new schools and the enrollment of new students is important, retention of these students in those schools is of equal importance to the overall development of Saudi Arabia's middle level manpower needs.

To overcome the problems involving public education, a number of companies in Saudi Arabia and the other Gulf States have developed elaborate programs for technical education. The most notable and lavish is the Aramco training program, designed to produce Saudi technicians. This program has been used as a model for similar programs in the region. The big push to localize the technical workforce came around 1980 stemming from the enormous expansion of Aramco's operations after the oil price rises. At that time the annual training budget totalled $636 million. It is now down to around $150 million a year and 5,000 trainees, selected on leaving school, have been through the program.

Aramco admits to the limitations of its program. Although all operators are now Saudi, most technicians are still expatriates and their jobs are filled by Saudis only as part of a natural fall-out. Despite careful screening there is at least a 20 per cent drop-out rate. Inevitably, there is competition from other industries, especially Jubail, in searching for the right candidates. Instilling a sense of discipline remains the hardest part of the program.

Training of locals is part of most industrial joint venture schemes in the Gulf, either in-house or outside, often at overseas institutions.

PROBLEMS FACED BY SAUDI WOMEN

One cannot discuss the economic development of Saudi Arabia and the Kingdom's manpower needs without discussing the subject, however controversial, of the role of Saudi women.

Today, Saudi women comprise one-third of the Kingdom's present university enrollments. The cost effectiveness of education for women can be severely challenged if the end product is never to find its way into the marketplace. At present there are a number of constraints against the employment of Saudi Women.[7]

(1) Most job opportunities for them are restricted to fields perceived to be in keeping with the traditional role of women as wives and mothers.

(2) Freedom of movement is restricted by the ban on women driving

and their need for male drivers to accompany them for business purposes. Public transportation for women does not exist.

(3) The paucity of child-care centers restricts the activities of those women who cannot afford live-in servants.

(4) Business initiatives are hampered by the inability of women to register a business in their own name, or obtain home loans or government land grants which might provide the wherewithal to establish a private business.

(5) A woman is prohibited from working if such work is contrary to the wishes of the male members of her family, upon whom she is dependent both socially and economically.

(6) The religious interpretations of some sectors of the society deem it inappropriate for women to work outside the home.

(7) Fear of the social stigma which may be attached to the working woman and/or her family, when suggestions are made relative to the family's economic status or the woman's morality is a further constraint on women working.

(8) The lack of incentives created by the relatively comfortable circumstances of much of the Kingdom's citizenry reduces the incentive for women to work. The same applies to the Islamic tradition which stipulates that the men of the family are responsible for the family's income.

(9) The inability of most working Saudi women to penetrate the decision-making process in the workforce has stifled women's opportunities.

(10) Decades of Saudi tradition which 'conditions' Saudi women to accept rather than challenge their role in life has been a subtle, but powerful, deterrent to the advancement of women's role in society.

Another important constraint which is extremely important in any developing nation striving for the enhancement of its human resources is the lack of women's networks, professional organizations or other such associations which could serve as catalysts for concerted action on the restrictions inhibiting women from entering the workforce and at the same time providing career counseling, management training, and other professional development opportunities for young Saudi women.

In most Arab countries work that is considered 'respectable' includes teaching, secretarial work and medicine. Even in Saudi Arabia, where attitudes toward women are the most conservative in the Arab World, efforts are made to create acceptable surroundings to facilitate their working.

The main conservative objection then is not to women's work but to their involvement in the public sphere. The fact that Gulf women's participation in the workforce is low shows that 'need' at the popular level is an important condition to be met before women are fully integrated into the modern sector.

Conservative attitudes are a factor, but not a primary one as some Gulf analysts are aware. It has been pointed out[8] that the number of Saudi women in the workforce does not reflect their numerical weight in the country. This cannot be ascribed to the fact that most women went into fields like education, medicine, and social welfare, since the government still had to depend on many foreign women for these skills. The reasons for the low numbers are more related to the fact that most women did not face an economic need to work.

It is interesting in this respect that in the 'poorest' Gulf states in per capita terms, Bahrain and Oman, there is a more positive attitude towards women's work, both at the government and popular levels. In Oman in particular the government is active in sponsoring seminaries and strives to encourage women's integration into the work force. In these countries the people need to earn more than one income per family, and the state cannot afford to finance the vast manpower imports of their neighbors.

In general it appears that cultural attitudes are not the major obstacle to women's integration into the labor force. Other factors are also important. These include: (a) the country's manpower situation, (b) the need for income at the family and individual level, (c) the encouragement provided by the state, and (d) the skills that job-seekers possess. If the conditions of need, opportunity and ability are met at the state and the popular levels, then women will be fully integrated into the workforce.

FUTURE TRENDS

Two future scenarios concerning migration to the Gulf can be suggested at this stage:[9]

(1) Further declines in oil prices may result in a new surge of foreign worker departures together with a slump in new work permit issues and the retention of only the most essential expatriate workers. However, local entrepreneurs, merchants and businessmen, whose interests are served by the expatriate communities' demands for consumer goods and housing, would resist the policy changes implied by this scenario.

(2) The patterns of migration will follow recent trends – the gradual decline in the number of expatriate workers is likely to continue, and may even stabilize, with a relatively low level of net labor outflows and a high rate of foreign labor retention. This will be accompanied by heightened foreign labor mobility within individual Gulf states. Immigrant communities themselves will supply an increasing proportion of new non-national labor market entrants as their demographic profiles mature, thus further reducing the level of new labor inflows.

Effectively, the Kingdom would repeat the experience of Western Europe where immigrant labor also proved exceptionally resilient. This was particularly the case after the first oil price shocks of 1973–74. Despite the recession and the closure of labor markets to the new foreign labor inflows,

> the number of Turkish *gastarbieter* in the Federal Republic of Germany increased from 590,000 (1974) to 623,900 (1980).

Regardless of which scenario holds, the government is likely to continue to favor arabization of the labor force. This is likely to be within the context of an overall reduction of the foreign population. This will be difficult to achieve, requiring considerable determination.

The private sector wishes to continue the option of mobilizing large numbers of cheap workers, usually of Asian origin. This approach tends to favor the arrival of non-national dependents, to bolster local consumption and trade. Increasing numbers of Saudi children will tend to stimulate short-term demand for foreign workers. Also, natural increase of the non-national communities will grow in importance.

The most likely scenario is one in which[10] Arabization will progress, especially of the public sector and professions, with the consequent tendency for dependent Arab populations to increase. Settlement of foreigners will be encouraged by the easing property market and landlords' desire for tenants. The process of arabization will occur in a labor market that contracts slightly for a few years, with some net re-exports of non-nationals, but which is then likely to grow again in the early 1990s, with a stable or increasing number of non-national workers.

Both the non-national and national populations will grow under these circumstances. While there is likely to be a significant increase in Saudi women in the labor force, there is unlikely to be a significant contraction of the foreign population. For a while, the shares of national and non-national populations are likely to remain constant. However, within the foreign population the share of Arabs will increase.

NOTES

1. Edmund O'Sullivan, 'Managing Gulf Economies', *Middle East Economic Digest* (27 January 1989), p.2.
2. Ibid.
3. Ibid., p.3.
4. Paul Stevens, 'The Impact of oil on the Role of the State in Economic Development', *Arab Affairs* (Summer 1986), pp.95–97.
5. Joy Winkie Viola, *Human Resources Development in Saudi Arabia: Multinationals and Saudization* (Boston: International Human Resources Development Corporation, 1986), pp.166–167.
6. Joy Winkie Viola, op.cit., pp.155–56.
7. Joy Winkie Viola, op.cit., pp.213–14.
8. Nadia Hijab, 'Arab Women at Work: A Checklist that Puts Culture into Perspective', *Arab Affairs* (Summer/Autumn 1987), pp.48–9.
9. Ibid.
10. Following J.S. Birks, 'The Demographic Challenge in the Arab Gulf,' *Arab Affairs* (Summer, 1986), p.81.

[18]

EMPLOYMENT IN SMALL-SCALE MANUFACTURING IN CAIRO: A SOCIO-ECONOMIC SURVEY

Günter Meyer

Editor's Note: *The author's own transliteration of Arabic names has been retained because of the technical difficulties that would have been faced in adjusting them to the* Bulletin's *system.*

i
Introduction

One of the major problems in the economic development of Third World countries is the low growth rate of the secondary sector. Since the number of jobs created in industry is insufficient to absorb the increasing urban labour force, the service sector is rapidly expanding, particularly in the large metropolitan areas. This general rule, however, cannot be applied to the Greater Cairo Region. Here the service sector lost almost 4 per cent of the share of total employment between 1960 and 1976. During the same period industry and construction were able to increase their share of the labour force from 25 to 34 per cent, with manufacturing alone accounting for 26 per cent of total employment in the Greater Cairo Region. The majority of these jobs in manufacturing (55%) were supplied by private sector firms with an average work force of around five (GOPP, 1983: 1.15–16). Compared with the national total, Cairo accommodated 50 per cent of private manufacturing employment and about 61 per cent of the nation's artisans (PADCO, 1981: 156). Thus, small private manufacturing is not only centred in Cairo, but within the city it is the largest source of industrial employment.

Since the late 1970s the rate of increase in the number of small-scale manufacturing establishments has accelerated in an unprecedented manner. The economic liberalization under the Open Door Policy (*infitāḥ*) and the general rise in demand, due to the massive influx of remittances from Egyptians working abroad, presented quite favourable sales conditions for small enterprises. In the lower-class quarters of Cairo, in particular, the number of workshops producing basic consumer goods for the local population has risen dramatically. So far, however, neither the extent of this development, nor the socio-economic situation of the labour force employed in this expanding sector of the metropolitan economy is known. What is the structure of the small-scale manufacturing enterprises? How is their labour force composed as regards social relations, age, origin, and place of residence? To what degree do the workers participate in international labour migration and what is its impact on the development of small-scale manufacturing? In order to find answers to these questions a socio-economic survey of small-scale manufacturing enterprises in Cairo was carried out by the author.

ii
Empirical Survey and Data Base

Since only a limited number of manufacturing firms could be included in the survey, six popular quarters with a relatively high concentration of workshops were selected as test areas. Two of these areas were situated in the centre of the Egyptian metropolis, i.e. in the northern and north-eastern part of medieval Cairo, whereas the four sample areas were spread over peripheral regions of Cairo, which had been settled mainly between 1960 and 1977 (cf. Fig. 1). The

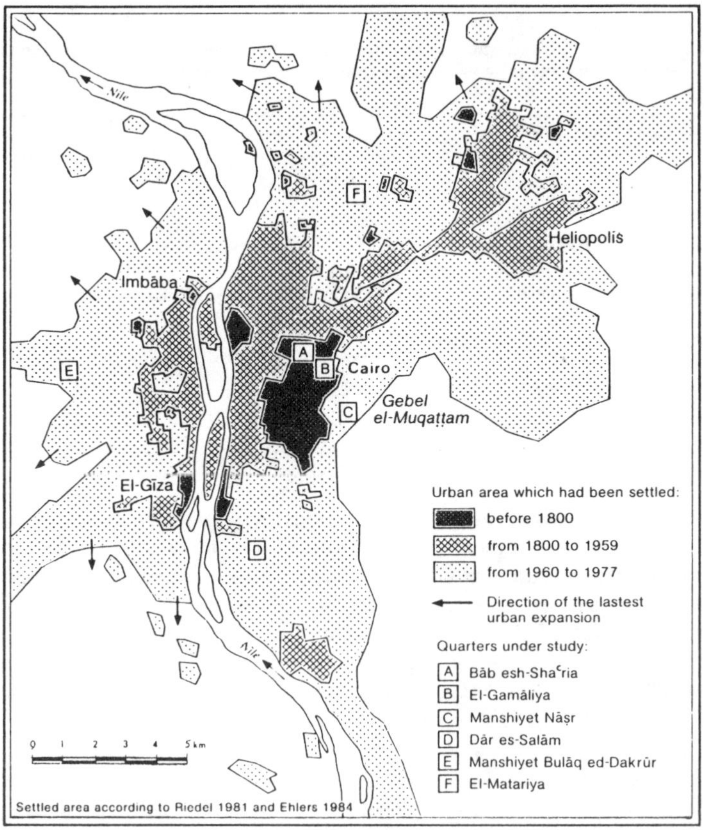

Figure 1. Position of selected quarters in Greater Cairo which were included in the survey on small-scale manufacturing enterprises

selected quarters covered areas of about 7–8 ha in the central parts of Cairo and of 30–45 ha on the periphery. All manufacturing enterprises in the sample areas and the labour force working in those firms were included in the survey, which was carried out between September 1985 and April 1986. During that time the author was able to interview 4,749 owners and employees of 1,149 manufacturing enterprises about the development, structure, and economic situation of the firms under study and about the socio-economic background of the labour force. Some of the general findings are presented in the following sections.

iii
Structure of the Manufacturing Enterprises

The vast majority of the enterprises covered by the survey are engaged in the production of basic consumer goods as Table 1 shows. The leading branch is

Table 1. Percentage of manufacturing enterprises, labour force, and average number of employed persons per enterprise according to manufacturing branches.

Manufacturing branch	Percentage of		Average number of employees
	enterprises (n = 1149)	labour force (n = 4749)	
Furniture	27.3	24.7	3.7
Shoes, leather products	18.1	17.7	4.0
Textiles, garments	15.1	9.0	2.4
Kitchen utensils of aluminium	9.8	13.6	5.6
Other houseware items	14.5	15.3	4.3
Construction materials and components	8.3	7.3	3.6
Bread, cake, sweets	4.0	9.9	10.3
Paper, printing, stationary	2.6	2.1	3.3
Others	0.3	0.4	5.0
Total	100.0	100.0	4.1

furniture-making, which accounts for about one quarter of the investigated firms and their labour force. These workshops, like most of the other branches of manufacturing industry which were investigated, are evenly distributed over the sample areas, whereas the production of shoes is concentrated in the quarter of Bāb esh-Sha'ria. In this ancient part of Cairo almost one out of two craftsmen makes shoes, which are mainly sold to retail shops in the central business district. Another important concentration of a specific manufacturing branch is to be found in El-Gamāliya. There the aluminium industry, which produces plates and pots not only for local demand but also for the whole Egyptian market, supplies about 40 per cent of total employment in manufacturing. Besides the dominant production of simple consumer goods, the manufacture of construction materials like tiles, and of building components such as doors and windows should also be mentioned. The firms in this manufacturing branch provide jobs for about 7 per cent of the studied labour force.

Most of the manufacturing enterprises are very young: two-thirds of them have been founded since 1980, and about 40 per cent had been in existence for less than two years at the time of the survey. Such figures indicate the dramatic expansion of the private manufacturing sector which has been taking place in recent years. This development is by no means confined to the newly-settled, peripheral quarters of Cairo, but is also to be found in the ancient parts of the metropolis as the age-lines for the enterprises in Bāb esh-Sha'ria and El-Gamāliya clearly demonstrate (Fig. 2). In Bāb esh-Sha'ria, for example,

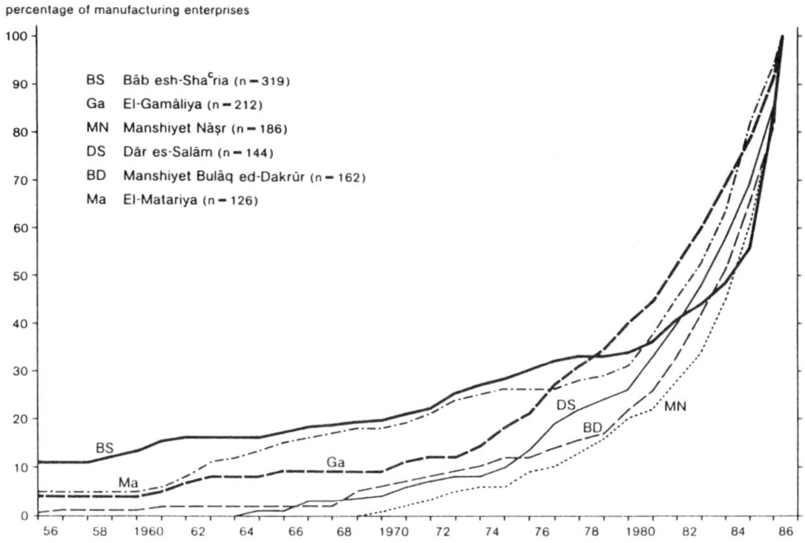

Figure 2. Age of the small-scale manufacturing enterprises

which is one of the most crowded and densely populated quarters of Cairo with more than 1,000 inhabitants per ha, the creation of additional space for workshops was made possible by the demolition of old residential houses and the construction of new multi-storied manufacturing centres. In the largest private building of this kind 63 workshops were accommodated.

As was described in numerous reports by the International Labour Organisation dealing with the 'informal sector' in developing countries (cf. Sethuraman, 1981), most small-scale manufacturing enterprises in Cairo are characterized by the application of very labour-intensive production methods, relatively low value-added per worker and consequently low labour productivity. In 58 per cent of all investigated cases the total value of equipment and machinery in the workshops was less than 1,000 Egyptian pounds. On the other hand, a considerable number of small workshops were encountered which did not fit at all into the conventional picture of informal-sector enterprises: they were equipped with very expensive and sophisticated machinery, often operated by highly skilled technicians and engineers.

If we look at the size of the manufacturing enterprises, relatively wide differences can be observed (Table 1 and Fig. 3). The average number of

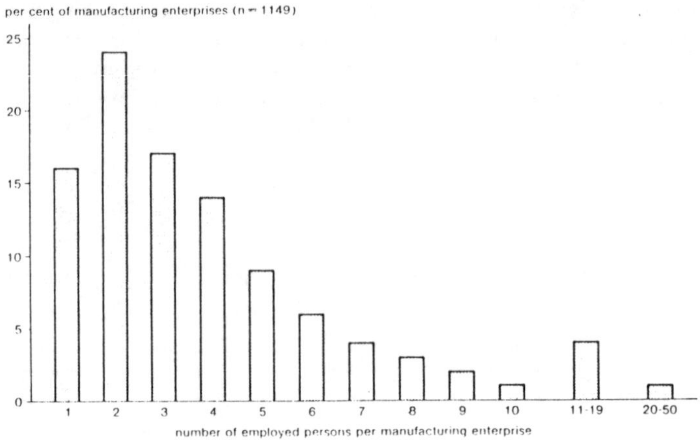

Figure 3. Number of persons working in the small-scale manufacturing enterprises

persons working in the selected firms is 4.1, and 80 per cent of the enterprises employ between one and five persons; but there are also 13 comparatively large firms with 20–50 workers. The highest average number of about ten labourers was found in the bakeries, most of which work two shifts per day. At the other end of the spectrum there are the small tailors' workshops, in which the average number of employees amounts to only 2.4.

iv
Composition of the Labour Force

A characteristic feature of the employment structure in small-scale manufacturing is the close social ties between the people working in the same enterprise. More than 50 per cent of the labour force under study is composed of the owners of the manufacturing firms, their family members, and their relatives (Fig. 4). In contrast with the mainly unpaid family members, nearly

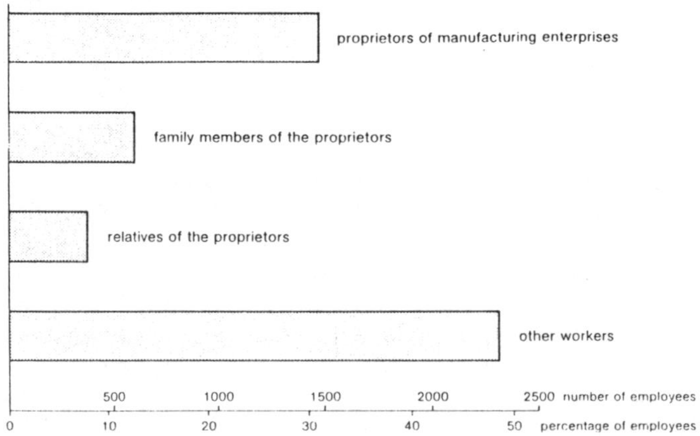

Figure 4. Employment structure of the small-scale manufacturing enterprises

all relatives of the firms' proprietors receive the same wages as other labourers who lack close social connections with their employers.

The age of the labour force of the investigated enterprises is in general relatively low. Almost every second worker is less than 25 years old. As regards the proprietors of firms, most of them are in their thirties (Fig. 5). The

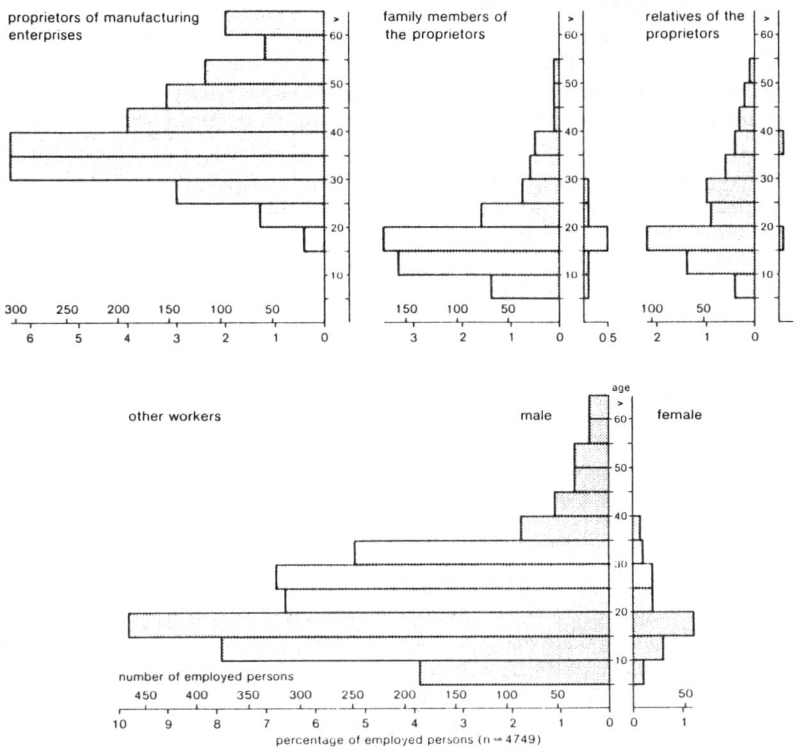

Figure 5. Age structure of the persons working in the small-scale manufacturing enterprises

majority of the family members and relatives of the owners of manufacturing firms are below 20 years of age. Among the other workers the age group of 20–24 years is significantly underrepresented because a large proportion of young men of this age are serving as conscripts in the armed forces. It is quite common, however, for many of those soldiers to try to raise their scanty service pay by working in manufacturing enterprises whenever they are on leave, particularly during evening hours and at week-ends.

Another important group of the labour force consists of children. Almost one out of five workers was less than 15 years old, and 6 per cent had not even reached the age of 10. As child-labour at that age is officially prohibited, the young boys are not referred to as 'workers', but as 'helpers', which in practice makes little difference, except for the lower wages. This problem is extremely acute in the aluminium industry, where the share of boys below 15 years of age has reached a record 34 per cent, while the proportion of children between 5 and 9 years amounts to 12 per cent of total employment. It is not uncommon for such children to work up to eight hours in the aluminium workshops. Although the tasks they perform are very simple, the working conditions are terrible: hours and hours spent in workshops where one can hardly breathe because the air is filled with grey aluminium dust, where the ears are harassed by the tremendous noise of the machines, and where one is constantly threatened with injury from the rotating parts of the lathes—such working conditions are almost unbearable for adults and completely intolerable for children.

Finally, the female part of the labour force has to be mentioned. In general, women play only a minor role among the employees of the manufacturing enterprises and account for no more than 3 per cent of total employment. Their main area of work is tailoring, where they represent about a quarter of the labour force. It is characteristic that the vast majority of the female workers are girls or young unmarried women. Most of them stop working as soon as they get married.

V
Origin and Migration of the Labour Force

According to the population census of 1976 about 73 per cent of Cairo's inhabitants were born in the Egyptian capital, and 17 per cent had moved from other cities to the metropolis. Only 10 per cent of the inhabitants were rural-urban migrants (CAPMAS, 1980, p. 220). For the labour force of the small-scale manufacturing enterprises the results are rather different as Fig. 6 shows. Among the workers in the ancient quarters of Cairo rural-urban migration (8%) is less important than among the total metropolitan population, and immigration from other urban centres is completely negligible. Instead, the vast majority of the labour force was born in the quarter of employment or in neighbouring parts of ancient Cairo. In the peripheral quarters of the capital, however, rural-urban migrants are widely over-represented: they account for nearly one-third of total employment in the studied enterprises.

By far the largest group of workers originating from rural areas is to be found in the bakeries. This branch of small-scale manufacturing is almost entirely the domain of rural migrants: 86 per cent of the labour force in the investigated bakeries were born in rural parts of Egypt. Most of them came from a few villages in the governorate of Assiut. We are here confronted with

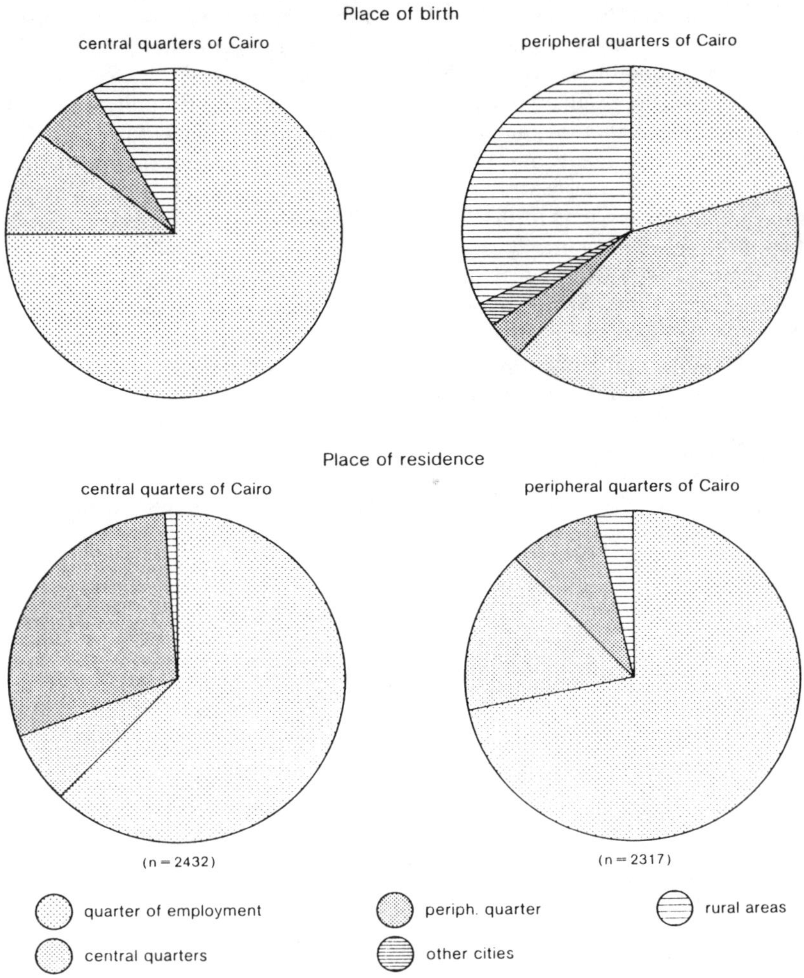

Figure 6. Place of birth and place of residence of persons working in small-scale manufacturing establishments in central and peripheral quarters of Cairo

another example of 'chain-migration', resulting in a massive concentration of rural migrants from the same place of origin in specific branches of the metropolitan economy (cf. Meyer, 1980 and 1987).

If we look at the residential areas of the labour force (lower half of Fig. 6), it becomes obvious that the majority of the employees live in close proximity to their place of work. Daily and weekly commuters from outside Cairo are very rare, particularly in the central parts of the capital. Instead, a considerable proportion of the workers in the ancient parts of Cairo (30%) commute daily between their dwellings on the periphery of the metropolis and their centrally situated workshops. Many of them live in the recently constructed residential quarter of Madīnat es-Salām, a vast public housing area situated about 21 km north-east of the ancient parts of Cairo. This means that the commuters have to spend an average of two hours every day in overcrowded buses to reach their place of work and to return home.

The dominant pattern of life-time migration among the people engaged in small-scale manufacturing is the move from the place of birth in the ancient overpopulated neighbourhoods of central Cairo to new residential quarters on the periphery (Fig. 7). As it is very difficult for young couples with a low

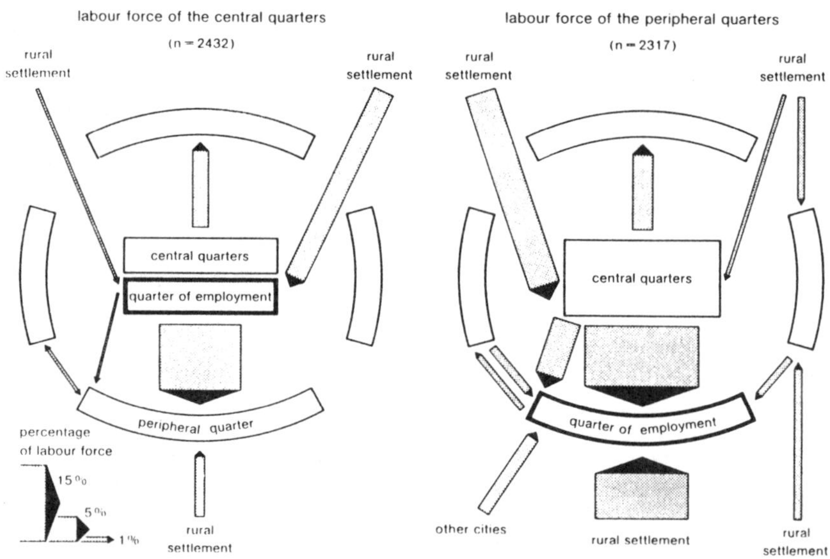

Figure 7. Migration patterns of the labour force in the central and peripheral quarters of Cairo

income to find an accommodation of their own in the ancient parts of the capital, most of them are forced to look for a rented apartment in one of the large public housing-blocks on the outskirts of the metropolis. Thus the typical male intra-urban migrant is between 23 and 28 years of age and just getting married when he moves out from the centre to the outskirts of Cairo. This migration pattern could be observed not only among the labour force which has been able to find employment in the manufacturing enterprises of the new quarters, but also among the workers in the ancient neighbourhoods who kept their former jobs in the central quarters in spite of their change of residence.

vi
The Importance of Temporary Labour Emigration

In addition to internal migration, a significant proportion of the labour force in the small-scale manufacturing enterprises has also participated in temporary labour emigration to other Arab countries with higher wage levels. Altogether 12 per cent of the interviewed employees had worked abroad at least once. At first sight the low rate of former migrants seems to indicate that labour emigration is only of minor importance in this sector of the metropolitan economy. However, if the data for the proprietors of manufacturing firms are viewed separately, the impact of labour emigration turns out to be much greater, since one out of four owners of the studied enterprises had worked abroad. The highest share in this respect was observed among the owners of shoe-producing firms: in that group the rate of former participation in labour emigration reached a record 37 per cent. Such a high rate can be explained primarily by the existence of a well-established private network via which workers from the shoe-producing center of Bāb esh-Sha'ria are channelled to shoe-making enterprises in Al-Rashīd Street in Baghdad.

It is characteristic that the highest propensity to take up work abroad is to be found among the better qualified sections of the labour market. This tendency becomes very obvious, if we compare the diagrams in Fig. 8: the ratio

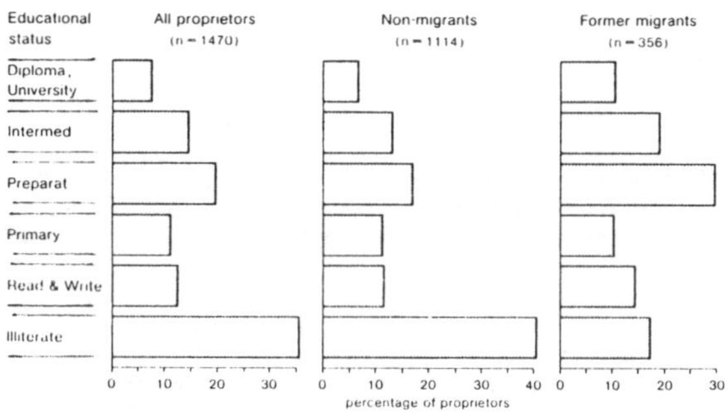

Figure 8 Educational status of proprietors of manufacturing enterprises according to former participation in labour emigration

of illiteracy is much lower and the proportion of owners of manufacturing firms who had been at least to a preparatory school or even graduated from a university is considerably higher among former labour emigrants than among those who had not been abroad. This result confirms the general observation by Birks and Sinclair (1980: 95) that in Egypt 'skilled good-quality workmen with formal qualifications for job-related training' are more than other occupational groups inclined to migrate internationally.

Finally, the question about the direct impact of labour emigration on the recent expansion of small-scale manufacturing has to be answered. To what degree did returning migrants use their savings from abroad to set up new workshops or to buy modern machinery? The results of the survey show that 35 per cent of the proprietors of manufacturing enterprises who were former labour emigrants had used their remittances as the main source of capital to establish a new workshop of their own. It was also evident that a large proportion of workshops which were equipped with the most advanced machinery belonged to returning migrants. Thus remittances are not only fuelling the demand for consumer goods, but are also providing the means for the creation of new enterprises in which those consumer goods are being produced.

References

Birks, J.S. and Sinclair, C.A. (1980), *International Migration and Development in the Arab Region* (Geneva, International Labour Office).

Central Agency for Public Mobilisation and Statistics (CAPMAS) (1980), *1976 Population and Housing Census, Fertility and Internal Migration and Movement of Workers and Students* (Cairo).

Ehlers, E. (1984), 'Ägypten—Zur Urbanisierung einer agraren Gesellschaft', *Geographische Rundschau*, Vol. 36. pp. 220–228.

General Organization for Physical Planning (GOPP) *et al.* (1983), *Greater Cairo Region Long Range Urban Development Scheme, Master Scheme* (Cairo).

Meyer, G. (1980), 'Die Zuwanderung aus den ägyptischen Oasen nach Kairo—zur räumlichen und beruflichen Integration von Fellachen in die Stadt', *Der Islam*, Vol. 57. pp. 36–50.

Meyer G. (1987), 'Waste-recycling as a livelihood in the informal sector—the example of refuse collectors in Cairo', *Applied Geography and Development* (in the press).

PADCO, Inc. *et. al.* (1981), *Working Paper on First Round Alternatives for the National Urban Policy Study*, Vol. II, Cairo concept plan (Cairo).

Sethuraman, S.V. (1981), *The Urban Informal Sector in Developing Countries—Employment, Poverty and Environment* (Geneva, International Labour Office).

Acknowledgements

I should like to thank Professor Dr Nabeel Embabi from the Department of Geography at the Ain Shams University in Cairo for his support of my survey in Egypt by providing me with a research permit. I would also like to thank the German Research Foundation for supporting my fieldwork in Cairo by means of a travel grant.

... ...

The foregoing paper was presented at the Fourteenth Annual Conference of the Society, held at the University of Exeter, 12–15 July 1987.

[19]

Int. J. Middle East Stud. 14 (1982), 159–171 *Printed in the United States of America*

Donald C. Mead

SMALL INDUSTRIES IN EGYPT: AN EXPLORATION OF THE ECONOMICS OF SMALL FURNITURE PRODUCERS

I. INTRODUCTION

In the analysis of the transition from low-income, rural-centered, capital-poor countries to modern, capital-rich, urbanized nations, small enterprises have received increasing attention in recent years. In rural areas, there is a belated recognition of the importance of nonfarm enterprises as supplementary sources of income and employment in village households. In towns and cities, there has been an explosion of interest in small producers, including but not limited to the so-called urban informal sector.[1]

This discussion of small enterprises has been characterized by strongly held and often conflicting opinions and evaluations. The sector has been praised by some as a training ground for entrepreneurs and as an experimental arena for the development of intermediate technology which may be both efficient and capital-saving. With relatively few restrictions or barriers to entry, anyone with a small amount of capital and some skills can start a business of his own, expanding as he overcomes production problems, uncovers markets, and determines which product types provide him with the best returns for his efforts. In this way, small firms have provided a source of income for large numbers of people who would otherwise have only low productivity in agriculture, but for whom modern, capital-intensive sectors do not generate adequate employment opportunities.

The very listing of the potential advantages of small producers raises questions about their limitations and disadvantages. The characteristics of easy access, freedom of entry, and low capital use per worker may result in stiff competition and low income to producers and workers alike. The very smallness of the individual enterprise may limit the potential for specialization, either within or between firms, thereby ruling out one of the major factors contributing to falling costs and rising incomes. Limited or negligible use of machinery may mean that small producers find it difficult to compete with larger, more modern, and mechanized firms. Squeezed by competition from modern, large-scale producers on one hand, and from large numbers of small firms on the other, individual small producers may find returns pushed down to unacceptably low levels. In this situation, efforts by governments to sustain the income of small producers may be justifiable as welfare payments, but the economics of the situation may imply that such efforts are attempting to swim against a strong and irreversible tide. Primary attention should then be given to speeding and facilitating the necessary transition by helping people move out of the small enterprise sector (although it is not clear what alternatives they would be moving to).

If small enterprises have been alternatively praised and condemned by scholars seeking to understand the development process, they have been generally ignored by statistical offices. It is difficult to collect comprehensive data about small producers. There are many such enterprises, and their numbers change quickly as existing firms go out of business and new ones are formed. Small firms generally have irregular input patterns, variable product quality and types, and are often managed by operators who have little facility for or interest in record keeping. All of these characteristics make data collection extremely difficult. The result is that policy is often made on the basis of inadequate information about what small firms are doing and what their needs are. To make matters worse, policies introduced in support of other sectors often operate unwittingly to the detriment of small producers, discriminating against them compared to their larger, more influential and better informed neighbors with regard to the availability and cost of credit, raw materials, and a variety of government support facilities.

This paper examines the validity of these alternative contentions through an exploration of small-scale furniture producers in Egypt. Section 2 presents background information concerning the small-scale industry sector as a whole in that country. Section 3 provides a more detailed examination of Egyptian furniture producers. Section 4 presents interpretations and generalizations concerning the present state and future prospects for these producers.

2. SMALL INDUSTRY IN EGYPT: AN OVERVIEW

Information about the activities of small enterprises in Egypt is relatively comprehensive, at least in terms of aggregative measures, although by now it is seriously out of date. The Census of Industrial Production of 1966/67 collected information concerning output, employment, capital stock, and value added in all industrial establishments, large as well as small; the results have been published, at a three-digit industrial breakdown, with separate figures for enterprises of different size.[2] The results of the survey show that, at that time, approximately one third of all manufacturing employment was in enterprises with less than ten workers (see table 1). This ratio becomes more striking if we exclude public sector enterprises, most of which are very large firms. In the private sector taken by itself, over 70 percent of all manufacturing employment was in enterprises with from one to nine workers.

These very small establishments produced a wide variety of products. Table 1 shows the most important components. As the table indicates, the majority of workers in very small establishments are engaged in producing basic consumer goods. In the case of clothing, shoes and furniture, the largest share of the total supply in the domestic market comes from these small producers. There are a number of other products (e.g., bread, cloth) for which small producers are an important supplementary source of supply,

TABLE 1 *Employment, selected industrial subsectors, 1966/1967 (in thousands)*

Products	Private sector small enterprises (1-9 workers) (1)	Private sector large enterprises (10+ workers) (2)	Public sector (all large) (3)	Total, large enterprises (2+3) (4)	Total, all enterprises (1+4) (5)
Clothes & garments	64	3	1	3	67
Furniture & fixtures	28	4	5	9	37
Metal products	28	11	15	25	53
Spinning, weaving	21	25	209	235	256
Shoes	19	4	2	6	25
Bakeries	14	19	5	25	39
Grain milling	14	1	14	15	29
Subtotal	188	67	251	318	506
All other subsectors	96	59	226	285	381
Grand total	284	126	477	603	887

Note: Totals may not add due to rounding. All subsectors providing as much as 5 percent of total employment in small enterprises are shown separately.

Sources: Census of Industrial Production [alternate translation of title: Data on Industrial Production], *1966/67*, Vol. 1 (April 1970) and Vol. 2 (April 1971).

even though the majority of the products in the local market come either from imports or from large-scale domestic producers. Particularly for lower-income people, small enterprises are important not only as sources of wages and employment but also as a major source of supply for products on which they spend their income.

There are no comprehensive data concerning trends in output or employment in small enterprises since 1967. A survey of small producers was undertaken in 1974, and while the results are interesting and informative, they are not comparable to the earlier census.[3] A subsequent study by the World Bank estimated that employment in small establishments had risen from 284,000 in 1967 to 330,000 in 1974; but the empirical basis for that estimate is uncertain, to say the least.[4] Discussion with a variety of officials suggests that employment in small enterprises has increased since 1967; the precise magnitude of the increase is not known.[5]

3. THE FURNITURE INDUSTRY

As indicated in the table, producers of furniture comprise one of the largest subsectors among small enterprises. The 1974 survey found 19,265 small furniture and woodworking establishments in Egypt in that year, employing over 35,000 persons. Employment in larger woodworking establishments (ten or more employees) at that time may have been about 10,000 workers. Thus, employment in furniture production is overwhelmingly dominated by small establishments.

What follows is an exploration of patterns of production and resource use among these small furniture producers. In addition to published and unpublished written materials about the sector, the analysis is based on interviews and discussions with some 50 woodworking establishments in Cairo and Alexandria. A brief questionnaire was completed for 25 of these establishments. For comparative purposes, visits were also made to several large furniture manufacturers, in order to be able to provide contrasts between the small enterprises and their larger competitors.

Output

Products made in the sector are highly diverse: coathangers and deck chairs, picture frames and wooden paddles for putting bread into ovens. Carpenters engaged in construction activities were excluded from the study. The great majority of establishments are engaged in producing basic furniture: dining rooms, bedrooms, and "salons" (living rooms). While it is possible to buy a couch or a dining room table separately, the products are generally sold as sets, or complete rooms. The analysis of this paper is concerned only with the production of furniture.

Inputs: Capital

Machinery use in small furniture enterprises is extremely low. In the 1974 survey, the average capital stock per worker in all woodworking establishments was 50 Egyptian pounds (hereafter, LE 50).[6] This may be compared with an estimate of capital stock per worker in all manufacturing firms in 1967 of over LE 800.[7] Alternatively, in 1976, capital stock per worker in all public sector enterprises in the food, textiles, chemicals, and metals industries averaged LE 1,466.[8] In two large and modern furniture factories visited, current book value of machinery averaged just under LE 3,000 per worker. The contrast with small firms is striking.

Even this low average figure for small furniture enterprises is in some ways a misleading one. An average for all firms in the sector, it suffers from the usual inadequacies of averages. Among the 25 firms for which a questionnaire was completed for this study, 22 had no power machinery at all in their work place. These small producers without machines of their own do not rely solely on hand tools. Scattered throughout the city are numerous small machinery workshops, some with only one or two machines, others with six or eight. Small unmechanized carpentry workshops make heavy use of these service centers; they mark the pieces of wood, then transport them by bicycle, by taxi, or by hand to the mechanical workshops where they pay a negotiated price for a particular cut, a particular shaping or planing. The service centers are privately owned, are extremely busy, and have modern and well-maintained machines.

The result is that although the average capital stock per worker among small carpentry shops is very low, the machinery is efficiently and continuously in use.

Skilled carpenters know which things are best done mechanically, and have ready access to the necessary machinery, even if they do not own the machines themselves. The situation provides a clear contrast with the larger producers, who generally have a range of modern machines on their own premises, but with only a few of these in use at any point in time.[9]

Inputs: Labor

There are several aspects of labor use in small enterprises which are of interest. In the 25 enterprises for which detailed data were collected, nearly a third of all workers were trainees. These are young boys who are paid a salary generally between LE 3 and LE 4 per (six-day) week. The trainees do all kinds of odd jobs around the shop: carrying, holding, fetching, cleaning up; in the process, they learn about the furniture business. A number of skilled workers indicated with some pride that they had started out as trainees, often in the same workshop where they are currently employed.

There is apparently little uniformity in the treatment of these trainees. The apprenticeship period can last anywhere from a few months to a few years, depending on the abilities of the learner and the teacher, the needs of the employer for another semiskilled worker, and the personal relationships between the people involved.

One of the questions asked in the questionnaire concerned the number of trainees employed five years earlier, and their wage rates then. The answers suggest that over that period wages paid to trainees rose by a factor of more than four (i.e., there was a 350 percent increase). During that time, the urban consumer price index may have risen by some 70 percent; real wages of trainees more than doubled. The supply of trainees, on the other hand, was contracting. Reported numbers in May 1979 were only about two-thirds of employment levels recalled for five years earlier. The explanation given was that young people are much less interested today in becoming apprentices, having set their sights on more formal education. Workshop owners complained about problems of finding trainees, in spite of the sharp increase in pay. Numbers reportedly go up during school vacation periods, but during the school year they are hard to find.

Turning to the rest of the labor force, it is clear that it is made up primarily of skilled workers. Among the 25 enterprises for which detailed data were collected, the average daily wage rate for all workers (excluding apprentices) was LE 3.72 per day; 56 percent earned LE 4 or more per day. For comparative purposes, a university graduate starting work in the civil service currently earns LE 30 per month. Judging from their wage rates, less than 25 percent of the labor force in small furniture workshops might be considered as semiskilled (earning less than LE 3 per day); virtually none were unskilled. These figures contrast sharply with the large-scale furniture factories visited, where semiskilled and unskilled workers (once again, excluding trainees) constituted between 60 percent and 70 percent of the total production labor force.

Wage rates for skilled workers in small enterprises have also been rising, although not as rapidly as for the trainees; based on employers' recollections of wage rates five years earlier, the average increase was 140 percent, approximately twice the increase in the consumer price index. With regard to changing levels of employment, 22 of the 25 polled firms had been in business five years earlier; for these firms taken together, employment in 1979 was precisely half what it had been five years earlier.[10] The explanations given for this decline were two: large numbers of skilled workers have left the country to find better-paying employment in other Arab countries; and (much less frequently reported) some workers have gone into business for themselves. Once again, the picture is one of an overall shortage of workers, this time due primarily to emigration of many of the most highly skilled workers. Employers look for ways of replacing those who leave, but with only limited success. Those who return from overseas—and increasing numbers are reported to be returning—often have enhanced skills as well as some savings; they are not inclined to go to work as employees, but rather prefer to go into business for themselves.

These findings are consistent with the overall picture that emerges in other studies of the Egyptian labor market in recent years. In the aggregate, growth in employment has lagged far behind the increase in the labor force; Egypt is still in an important sense a labor-surplus country. But occupational and career choices have matched very poorly the patterns of expanding demand, with the result that there are clear labor shortages in a variety of occupational as well as geographical areas. Wage rates have increased sharply for unskilled laborers in both urban and rural districts, as the spread of schooling has left fewer people ready to undertake these jobs; and in a variety of occupations requiring particular vocational skills (e.g., carpentry, plumbing, bricklaying), wage rates have risen sharply in real terms. There continues to be a large and increasing surplus of general, all-purpose preparatory school, secondary school, and university graduates, at the same time that other occupations—both skilled and unskilled—show clear signs of labor shortage, either because people are no longer willing to work in those lines at wage rates offered or because there are not people with the requisite skills.

Specialization by activity

In the discussion of capital use among small furniture producers, the point was made that there is considerable specialization in the sense that wood parts are often transported to the machines for sawing and shaping in mechanical workshops. To some extent, the same thing happens for specialized labor skills. Makers of chairs will send a partially completed product to another workshop for carving, paying a fee for this service. Polishing of wood or caning of seats may be handled the same way.

A more general form of specialization is reflected in an active market for parts or products at any of a variety of stages of completion. One can buy chair legs, finished but unassembled; one can buy chairs completed except that they have no seat in them (caned or upholstered); one can buy chairs which are complete, but with the wood unfinished ("white"). There is specialization among producers, and a ready market for the products, both for manufacturers and consumers, at each of these stages. A consumer can buy an unfinished chair, pay one man to upholster it and another to finish and polish the wood; or an entrepreneur may buy furniture in the white stage, polish it, and resell it finished. Extensive furniture production takes place in one of the governorates 200 kilometers north of Cairo, with the products transported to Cairo in the white stage for finishing and sale there. There exists a ready market particularly for the lowest-cost furniture, for white products, which a low-income consumer can either use as is, finish himself, or pay a less-skilled worker (perhaps in his village) to stain and polish for him.

Specialization by product

One of the characteristics of furniture is its highly differentiated nature. In part, this reflects the fact of continuously variable quality; if one is willing to pay a bit more, one can get a product with more skilled labor embodied in it, produced more carefully and with greater precision. In part, the product differentiation has to do with styles: ornate or straight, modern or traditional.

Different products are sold in different markets; they are also produced in different types of firms. At the low end of the price and quality scale, small producers generally have the market to themselves. As suggested above, these low-cost products are often sold in an unfinished (white) stage. The raw materials used are of low and sometimes irregular quality, which makes them unsuitable for use in standardized, mechanized production lines, but which also lowers their cost. Machine work is limited, the workers are less skilled (and therefore less well paid) than those producing higher quality products, and each product uses fewer labor hours for its production. No large-scale mechanized producer has yet succeeded in manufacturing these low-cost, low-quality products at prices that can compete with the output of the very small producers.

At the opposite end of the quality range, the product is often delicately carved or otherwise elaborately finished. Only the best quality raw materials and fittings are used. Small workshops may have individual skilled craftsmen of requisite abilities, but generally they do not have the range of specializations as well as the specialized machines needed to produce this very best quality output. The top of the line generally comes from intermediate-sized establishments, which combine considerable machinery with a number of highly skilled craftsmen with a diverse range of skills.

In the intermediate-quality range, competition in the market exists between two different types of products: the more traditional embellished furniture, with its carving, gilding, and fancy finishes; and the modern furniture, with its simple straight lines. The latter type of product is currently being produced by both large and small producers, although the larger, more highly mechanized enterprises are rapidly increasing their share of this market. The more traditional furniture, on the other hand, uses considerable skilled labor, but not the diversity of very highly skilled workers which the top-of-the-line products require; on the other hand, it is less dependent on machinery, either for repetitive, standardized processing (as is used in the middle range modern furniture) or for the specialized drying and pressing machines needed for the top quality products. To date, this medium-price traditional furniture is firmly under the control of the small producers; the larger enterprises have made only limited inroads into the manufacture of these traditionally styled products.

4. SMALL FURNITURE PRODUCERS: AN EVALUATION

Based on this description of patterns of production among small furniture producers in Egypt, it is possible to comment on the alternative perceptions of the strengths and weaknesses of small enterprises discussed at the beginning of this paper. The discussion is presented under four headings: factor proportions; specialization; incomes; and future prospects.

Factor proportions

If capital is measured in terms of machines only, then small furniture producers are characterized by very low average capital use per worker, as expected. In an important sense, though, this is too narrow a view. From a broader perspective, one can say that both small and large furniture enterprises use considerable amounts of capital in the production process. In small workshops, this capital is embodied in skilled workers, whose role is central to the technology used. For the larger enterprises, by contrast, the capital primarily takes the form of machinery, combined with a much less highly skilled labor force.

The distinction between these two types of capital is significant for a variety of reasons. In one case, capital formation takes place through training, often on-the-job training. While "investment" is taking place in the economy, the corresponding "saving" has no financial dimension, and in fact can be thought of as saving only in a forced kind of national income accounting sense; it may be that no one is in fact holding back on current consumption in order to be able to enjoy higher levels of consumption in the future, a key characteristic of the normal concept of saving. Furthermore, access to this type of capital formation is far less restricted. The opportunity to participate in "investment in people" (in particular, one's self) is available not only to those who already have money or who have access to financial institutions willing to lend it; it is open to any who can acquire the requisite skills, either by enrolling in one of the government-run vocational training programs or by working as a trainee in an existing workshop. As indicated above, there are plentiful opportunities to do this. Finally, the difference in import coefficients of the two types of capital is significant. The machinery is virtually all purchased from abroad, while the training process has a negligible import component. For a country with large and continuing balance of payments problems, the difference is important.

Specialization

The idea that small firms have higher costs since they are not big enough to permit specialization within the production process is not supported by this study. On the contrary, even the smallest firms have often been able to attain a high degree of specialization, concentrating on only one or a few steps in the production process. They may buy semifinished inputs, selling their output after one further stage of processing; they may undertake a certain step in the production process, working for others on a contract basis; or they may send out their goods-in-process to other workshops for such jobs as sawing and carving. With this tightly woven set of market interrelationships, smallness of size has not proven a barrier to a high degree of specialization.

Incomes

The generalizations most often heard about small producers indicate that ease of entry results in much competition with other small producers, while primitive technology in use among small producers makes it difficult for them to compete with modern, large-scale factories. These generalizations clearly do not apply to small furniture producers. For the most part, incomes of producers and workers in the sector have been high and rising. In large measure, this reflects the shortage of workers who either have or are interested in obtaining the requisite skills. One way of expressing this is in terms of the point made above with regard to capital use. With demand pressing hard on capacity in recent years, capital is earning good returns both among large and small producers. In one case, these returns take the form of high wages for skilled workers, while in the other case it is the owners of the enterprise who are earning high returns. In both cases, incomes seem to be more than satisfactory.

Future prospects

There are a number of factors which will determine the future outlook of small furniture producers. On the demand side, three considerations have an important role to play: the growth in total demand for furniture products, the distribution of income among different groups, and changing patterns of taste. On the first of these, the overall demand for furniture products rises as a result of population growth (currently about 2 percent p.a.) as well as increases in real income per capita. Income elasticity of demand for furniture is high in Egypt today, probably over 2 in the aggregate; as people get richer, the proportion of their income spent on furniture increases markedly.[11] Of equal importance to the growth in aggregate income is the distribution of this increase among different groups in the society. As indicated above, the highest cost, highest quality furniture is produced primarily by middle-sized, skill-intensive, selectively mechanized enterprises; the lowest cost products, by contrast, which are consumed by the poorer groups in the country, are made predominantly in very small, essentially unmechanized establishments. For the intermediate-priced products purchased by middle-income consumers, the market is shared among a variety of different types of producers ranging from small workshops with one or two skilled workers and no machines to the large mechanized establishments relying heavily on semiskilled and unskilled workers. Egyptian leaders have often talked in recent years about the need to ensure that a major part of increases in national income will be captured by lowest-income people; whether this result will in fact emerge from the current economic policies is problematical.

The third major influence on demand concerns changing patterns of taste among different types of furniture products. This question is particularly important for the medium-priced furniture, where widely differing furniture styles—produced by quite different types of enterprise (in terms of firm size, factor proportions, and production technology)—are in direct competition. A shift in tastes from traditional, elaborate furniture produced primarily in very small workshops to more modern, streamlined products generally made in the larger, mechanized establishments would clearly have important implications for the small producer. So far the demand for the traditional products has remained strong; but one might expect a shift in this pattern over the coming decades, operating to the detriment of the small producer.[12]

In addition to these demand considerations, one must also take account of questions arising on the supply side. In recent years there has been a clear constraint on small producers imposed by the limited numbers of skilled workers available in the industry. Demand has pressed hard on supply; prices of furniture have risen, and the returns to factors of production in the sector have been high and rising. While this has provided good incomes for those in the sector, it is a risky basis for future growth. The larger-scale, more highly mechanized modern producers can expand their output more easily without facing the same supply limitations. There are plenty of unskilled and trainable workers in the country, and the necessary machinery can be freely imported. The binding constraint here may be managerial talent; as the requisite entrepreneurial ability develops, it will be relatively easy for larger producers to respond to increases in demand with relatively little increase in costs.

The risk for the small enterprises, then, is that even if demand for their products does grow, supply problems may work to price them out of the market, shifting tastes more rapidly away from the traditional products which are their specialty in the middle-income range, perhaps even raising the price of lowest-cost furniture to the point where mass-produced products can out-compete them.

One would expect there to be some supply response in the factor markets to these developments. High wage rates should draw more skilled workers into the sector, both by pulling home some emigrants and by causing people to seek to gain new skills in this area; but this is a relatively slow and uncertain process. Training takes time, the differentials with incomes abroad are still significant, and the choice of careers in Egypt is strongly influenced by considerations of security and prestige, which may slow the inflow of people into the furniture industry.

The question arises as to whether small-scale producers might be able to adapt to changing supply and demand conditions, shifting their production in the intermediate price range toward more modern production, relying more on machinery and less on skilled craftsmen. To some extent this is happening already, as small enterprises seek to adapt to market demands by producing more modern furniture. Yet this is not an easy transition for them to make. The type of mechanization which is called for is significantly different from what they are used to; the sending of parts to the service center will need to be replaced by well-organized and integrated production lines, with much higher capital per worker. Traditional skills as craftsmen become increasingly inadequate relative to the new managerial skills which are required for medium and larger scale enterprises. On the whole, one might say that in the production of intermediate-priced modern products, small enterprises are in the process of being replaced today by larger, more highly mechanized workshops. The sooner these small producers recognize this and change the focus of their activities, either by growing and expanding their mechanization or by shifting into other product lines, the less painful the transition will be. In the meantime, small producers will be able to keep on earning a living in these lines of work, but their incomes will be increasingly squeezed by competition from larger, more highly mechanized firms, which can produce similar or better products at lower cost.

The continuing strength of the small producers lies in two other areas: the production of lowest-cost, simple furniture, where it seems likely that they will control the market for the foreseeable future; and in the intermediate price and quality range traditional furniture, which depends on considerable skilled craftsmanship in the production process. Current production patterns for this type of product among small producers are impressively efficient; as long as the consumer tastes do not shift too rapidly away from their traditional roots, the future prospects for small producers of these products are bright.

5. CONCLUSIONS

The furniture producers examined in this study constitute something of a special case. With domestic demand growing while productive capacity has faced significant supply constraints, it is perhaps not surprising that many of the usual generalizations concerning small producers have been found not to apply. One would need similar studies of other product groups to determine the extent to which conclusions reached here are valid for other product lines. This is a rich and promising area for future research.

Perhaps the most important lesson to be learned from this study concerns the difficulty of generalizing about small industries, and the importance of disaggregating by product group. There is very little that one can usefully say about small furniture producers in general, much less about small firms taken as a whole. This study has been restricted to only one, fairly narrowly defined industry; yet even within that industry, prospects look bright for small producers of certain product groups, while in other lines the future appears to be considerably less hopeful.

There is a widespread presumption in at least part of the development literature today that, far from being "beautiful," one might say that "small is backward": small enterprises use primitive technology, providing low incomes to people who cannot find jobs in more dynamic sectors of the economy. As the modern sector grows, this reasoning implies, small enterprises will disappear. The analysis of this paper suggests that, at least in certain product groups, small enterprises in Egypt are alive and well. They use resources efficiently, provide a good income to factors of production employed in the sector, and produce products well suited to diverse consumer demands. In a country where government involvement in the economy has been pervasive over the past two decades, the vitality of these private-sector enterprises is impressive. For the future, it seems likely that in some lines of production small producers will not be able to stand up to competition with more highly mechanized modern producers. But in other segments of the market, prospects look bright; in these areas, one might hope that small producers will continue to thrive and expand for years to come.

MICHIGAN STATE UNIVERSTY

NOTES

Author's Note. This study could not have been completed without the generous cooperation and encouragement of the Handicrafts Industries and Productive Cooperatives Organization (HIPCO). In particular, Mohamed Gamal Morsy, General Director of HIPCO, and Mohamed Nasr el Din were helpful above and beyond the call of duty. The paper also benefited from helpful comments by participants in a joint Social Science Seminar at the American University in Cairo, where this material was presented for discussion. Thanks are also due to numerous individual businessmen in both large and small enterprises who gave generously of their time.

[1]See, for example, *Rural Enterprise and Nonfarm Employment: A World Bank Paper* (Washington, D.C.: World Bank, January 1978); E. Chuta and C. Liedholm, *Rural Non-Farm Employment: A Review of the State of the Art*, MSU Rural Development Paper No. 4 (East Lansing, Mich.: Dept of Agricultural Economics, Michigan State University, 1979); *Employment and Development in Small Enterprises* (Washington, D.C.: World Bank, 1978); and various publications of the International Labor Organization World Employment Program.

[2]The strengths and weaknesses of this census have been well discussed in R. Mabro and S. Radwan, *The Industrialization of Egypt, 1939-1973: Policy and Performance* (Oxford: Clarendon Press, 1976), pp. 118-119.

[3]This survey was undertaken by HIPCO, in cooperation with the Central Agency for Public Mobilization and Statistics. Some of the results of this survey have been published in World Bank documents. Details are available in the offices of HIPCO.

[4]International Bank for Reconstruction and Development, *Arab Republic of Egypt: Survey of Small-Scale Industry* (Washington: December 2, 1977).

[5]Other recent studies of small enterprises in Egypt include the following: Suzanne Berger, "Problems and Prospects of Egyptian Small-Scale Industry," August 1978 (mimeo); B. H. Daniels, "Preliminary Analysis of the Feasibility of New Development Finance Institutions to Support the Small-Scale Industrial Sector in Egypt," December 1978 (mimeo); Fouad Gabril, "Industrial Estates and Their Role in the Development of Small-Scale Industries," June 1978 (mimeo); HIPCO, "Coordination among Agencies Concerned with Small Industries and Handicrafts, ARE," n.d. (mimeo); HIPCO, "Vocational Training in Egypt: Coordination among Ministries and Authorities," n.d. (mimeo).

[6]At the start of the period discussed in this paper, the official exchange rate was LE 1 = $2.30. A second or "parallel market rate" was officially sanctioned for selected transactions. This second rate gradually gained in importance as increasing numbers of transactions came to be governed by it; at the start of 1979 it became the single unified rate, established at approximately LE 1 = $1.45.

[7]This figure is derived by dividing Radwan's estimate of net fixed capital stock in industry (*Capital Formation in Egyptian Industry and Agriculture, 1882-1967*, London: Praeger, 1974, p. 99) by Central Agency for Public Mobilization and Statistics estimates of employment in manufacturing in that year (from the Statistical Yearbook).

[8]Ministry of Industry, *Report on the Results of Operations of the Public Sector in Industry and Mining for 1976*, Part I (September 1977).

[9]A recent visit to a middle-sized carpentry workshop showed a labor force of 19, with 9 modern machines. At the time of the visit, 2 of these machines were in use; at a workbench, one worker was

sawing a large sheet of plywood—by hand!—while another helped to hold the wood. In another visit to a large, highly mechanized enterprise with several production lines, one whole line (4 large machines) was standing idle. Its capacity far exceeded that of other stages in the production process it was designed to serve. The capable manager indicated that he was taking steps to bring these different components into balance, by expanding those currently operating as constraints. By contrast, though, in visits to 5 service centers, ranging in size from 1 to 8 machines, I never observed a single machine not in use.

[10]Of these 22, 6 reported no change in employment, 2 reported increases, 1 had incomplete data, and 13 showed decreases.

[11]A recent consumer expenditure survey indicates that, in urban areas, as family income rises from LE 100 to LE 500 per year, expenditure on furniture rises by a factor of nearly 12, implying an expenditure elasticity of just over 3. As income rises further to LE 1,500, spending on furniture expands by a factor of 5, implying an expenditure elasticity of nearly 2. In rural areas, the largest increases in spending on furniture come at higher income levels; expenditure elasticity is below 2 over the range LE 100-500, while it is nearly 5 over the range LE 500-1,500 per year. These differences make clear once again that the effects of income growth on demand for furniture products depend crucially on who gets the additional income.

[12]Buying patterns have so far limited the effects of this shift in tastes on actual purchases. Furniture for a couple's first household is generally bought by the bride's parents, as a gift to the young couple; the choice of furniture is generally made with some consultation, but the parents are the ones who ultimately make the decision. Their tastes are often much more traditional than those of the younger generation. The result is that the effects of changing tastes are postponed, in terms of their impact on the market.

[20]

The Hidden Economy in Egypt

DELWIN A. ROY

A hidden economy in Egypt has been a feature of this centrally-planned state for several decades. Although this aspect of the economy has more typically been known as the 'informal' sector, after 1973 and the initiation of the economic liberalization policy – the *infitah*, it became considerably easier to engage in all forms of private economic activity that could be more readily 'masked'. That is, the scope, range and the specific kinds of economic activities being conducted, and the amounts of money involved, are largely indeterminate and unknown.

Accordingly, the term 'hidden economy', as defined here, refers *inter alia* to a number of spheres of this unknown activity: traditional informal economic activity; 'black' market operations; 'gray' market operations; and, the more purely domestic economic activities of the military establishment. In addition, two major enabling mechanisms, remittances and the primary agents for these, the money dealers (changers), the Islamic companies and other Islamic banking and financial institutions which are integral to the operation of the hidden economy, are included in the term 'hidden'.

The main components of the hidden economy represent economic activity – capital flows, imports, production, factor payments, rents, etc. – that is mostly unreported and unrecorded, legal, illegal or quasi-legal but nevertheless the effects of which are not entirely invisible. For example, there has been a construction boom in the rural areas of Egypt, financed largely by vastly increased capital flows (through the informal remittance process) of rural-based migrant laborers that travel to Saudi Arabia, Iraq and the Emirates for employment. The evidence, marked improvement in the number of dwellings (an average of 211,000 new units per year since 1980) and the quality, size and furnishings of these rural dwellings is clearly there, but the capital which financed this is largely unaccounted for and is therefore classed as 'unreported'.

There are many other examples that amply demonstrate the concept of the hidden economy. In 1979, President Sadat made a gift of 5,000 hectares (approximately 12,500 acres) of unimproved, desert land to a friend. In turn, the friend used government machinery at no personal cost to reclaim this land rendering it arable and therefore livable. In 1986 the

Middle Eastern Studies, Vol. 28, No. 4, October 1992, pp. 689–711
PUBLISHED BY FRANK CASS, LONDON

land was sold for LE 25,000,000, or, at the then prevailing exchange rate, about US$13 million, the sale proceeds being deposited outside the country. A woman who owns a block of flats rents one to an international bank, asks that the bank pay only a third of the rent to her in domestic currency and that the remaining two-thirds be deposited outside the country, in dollars. The bank agrees.

This hidden economy is to be distinguished from the formal economy, that portion of economic activity which is recorded in the Central Bank, the Ministry of Planning, and CAPMAS statistics, and has, since 1976 when the real effect of remittance earnings began to take hold, gained momentum and sophistication. To continue to refer to it as 'informal' is thus somewhat a misnomer. Consistent with the events of 1973 and the changes in the political economy of the region, there is strong evidence that the 'hidden economy' is not a phenomenon confined to Egypt. Rather, Egypt is but one player, albeit an important one, in the hidden but growing economy of the Middle East. This region-wide economy, linking Egypt and other Arab countries, is built by large-scale capital flows across national borders, mostly unrecorded and unreported, and to a large extent escaping the traditional means by which these countries account for formal economic activity. It remains hidden because the points at which its transactions surface are not always legal and therefore do not appear in the economy's formal record of performance. Even when legal, transactions that are based on unrecorded capital inflows do not leave clear traces.

The creation of a hidden economy and the unrecorded capital flows upon which it is largely based, has created effects that differ from those capital flows which are recorded and conventionally accounted for as 'remittances'. When predominantly informal channels are used for these transfers, the government cannot access this foreign exchange and, therefore, the policies which it has in force to allocate this scarce resource are rendered increasingly inoperable. Further, when the true magnitude of the productivity of nationals abroad remains unknown, the result is a distorted view of macroeconomic parameters.

There are essentially two main components that fuel the growth of the hidden economy in Egypt: remittances, the source of capital for much of the hidden activity *and* the institutional means by which remittances are transmitted, thought to be predominantly the money dealers and the Islamic financial and banking institutions.

Remitted earnings constitute the most visible consequences of the migration for employment. Balance-of-payments statistics conventionally record such flows as 'unrequited private earnings', and the conventional view of remitted earnings focuses on the formally recorded flows, their effect on labor markets and the broader economic impacts, primarily on consumption and savings.

The size of actual remittances as opposed to those formally recorded has been a subject of debate for some time. Officially, remitted earnings initially appear as added income in the hands of consumers who can either decide to consume or save and invest. The relative split of remittances between consumption and investment is an important determinant of further consequences. Thus, if the consumption portion is small relative to investment, the impacts on output are correspondingly greater. The most conventional view is that these remitted earnings are 'squandered', that is, expended in a largely frivolous fashion. It is in viewing the informal channels that have been created to transfer remittances that one immediately senses that the official channels for effecting such transfers are in the main being bypassed. Officially recorded remittances have never exceeded $4 billion, a figure totally inconsistent with the number of Egyptians known to be working abroad and then pattern of remittance behavior.

It is generally conceded that in the early 1980s the then prevailing level of official remittances – approximately US$ 2.5–3.0 billion – reflected only a portion of actual remittances entering the country. It was estimated by Egyptian economists and officials of the Ministry of Economy and the Central Bank that there was 'probably' an additional US$ 3–4 billion entering the country, in the form of either cash or goods that were not officially recorded. Accuracy was a problem as estimates of the number of Egyptians working abroad were very unreliable, placed anywhere from 1.6 to 3.2 billion.

Since 1981–82, the data have become more reliable, and a 1984 and 1988 study by Nazli Choucri (MIT) puts forth a methodology that in general is being accepted as accurate by American and Egyptian economists knowledgeable in the matter. The 1984 study tended to overstate the volume of actual remittances, and was methodologically weak. The more recent study (1988) still probably overstates actual remittances (Choucri places these at US$18 billion) but methodologically makes a much stronger and more compelling case for the significant under-reporting evident in government economic data.

To Choucri's studies must be added the fact that since 1982 more evidence is available on these informal remittance flows because rampant inflation and currency rate instability have led more Egyptians working abroad to seek protection against loss in real value terms. The most spectacular example of this is the meteoric rise in the deposits held by the Islamic companies and the rural construction boom.

Taking Choucri's methodology into account and reasonable estimates of the deposits in the Islamic Companies and 1986 Census data on residential construction, coupled with the trend more or less officially acknowledged by the Ministry of Economy and Central Bank officials in 1981, and the fact that the informal money changers both abroad and in Egypt have become very sophisticated in by-passing official banking channels, it is *reasonable* to assume that remittances are in the region of US$ 12+ billions (from both officially recorded and informal sources).

There is mounting evidence that remittances flow predominantly through these informal channels and that they are, literally, 'hand carried'. Among the most important channels for remitting earnings is the extensive network of currency dealers, or money merchants, to whom the foreign workers turn for conversion of their hard currency. The workers are virtually assured that their families in the home country will receive the equivalent in local currency. The currency dealers extract a fee for their service. The real profits, however, are to be made by the time-lag in delivering the local currency, thus allowing for short-term interest profits as well as to 'ride' fluctuations when the local currency is depreciating with respect to foreign currency. The parties to this exchange are all satisfied: the workers, because they are confident that their families will receive the transferred funds; the families, because they have extra income; and the intermediaries, because they profit from the intertemporal exchange and transmission service.

The hidden economy in Egypt is so massive that the value of transactions remitted in the informal process must at a minimum stand at several times the value of export earnings. It is a main form of economic activity. The quasi-institutional character of the informal transfer processes is sustained by the induced deterioration of exchange rates. As long as the value of the local currency worsens (as has clearly been the case in Egypt), the dealers profit. Taken one step further, there is some point at which the expectation of future profits by these dealers merely sets in train future induced pressure on exchange rates, again a process clearly in evidence in Egypt.

In 1985 the Central Bank in Egypt actually had to borrow foreign exchange from the money dealers due to the critical shortage prevailing at that time. This act at least partially acknowledges the importance of these agents. More importantly, it represents more than a tacit admission by the government that the volume of funds moving through these 'informal' channels is indeed large and important. The transfer of funds in this manner is not illegal. Technically, no hard currency transaction takes place inside Egypt. The reality is that labor migration has led to the restructuring of labor markets, income generation and the resulting operations of financial agents involve currency transfers on a permeable basis. National borders, as barriers to or constraints upon the flow of economic resources, are no longer meaningful and this is especially critical for a large labor exporter such as Egypt. Foreign earnings shape the hidden economy. It is created by the unrecorded hard currency transfers from workers abroad to their domestically domiciled families and is controlled and manipulated by foreign exchange dealers. The holdings of hard currency by these dealers influences the fluctuation of the relative exchange rate of local currency and hard currency and is the central monetary feature of the hidden economy.

The hidden economy interacts with the formal economy on an institutional and financial basis and it is here that the Islamic banks, investment companies and other financial institutions enter the process. These Islamic financial intermediaries have proliferated in Egypt since 1982. Operating at the margin of Civil Law, Islamic financial intermediaries are an integral part of the Egyptian economy and are powerful political players. Islamic investment companies are particularly notable, both because the majority are led by individuals who started out as smugglers and black market speculators in currency and because their activities are of an increasingly dubious character.

Most Islamic companies are built on attracting on a large-scale small depositors, the majority of whom are Egyptians working abroad. Hence, the labor-remittance link provides the backbone of these investments. As a result, both because they lie largely outside the realm of civil law in Egypt, and their link with the externally-transacted hard currency conversion activities of the money changers, not to mention their presumed 'religious' character, Egypt's formal economy is unable to extend control over the hidden economy.

Reliable sources in Egypt's financial community, including Central Bank officials, the leaders of several major Islamic banks and former economics ministers, place the total number of depositors in the Islamic companies at about 500,000. Estimates of current deposits range from $5 billion to $15 billion. At their peak (1985–86), it is reasonable to put deposits at about $7 billion. Given the declining employment of Egyptians abroad and extensive losses in the global stock market adjustment in 1987, current holdings may be no more than $4 billion.

The less reputable of these Islamic investment companies, such as Rayan, have incurred substantial losses in their external investment portfolios, largely as a result of the market crash in October 1987. Typically, the ICs have done reasonably well in speculating in currency fluctuations, real estate and gold. They have done less well in attempts to corner domestic markets for selected high value goods and commodities, and probably fared no better nor worse than most investors in the 1987 crash. It is estimated that about one-half of the deposits of the ICs have been converted to foreign currency and are held offshore. All of the activity, good or bad, is largely 'hidden' and unreported owing to the 'hands off' policy of the government.

While the ICs are private and involve no government control or investment, highly placed government officials, both former and current, have been engaged as consultants by the ICs. For example, Abdel Razzak Abdel Meguid, former Minister of Planning and Minister of Economy under the Sadat regime, is a 'consultant' to the Rayan group. More recently, he is known to be actively lobbying President Mubarak to prevent the government from stepping in to save the foundering Rayan operation, both as a means of hedging his economic position and for other reasons.

In summary, remittances provide the capital for the hidden economy and, increasingly, the Islamic financial institutions, particularly the Islamic companies, represent the main channels through which the remittances flow and exert their effect on the domestic economy. As will be seen, it is only in a few instances that these Islamic entities exert positive and constructive influence over the economy. The more typical case involves speculation, capital flight and the financing of the burgeoning trade in illegal drugs and weapons in Egypt, a point to be taken up in greater detail.

As already observed, the term 'hidden economy' incorporates a number of components, perhaps best considered to be different strata of the same formation. While these subcomponents – the 'black' and 'gray' markets, the traditional informal economy and the military economy – are rather distinct from one another, they are nevertheless increasingly linked by the commonality of funding sources described above and the kinds of economic activity that groups and interests in each component undertake.

These links are often imperfect, difficult to identify, but nevertheless the actions of any one component cannot often be isolated from those of the others. For example, the military are actively involved in currency speculation, selling off portions of unimproved lands under their control. The Islamic companies, as noted, are actively engaged in real estate speculation. In the traditional informal economy, the surge in 1978 and after in external employment of rural-based labor has infused new and vast capital resources for the improvement of housing in rural areas, resulting in rising prices for land previously used for agriculture. Land prices in rural areas that varied in the early 1980s from LE 2,500 to LE 5,000 per feddan are now LE 8,000 – 70,000 per feddan, the latter price prevailing if they are in the vicinity of a rapidly growing urban area. Much of the land controlled by the military is this kind of land. Thus, prospective buyers and sellers, be the latter the Islamic companies or the military, are all interacting around the same phenomenon: land-price speculation.

Interconnected as these strata may or may not be, it is useful to describe the characteristics of each on a separate basis.

THE 'BLACK' MARKET: THE ILLEGAL ECONOMY

The economic activities included in this category are:

- Smuggling (of goods, drugs, weapons).
- Smuggling of capital; other illegal currency transactions.
- Illegal sale of public property (equipment, production, raw materials) and use of equipment and labor for private gain.
- Tax evasion and tax avoidance.
- Corruption and graft.

Of these activities, there appear to be four that are of considerable scope and generate large amounts of cash: smuggling, corruption and graft, and illegal currency transactions (primarily smuggling of capital).

Smuggling is a multi-billion dollar business in Egypt; to some extent it involves the military and is alleged by reputable sources to involve the less savory of the Islamic investment companies. Drug smuggling, primarily hashish for domestic consumption, is currently estimated to be between $2 and 4 billion. As a large cash flow is required to finance this scale of operations and because profits need to be 'laundered' in some fashion (although it is conceded that this is less of a problem for those in developing countries), the unregulated Islamic companies are ideally suited to act as agents. The ICs have the flow of funds, the ability to secrete large transactions and in the case of the owners of the less reputable organizations, the predilection and, in some cases, the experience.

The military have for some time been active in the goods-smuggling business. As the military control access to the Suez Canal free zones (Port Said and Suez), the illegal flow of goods to the domestic economy from these regions cannot take place without its collusion. Initially, circa 1976, this might have involved sentry posts and those manning roadblocks taking 'bakhshish' and permitting the private consumer to pass through with the car trunk full of Levis. However, as will be seen when reviewing the flow of Israeli-produced goods, considerably more volume is now passing through these zones. To effect this requires the knowledge and permission of senior officers. It is worth noting in this regard that one of the main recommendations of a committee of noted Egyptian economists, convened by Mubarak in 1982, was that the Port Said free zone be closed. The group found that the volume of goods being smuggled from this source was in the words of the two senior conference leaders, 'monumental', and that this practice was responsible for a major portion of 'hidden' economic activity, much of it illegal. The proposal was rejected outright by the Mubarak government, owing as one well-placed source put it, to 'pressure from the senior levels of the military'.

Any attempt to assess accurately the full value of smuggling is extremely difficult, owing both to the nature of what is being smuggled in some instances (drugs and weapons, for example) and to the power of those involved – the military (by definition above reproach) and Islamic institutions (by definition above question). In Israeli-produced goods alone, $65 million above officially recorded trade in 1986 passed through the Canal free zones to the Egyptian domestic market. Drugs, as noted, range above the $2 billion mark.

Tax evasion and tax avoidance are legion in Egypt and take place in every conceivable fashion imaginable. The major taxes being evaded include: taxes on the liberal and non-commercial professions; commercial and industrial profits; and, general income. Implicit in the evasion and avoidance process are the following practices: non-reporting or under-reporting of income (especially from informal-sector activity such as moonlighting) from employment; escaping Social Security Tax payments; under-reporting of actual production and sales; the non-reporting and under-reporting of rental payments; and, the non-reporting of illegally obtained income – from corruption and graft – and the private use of public property. A former prime minister (and former minister in a number of economic ministries in the course of his career) states that no more than '20–30 per cent of those required actually submit returns – and these only do it because they have always been under scrutiny.' The latter remark clearly implies that tax evasion is one of the primary means of exacting political retribution or at least holding out the prospect of it.

Corruption and graft are two of the most pervasive forms of black-market activity currently in evidence in the Egyptian economy. They percolate to the most minute and seemingly insignificant levels, such as the housewife who bribes the operator of the village water-pump to operate it after hours so that she would not miss televized soap operas. And there is corruption at the very top – involving present and former ministers, members of presidential 'inner circles' and leaders and members of parliament.

From time to time, as in the case of Sadat's brother, a 'show trial' is conducted, but for the most part corruption at the major and minor level goes unchecked and is unabated. Those involved in major graft are able to secrete their income abroad; the more brazen and confident do not bother, keeping it in domestic banks that have offshore status. It involves millions of dollars and thousands of government officials.

THE TRADITIONAL INFORMAL MARKET: THE UNRECORDED ECONOMY

A large and active informal sector of economic activity is a relatively longer-term feature of the Egyptian economy than other major components of the hidden economy. It is called 'traditional' here to distinguish it from those activities that emerged after 1973 with the onset of the liberalization policy. It must be noted, however, that this traditional informal economy saw tremendous growth as a result of increased oil prices, the resulting migration of Egyptian labor and the remittances stemming from it.

This component consists of the following main activities:

- Barter.
- Self-employment; small scale (under 10 employees) enterprises.
- Self-help construction.
- Self-help social, medical and health and education services (from Islamic organizations).

That the Egyptian government continues to report that 30 per cent of energy sources used in the country come from 'animal dung, random collections of wood' attests to the true informality of this sector as well as to the potential value of economic activities 'hidden' in this sector.

The sector is primarily based on a barter arrangement, monetized and non-monetized transactions, the self-employed operating beyond the formal recording processes of the government or outside the purview (or interest) of government regulatory bodies and small-scale producers of goods and services of all kinds. Not all activities in this sector are legal *per se*, but there is a difference in the legal issues attached to the under-reporting or non-reporting of personal and business income derived from such activities and the actual activity itself. Income is legally earned but illegally treated for tax purposes. Perhaps the segment of this informal sector that is most significant is the small-scale enterprise. Self-help construction is the second most important.

In 1970 the then Director of the National Institute of Planning placed the size of the informal sector at approximately 25–30 per cent of total industrial output in the formal (and predominantly public) sector. It is of interest to note that, although acknowledged, the Ministry of Planning statistics made no attempt to incorporate an estimate of the value of output of the informal sector in its official economic data.

It was assumed in large part and correctly that the bulk of this informal sector activity was to be found in major urban areas. With the onset of economic liberalization and the shift of demand for migrant labor to include those from rural areas after 1978, there has been a dramatic increase in the size and scope of activities of the rural-based informal sector. Small-scale enterprises offering goods and services, like their urban counterparts, have proliferated.

Migration has been a key to this development and has brought with it two substantive changes in the process of diminishing the importance of the traditional agricultural sector in Egypt: it has opened urban-based employment opportunities to a much larger portion of the agrarian population (particularly given the rapid growth of secondary and tertiary urban centers such as Damietta, Zagazig, etc.), *and* it has internationalized the agrarian labor market. There are signs that, for a growing number of Egyptian farmers, outside sources of income, especially that earned abroad, have assumed enough importance to marginalize further traditional agricultural activity.

Nowhere is this more pronounced than in the growth of the rural-based, non-agricultural production and services-oriented informal sector. There has been a distinct shift of wages and returns on non-traditional agricultural output. Markets for such services as equipment repair, public transport, maintenance, housing and food supplies, previously confined to the village, have been transferred to the rapidly urbanizing rural towns. The village-based market is, as a result, becoming extinct.

This dramatic shift of income to the rural areas, spawning growth in the demand for informal sector goods and services, has no doubt increased the size of the hidden dimension of the Egyptian economy. Agricultural productivity has always been under-valued and poses special problems for those who are accounting for formal economic activity. It is worth noting that the most recent economic plan continues to estimate private sector activity (including informal) at about '30 per cent of total industrial' output. It might conceivably be the case that in the period 1970–88, total industrial output, particularly that of the public sector, grew so dramatically that the burgeoning growth evident in the informal sector, urban- and rural-based, maintained only the same share. However, the statistical evidence offered by various official agencies hardly substantiates this conclusion.

Nowhere has evidence of the surge in rural development been more apparent than in the case of construction. The stock of wealth in the informal sector is somewhat accounted for by the evidence accumulated in the 1986 Census; rural construction growth can only be described as dramatic. Preliminary 1986 Census results show that in the period 1976–86, 75 per cent of all urban housing starts occurred after 1980 (attesting to the full impact of remittance earnings coming into play). Starts (non-traditional, that is, modern, not 'baladi', housing) in the rural sector averaged 171,000 per year in the period 1976–86, but averaged 211,000 per year *from 1980 to 1986* and represented 53 per cent of the total stock of new housing starts for the decade. This represents a significant shift of income to the agriculture sector. Very few of the major implications of this income and construction sector shift to rural Egypt is captured in the official economic (against census) data for the formal economy.

A final dimension of the informal economy that is a relatively new phenomenon is the provision of social, medical and health, and education services offered to the Egyptian public primarily by Islamic organizations. While such services are provided in both urban and rural settings, they appear to be more heavily concentrated in rural areas. The impetus for the provision of such services is, at least on the surface, occasioned by the rapid deterioration in government-provided services, both in terms of quantity and quality. A partial reason for the more 'rural' emphasis of Islamic organization-provided assistance is that the rural areas have always been poorly treated in the supply of government services; urban areas were (and are) clearly favored. There is also a political reason for this emphasis.

There is no real way to estimate the value of such services. One source, a former Minister of Economy, notes that the primary reason for the provision of these services is not 'economic'. Rather, 'Islamic adherents are objectively containing the discontent in Egypt – through teaching teams in schools, operating medical clinics, offering low-priced clothing ... at a time when government services are diminishing. The Islamic movement is stepping in on an efficient, low-cost basis.' As a result, he notes further, 'Islamic political movements are contacting and controlling the most mobile elements of society, the educated youth – especially that located in provincial universities.'

THE 'GRAY' MARKET: THE UNREPORTED ECONOMY

The 'gray' market is comprised of actions perhaps best described as hidden economic activities that are of doubtful legal origin, the economic consequences of which are largely unreported. Of all the components of the hidden economy, it encompasses outcomes that are the most difficult to detect.

Applying the concept of the 'quasi-legal' transactions in practice poses some methodological difficulty. Trading and dealing in foreign currency, for example, is 'legal', as in the case of the money dealers who conduct the transaction offshore; 'illegal', when it is smuggled in or out of the country; and 'quasi-legal', when it involves any Islamic financial or banking institution. Hence, foreign currency dealing is included in 'black' and 'gray' market activities and forms the backbone of the remittance transfer process.

The 'gray' market also includes that which in the purely legal sense is but illicit, given a more social and moral stance, considered honest. Moonlighting is perhaps the best example of this as are other activities to which the government finds it useful to turn a 'blind eye'. Given rampant inflation and the poverty of certain classes of Egyptians, and the potential political consequences of attempting to do something about it, it is easier to legitimize 'gray' market activity rather than attempt to observe the letter of the law. Perhaps the leading example is to be found in the illegal tapping of electricity for 'informal' housing, those ramshackle dwellings that are to be found in urban areas. It is estimated that almost 20 per cent of the total electricity supply generated in Egypt is tapped illegally.

Activities considered to be part of the gray market include:

- Foreign currency transactions, especially of the Islamic Companies; currency speculation.
- Multiple job-holding; 'moonlighting'.
- Imports financed by remittances held offshore.
- Real estate speculation.
- Goods and commodities speculation.

The foreign currency transactions of Islamic financial organizations have already been discussed at length and therefore are not to be mentioned further here. Multiple job-holding is, in addition to corruption, one of the most prevalent hidden economic activities in Egypt. For the most part, its participants include government and public-sector employees trying to keep pace with inflation. Government salaries and wages are meager at best and the need to hold a second job is almost axiomatic. The hidden economic dimension of moonlighting is manifest in several ways. Those in government and public-sector positions tend to perform less in their 'official' positions, either taking time off to attend to their other job, simply not showing up or using government supplies and equipment in the performance of their other job. Productivity is therefore shifted to the informal activity but not lost to the economy, assuming that the moonlighting is 'productive'.

In the accounting sense, the productivity shifted and implicit in the other employment *is* lost. Wages and salaries in such positions are unreported for the most part as is the product of the activity. Hence, when one considers that there are over 3 million government and public-sector employees, the leakage may be quite substantial. It might be assumed that some of this leakage is recaptured in the official economy through increasing marginal productivity. That is, the sheer number of government and public-sector employees has acted detrimentally in achieving productivity.

Imports financed with remittances held offshore are one of the most interesting of the gray-market activities, involving legal currency transactions, the import of legal products to free zones, the quasi-legal (possibly illegal) transit of those goods from the free zones to the domestic market, and, among goods of undoubtedly varied origins, those from Israel. These imports and the means by which they move to domestic markets are an example of the degree of sophistication being achieved in the hidden economy and, more importantly, an example of how the various components of the hidden economy interact.

Officially, trade between Egypt and Israel is reported to stand at about $170 million annually, with a $166-million balance in Egypt's favor. The bulk of this is in oil shipments to Israel, ranging from $150–160 million a year. These exports are officially recorded but do include a hidden dimension. Foreign oil companies operating in Egypt opt to take payment 'in kind' rather than run the risk of finding the hard currency on the local market in order to expatriate earnings. This payment in kind is pumped along with the oil destined for final use in Israel, shipped to Europe, where it is sold, and proceeds credited to the companies.

Officially recorded trade stands at about $8–10 million, but commerce between the two countries is more active than is thought or conceded by official statistics. Another $65 million is transiting through the Port Said free zone, financed for the most part by a variation on the remittance transfer process noted earlier and involves final users in both the public and private sectors.

The imports are bought with hard currency held offshore and provided by Egyptian migrant workers. The goods are then sold to the domestic market, paid for in local currency by the buyer, who makes payment directly to agents who in turn remit it to the families of workers abroad, or in some cases (hotels and other tourist facilities, for example) the buyer literally opens a 'tellers' cage and pays the families directly. The goods imported in this fashion are unrecorded, owing in part to an accounting convention practiced by CAPMAS. Imports are only 'official' when they establish a current claim against foreign exchange holdings. As the Israeli imports are financed offshore and thus, outside the official banking system, they are not identified or acknowledged by CAPMAS. The imported goods are legal; there are no provisions against the import of Israeli goods *per se*. The products are mostly high-value processed agricultural goods and industrial chemicals. They simply are not counted.

Real estate and scarce, high-value goods and species speculation is an activity engaged in by many parties: the private sector, Islamic finance and banking institutions, the military, etc. Owning land or real estate or goods or species likely to increase rapidly in value is one of the main savings channels in developing countries. With a rising inflation rate, the preference is to hold wealth in any form other than local currency, or even hard currency. Gold, land, improved real estate, and goods and commodities which are at least likely to hold their absolute value, if not experience an increase in it, become a superior store for wealth accumulation. Because of inflation, there is the expectation that the price of such items will rise in relation to the stock of all other goods and commodities. It follows that speculation and inflation move hand in hand and if the stock of capital in pursuit of hedging activities is large enough, become a self-perpetuating process.

In the case of Egypt, speculation in real estate is of great importance owing to a number of factors:

- Increasing population faced with a relatively limited supply of urban land lends strong impetus to rising prices and in turn the lump-sum profits of landowners.
- The construction boom has markedly increased the capital gains to be made from subcontracting, brokerage and speculation in real estate.
- Indirect bidding on land and improved real estate contracts leads to capital gains in the form of commissions, brokerage and monopolistic profits, all of which go untaxed.

There is in effect a vast sum of capital chasing a fixed and increasingly scarce resource, allowing huge profits to be made, which in turn go unreported as income. Values are rendered somewhat meaningless because the process of speculation becomes a value-creating device in its own right; the real intrinsic economic value of land, or for that matter other goods or services, becomes increasingly irrelevant.

The hidden economic dimension is in the form of artificial or windfall gains realized but unreported. Wealthy landowners do not pay taxes and are more prone to keep their funds offshore. Agent and broker commission revenues are significant but not nearly as great as are the capital gains of landowners.

THE MILITARY: THE SECRET ECONOMY

The role of the military in the domestic economy of Egypt is a phenomenon that has markedly increased in the past seven or eight years. In the late 1970s Sadat directed the Egyptian military to expand their economic role. It appears that Sadat had in mind the need to offset the rising costs of maintaining a standing military force, but it also seemed to imply that the military could enter into all forms of economic activity, irrespective of its direct relevance to the performance of their main mission, that is, national security. Whatever the intent, the military have taken Sadat's direction literally.

The range of economic activities in which the military now engage is extensive. A number of them are not substantially different from what one would find the military performing in other countries: improvement of the transport system; waterway construction and improvement; and, other engineering projects in telecommunications and bridge construction. Self-sufficiency in producing their own food requirements is purposeful. Assistance to the civilian sector – housing for officers at a very high standard, automated bakeries, imports of goods for resale to the domestic sector, office buildings and real estate sales and development – seems to go beyond what the military might normally undertake.

The issue here is not a moral one, that is, what should the military be allowed to undertake in economic activity; rather, it is the hidden dimension of this activity and its often secretive nature. Military debt (now thought to be in the range of $9–11 billion) is not part of the national budget, nor are the earnings gained from income-generating economic activities of the military. These are 'retained', often for the sole benefit of the officer corps.

If the notion is that economic activity in the military is an offset to budget costs, there is little evidence that this is in fact occurring. The budget, excluding debt creation on capital account and debt servicing and repayment on current account, was LE 1.1 billion in 1980–81. In 1984–85 it was LE 2.4 billion; 1986–87, LE 2.5 billion; and, in 1987–88, LE 2.7 billion. Admittedly, the Egyptian pound has become devalued, but the primary cost in the current account budget is for wages and salaries, a local-currency cost. Hard-currency costs are buried in the capital account and financed almost entirely by foreign borrowing. As one former senior official puts it, 'the military are benefiting themselves, they rely on imported components and engage in sales of land. This process of market intermediation creates big profits – which they keep – but does not create jobs or products for the public good.' A noted Egyptian economist views the military 'as well managed; increasingly diversified in their economic activity; destined to be the largest importer in Egypt, but they report no "profits" out'. As these profits are totally absorbed within the military themselves and created by economic activity of unknown dimensions, it must be true that cumulatively such activity represents a major component of the hidden economy.

This 'secret' economy includes the following activities:

- Land sales, primarily from vast tracts set aside for military use.
- Food production for domestic markets.
- Real estate development, investment and speculation.
- Fee-based health and medical plans for civilian use of military hospitals and dispensaries.
- School-book and text production.
- Import of goods for resale to the domestic market.
- Smuggling of goods, through free zones, etc.
- Use of military personnel for private construction and other non-military purposes.
- Land reclamation.

It is extremely difficult to obtain a sense of the full value of activity being conducted by the military in the national economy. The military are 'unaccountable' and their economic activity 'unaccounted for' in any official statistical sense. While thus far the Egyptian military have not opted for the creation of the military economic enterprise (MEC) form of organization that one sees in Yemen and the Sudan, this cannot be far off and in any event may already be a *fait accompli*.

Several years ago imports for domestic resale were placed at about $400 million. More recently the auditor for the military economic offices (two of these exist, each headed by a general) noted that 'the government told the military to quit importing goods for the domestic market', and that now such imports are no more than '$100 million'. The truth of the matter is difficult to determine. In the area of land sales, real estate development and speculation, there is no doubt as to the military's active and profitable participation. As much of the military's land holdings are in the Canal Zone and the Western Desert, the creation of the New Cities led to the opportunity for significant profits. Not all of these newly created cities prospered, but many have. The rapid population growth in secondary and tertiary urban centers in the Delta also provided the military with new opportunities for land sales. Typically, large-scale military reservations are located in the Delta, near these growing urban areas and land values, as noted, have sky-rocketed.

Finally, it is worth noting the 'mix' of military economic activities. In the public domain these include major projects in civilian air facilities, bridges, telecommunications and electric power-generation plants. In the private domain, it includes health and medical services (fee-based), food production, textbook production and real estate development. It does not take a political wizard to sense the strategic character of this kind of penetration of the national economy.

It is important to observe the distribution of the profits of this hidden economic activity. The proceeds have in part been used to increase the living standard (housing and subsidized services and foodstuffs) of the officer corps, the wages and salaries of senior NCO's and junior officer ranks and the 'perks' of officer cadre: improved and expanded clubs, recreation and sports facilities, the provision of automobiles, etc.

As to the illegal activity of the military, the term 'illegal' poses difficulty. One is almost disposed to say that if the military do it, that fact alone makes it 'legal'. Yet, the military must be engaged, tacitly or otherwise, in the growing unrecorded import activity coming through the Sinai and Port Said. The Sinai is under military control as is the Canal Zone and it is unwarranted to assume that individual officers are making decisions about what passes through. Some of this occurs no doubt, but the scale of illegal importing activity (not necessarily of illegal substances or goods) is such that complicity at the highest levels must indeed exist.

Such matters are not of direct interest here. What is, is the scale of the hidden economic activity involved. In this respect, it is concluded that while one cannot measure it accurately, it must at a minimum be of the order of $1–2 billion.

MEASURING HIDDEN ECONOMIC ACTIVITY IN EGYPT

The difficulty of obtaining an accurate assessment of the value of all of the forms of hidden economic activity – beyond conjecture, innuendo and guestimates – has been discussed already. There is one study that attempts to measure the key elements of this economy circa 1980–81. While weak in many respects, it does give a perspective that appears to be methodologically correct and can serve as a baseline for an estimate of the overall magnitude of hidden economic activity as it stood in 1988.

The following Table sets forth what is known quantitatively about the hidden economy as contained in J.K.T. Diab's *The Hidden Economy in Egypt* (1983, an MA thesis submitted at the American University of Cairo). The caveats to this quantification are, however, legion:

- For determination of moonlighting activity, the random sample for survey purposes was extremely small; the results may not be representative.

- The values for real estate dealings, upon which the profits from speculation estimate is based, are seriously underestimated as it is common practice to list transactions at less than one-third value to avoid property taxes.
- Data on smuggling of hashish and other goods are based solely on the amount of goods seized.
- The estimate of self-help construction is put at an aggregate of 40 per cent of the total volume of housing construction. There are no survey results in support of this conclusion.
- Tax evasion is based on only 400 cases involving government seizure of property or bank accounts.

This study concluded that on a seriously underestimated basis (the only one feasibly adopted given the secretiveness of such activity) hidden economic activity in Egypt amounted to about '13 per cent of formally generated GNP'. It is important to bear in mind that this 1983 study worked almost entirely from minimal evidence, for example, the actual cases of smuggling reported and prosecuted, and the actual number of prosecutions for tax evasion and avoidance. What it did accomplish was to establish a reasonable floor for an acceptable estimate of the size of the hidden economy. In this respect, the estimate that the hidden economy represented about 13 per cent of GNP is in effect that 'floor'. This clear underestimation was recognized by the researcher conducting the study and in an article published in 1985 it was stated by them that 'no doubt, the actual hidden economic activity in 1982 was closer to 20 per cent of GNP rather than the 13 per cent indicated in the study completed in 1983'. Notwithstanding this adjustment with respect to the validity of the 1983 study, the revised estimate did not take into account the economic activity of the military or the Islamic Companies.

What is a sensible conclusion as to the current level of hidden economic activity in Egypt? A major difficulty is breaking down the activity in remittances and other currency transfers. If it is treated simply on the supply side, then one avoids the problem of double-counting. However, there are demand side-effects in the form of commissions, float, profits from currency speculation, etc., that are potentially buried in such an approach.

Even allowing for the supply side definition, if there are indeed some $8–12 billion in non-officially transmitted remittances involved in the hidden economy, then correspondingly, one must expect that the hidden economy is of equal dimension, if not greater. Smuggling of illegal

TABLE 1
MEASURING THE HIDDEN ECONOMY OF EGYPT, 1980–81
(in millions US$)

Category	*Amount*
'Black' Market	
Smuggling, Total	667.9
Illegal substances, volume	(303.6)
Illegal substances, profits	(152.4)
General goods, volume (Port Said)	(211.9)
Currencies	123.0
Tax Evasion, Total	427.4
On business profits	(297.6)
Customs duties	(129.8)
'Gray' Market	
Multiple job-holding	742.9
Real estate, Total	431.0
Speculation	(391.4)
Commissions	(39.6)
Traditional/Informal Market	
Self-help construction, Total	342.9
Miscellaneous, Other	1.6
GRAND TOTAL	2,613.7
GNP	20,833.3

substances alone might be conservatively placed at $2 billion; the hidden economic activity of the military at $1 billion; the Islamic companies command at least $2.5 billion (much of it, no doubt, fugitive income) that is funneled into gold and real estate speculation, possibly drug and weapons smuggling, and currency speculation; and, thus far one has not taken account of traditional informal economic activity, moonlighting, or the full ramifications of tax evasion and tax avoidance and graft and corruption.

The conclusion, therefore, albeit extremely difficult to support with irrefutable evidence, is that the hidden economy of Egypt in 1988 was in the order of a minimum of 35 per cent of officially recorded GNP. A more realistic figure would put it in the 45–55 per cent range. Part of the difficulty in solidly defending this latter level lies in accurately assessing the volume of capital flows, or the supply side of the monies that finance much of the hidden economic activity – money flowing into Egypt through informal channels and the end-use of those monies. Not enough is known as to how large the leakage is; that is, how much of the money is simply 'passing through' the Egyptian economy on its way to somewhere else as against how much is retained in the country (whether hidden in mattresses, held in the form of highly liquid assets such as gold, goods inventories, or in current accounts). Therefore, the 35 per cent of GNP level is more easily defended notwithstanding the author's firm belief that it is indeed higher.

ANALYSIS AND THE GENERAL IMPLICATIONS OF THE HIDDEN ECONOMY

What is to be observed in this growth of the hidden economy is the full effect of the economic transition begun in 1973. This is not to say that the 'effect' observable was intended; it most certainly was not anticipated by the architects of the liberalization policy. Egyptians who under the restrictive regime of Nasser had become highly innovative in overcoming the inimical effects of the 'legislated and planned economy' have turned that experience to profit by the partial dismantling of the foreign currency control and import mechanisms and the partial freeing of domestic market constraints.

On the positive side, one can identify several major results:

1. The Egyptian economy is far more buoyant than official economic data indicate. There is high liquidity and observable increase in the stocks of wealth of the private sector. Accordingly, political stability is no doubt more assured as a result of this privatization of income and wealth accumulation outside the control and influence of national planning directives and policies.
2. The redistribution of wealth away from urban centres to the countryside is also significant. Central plans had always had an urban bias. The rural sector has now generated its own resources and in the area of housing and in the wide range of services now available, there has been vast improvement. Again, this is a factor that, politically, is stabilizing.
3. The ability of the central government to control the hidden economy is limited; therefore, it cannot bring that economy's resources into the wasteful and inefficient public sector and bureaucracy. In view of the rapid growth of competition from the hidden economy, the public sector has had to try to become more lean and efficient. It remains lethargic for the most part, but the degree to which it can continue to do so is clearly diminished.
4. There has been a vast accumulation of wealth in private hands. *In principle*, this represents a stock of capital that can be invested, not just in quick turn-around import and speculative activities, but in medium- and long-term productive projects.
5. The private sector is vastly more experienced than was the case in

1973 and again, *in principle*, should be able to undertake successfully increasingly more complex financial and technological investments. In the financial intermediation area in particular, there is evidence of extremely successful arbitrage and financial packaging activities. Institutions and individuals involved are making good use of electronic means to move currency and make external capital investments.

6. The ability of the hidden economy increasingly to compensate for the failings of the public sector and the central government to provide necessary goods and services of a reasonable quality, is also potentially politically stabilizing. As long as the stock of goods is there, albeit at inflated prices, the extent and degree of public dissatisfaction at least partially decreases.
7. Politically, this new class of wealthy private sector interests is exerting power. When the question of what comes after Mubarak is raised, the most frequently stated opinion of those most qualified and informed is 'a coalition between big business and the Egyptian military'. These business interests are decidedly pro-American.

Casual factors – frequent and erratic local currency movements, rampant inflation (of the order of 30 per cent plus) and the devaluation of the US dollar – have been instrumental in providing the impetus for the extensive growth of the hidden economy since 1982. Equally important has been the continued demand, albeit lessened, for Egyptian labor in Saudi Arabia and the Gulf (with Jordan and Yemen drawing increasingly upon Egypt's labor supply). OPEC's ability to drive up oil prices once again would only mean that Egypt's hidden economy would experience a new surge of growth. Hence, it is concluded that for better or worse, over the next decade the character of the hidden economy will determine more and more the character of Egypt's economic future.

There is, however, a negative side to the effects of the hidden economy:

1. The hidden economy feeds primarily on the inefficiencies of the public sector, not on any inherent ability the private sector may have to operate successfully and competitively in an open, free-market situation. Also, it co-exists with the public sector behind a tariff wall that often benefits the private sector as much as, or more so than, the public sector. Hence, the experience gained by those operating in the hidden economy, feeding on distortions as this sector does, is itself 'distorted'.
2. The old ideals of 'social justice' and 'national unity' are clearly suffering by increased wealth accumulation in private hands on an

inequitable basis. Whole classes of Egyptians, especially those in government or public-sector service, have become increasingly impoverished while a very few have accumulated massive sums of money. This unequal distribution of income is potentially explosive and politically destabilizing.

3. While there has been accumulation of wealth of a significant order, there is little evidence that the most wealthy are willing to make longer-term investments in the domestic economy. Those with substantial wealth have all the means to move that wealth abroad and do. It is conceivable that over time, as the power and confidence of the new private business class grows, it will indeed undertake such investments. To date there is no evidence that this is happening.
4. The hidden economy is highly dependent upon corruption as a main enabling factor. As such, it has incorporated the practice of making 'under-the-table payments' as a standard means of doing business. Corruption in turn exacts a very high price on a public that increasingly believes that the government is perhaps the most immoral that Egypt has ever witnessed. The Islamic fundamentalists are able to make considerable political capital from this situation. Socially, it is destabilizing and the prospect of its weakening the present regime is real.
5. There is no evidence that, cumulatively, the varied practices of the main players in the hidden economy add up to and form a potentially efficient, modern, innovative and competitively able private sector for the future. Many operations are no more than 'bazaar-like' in management style and scope of activities. Feeding as it does off the distortions in the economy, this business class has much at stake in avoiding reforms of any kind. There is little evidence to date that this new private business class can reform itself or police its own ranks, or that it could ever enter into 'head-to-head' competition in international markets.
6. The evolution of a fascist-like state, involving a coalition between big business and the military, is not too attractive, especially to those intellectuals and educators of a more liberal persuasion. More broadly speaking, it is not clear that the Egyptian public would stand by and watch it happen. At a minimum it would polarize internal opposition along religious, economic, social and ideological lines.

On balance, it is concluded that for the most part the growth of the influence of the hidden economy in Egypt is a positive development. Its remaining so is dependent in large part on how quickly it evolves into a more efficient and responsible sector and is able to have a more widespread and positive effect on income distribution. In the longer run, it will lead to political change (in fact, it already has), but there is little indication thus far as to what exactly this political change will bring to the domestic scene. The pro-Nasserists and the Islamic fundamentalists are also well aware of the long-term political stakes involved in the economic changes that have occurred thus far and will continue to occur in the future. As described, these interests – particularly the fundamentalists – have quickly learned how to tap into the hidden economy to generate the resources needed to sustain their political efforts. Indeed, this is also true of the military.

That one is witnessing the rapid formation of a large number of highly disparate political groupings is a product of the liberalizing trend observed in Egypt over the past 15 years. The political center, the National Democratic Party, has not completely eroded but it is on its way to becoming less able unilaterally to impose its will. However, with the decreasing strength of the political center, it is not clear that anyone is 'in charge' and this, increasingly, is the complaint one hears about the Mubarak regime. The hidden economy, the purest form of free market enterprise that Egypt has, is, politically, neutral. It is an arena in which anyone, of whatever political persuasion, can operate. It is also composed of markets in which a well-organized political group can 'corner' activities and thus be able to exert strong influence over future political directions. There is no reason to believe that these political interests would always be disposed to favor the alliance with the United States or be moderate in character.

One might speculate further about the possible future political consequences of the economic transformation taking place in Egypt. This phenomenon is not confined to Egypt. Practically speaking, what had started as a process of regional economic integration through labor migration will now extend to many other realms of economic interaction. This has already started informally and will lead to more formal economic integration in the region in the next decade, something that in the past has eluded Arab governments' ability to bring about.

In a sense, economics is beginning to exert its own influences over what in the past were more politically determined issues. The hidden economy is moving independently of the solution of outstanding and unresolved political issues between Arabs and Israelis and between Arabs and Arabs. It may well be a mistake to assume that business as usual among the Arabs will remain 'business as usual'.

Name Index

Abd al-Halim, Musa 56
Abdel-Rahman, I. H. 39
Abu Ali, M. S. 39
Abu Basha, H. 61
Abu Ghazala, 'A. H. 60, 62
Ahmad, S. M. 252, 253
Al-Alfi, H. 58, 61
Al-Asad, H. 98, 99, 114, 187
Al-Banna, J. 249
Al-Bashir, U. H. 65
Al-Hossari, A. M. 144, 149, 152
Al-Imadi, M. 109
Al-Kasm, A. R. 98, 104, 110
Al-Latif Bultiya, A. 251
Al-Mughni Said, A. 249, 255
Al-Nasser, G. A. 4, 36, 38, 40, 47, 48, 53, 55, 178, 179, 180, 191, 244, 245-6, 247, 248, 249, 250, 349
Al-Sabah, J. A. 228
Al-Sadat, A. 8, 36, 47, 48, 52, 55, 59, 244, 246, 250, 252, 256, 330, 344
Al-Sayid, G. 59
Al-Shafai, H. 248
Al-Zu'bi, M. 98, 110
Ali, M. 36
Amid, M. J. 198
Anand, R. 89
Arslan, I. 91
Ashraf, A. 198
Ashraf, B. 210
Ashraf, J. 210
Ayrout, H. H. 142, 155
Azmeh, B. 181
Azmi, Z. 56

Badr, Z. 56
Bell, C. 145
Beneria, L. 211
Benton, L. A. 211
Bianchi, R. 241
Birks, J. 124, 315
Borjas, G. J. 210
Bunster, X. 216

Castro, M. G. 221
Çeçen, A.A. 78
Celasun, M. 91
Chaney, E. M. 216, 221
Chenery, H. D. 81
Chhibber, S. 89
Choucri, N. 332

Dawalibi, M. 181, 190
Diab, J. K. T. 346
Disuqi, M. 61
Dogruel, A. S. 78
Dogruel, F. 78
Dornbusch, R. 96-7
D'Silva 165

El-Tobgy, H. A. 144, 145
Eldin, A. M. 146

Fahim, A. 251
Fahmy, S. 39
Feiler, G. 222
Fields, G. S. 21, 22
Freeman, O. 166, 176

Gaitskill, A. 176
Garrett, R. 146
Geertz, C. 2
Gharib, S. 251-2

Hakim, C. 210
Halim, A. 246
Hamid, A. 178
Hashemi-Rafsanjani, A. A. 68, 75, 77
Hassan, Crown Prince 265
Hassan, King 55
Hussein, King 55, 259-60

Jones, G. 198

Karen, R. 166
Karshenas, M. 196, 205-6, 207
Khayrat, R. 61
Khomeini, R. 67, 68, 74
Kontos, S. 159
Krishna, R. 152
Krueger, A. 82
Kuznets, S. 22

Lewis, O. 17

Mahfouz, N. 57
Meguid, A. R. A. 335
Mellor, J. 152
Mohtadi 205, 206
Mordoglu, K. 215
Moskoff, W. 215
Mubarak, H. 38, 44, 46, 47, 48, 52, 53, 54, 55, 56, 58, 59, 60, 62, 63, 246, 250–1, 256, 335, 337, 350
Muhieddin, K. 249
Muhieddin, Z. 248
Murad, H. 249, 255

Naguib 247, 249
Nasser *see* Al-Nasser
Nattagh, N. 195
Numayri 171, 172
Numayri, J. 161

Omer, E. H. B. 174

Papps, I. 220–1
Perthes, V. 98

Radwan 26
Rafsanjani *see* Hashemi-Rafsanjani, A.A.
Rifaat, K. 248-9
Rodrik, D. 91
Roldan, M. 211

Sa'ad, H. A. G. 146
Sabri, A. 248
Sadat *see* Al-Sadat
Salama, A. 251
Salim, M. 252
Salmanzadeh, C. 198
Schmitter, P. C. 241
Sidqi, A. 54, 248
Sidqi, I. 246
Sinclair, R. 124, 315
Springborg, R. 53
Swearingen, W. D. 127

Tantawi, H. 60
Tu'ayma, A. 247
Tuncer, B. 82

Waterbury, J. 51
Wijnbergen, S. van 89, 91
Wikan, U. 1, 2, 3, 4, 7, 10, 11, 16, 17, 18, 19
Wilson, F. 215

Yinon, O. 2
Youssef, N. H. 215

Zaydan, H. 255
Zusman, P. 145